The Wealth of the Nation

Scotland, Culture and Independence

Cairns Craig

EDINBURGH
University Press

Edinburgh University Press is one of the leading university presses in the UK. We publish academic books and journals in our selected subject areas across the humanities and social sciences, combining cutting-edge scholarship with high editorial and production values to produce academic works of lasting importance. For more information visit our website: edinburghuniversitypress.com

Edinburgh University Press Ltd
The Tun – Holyrood Road
12(2f) Jackson's Entry
Edinburgh EH8 8PJ

Typeset in 11/13 Sabon by
Servis Filmsetting Ltd, Stockport, Cheshire,
and printed and bound in Great Britain

A CIP record for this book is available from the British Library

ISBN 978 1 4744 3557 4 (hardback)
ISBN 978 1 4744 3558 1 (paperback)
ISBN 978 1 4744 3559 8 (webready PDF)
ISBN 978 1 4744 3560 4 (epub)

Contents

Acknowledgements

This book began in work of Phase 2 of the Arts and Humanities Research Council (AHRC) Centre for Irish and Scottish Studies at the University of Aberdeen in the period between 2005 and 2010, and, in particular, from two conferences held in 2007 and 2009 in Aberdeen and in Trinity College Dublin on the theme of 'The Arts, Culture and the Wealth of the Nations'. By accident these dates straddled the financial crisis of 2008 and, as result, provided very different perspectives on the issues that were addressed, as can be seen in the issue of the *Journal of Irish and Studies,* Vol. 2:2 (Spring 2009) in which some of the papers are collected. My thanks to the AHRC for their support for those and many other events during Phase 2 of the Centre. Some of the research which underpins these chapters was published during and after the lifetime of the AHRC Centre: Chapter 1 draws on my contributions to Liam McIlvanney and Ray Ryan (eds), *Ireland and Scotland: Culture and Society 1700–2000* (2005) and on my contribution to John Mackenzie and T. M. Devine (eds), *Scotland and the British Empire* (2011); Chapter 2 draws on my contribution to *The Journal of Scottish Thought*, Vol. 2:1 (2009), *Race, Scripture and Science*; Chapter 3 had its origins in my contribution to Jonathan Murray, Fidelma Farley and Rod Stoneman (eds), *The Scottish Cinema Now* (2009); Chapter 4 synthesises some central concerns in my recent writing on modern Scottish literature. I would like to thank those editors whose commissions helped stimulate some of its ideas – Matt McGuire, Colin Nicholson, Gerrard Caruthers, Liam McIlvanney, Alan Riach, Ian Brown and Caroline McCracken-Flesher. The final chapter draws on a paper I gave at the conference of the *Société des Anglicistes de l'Enseignement Supérieur* at Toulon in June 2015 and which was subsequently published in the *Observatoire de la Société Britannique* (No. 18, février 2016) – my thanks to Gilles Leydier for the invitation.

More general thanks are owed to my colleagues in the Research Institute of Irish and Scottish Studies and in the School of Language, Literature, Music and Visual Culture at the University of Aberdeen, who have provided such a stimulating environment in which to work over the last decade – if I mention Michael Brown, Catherine Jones, Ali Lumsden and Tim Baker it is only because their research and publications have most closely intersected with my own.

My thanks, as always, go to Linda and Conan, who have travelled with these chapters over several years.

Cairns Craig

Introduction: The Wealth of the Nation

1 Wealth and Poverty

Opinion polls in the week before the referendum on Scottish independence in September 2014 indicated that the 'Yes' side had taken a narrow lead over the 'Better Together' side. When the result was announced, with 55 per cent voting to remain in the United Kingdom (UK), it was unclear whether the polls had simply been wrong or whether the demand for independence had been quelled by the much publicised promise by the three leaders of the Westminster unionist parties to devolve further powers to the Scottish parliament; or, indeed, if people had simply voted on the side of caution after a blitz of scare stories about the possible economic consequences of independence. The central question in the two-year debate leading up to the referendum was, could Scotland afford to be an independent country, especially given the winding down of the oil industry in the North Sea, in which revenues had peaked as far back as the turn of the century? As though in ironic response to those debates, in the months following the referendum the price of oil collapsed from nearly $100 to less than $40 a barrel, leaving a hypothetically independent Scotland with a 'black hole' in the finances projected by the Scottish Government's White Paper *Scotland's Future*, that had set out the economic opportunities of independence. In the space of a few months, Scotland had gone from being a potentially wealthy independent country to being apparently dependent on the largesse of the rest of the UK for its future standard of living. As the oil price showed no sign of significant recovery in the following years, the economic forecasts for Scotland's future, whether within or outside the UK and, after the UK's decision to leave the European Union in 2016, whether within or outside the European free trade area, were painted by many as bleak – the country was running a £15 billion deficit.[1] The wealth of the nation had evaporated and, in the 'snap' UK general election called by Prime Minister Theresa May in June 2017, the number of Westminster parliamentary seats won by the Scottish National Party (SNP) collapsed from fifty-five to thirty-four. The SNP were still, by a long way, the largest party in Scotland and the third largest in the UK, but this decline indicated a substantial loss of confidence in the SNP's vision for the future of Scotland.

Scotland's likely ongoing poverty as an independent country had been one of the arguments advanced by those in favour of the Union of 1707. Thereafter, however, the lack of immediate economic benefit became a source of complaint. As Adam Smith wrote to his publisher in London, William Strahan, on 4 April 1760:

> Nothing . . . appears to me more excusable than the disaffection of Scotland at that time. The Union was a measure from which infinite Good has been derived to this country. The Prospect of that good, however, must then have appeared very remote and uncertain. The immediate effect of it was to hurt the interest of every single order of men in the country. The dignity of the nobility was undone by it. The greater part of the Gentry who had been accustomed to represent their own country in its own Parliament were cut out forever from all hopes of representing it in a British Parliament. Even the merchants seemed to suffer at first. The trade to the Plantations was, indeed, opened to them. But that was a trade which they knew nothing about; the trade they were acquainted with, that to France, Holland and the Baltic, was laid under new embarrassments which almost entirely annihilated the two first and most important branches of it. The Clergy too, who were then far from insignificant, were alarmed about the Church. No wonder if at that time all orders of men conspired in cursing a measure so hurtful to their immediate interest. The views of their posterity are now very different; but those views could be seen by but few of our forefathers, by those few in but a confused and imperfect manner.[2]

By 1914 Scotland had a Gross Domestic Product that was among the highest of any country in the world, an outcome which itself could be seen only in a 'confused and imperfect' manner, because many among the working classes lived in squalidly poor housing conditions and had to compete for their jobs with cheaper immigrant labour from Ireland and from Eastern Europe. The interaction of wealth and poverty is summarised in Devine, Lee and Peden's *The Transformation of Scotland* (2005):

> One estimate for 1914 suggested that overseas investment was equivalent to £110 for every Scot compared to an average of £90 for the UK as a whole. This indicates, as there is neither evidence nor complaint of investment shortages in Scotland before 1914, that the process of growth had generated a considerable accumulation of capital. That it should seek outlets abroad to take advantage of better returns is completely reasonable. It is clear evidence of the success of Scottish economic advance in producing such a surplus, sufficient to account for over 8 per cent of national income as its return on those investments. But from a different perspective it further confirms the deep and inherent inequality in prosperity in Scotland. The investors were primarily men of substance who had made fortunes or at least a good income in business or the professions. While the aspiring middle classes were able to add their own modest savings, the vast majority of the less prosperous were excluded by their poverty. Unfortunately for them, investment in housing construction, especially for those on the lowest incomes, constituted a much less attractive investment opportunity than ranching or real estate in North America. The market forces that guided these funds abroad further exacerbated the economic and social divide within Scotland.[3]

In 1914, Scotland was both wealthy and poor, a paradox which was repeated in the Scotland of 2014, an oil-rich country with some of the highest levels of multiple deprivation in Europe. Part of the SNP's political success after 2007 was based on its claim that it would use the country's wealth to address its inequalities: an independent Scotland with control over oil revenues would be a country capable of eradicating the nation's poverty. A collapsing oil price undermined, however, the optimistic expectations of what Nicola Sturgeon described as her 'utilitarian nationalism'. Scotland, briefly rich because of oil, was, apparently, a poor country getting poorer and, therefore, more than ever economically dependent on the Union.

The most effective index of Scotland's poverty, however, was not the level of its monetary wealth but its declining population. Scotland was almost alone among European nations in having stagnant population growth through the twentieth century. In 1921, the population was 4.8 million and growing. In 2001, the population was 5 million and declining from a peak of 5.2 million in 1971. It looked likely that within a decade the population would be back to the level of 1921. The reason for the lack of growth – England's population had grown from 35.2 million to 53 million in the same period – was in large measure due to outward migration. Many Scots were forced to move as the industries in which they worked were relocated to England – as in the case of the Massey Ferguson tractor plant, the Saxone shoe factory and BMK carpets[4] – or scaled back, resulting in places in England, like Corby, becoming known as Little Scotland because of the number of Scots who had moved to its steelworks for employment. Many others moved because they were ambitious and the headquarters of UK Government organisations, public institutions and major companies were in London. Many more, however, sought a better life by emigrating to the United States of America (USA) or to Canada, to Australia or New Zealand, or even to South Africa. The numbers for a country with such a small total population are challenging: T. M. Devine suggests that 600,000 Scots moved to England between 1841 and 1911 and that between 1825 and 1938 over 2.3 million people left Scotland for overseas destinations.[5] It is a continuing trend, with a net population loss of 825,000 between 1952 and 2006, despite significant inward migration from the Indian subcontinent in the latter part of the twentieth century and, in the early years of the twenty-first century, from eastern Europe.[6] Looked at from this perspective, Union and Empire could be regarded as Scotland's salvation, allowing it to maintain its total population at levels appropriate to its ability to generate income, or it could be seen as the detrimental outcome of being tied into a state over which it had very little control, and which, despite the efforts to establish new manufacturing plants at places like Linwood and Bathgate in the 1960s, had little interest in its infrastructural requirements. During the Thatcher years, a campaign seeking improvements to the Edinburgh–Aberdeen rail line was met with the caution that they could have their existing railroad or none at all. Migration might not, as in the Ireland of the 1950s and 60s, have been an explicit assumption of government planning, but Scotland was, nonetheless, a country where government did not need to plan for growth since it could depend on migration to allow it to service the needs of a contracting population.

II The Shadow of Adam Smith

In 1968, one of the most influential international economic associations, the Mont Pèlerin Society, met in Aviemore in the Scottish Highlands – largely by accident as the meeting had been scheduled to take place in Budapest before the venue was changed in protest at the Russian invasion of Czechoslovakia. The Mont Pèlerin Society – often referred to as the 'Friends of Friedrich Hayek' – was named after the location of the first meeting of a group of economists and historians invited by Hayek in 1947 to discuss how to develop the defence of freedom that he had set out in his 1944 book, *The Road to Serfdom*. Hayek, then at the London School of Economics, would shortly after leave for the University of Chicago, where, with Milton Friedman, he would become part of the influential 'Chicago School of Economics', a school that promoted Adam Smith as the founder both of free market liberalism and of the need to limit the state's role in the economy.

One of the speakers at that 1968 conference was Robert Schuettinger, an American who was lecturing at St Andrews University, where the heritage of Adam Smith's economics had been developed by James Wilkie Nisbet, appointed in 1927, and himself a former student of W. R. Scott, then the most recent biographer of Adam Smith. Nisbet promoted Smith's economic views in books such as *The Case for Laissez Faire* (1929) and opposed the developing consensus around the economic theories of John Maynard Keynes, whose *General Theory of Employment, Interest, and Money* was published in 1936, arguing for the role of the state in counteracting the kind of economic collapse that had followed the stock market crash of 1929. For Nisbet, Keynes's notions of government intervention in the economy went against the fundamental principles of the free market as they had been expounded by Smith. In 1979 Schuettinger co-wrote with Eamonn Butler, who had been a student at St Andrews, *Forty Centuries of Wage and Price Controls*, a book which tried to demonstrate how, over a very long period, government intervention in markets always failed. At that time Butler himself, after working for some years in the USA, was Co-Director of the Adam Smith Institute which he had established in 1977 along with another St Andrews graduate, Madsen Pirie. Pirie too had spent time in the USA working for the Republican Study Committee, a group of Republican politicians committed to proselytising for limited government. The Adam Smith Institute was to be the source of many of the privatisation initiatives of the Thatcher government in the 1980s, as well as the source of the idea of replacing existing local government taxes – 'rates' in Scotland – with a charge on each individual – what became known as the 'poll tax'.[7] Thatcher herself could never understand why the Scots were so antipathetic to her ideas, since they derived, in her view, from a great Scotsman, of whom Scots should not only be proud for his contemporary influence through the work of Hayek and Friedman, but whose ideas they should accept, since those ideas had contributed to the great achievements of nineteenth-century industrial Scotland: Hugo Young records her as having said that 'the Scots invented Thatcherism, long before I was thought of', and declaring, 'Tory values are in tune with everything that is finest in the Scottish character. Scottish values are Tory values – and vice versa'.[8]

On 21 May 1988, Margaret Thatcher gave an address to the General Assembly of the Church of Scotland. It was a moment that came to be known as 'the sermon on the Mound'. The address was a statement both of Margaret Thatcher's version of Christianity and her views about dependency on the state, a dependency that many of her followers believed was not only endemic in the parts of Scotland where unemployment was persistently high but was a structural principle of the Scottish economy because of its resistance to free market solutions, with the result that a far higher number of people were employed by government and government agencies than in England. Thatcher's emphasis was on economic individualism, an individualism underlined in her *Woman's Hour* interview in which she declared, of the poor and unemployed,

> they are casting their problems on society and who is society? There is no such thing! There are individual men and women and there are families and no government can do anything except through people and people look to themselves first.[9]

The apparent acceptance of an atomised individualism in which 'the great driving engine, the driving force of life' is money, because '[t]here is nothing wrong with having a lot more money',[10] clearly angered many who saw their Christian duty in terms of fellowship and renunciation rather than personal acquisition. The irony, as revealed by Ian Lang, Minister of State for Scotland 1987–90, was that Mrs Thatcher had taken the phrase 'there is no such thing as society' from the Scottish philosopher John Macmurray,[11] who had argued that 'society' and 'community' were opposed to each other, the former being merely an instrumental set of relations in which we engage out of economic necessity while the latter is the real context of our existence as 'persons':

> Men need one another for the purposes of providing for their necessities through co-operation. But they need one another in an even deeper sense because of the essential mutuality of their personal being. It is thus in the fact of mutuality, of friendship, of communion between man and man that we must discover the core of religion. It is those fully personal relationships – independent as they are of changing conditions, because they are not forms of co-operation for particular purposes – that the eternal substance of humanity is to be found.[12]

In denying 'society', however, Thatcher appeared to be denying 'community', the community that had been fundamental to much Scottish religion and to its various philosophical expressions. By focusing on the issue of economic individualism as the core of Smith's account of economics, Thatcher was effectively following the Chicago School, for whom Smith's work justifies 'the assumption that humans can be represented as *homo economicus*, beings driven by a single motive: personal utility maximization.'[13] What this reading of Smith set aside, however, was what, in late nineteenth-century Germany, had come to be known as '*Das Adam Smith Problem*'[14] – how could the economics of *The Wealth of Nations* be reconciled with the moral philosophy of *The Theory of Moral Sentiments*? It was an issue taken up by Andrew Skinner of the University of Glasgow in an edition of *The Wealth of Nations* he edited in 1970. Skinner emphasised not Smith's belief in the self-interested nature of human actions but his commitment to 'fellow feeling', as expressed in the opening sentences of *The Theory of Moral Sentiments*:

> How selfish soever man may be supposed, there are evidently some principles in his nature which interest him in the fortune of others, and render their happiness necessary to him, though he derives nothing from it except perhaps the pleasure of seeing it.[15]

The consequence is two different ways in which morality may operate in a society, one based on fellow-feeling and one based simply on the application of the rules of a justice system:

> Smith argued that where men act with an eye to the positive rules of morality, and where their behaviour is characterized by 'beneficence' rather than justice, then the society 'flourished and is happy'. Where, on the contrary, only the negative virtue of justice is observed, then life in society can be characterized by nothing more than 'a mercenary exchange of good offices according to an agreed valuation'.[16]

Skinner's account of Smith's thought was based on what he asserted was Smith's own belief that he 'regarded *The Moral Sentiments* and *The Wealth of Nations* as but parts of a single, greater whole';[17] Hayek, on the other hand, believed that the 'negative virtue' of justice was sufficient to produce an effective social order, and that the failures attributed to capitalism were directly the outcome of inadequate systems of justice:

> Much that has been blamed on the capitalist system is in fact due to remnants and revivals of precapitalist features: to monopolistic elements which were either the direct result of ill-conceived state action or the consequence of a failure to understand that a smooth working competitive market order required an appropriate legal framework.[18]

Under Hayek's influence, the Smith of *The Moral Sentiments* became the Smith not simply of *The Wealth of Nations* alone but of one single element in it: the systematic analysis of the behaviour of individuals pursuing their self-interest under conditions of competition, and the ways in which the 'invisible hand' would lead inevitably to the benefit of a whole society. As E. K. Hunt put it 1979, 'The invisible hand was not the intentional design of any individual but was simply created by the systematic working out of natural laws'.[19] Insofar as those laws were 'natural', calculated government interference was more likely to disrupt them than to make them work more effectively.

This 'modernisation' of Smith as the fundamental defence of the necessary connection between free markets and a free society added significance to the work of American scholars who, since the 1920s, had been researching the roots of rapidly developing modern disciplines such as economics and sociology, and who had discovered that many of the most important progenitors of those disciplines were to be found in eighteenth-century Scotland. The first step in this excavation was probably W. C. Lehmann's *Adam Ferguson and the Beginnings of Modern Sociology*, published in 1930 as part of a series entitled *Studies in History, Economics, and Public Law* which was edited by the Faculty of Political Science of Columbia University. The location is significant because a prominent contributor both to sociology and to political science in the USA in this period was Robert Morrison MacIver, professor at Columbia, and who, when he was a junior lecturer at the University of Aberdeen, had been among the first in the UK to teach sociology as a modern discipline. MacIver would later provide a preface to another of Lehmann's recuperative studies of Scottish eighteenth-century thinkers, *John Millar of Glasgow, 1735–1801*.[20] Ferguson and Millar were, for Lehmann, pioneers of sociology and, therefore, the foundation on which modern American social science was built. American sociology, he argued, needed to recognise its origins in order to better understand its own assumptions: Ferguson's perspective directed contemporary sociology to return to 'a method that aimed to be severely empirical, at once psychological and historical'.[21] Lehmann's work was to be given substantial support by Gladys Bryson's *Man and Society: The Scottish Inquiry of the Eighteenth Century* (1945), which even more ambitiously sought to situate Scotland's eighteenth-century thinkers not only as the origin of modern American social science but as a compass by which it ought to navigate its future development: 'We shall be concerned chiefly with the effort of this earlier group [Hume, Smith, Ferguson] to lay the foundations for an empirical science of man, a goal which we have not yet completely achieved'.[22] The focus on Scottish thinkers as a group was justified by the fact that they 'were so closely connected by ties of friendship and by the relation of teacher to pupil that we may fairly speak of them as composing a school'[23] but, just as importantly, because of the 'degree to which the Scottish thought was spread in the United States'.[24] Bryson's argument was not just that Scots were the origin of the attempt to construct a 'science of man' but that if there were to be a modern 'science of man' it had to be built on the foundations established by eighteenth-century Scotland. Lehmann's and Bryson's researches, in arguing the close ties between modern America and eighteenth-century Scotland, had already provided a broader historical justification for Hayek's claim that Adam Smith was both the foundation and the justification of contemporary American free-market ideology.

This rediscovery of Smith after the Second World War – his theories had long ceased to play any but a historical role in the main developments of economics in the late nineteenth and early twentieth centuries – brought to the fore one of the problematic distinctions in Smith's writings with which later economists wrestled – the contrast that Smith draws between 'productive' and 'unproductive' labour. How do we identify that labour which adds to the wealth of nations and labour which adds nothing or, indeed, subtracts from it? For Smith, an increase in wealth is only possible if something is created which is carried forward from one cycle of production to the next, so that it can be added to the resources available for production in the following period, whether because additional productive labour can be hired or more efficient machinery deployed. Unproductive labour can have its uses and may, indeed, be essential in the workings of society, but it does not contribute to expanding the wealth of the nation:

> The sovereign, for example, with all the officers both of justice and war who serve under him, the whole army and navy, are unproductive labourers . . . In the same class must be ranked, some both of the gravest and most important, and some of the most frivolous professions: churchmen, lawyers, physicians, men of letters of all kinds; players, buffoons, musicians, opera-singers, opera-dancers &c.[25]

These are all a cost to the national wealth, as what they produce is consumed as it is produced and leaves nothing additional for investing in the next cycle of production. What we now designate as 'the arts' or 'culture' are, in this perspective, a drain on the wealth of the nation, a drain which must be made up by the additional productivity of others. The consequence, among some modern Smithians, is that the arts and culture are regarded as being of no value to the wealth of the nation and, like other 'unproductive labour', should be constrained in order not to limit the resources that could be directed to increased productivity – which is one of the reasons that proposals to end both the National Endowment for the Arts and the National Endowment for the Humanities in the USA were announced by Donald Trump early in the first year of his Presidency.[26] Those US Endowments, brought into existence by Lyndon Johnson in 1964 as evidence of America's greater degree of civilisation than its Cold War opponent, were modelled on the Arts Council of Great Britain,[27] which had itself come into existence in 1946 as a continuation of the work of the Committee for the Encouragement of Music and the Arts (CEMA), set up in 1939 to try to bolster morale among the civilian population in the UK. So successful was CEMA at discovering new audiences among those previously shut out from the arts, it was argued at the end of the war that it ought to be made permanent and it was transformed, in 1946, into the Arts Council of Great Britain. The person who made the argument to government for this extension of the wartime use of the arts was John Maynard Keynes,[28] against whose interventionist approach to the running of a modern economy the virtues of the 'self-interested individual' were mobilised in the name of Adam Smith.

Throughout its history, however, the Arts Council of Great Britain struggled with two major dilemmas. The first was its relationship to the constituent parts of the UK. Keynes saw the Arts Council he was creating as a vehicle for promoting a unifying conception of English cultural identity: thus in a broadcast in 1945 in which he set out his ambitions for the continuation of CEMA he insisted that 'nothing can be more damaging than the excessive prestige of metropolitan standards and fashion' but suggested that the consequence was that we should 'let every part of Merry England be merry in its own way'. A renewed 'merry England' would, he suggested, be 'death to Hollywood'.[29] At the same time, he insisted on the importance of making London 'a great artistic metropolis, a place to visit and to wonder at', which would be achieved by the establishment of 'national' opera and theatre companies, the nation in question being England, as is evident from the titles of the four 'national' companies which the Arts Council helped establish, Covent Garden, English National Opera, the National Theatre, and the Royal Shakespeare Company. Robert Hewison suggests that what Keynes's broadcast implied was an Arts Council agenda focused on 'anti-Americanism and the promotion of a conservative image of English identity'.[30] The wartime origins of the Arts Council of Great Britain contributed not only to this cultural agenda but was built into its administrative structure, which was based on 'eleven regional offices . . . corresponding to the geographical areas covered for Civil Defence: ten in England and one in Scotland'.[31] It was an organisation, in other words, oriented not to the four nations of the UK but predominantly to the support of a specifically English cultural agenda.

The second problem with which the Arts Council struggled was the perception that what it supported was elite culture, and that whereas the 1945 Labour Government was committed to redistributing wealth through the tax system and through free health care, the Arts Council was effectively taking tax payers' money to subsidise the pleasures of the well-educated and the well-off. This led to a series of contradictory investigations and reports aimed, on the one hand, at finding ways in which the Arts Council's funds could be directed at those who would not normally attend events by the 'national' companies, and, on the other hand, at providing justification for the spend on the 'national' companies because of the benefit they brought to the British economy through tourism, or through the encouragement to major businesses to set up in London. Much of this was driven by the appropriation of Adam Smith's economic theories as defined by the Chicago School and as promulgated by the Adam Smith Institute in London. Indeed, throughout the Thatcher years the Arts Council was in constant turmoil in trying to develop a strategy that would co-ordinate these competing demands, prevent ongoing cuts to its budget and justify its future existence. When a strategy document was finally published in 1984, its title, *The Glory of the Garden*, was taken from a poem by Rudyard Kipling, which contained the lines, 'Our England is a garden, and such gardens are not made/By singing "Oh How beautiful!" and sitting in the shade'. The Arts Council of Great Britain's mission was the promotion of English culture, a mission that was gradually incorporated into the potential of the heritage industry and then into 'The Department of National Heritage', inaugurated as part of John Major's Government in 1992 under the stewardship of David Mellor; the 'nation' whose heritage was being preserved did not need to be stated, for effectively England had declared cultural independence and was determined no longer to be constrained by the effort to fulfil the requirements of 'Britishness'. It was a transition symbolised in 1983 when the National Heritage Act produced, as its outcome, an organisation called 'English Heritage'.

III Base and Superstructure

The inauguration of the Edinburgh Festival in 1947, and the international audiences that it began to attract, was a major inspiration to the redevelopment in Scotland's cultural infrastructure. Organisations like the National Trust for Scotland (founded 1931) and the Saltire Society (1936), whose activities had been restricted during the war, began again to promote Scottish culture. The Festival itself spawned the Edinburgh International Film Festival – originally focused on documentary film but then extending to the whole range of contemporary, and, indeed, historical film-making – and the Festival Fringe, which grew through the 1950s from an initial eight visiting companies in 1947 to nearly 500 by the early 1980s and to over 3,000 by 2016. The Fringe, in turn, spawned the Traverse Theatre in 1963 as an 'all-the-year-round' Fringe venue, from which was created, in 1966, the Richard Demarco Gallery, presenting the work of avant-garde European artists. In Glasgow, the Citizens Theatre, founded in 1943, became the focus of experimental theatrical productions after Giles Havergal took over as its Director in 1969; the 7:84 Theatre Company started touring in 1971, spinning off David MacLellan and David Anderson's Wildcat in 1978, and setting the stage for the launch of Communicado in 1983. The Byre theatre in St Andrews, which went back to the amateur theatre movement of the 1930s, was established in a new building in 1970 and moved to a purpose-built location in 1989, while the Pitlochry Festival Theatre, which also derived from the amateur theatre movement in the early 1950s, was finally established in a specially commissioned permanent home in 1981. In the early 1980s a series of May Day Festivals in Glasgow, in part sponsored by the Scottish Trades Union Congress, turned into 'Mayfest' in 1983 while the Celtic Connections Festival, founded in 1994, indicated how much the axis of Scotland's cultural life had moved towards Ireland and North America. A major cultural opportunity was opened up by the establishment, in 1983, of the Edinburgh International Book Festival, which ran alongside the Edinburgh Festival: it switched from being a bi-annual to an annual event in 1997 and by 2015 it had over two hundred thousand attendees. Its success generated similar initiatives around the country: Aberdeen's *Word* festival was established by Alan Spence in 1999, while Glasgow's version, *Aye Write*, was launched in 2005 and though planned to be bi-annual became almost immediately an annual event. Other book festivals were launched in more remote parts of the country – the Wigtown Book Festival in 1999 and the Ullapool Book Festival in 2005. The musical component of the Edinburgh Festival was to help the BBC Scottish Orchestra, founded in 1935, to become a full symphony orchestra in 1967, and inspired the Aberdeen International Youth Festival in 1973. In the media, the 1957 launch of Scottish Television provided an alternative Scottish dimension to the BBC's television broadcasts in Scotland, and the subsequent establishment of commercial radio – Radio Clyde in 1973 and Radio Forth in 1975 – provoked the BBC into the introduction of Radio Scotland in 1978 and then the launch of BBC Radio nan Gàidheal in 1986, with BBC Alba television coming on-stream in 2008.

The development of this rich cultural infrastructure was matched by developments in the visual arts: the first Scottish Gallery of Modern Art opened in 1960 in Inverleith House in Edinburgh's Botanic Gardens and moved in 1984 to a neo-classical building on Belford Road, becoming 'Modern One' in 1999 when the gallery was extended by the acquisition of another neo-classical building, 'Modern Two', on the opposite side of the road. These facilities in Edinburgh were extended by the establishment of the Fruitmarket Gallery in 1974, directly opposite where the City Art Centre would be established in a former warehouse in 1980, and by the addition of photography to the National Galleries' collections in 1984. In Glasgow, the opening in 1983 of the building that would house the Burrell collection, gifted to the city by Sir William and Lady Burrell in the 1940s, began a period of intensive cultural investment that would allow the city to capture the European City of Culture accolade in 1990. Contentious as it was to many, because it seemed to take little account of the actual culture of working Glaswegians, Glasgow became symbolic of how 'culture' could produce urban regeneration in a post-industrial city,[32] with the City investing in a range of ambitious new cultural venues including Trongate 103, a £7 million visual arts centre, a £6 million headquarters for Scottish Ballet at Tramway, and the Riverside Museum, an £80 million building opened in 2011 as home to the Museum of Transport. The Gallery of Modern Art in Glasgow was opened in Royal Exchange Square in 1996 and Dundee launched its Contemporary Arts Centre in 1999.

Indicative of the importance of museums to the cultural infrastructure was the opening of the National Museum of Scotland in 2006, housed in a distinctive new building that was linked to the former nineteenth-century Royal Scottish Museum in Edinburgh's Chambers Street. The National Museum's aim was to present, through physical artefacts, the history of Scotland from the earliest times – from long before Scotland itself as a political entity had come into existence. The flourishing of museum curation – Glasgow was spending £14m a year on museums by 2010, the equivalent of £23 per head of population[33] – was recognised by the establishment of the Scottish Museum Council's Recognition Scheme which, by 2017, had accredited forty-seven 'Nationally Significant Collections'.[34]

In the immediate aftermath of the Second World War, Scotland's cultural infrastructure depended largely on cultural initiatives that dated back to before the First World War – the Scottish National Gallery in 1853, McLellan Galleries, Glasgow in 1855, the Royal Scottish Museum in 1861, the McManus Gallery in Dundee in 1867, Theatre Royal Glasgow in 1867, the Aberdeen Art Gallery in 1884, the Scottish Portrait Gallery in 1890, the Empire Palace Theatre in 1892, the Glasgow School of Art in 1899, the Kelvingrove Museum and Gallery in 1901, King's Theatre Glasgow in 1904, His Majesty's Theatre Aberdeen in 1906, Usher Hall Edinburgh in 1914, as well as the host of libraries funded by Andrew Carnegie[35] – Dunfermline 1883, Grangemouth 1889, Edinburgh 1890, Aberdeen 1892, Airdrie 1893, Wick 1898. When the first Edinburgh Festival took place in 1947 that cultural infrastructure was largely unchanged but by the 1990s Scotland's cultural infrastructure had been enriched with a wealth of new buildings, new spaces for display and for theatre, and opportunities for new cultural organisations. Scotland, by the turn of the century, was a nation culturally transformed and part of that transformation can be dated to 1967, when the reorganisation of the Arts Council of Great Britain resulted in the establishment of a separate Scottish Arts Council (SAC). The date, the year of the first parliamentary victory for the SNP since the 1940s – Winnie Ewing's in the Hamilton by-election – is significant. The rise of Scottish nationalism and the sense of injustice in the English regions about the fact that the Arts Council had been pouring resources into the 'national companies' and the national institutions in London – twice as much was spent in London and the South-East as in the rest of the country[36] – led to a review of its charter and a restatement of its mission: 'To develop and improve the knowledge, understanding and practice of the arts' and 'to increase the accessibility of the arts to the public throughout Great Britain'.[37] The latter ambition was to be achieved by having separate Arts Councils for Scotland and Wales, even if they were to remain technically subcommittees of the Arts Council of Great Britain. The devolution of culture in 1967 prefigured – perhaps, indeed, promoted – the devolution of political power in 1997. The Arts Council in Scotland became a mirror version of the Arts Council of Great Britain as envisaged by Maynard Keynes, supporting four major companies in the elite arts: the Scottish National Orchestra (SNO) (founded in 1891 and given 'Royal' status in 1991); Scottish Opera (an off-shoot of the SNO created in 1962 by Alexander Gibson, then its conductor); Scottish Ballet (which was established in 1969 from a company that had previously operated in Bristol since 1957), and the Scottish Chamber Orchestra (formed in 1974). By its separation from the Arts Council of Great Britain, Scotland was effectively allowed to pursue a specifically Scottish agenda, one which would not necessarily aim at integration of the arts in Scotland with the overarching agenda of the arts in the rest of the UK, as was illustrated by the very different treatment of the 7:84 Company north and south of the border: despite many difficulties, 7:84 survived in Scotland from the 1970s until 2007 because of the SAC's desire to support popular Scottish theatre, whereas its sister company in England collapsed after its Arts Council support was withdrawn in the politically confrontational atmosphere of 1984.

The impact of the SAC can be seen in how rapidly, after 1967, Scottish publishing was re-energised. Particularly significant was the establishment in January 1968 of the magazine *Scottish International*, a journal aimed at addressing a broad range of cultural and social issues. There had been small Scottish magazines publishing poetry and some literary criticism, such as Callum MacDonald's *Lines Review* (1952), Gaelic language magazine *Gairm* (1952) and Duncan Glen's *Akros* (1965), but there was a regular complaint that Scotland had no equivalent to *The Spectator* or *The New Statesman*, a gap that *Scottish International*, with SAC support, aimed to fill, moving from its initial high-quality, glossy quarterly format to a newsprint, monthly format in 1970 that aimed to respond more rapidly to the changing cultural environment. *Scottish International* set the model for later Scottish literary magazines, many of which at some point received SAC support, including *New Edinburgh Review* (1969), *Chapman* (1970), *Tocher* (1971), *Calgacus* (1975), *Crann Tàra* (1977), *Cencrastus* (1981), and *Radical Scotland* (1982). While Edinburgh's publishing industry, though much diminished since its high point before the First World War, had managed to retain a few book publishers into the 1960s, it was focused mainly on specialist areas, such as the religious publishing of T. & T. Clark, the dictionaries and encyclopaedias of Chambers and the medical and scientific imprint of Churchill Livingstone. Collins, with its large fiction list, was still printing books in Glasgow but was editorially controlled from London and focused on best-sellers (some of whom, like Alastair MacLean, happened to be Scottish). 'Serious literature' was almost entirely restricted to the activities of printing companies who acted as publishers as a side-line to their main business: William MacLennan in Glasgow produced Hugh MacDiarmid's *In Memoriam James Joyce* in 1955, and MacDonald's in Edinburgh, as well as publishing *Lines Review*, produced the occasional novel, such as Stuart MacGregor's *The Myrtle and the Ivy* (1967). SAC support was to help underpin literary publishing in Scotland in the 1970s and 80s, even if many of the companies remained small and vulnerable: Mainstream was launched in 1968, Canongate in 1973, and Polygon was spun off from the Edinburgh University Students Publications Board in 1977. With SAC subventions these publishers could provide an outlet for authors whose work was unlikely to be promoted by London publishers – Alasdair Gray's first novel, *Lanark*, was published by Canongate in 1981 (though they could not keep him for his second novel, *1982, Janine*, which went to Jonathan Cape in London); James Kelman's *The Busconductor Hines* (1984) and Janice Galloway's *The Trick is to Keep Breathing* (1989) were published by Polygon (though Kelman's Booker Prize-winning novel, *How late it was, how late* would be published by Secker & Warburg in London, and Galloway's *Foreign Parts* in 1994 would be published by Cape);

Ian Rankin published his first novel, *The Flood* (1986), with Polygon but it was Bodley Head who eventually took the first Rebus novel. French-based Kenneth White's work was introduced back into Scotland first by Mainstream in 1989[38] and then by Polygon in 1998.[39] London publishers subsequently found that it was well worth investing in Scottish writers, providing a promotional environment in which Scottish writers could flourish, most notably, perhaps, in the case of Iain Banks's *The Wasp Factory* (1984) and the subsequent science fiction novels (under the pseudonym of Iain M. Banks) which were initially taken up by Macmillan, as well as Secker & Warburg's publication of Irvine Welsh's *Trainspotting* in 1993.

The impact of an independent Scottish Arts Council was equally clear in the visual arts, when it supported in 1968 a group of related exhibitions focused on late nineteenth-century Glasgow: the first, a comprehensive exhibition of the work of 'The Glasgow Boys' in the period between 1880 and 1900; the second, under the title of 'A Man of Influence', on the art dealer, Alex Reid (1854–1928), who had helped promote their work in Europe and the USA; the third, on the photography of James Craig Annan (1864–1946), who became a member of the Glasgow Arts Club in 1891 as a 'photographic artist'; and, finally, an exhibition under the auspices of the Edinburgh Festival on Charles Rennie Mackintosh (1868–1928), whose work was only then beginning to be recognised as a major contribution to modernism in both Scotland and Europe. This was a determined attempt at the revaluation of late nineteenth-century art in Glasgow. William Buchanan wrote in his notes to the exhibition: 'that they were highly regarded in their own day is abundantly clear: that they are now almost forgotten is painfully evident',[40] but the 1968 exhibition was to bring them – and, later, the work of the Glasgow Girls – to such public prominence that an exhibition in 2010 entitled 'Pioneering Painters: the Glasgow Boys 1880–1920' attracted 120,000 visitors. There was a similar transformation in the appreciation of the Edinburgh-based Scottish Colourists. When the National Gallery of Modern Art mounted an exhibition of all the Colourist works they had access to in 1980, an apologetic roneoed list of the paintings admitted that there was no proper catalogue because the diversity of the four artists known as the 'Colourists' – S. J. Peploe (1871–1935), G. L. Hunter (1877–1931), F. C. B. Cadell (1883–1937) and J. D. Fergusson

(1874–1961) – made 'it difficult to provide a critical account of the paintings'.[41] Twenty years on, however, the Colourist exhibition that was shown in London at the Royal Academy of Arts (June–September 2000) and then at the Gallery of Modern Art in Edinburgh (November 2000–January 2001), not only attracted huge audiences but was accompanied by a lavish publication by Philip Long and Elizabeth Cumming.[42] Such was the success of the Colourist exhibition that by the end of the decade the Gallery of Modern Art had committed to an annual exhibition devoted to each of the four members of group in turn, and when that was complete they then held an exhibition of *Modern Scottish Women Painters and Sculptors 1885–1965* in 2015.[43] The SAC's most radical intervention, however, in its early years was possibly the purchase of an Alexander 'Greek' Thomson building in Glasgow which had been the home of the Glasgow Society of Lady Artists and which became, under the guidance of Tom McGrath, 'The Third Eye Centre', a venue for *avant garde* art and poetry. It was, perhaps, the launch pad for what has come to be known as 'the Glasgow Miracle' – an idea first voiced by the curator of the 1996 Turner Prize, Hans-Ulrich Obrist, when Douglas Gordon won the prize, but a designation which proved to be prescient as Glasgow-based artists were regularly nominated for the Turner, eventually winning the prize four times between 2005 and 2011.[44]

Adam Smith may have regarded cultural production as something which did not add to the wealth of the nation, even if it was a sign of opulence, but the fortunes of the Glasgow Boys, the Glasgow Girls and the Scottish Colourists tell a different story. W. Y. Macgregor, sometimes described as the 'Father of the Glasgow School',[45] was the son of a family who owned a shipbuilding business that had been a pioneer in the design and construction of iron steamships – indeed, Tod and Macgregor had built the first ships that made regular crossings from Glasgow to New York.[46] Their shipbuilding contributed considerably to the wealth of the nation, both through the sale of ships but also by their investment in the various dry docks and engineering facilities needed to build them. In the 1870s, however, the business began to fail and the Macgregors sold their share to the Henderson family who owned the Anchor Line, which made its money conveying emigrants to North America. Anchor itself was taken over by Cunard in 1911 but in the post-war economic decline Cunard was forced to put the

Anchor Line into liquidation in 1935. The dockyard which Tod and Macgregor had built at Meadowhouse in Glasgow was still in use in the Second World War, building landing craft for the army, but their dry dock was to be filled in with the rubble of the city's demolished St Enoch Hotel when the St Enoch Centre was built in 1988.[47] Tod and Macgregor's investments have not only entirely disappeared from the industrial infrastructure of Scotland, they have disappeared from its landscape. Macgregor's paintings, however, not only remain as part of the assets of the country, they have gathered value with the passing of time, as the significance of the Glasgow Boys not just to Scottish but to European art has been increasingly recognised. Rather than being a drain on the national economy, the arts accumulate value over time and, in a globalised economy, advertise how the nation can be both distinctive and distinguished. Culture is not only fundamental to the wealth of the nation but fundamental to its self-perception as a nation. It is symptomatic of Scottish historians' blindness to the role and influence of culture that the SAC is not listed in the index of Christopher Harvie's *No Gods and Precious Few Heroes* (1981), T. M. Devine's *The Scottish Nation* (2000), Jo Eric Murkens' *Scottish Independence: A Practical Guide* (2002), Richard Finlay's *Modern Scotland 1914–2000* (2004), Ewen A. Cameron's *Impaled Upon a Thistle: Scotland Since 1880* (2010), or James Mitchell's *The Scottish Question* (2014). It gets brief mention in Catriona M. M. MacDonald's *Whaur Extremes Meet: Scotland's Twentieth Century* (2009), but only in relation to the work of individual artists who had SAC support. To modern historians, trained in the traditions of economic history, cultural wealth is, it seems, invisible.

The further irony of this accumulation of cultural wealth in Scotland that goes largely unnoticed by the nation's historians is that there is probably no nationalist party in the world that has been less focused on mobilising culture as part of its political strategy than the SNP. Although founded in the 1920s by writers and cultural activists – the original founders of the National Party of Scotland in 1928 included R. B Cunninghame Graham, Compton Mackenzie and Hugh MacDiarmid (C. M. Grieve) – the SNP's mission since the 1960s has been framed almost entirely in terms of Adam Smith's definition of wealth, from the claim in the 1970s that 'it's Scotland's oil' to the 2014 White Paper's insistence that an independent Scotland would make 'Scotland's vast wealth and resources work much better for everyone in our country, creating a society that reflects our hopes and ambition'.[48] The SNP Government might be proud of the amount of money that is spent on the arts in Scotland but it shows little evidence of understanding what value the arts bring to the nation, even though the SNP may have been one its principal beneficiaries because of what, among political scientists, has come to be known as the 'devolution paradox'. Sociological studies consistently show almost no difference in the economic standing or the range of social attitudes of people in Scotland as compared with those in England: 'in key respects', David McCrone suggests,

> Scotland is far less 'different' from the rest of the UK than we might imagine, or than some writers have claimed. Over the long-term, its industrial and occupational structures have been much closer to the British mean since the nineteenth century, and certainly more so than particular English regions, or Wales and Northern Ireland. Its employment and wages structure reflect a common UK labour market.[49]

Such a confluence of Scotland's economic and social values with those in England might suggest that there is nothing to distinguish Scotland from British norms: for practical purposes, Scotland might as well not exist and, indeed, McCrone begins his study in the past tense, with a chapter entitled 'When was Scotland?'[50] But as Scotland and England have converged in standards of living, in social values and in participation in a globalised world of consumerism and international entertainment, Scottish politics has significantly diverged from England's, in part of course because of the existence of the SNP as an alternative to the two main UK parties, but even when what is offered in both Scotland and England is the same yes/no option, Scotland votes differently, as revealed in the 2016 Brexit referendum, when 62% of Scots were in favour of remaining in the EU as compared with only 48% in the UK as a whole. What makes the difference is not the potentially 'vast wealth and resources' of Scotland's economy, which has always fluctuated with its economic environment, but the vast wealth of its cultural inheritance, a cultural inheritance which was assumed, from the eighteenth century to the 1980s, to be incapable of surviving the incorporating Union or the internationalism of the modern economic system. That Scotland should continue to be able to assert its difference from England rather than being assimilated by it, that it should continue to produce a distinctive and internationally recognised culture and that it can continue to generate cultural wealth is the paradox that the following chapters explore.

Notes

1. Gardham, M. (2016), 'Sturgeon lays blame for Scotland's record £15billion deficit at UK Government's door' *The Herald*, 10 March, <http://www.heraldscotland.com/news/14336255.Sturgeon_lays_blame_for_Scotland_s_record___15billion_ deficit_at_UK_Government's_door>; Cramb, A. (2016), 'Scotland's huge deficit 'blows £15bn hole in case for independence'', *The Telegraph*, 24 August, <http://www.telegraph.co.uk/news/2016/08/24/scotlands-huge-deficit-blows-15bn-hole-in-case-for-independence>; Carrell, S. (2016), 'Scottish deficit grows to nearly £15bn as oil revenues collapse', *The Guardian*, 24 August, <https://www.theguardian.com/society/2016/aug/24/scottish-finances-worsen-fall-oil-revenues-15bn-deficit> (last accessed 30 May 2017).
2. Mossner, E. C. and I. S. Ross (eds), *The Correspondence of Adam Smith* (Oxford: Clarendon Press, 1977), p. 68.
3. Devine, T. M., C. H. Lee and G. C. Peden (eds), *The Transformation of Scotland: The Economy since 1700* (Edinburgh: Edinburgh University Press, 2005), pp. 153–4.
4. All lost to one town, Kilmarnock, between the 1960s and the 1980s.
5. Devine, T. M., *To the Ends of the Earth: Scotland's Global Diaspora 1750–2019* (London: Allen Lane, 2011), p. 85.
6. Ibid. p. 271.
7. Eamon Butler wrote in 2009: 'It was an ASI [Adam Smith Institute] report *Revising the Rating System*, written by my colleague, the late Douglas Mason, that put the idea on the public agenda. Mason recommended a flat-rate, per capita charge for local services, balanced by improvements in welfare benefits . . . If anything sunk the poll tax, it was disastrously bad implementation, rather than the idea itself'; Available at <https://www.adamsmith.org/blog/tax-spending/the-rates-the-poll-tax-and-council-tax> (last accessed 30 May 2017).
8. Young, H., *One of Us* (London: Macmillan, 1989) p. 528.
9. Available at <http://www.margaretthatcher.org/document/10668 9> (last accessed 29 June 2014).

10. Available at <http://www.margaretthatcher.org/document/106689> (last accessed 29 June 2014).
11. Available at <http://www.spectator.co.uk/the-week/10293/who-inspired-thatchers-most-damaging-remark-tony-blairs-favourite-guru/> (last accessed 29 June 2014).
12. Macmurray, J., *Creative Society: A Study of the Relation of Christianity to Communism* (London: Faber, 1935), pp. 97–8.
13. Evensky, J., *Adam Smith's Moral Philosophy: A Historical and Contemporary Perspective on Markets, Law, Ethics and Culture* (Cambridge: Cambridge University Press, 2005), p. 245.
14. Teichgraeber, R., 'Rethinking *Das Adam Smith Problem*', in Haakonssen K. (ed.), *Adam Smith* (Dartmouth: Ashgate, 1998), p. 489.
15. Skinner, A. (ed.), 'Introduction', *Adam Smith: The Wealth of Nations* (Harmondsworth: Penguin, 1970), p. 17; quotation from *Theory of Moral Sentiments*, I, I, i.
16. Ibid. pp. 27–8.
17. Ibid. p. 13.
18. Hayek, F. A., *Capitalism and the Historians* (London: Routledge, 1954), p. 28.
19. Hunt, E. K., 'The Categories of Productive and Unproductive Labour in Marxist Economic Theory', *Science and Society* 43: pp. 303–25; quoted in Samuels, W. J. (with M. F. Johnson and W. H. Perry), *Erasing the Invisible Hand: Essays on an Elusive and Misused Concept in Economics* (Cambridge: Cambridge University Press, 2011), p. 35.
20. For details of Morrison's career and thought, see Craig, C., 'Intended Communities: MacIver, Macmurray and the Scottish Idealists', in *Intending Scotland: Explorations in Scottish Culture Since the Enlightenment* (Edinburgh: Edinburgh University Press, 2009), pp.179–202.
21. Lehmann, W. C., *Adam Ferguson and the Beginnings of Modern Sociology* (New York: Columbia University Press, 1930), p. 257.
22. Bryson, G., *Man and Society: The Scottish Inquiry of the Eighteenth Century* (Princeton: Princeton University Press, 1945), p. 3.
23. Ibid. p. 2.
24. Ibid. p. 3.
25. Campbell, R. H., A. Skinner and W. B. Todd (eds), Adam Smith, *An Inquiry into the Nature and Causes of the Wealth of Nations* (Oxford: Clarendon Press, 1976), Vol. I, pp. 330–1.
26. Available at <https://www.nytimes.com/2017/03/15/arts/nea-neh-endowments-trump.html> (last accessed 28 May 2017).
27. Upchurch, A., 'John Maynard Keynes, the Bloomsbury Group and the Origins of the Arts Council Movement', *International Journal of Cultural Policy*, 10:2 (2007), pp. 203–17.

28. Hewison, R., *Culture and Consensus: England, Art and Politics since 1940* (London: Methuen, 1997), p. 40.
29. Ibid. p. 40.
30. Ibid. p. 45.
31. Ibid. p. 45.
32. O'Neil, M., 'Museums, Meaning and Money in Glasgow', *Journal of Irish and Scottish Studies*, 2:2 2009, p. 139.
33. Ibid. p. 140.
34. Available at <https://www.museumsgalleriesscotland.org.uk/accreditation-recognition/recognition-scheme/> (last accessed 25 June 2017).
35. Available at <http://www.scotcities.com/carnegie/early.htm> (last accessed 26 May 2017).
36. Hewison, *Culture and Consensus*, p. 253.
37. Ibid. p. 139.
38. White, K., *The Bird Path: Collected Longer Poems* (Edinburgh: Mainstream Publishing, 1989); White, K. *Handbook for the Diamond Country: Collected Shorter Poems* (Edinburgh: Mainstream Publishing, 1990).
39. White, K., *On Scottish Ground: Selected Essays* (Edinburgh: Polygon, 1998).
40. The Scottish Arts Council: An exhibition of work by the group of artists who flourished in Glasgow 1880–1900, *The Glasgow Boys* (Edinburgh: Scottish Arts Council, 1968), p. 7.
41. Scottish Artists in the Collection of the National Gallery of Modern Art, Edinburgh, Number 4, The Scottish Colourists, November 1980, p. 1.
42. Long, P. and E. Cumming, *The Scottish Colourists 1900–1930* (Edinburgh: National Galleries of Scotland, 2000).
43. Strang, A. (ed.), *Modern Scottish Women Painters and Sculptors 1885–1965* (Edinburgh: National Galleries of Scotland, 2015).
44. Simon Starling (2005), Richard Wright (2009), Susan Philipsz (2010), Martin Boyce (2011).
45. Buchanan, W. *The Glasgow Boys* (Edinburgh: Scottish Arts Council, 1968), p. 9.
46. Available at <http://www.gregormacgregor.com/Tod&Macgregor/> (last accessed 26 June 2017).
47. Available at <http://clydeserver.com/shipping/viewtopic.php?t=18148> (last accessed 26 June 2017).
48. *Scotland's Future* (Edinburgh: The Scottish Government, 2013), p. 1.
49. McCrone, D., *The New Sociology of Scotland* (London: Sage, 2017), p. 214.
50. Ibid. p. 3.

1 Cultural Capital and the Xeniteian Empire

1 Revivalism and National Memory

The *Proposals For Carrying on Certain Public Works in the City of Edinburgh* which inaugurated fundraising in 1752 for the construction of Edinburgh's New Town, opens with a description of the requirements of a national capital:

> Among the several causes to which the prosperity of a nation may be ascribed, the situation, conveniency, and beauty of its capital are surely not the least considerable. A capital where these circumstances happen fortunately to concur, should naturally become the centre of trade and commerce, of learning and the arts, of politeness, and of refinement of every kind. No sooner will the advantages which these necessarily produce, be felt and experienced in the chief city, than they diffuse themselves through the nation, and universally promote the same spirit of industry and improvement.[1]

The capital generates capital: it spreads through the nation the spirit of industry – or capitalism as it would come to be known – and it capitalises on the spirit that makes 'learning and the arts' a necessary adjunct to 'trade and commerce'. Scotland's future depends on overcoming 'the meanness of Edinburgh [which] has been too long an obstruction to our improvement, and a reproach to Scotland' by 'a project for enlarging and beautifying this city',[2] and by bringing Edinburgh up to a condition similar to that of London or Dublin, where, the *Proposals* note, Ireland's advances 'in manufactures and commerce' have encouraged the nobility to 'go more rarely to London, and reside more at Dublin'. This not only adds 'vigour to their manufactures' but allows Dublin a theatre that 'even rivals that of London'.[3]

> The national advantages which a populous capital must necessarily produce, are obvious. A great concourse of people brought within a small compass, occasions a much greater consumption than the same number would do dispersed over a wide country. As the consumption is greater, so is it quicker and more discernible. Hence follows a more rapid circulation of money and other commodities, the great spring which gives motion to general industry and improvement.[4]

In recognition of the value to culture of the national capital and of the value to capital of the national culture, the *Proposals* combine two principal aims – the building of new exchange as 'proper accommodations for our merchants'[5] and a new Register Office and Advocates Library 'which may be justly styled *The great charter-room of the nation*'.[6] The security of the recorded heritage of the nation is the foundation of the growth of its capital, in both senses of that word.

The concerns of the *Proposals* anticipate Adam Smith's argument four years later in *An Inquiry into the Nature and Causes of the Wealth of Nations*, that 'the capital . . . that is acquired to any country by commerce and manufactures, is all a very precarious and uncertain possession till some part of it has been secured and realized in the cultivation and improvement of its lands'. Indeed, because a merchant 'is not necessarily the citizen of any particular country', it being 'in a great measure indifferent to him from what place he carries on his trade', capital is not securely a national asset until the wealth it generates 'has been spread as it were over the face of that country, either in buildings or in the lasting improvement of the lands'.[7] The success of the Edinburgh *Proposals* of 1752 was signalled precisely by the spread of the new wealth of Scotland across the 'face of the country' to create the 'Athens of the North' that would allow Edinburgh, despite its size, to claim the equality with London that *Blackwood's Magazine* envisaged when proposing, in 1819, the construction of a 'National Monument':

> while London must always eclipse [Edinburgh] in all that depends on wealth, power, or fashionable elegance, nature has given to it the

> means of establishing a superiority of a higher and more permanent kind. The matchless beauty of its situation, the superb cliffs by which it is surrounded, the magnificent prospects of the bay, which it commands, have given to Edinburgh the means of becoming the most *beautiful* town that exists in the world . . . And thus while London is the Rome of the empire, to which the young, and the ambitious, and the gay, resort for the pursuit of pleasure, of fortune, or of ambition, Edinburgh might become another Athens, in which the arts and the sciences flourished, under the shade of her ancient flame, and established a dominion over the minds of men more permanent even than that which the Roman arms were able to effect.[8]

Edinburgh's real capital is its culture, its contemporary reputation as a 'hot-bed of genius',[9] as Tobias Smollett described it in his novel of 1771, *The Expedition of Humphry Clinker*, but also the value of its 'ancient flame', its pre-Union culture dating back, as James Macpherson claimed on the publication of his *Fragments of Ancient Poetry* in 1760, to a heroic bard of Gaelic culture named Ossian, who had lived in the third century AD. The claim was not merely that the Ossianic poetry was the earliest known poetry of the British Isles but a poetry to compare to the greatest achievements of classical Greece. As Hugh Blair put it in his 'Critical Dissertation on the Poems of Ossian':

> As Homer is of all the great poets, the one whose manner, and whose times come the nearest to Ossian's, we are naturally led to run a parallel in some instances between the Greek and the Celtic bard . . . It was not to be expected, that . . . Ossian could equal Homer. For Homer lived in a country where society was much farther advanced . . . But if Ossian's ideas and objects be less diversified than those of Homer, they are all, however, of the kind fittest for poetry . . . In a rude age and country, though the events that happen be few, the undissipated mind broods over them more; they strike the imagination, and fire the passions in a higher degree; and of consequence become happier materials to poetical genius . . .[10]

In a world where 'poetry, which is the child of the imagination, is frequently most glowing and animated in the first stages of society',[11] Homer is a mere 'modern' in comparison to the truly ancient poetry of Ossian, whose work is imbued with 'the fire and enthusiasm of the most early times . . .'[12] Gaelic Scotland, in economic ruin in the aftermath of the Jacobite defeat in

1746, was transformed by Macpherson's poetry into one of Scotland's most valuable cultural assets, and while for Adam Smith a nation's capital was effective only when 'spread as it were over the face of that country', Macpherson demonstrated that there was another kind of capital, one that derived from the face of the country when that country had been made the object of intense aesthetic experience. Smollett's Welsh travellers in *Humphry Clinker* are prophetic of generations of cultural tourists for whom the terminus of their travels is the landscape of Ossian:

> We have had princely sport in hunting the stag on these mountains – These are the lonely hills of Morven, where Fingal and his heroes enjoyed the same pastime; I feel an enthusiastic pleasure when I survey the brown heath that Ossian wont to tread; and hear the wind whistle through the bending grass – When I enter our landlord's hall, I look for the suspended harp of that divine bard, and listen in hopes of hearing the aerial sound of his respected spirit – The poems of Ossian are in every mouth.[13]

The recollection of the poetry of the ancient bard has created a new geography – 'the lonely hills of Morven' – and new models for contemporary manners. Out of that long-dead, perhaps entirely fictional mouth, a landscape once considered barbarous has been imbued with a 'respected spirit', the spirit both of art and of nation.

Macpherson's 'discovery' of the Ossianic literature was only, however, the most grandiose gesture in what had already become, and was, over the following two hundred years, to be foundational to Scotland's acquisition and accumulation of cultural capital – revivalism, the recovery of nearly forgotten literary treasures from Scotland's pre-Union past. Even in the midst of the negotiations over the Union with England, Edinburgh printer James Watson, a man of Jacobite sympathies, published in 1706 the first volume of his *Choice Collection of Comic and Serious Scots Poems Both Ancient and Modern* in order, he claimed, to make available the poetry of 'our own native Scots Dialect', poetry which had either been printed 'most uncorrectly' or 'never before printed'.[14] Watson's *Choice Collection*, containing some poems which went back to pre-Reformation Scotland, such as 'Christ's Kirk on the Green', attributed to King James V, was to inspire two collections by Allan Ramsay, both published in 1724. His *Tea Table Miscellany* was a collection of lyrics, mostly in Scots, intended for domestic performance: it went through more than twenty editions in the following three-quarters of a century, as well as through many imitations by other editors, and contributed to the fashion for 'national' songs which became part of the emerging 'British' culture of the eighteenth century. It was his *Ever Green* of the same year, however, which seriously attempted to reconstitute the culture of the national past through 'a collection of Scots Poems, wrote by the Ingenious before 1600'. The *Ever Green* made available for the first time a substantial number of poems by Dunbar, Henryson and Montgomerie preserved in the Bannatyne manuscript. Ramsay's effort to recover the Scottish literary past and to collect Scottish popular song was in turn to be the inspiration for generations of Scottish writers and scholars. Bishop Percy's *Reliques of Ancient English Poetry* (1765) had much of its impact because of the twenty Scottish ballads and songs supplied by his Scottish correspondent, Lord Hailes, who himself re-edited material from the Bannatyne manuscript in *Ancient Scottish Songs* (1770). David Herd's *Ancient and Modern Scots Songs* (1769), claimed that the fragments of the past had at last been gathered into 'one body' – but the dismembered past was to continue to give up new fragments to each succeeding generation. Burns, at the end of his career, in the songs he collected for James Johnson's *Scots Musical Museum* (1787–1803) and Walter Scott, at the beginning of his career, in his *Minstrelsy of the Scottish Border* (1802), both confirmed the as yet undiscovered riches of the oral tradition in Scots, riches which were to be further excavated by James Hogg's *Jacobite Relics* (1819), Lady Nairne's *The Scottish Minstrel* (1821–4), William Motherwell's *Minstrelsy, Ancient and Modern* (1827) and by William Aytoun's *Ballads of Scotland* (1858). The lore of Gaelic Scotland was collected in *Carmena Gadelica* (1900) by Alexander Carmichael, while the *Greig-Duncan Folk-Song Collection*, gathered in the North-East of Scotland in the decade before the First World War, required eight volumes for its publication in the 1970s and 80s. Modern Scottish literature and culture was no less underpinned by revivalism. The 'Scottish Renascence' of the 1890s, led by Patrick Geddes, and the 'Scottish Renaissance' of the 1920s, led by Hugh MacDiarmid (C. M. Grieve), were both inspired by the revival of earlier Scottish art and literature, in MacDiarmid's case by a linguistic return to the language of the Scots Makars of the fifteenth and sixteenth centuries. After the Second World War, the second Edinburgh International Festival in 1948 was astounded by the revival of Sir David Lyndsay's *Ane Satyre of the Thrie Estaitis*, in a version written by Scottish dramatist Robert Kemp and directed by Tyrone Guthrie, a play which had not been performed in Edinburgh since 1554. Such was its success, it was revived again in 1949, 1951, 1959, 1973 and 1984. In the same period Hamish Henderson was tape recording story and song among Scotland's travelling people and contributing to the 'folksong revival' of the 1950s and 1960s, led by singers like Jeanie Robertson and Ewan McColl, and generating large audiences for groups such as the Corries, one of whom, Roy Williamson, penned what was to become Scotland's sporting national anthem – 'Flower of Scotland' – a song which celebrates revivalism:

> Those days are past now,
> And in the past
> They must remain,
> But we can still rise now,
> And be the nation again,
> That stood against him,
> Proud Edward's Army,
> And sent him homeward,
> Tae think again.

Each of these revivals was an attempt to wrest from forgetfulness the memory of the nation which seemed, by the Union of 1707, to have consigned to oblivion its cultural past – the 'end of auld sang' as the Earl of Seafield is reported to have said on signing away Scotland's independence. But far from being the end of the auld sang, it was, in effect, the discovery of the importance of that sang, with new acts of recovery of Scotland's older culture being instigated by generation after generation of Scots born into the Union with England.

Revivalism was the medium by which Scotland's difference and distinction was continually reasserted through the years of the 'incorporating union' that ought to have made Scotland an indistinguishable part of the cultural polity of the United Kingdom (UK). Resistance took the form of refusing to allow an older – and once independent – Scotland to pass out of contemporary memory. The intensity of the commitment to those acts of revivalism was an index of a double threat: first, assimilation to English mores that would make a modern Scotland indistinguishable from its more powerful neighbour and, second, in so doing, disconnect modern Scotland from its distinctive past. The generation born immediately after the Union and which grew to maturity in the years when the Union, post-1750, was beginning to deliver economic benefits in Scotland, saw assimilation in language and in culture as the necessary price of the country's progress in civilization. David Hume's *History of England* (1754) and William Robertson's *History of Scotland* (1759) both presented the Scottish past as something which, because of the weakness of its monarchy, the feebleness of its parliament and its disputatious religious enthusiasms, could only be represented by historians as a warning against allowing the nation's past to infect its modern existence: as Murray Pittock puts it, 'Scotland was "the rudest, perhaps, of all European Nations" in Enlightenment eyes. Its conversion to civility must involve in part the despising of its own past'.[15] Pre-Union Scotland was to be remembered only to be rejected. Revivalism, on the other hand, sought to build a bridge between the culture of the past and that of the present, and, in a fashion similar to the religious revivalisms of the eighteenth century, sought to infuse the present with the virtues of that past. Adam Ferguson, in his analysis of the division of labour in *An Essay on the History of Civil Society* (1767), noted how the progress of civilisation might also destroy the virtues upon which civilisation depended for its future security:

> It is difficult to tell how long the decay of states might be suspended, by the cultivation of arts on which their real felicity and strength depend; by cultivating in the higher ranks those talents for the council and the field, which cannot, without great disadvantage, be separated; and in the body of a people, that zeal for their country, and that military character, which enable them to take a share in defending its rights.
>
> Times may come, when every proprietor must defend his own possessions, and every free people maintain their own independence.[16]

The wealth produced by modern commercial societies might be of no value where, as in many previous civilisations, 'the polished have fallen a prey to the rude, and where the pacific inhabitant has been reduced to subjection by military force'.[17] Ferguson, who had been a chaplain to the then recently formed Black Watch regiment (established as a unit of the British army in 1740) believed – unlike many of his eighteenth-century compatriots among the literati – that the erosion of martial virtue diminished the values of a civilisation:

> We may, with good reason, congratulate our species on their having escaped from the state of barbarous disorder and violence, into a state of domestic peace and regular policy; when they have sheathed the dagger, and disarmed the animosities of civil contention; when the weapons with which they contend are the reasonings of the wise, and the tongue of the eloquent. But we cannot, meantime, help to regret, that they should ever proceed, in search of perfection, to place every branch of administration behind the counter, and come to employ, instead of the statesman and warrior, the mere clerk and accountant.[18]

In the aftermath of 1746 and the banning of tartan except for use by the British army, the re-adoption of Highland dress by aristocrats in the 1780s and 1790s, and its promotion by the Highland Society of London (formed 1778), suggests, as Murray Pittock has pointed out, 'that the widespread and already iconic use of Government tartan in the British army helped to consolidate a sense of tartan as a vehicle for collective, regimental (and hence in the context of the Jacobite Rising, family and clan) identities'.[19] In the context of Ferguson's account of modern commercial society, however, the revival of tartan was a symbol that a leader of society, at least in Scotland, could resist the fragmentation of the division of labour and remain a 'statesman and warrior' rather than just a 'clerk and accountant'. Walter Scott's orchestration of tartan-clad clan leaders to greet King George IV on his visit to Scotland in 1822 has regularly been presented as Scott's substitution of Highland glamour for Lowland industry,[20] the Highlands that were being celebrated having disappeared 'other than as a sentimental entity based on chiefdoms, tartan and yearning for a lost past'.[21] But the bridge of revivalism is not built simply to allow a sentimental escape from the present to the past, it also provided a route by which the virtues of the past could march into the territory of the present and question, if not overthrow, its values.

In the context of revivalism, Scott's invention of the 'historical novel' with the publication of *Waverley* in 1814 was neither accident nor act of individual genius: it was the product of a country and a city which, deprived of political power after 1707, became a memory machine for the recollection of the nation's past: as David Masson, Professor of Rhetoric and English Literature at Edinburgh University and later the Historiographer Royal, put it, 'partly from the very intensity and compactness of the little national history which Edinburgh was bound to transmit . . . the mere aspect of things around one compels a constant sense of the antique, and cultivates in the mind of every resident a definite habit of historical reminiscence'.[22] Scott himself was to be memorialised by the Scott Monument (opened in 1844) on the principal street of the city, as Allan Ramsay's contribution to the revival of Scottish culture was to be memorialised in Patrick Geddes's renovation of the tenements of Ramsay Garden in Edinburgh's Old Town in the 1890s. Scotland might have been a nation which had lost its statehood, but in its commitment to the remembrance of its national past it became an almost exemplary case of the hypotheses of recent theories of the nation and of nationalism which, whether from the 'modernist' perspective of Gellner, Hobsbawm and Anderson, or from the 'ethno-symbolist' perspective of Smith and Hutchinson,[23] have laid an ever-increasing stress on the role of memory in national identity and in the politics of nationalism. Without a core of shared symbolism resting on an accepted body of cultural memory, the argument goes, the modern nation could not maintain the social solidarity which makes its existence possible. In old nations a selective tradition of its past experience has to be constructed to justify its continued existence in the modern world; in 'new' nations the symbols of a shared past must be 'invented' if they cannot be retrieved, reshaped and re-imagined from some pre-existing recollection of a non-national past. As, for the 'modernist' theorists, all nations are 'new' in the aftermath of the French Revolution, all nations are the inventions of reconstructed memories, thereby generating the central paradox that Ernest Gellner's influential account of nationalism in the 1980s posed to later theorists: 'Nationalism is not the awakening of nations to self-consciousness: it invents nations where they do not exist'.[24] For the ethno-symbolists, on the other hand, the modernist account of nationalism as arising only in the context of the challenge to the absolutist conceptions of the state in the seventeenth and eighteenth centuries mistakes its links with earlier forms of social solidarity:

> A time dimension of many centuries (similar to the *longue durée* emphasised by the *Annales* school of French historiography) is essential for disentangling independent ethnic experiences from the effects of diffusion and mimesis. An extended temporal perspective is especially important as a means of perceiving modern nationalism as a part of a cycle of ethnic consciousness. Because the epoch of Absolutism that immediately preceded European nationalism involved, at least for elites, an exceptionally strong rejection of ethnic differentiation, nationalism is often seen as utterly unprecedented. A longer look suggests that widespread intense ethnic identification, although expressed in other forms, is recurrent.[25]

As Anthony Smith notes in this context, 'the terms "ethnic" and "nation" form part of a continuum, and . . . what matters is not the form they take in different epochs, but the persisting group perception and sentiments themselves';[26] modern nationalisms tap into the symbolic structures of pre-existing communal memories, even if the territory of those memories is not identical with the boundaries of the modern nation. In either case, however, the fundamental asset of the nation is the stored cultural capital it can draw down for future investment in the memorial solidarity upon which its continued existence depends. The impact of Macpherson's Ossian throughout Europe, and the search across many cultures for local equivalents, was testimony to the developing awareness of the significance of cultural memory to the prospects of the nation, and to the awareness of a new kind of cultural capital which, rather than being merely civic – 'the centre of trade and commerce, of learning and the arts, of politeness, and of refinement of every kind' – was founded on the richness of the memories derived from national legend and from national history that could be attached to, and celebrated in, the national landscape.

The apparent diminution of the significance of Macpherson's Ossianic works in the face of accusations that they were the fraudulent inventions of modernity, rather than the recovery of the ancient virtues of the nation, prefigures debates within recent theories of the nation and of nationalism about the status of the memories around which the nation coheres – are they 'real' memories or simply invented fictions; are they actual inheritances from the past or modern creations designed to delude the population that they have a past? The very richness of this investment by the Scots produced what has been seen as the ongoing paradox of modern Scotland: how could a country with all the fitments necessary for the development of nineteenth-century nationalism progress through the era of nationalisms without itself giving birth to, or being politically influenced by, a nationalist movement? Scotland was, indeed, in many ways, the pathfinder into the new world of nineteenth century national cultures, inspiring others across Europe to search for the cultural origins which would justify their political independence. But in Scotland, unlike in its near neighbour Ireland, the recovery and the assertion of the nation's cultural capital did not produce a political nationalism.

Since the 1960s and the rise of modern Scottish nationalism, Scotland's 'absent nationalism' in the nineteenth century has been the issue which has inspired – and perplexed – many of the country's historians and theorists, from Tom Nairn's *The Break-up of Britain* in 1977, through the various rewritings of Christopher Harvie's *Scotland and Nationalism* (1977, 1994, 1998), to the flood of books that accompanied the three hundredth anniversary of the Union of 1707,[27] and to the equally vigorous publishing campaign that accompanied the referendum on Scottish independence in 2014, which included former UK Prime Minister Gordon Brown's *My Scotland, Our Britain*. Why, Brown asks, should Scotland have turned to nationalism in the twenty-first century when, in historical circumstances much more pressing than those in which it now finds itself, it has previously disdained to follow the path of national assertion that dominated European history in the nineteenth century? Brown asks why,

> the trajectory of Scottish nationalism is so unlike the other forms it claims to parallel. Can we explain why there was no significant Scottish-led rebellion in 1832 or 1848, when Britain was convulsed by riots over political reform; and why no significant Scottish nationalist uprising in 1919, when there was a huge sense of injustice as British promises of 'Homes fit for Heroes' were swept aside and workers left to the mercy of a post-war depression? If repression is the trigger for an assertion of national identity, why not in the period from 1746 when Highlanders were brutally suppressed in the aftermath of Culloden? If religious differences are

> a potential starting pistol for a secessionist movement, why not in 1712 when the British Parliament usurped the authority of the Scottish Church?[28]

The absence of Scottish nationalism in periods when it might (to Brown) have made sense, either because of apparent breaches in the agreements in the Treaty of Union, or in terms of the general development of European nationalisms, makes modern Scottish nationalism a historical anomaly, a solution to a problem that might have had relevance in the past but has no relevance in the contemporary world. A nineteenth-century Scottish nationalism would have made historical sense; Scottish nationalism in the late twentieth and early twenty-first centuries is a historical anomaly and, for Brown, a political mistake.

II Cultural Capital

Karl Marx, developing and extending Adam Smith's labour-based theory of value insisted that it was 'only the dominion of past, accumulated, materialized labour over immediate living labour that transforms accumulated labour into capital'.[29] Marx also underlines how capitalism produces the mutual interdependence of all areas of the world in the process of capital accumulation:

> The bourgeoisie has through its exploitation of the world market given a cosmopolitan character to production and consumption in every country. To the great chagrin of reactionaries, it has drawn from under the feet of industry the national ground on which it stood . . . In place of the old local and national seclusion and self-sufficiency, we have intercourse in every direction, universal inter-dependence of nations.[30]

'Interdependence', however, is not equality. The flow of resources accumulates at the centres of the global economy to the relative impoverishment of those beyond such centres, and thereby provides the platform for further accumulations of wealth. And that wealth is cultural as well as financial. Culture accumulates in commercial and imperial centres – whether looted from military conquest as in the collections of the British Museum or the Louvre, or bought by access to disposable wealth, as in the museums of New York and Chicago – and the power of that accumulated culture then underpins the imposition of the centre's cultural authority wherever commerce erases the 'national ground' of local industry. As Ngũgĩ wa Thiong'o put it, 'to control a people's culture is to control their tools of self-definition in relationship to others':[31]

> For colonialism this involved two aspects of the same process: the destruction or undervaluing of a people's culture, their art, dances, religions, history, geography, education, orature and literature, and the conscious elevation of the language of the coloniser. The domination of a people's language by the languages of the colonising nations was crucial to the domination of the mental universe of the colonised.[32]

If, in 1986, an African writer could still believe in the possibility of 'decolonising the mind', Western Marxism, from Adorno to Jameson, had long since given up on such possibilities, believing that 'culture' in (post-)modern capitalist societies had become so powerful, so totalitarian and so ruthlessly pervasive as to erase all alternatives. Frederic Jameson, for instance, differentiates 'postmodern' culture from earlier forms of capital and culture on the basis that it represents:

> a new cultural realm or dimension which is independent of the former real world, not because, as in the modern (or even the romantic) period, culture withdrew from the real world into an autonomous space of art, but rather because the real world has already been suffused with it and colonized by it, so that it has no outside in terms of which it could be found lacking.[33]

In an earlier period of colonialism, local culture is displaced or marginalised by the intrusions of the cultural capital of the coloniser. In our postmodern world, finance capital and instantaneous flows of information turn everything into 'culture' and make global culture inescapable in almost any geographic location. As Edward Said noted in *Culture and Imperialism*, 'direct colonialism has largely ended' but imperialism continues in a 'general cultural sphere, as well as in specific political, ideological, economic, and social practices'.[34] It is through cultural power that post-colonial imperialism asserts the 'domination of the mental universe' which underpins economic domination.

But the drive towards a singular universality, which has been both the ambition of all imperial systems and the underlying reason for their conflicts, has never been able to overwhelm the equally tenacious desire of people to maintain, protect and assert local cultural values which are, for them, no less valid just because, at a particular point in time – and perhaps at any time – they are incapable of enforcing a similar claim to universalizability. They become, in Homi Bhabha's term, 'cultures of survival'[35] – cultures which have (so far) survived being overwhelmed by the dominant powers of the world. In these processes, the colonising states, competing for the territory that had been opened up by the discovery of the Americas, spurred on by the increasing efficiency and reliability of navigation and empowered by the technologies made available to Europeans by the scientific revolution of the seventeenth and eighteenth centuries, developed their own narratives of national identity as justifications of their colonial ambitions: their 'nationalisms' were projected outwards as indicators of their superiority over those whom they ruled. But from the time of Napoleonic Wars to the decolonisation of the European empires after the Second World War, nationalism was also the local vehicle of resistance to the singular universality of imperialism. It is this which has made 'nationalism' such an ambiguous category – the 'Janus' of Tom Nairn's *Faces of Nationalism*.[36]

'Nationalism' is both the justification of colonial subordination – it is the duty of a more advanced culture to impose its cultural order on the barbarian and to set those cultures of lower status on the road of progress – and, at the same time, the medium of resistance to that subordination. Both forms of nationalism were, however, according to Marshall McLuhan's radical interpretation of the influence of the introduction of moveable type into European culture, the product of the printed word: 'the hotting-up of the medium of writing to repeatable print intensity led to nationalism and the religious wars of the sixteenth-century'.[37] It was an insight taken up by Benedict Anderson in *Imagined Communities*, in which he argued that nationalism was the product of a 'print capitalism' which fragmented the 'universal' language of Latin into a series of vernaculars and created a book- and newspaper-reading public who, because they shared the same written language, came to inhabit the same national 'imaginary': 'These fellow-readers, to whom they were connected through print, formed, in their secular, particular, visible invisibility, the embryo of the nationally imagined community'.[38] As these 'imagined communities' became, in Western Europe, the core cultures of imperial expansion, they acquired fellow-readers in the colonies who gained 'access, though the European languages-of-state, to modern Western culture in the broadest sense, and, in particular, to the models of nationalism, nation-ness, and nation-state'.[39] Colonialism inevitably confronts the 'nationalism' of the coloniser with the 'nationalism' of the colonised. In what follows, these two forms of nationalism are distinguished as 'projective nationalism' – the imperial variety – and 'resistant nationalism', that of the subordinated or colonised territory. These are not mutually exclusive, because a 'projective nationalism', like England's in the period of its imperial expansion into the 'British' empire, could, at a later point in time become a 'resistant nationalism', as England's did after the Second World War, when it sought to fend off the growing power of American culture. Equally, Germany's 'resistant nationalism' early in the nineteenth century, as it sought to divert domination by French-language culture, became a 'projective nationalism' by the end of the nineteenth century as it competed with Britain and France for imperial territory.

Both to projective and to resistant nationalisms in the era of print culture, the identification and promotion of a 'national literature' became one of the key cultural justifications of a nation's political aims. A significant national literature was a means of proclaiming the superiority of the values that colonising powers projected, and underlined the need for those whom they ruled to become students of the imperial literature if they were to rise above barbarity; equally, for those who inhabited countries whose boundaries were the arbitrary construction of imperial agreements or disagreements, a national literature was a means not only of generating the social cohesion which their populations lacked but also a means of winning international recognition for their cultural distinctiveness. Literature, the 'highest' achievement of the language of print capitalism, became one of the most valued – and contested – forms of national cultural capital. That the emergence of the discipline of Rhetoric and Belles Lettres – at least in the Anglophone world – should be traceable to Scotland between 1748, when Adam Smith delivered his first course of lectures in Edinburgh, and 1783 when Hugh Blair finally published the lectures which he had been giving in Edinburgh since the 1750s,[40] has often been presented as symptomatic of Scottish concerns that their corrupt dialect would impede their progress in the British state. 'Blair's work', Robert Crawford writes, 'had been geared to the task of cultural conversion, of Anglicizing upwardly mobile Scots to make them acceptable Britons'.[41] The eighteenth-century Scottish literati thus become a cultural and linguistic 'fifth column' – the willing promulgators of a projective English nationalism. Blair, however, was also the most enthusiastic promoter of James Macpherson's Ossianic poems, first published in 1760 as *Fragments of Ancient Poetry* and then completed in 1763 as *The Poems of Ossian*, and which claimed to be nearly fifteen hundred years old. Blair's *A Critical Discourse on the Poems of Ossian* first appeared in 1763 and, in a revised version, was included with the second edition of Macpherson's *Poems of Ossian* in 1765, giving considerable support to Macpherson's claim to have uncovered a British poetry as important as the epics of ancient Greece. On the one hand, Blair's lectures might be inducting a Scottish audience into appreciation of the superior virtues of 'English' literature; on the other hand, however, his support for Macpherson – as, indeed, his later support for Burns – insisted that English literature was the medium for projecting Scottish values at an English audience and seeking to convince them that the liberty on which the modern British state congratulated itself had Scottish foundations. Blair had no means of verifying the literary quality of the Ossianic texts, since he could neither read nor speak Gaelic, but he claimed that the poetry in English itself testified to the qualities of the original:

> To transfuse such spirited and fervid ideas from one language into another; to translate literally, and yet with such a glow of poetry; to keep alive so much passion, and support so much dignity throughout, is one of the most difficult works of genius, and proves the translator to have been animated with no small portion of Ossian's spirit . . . We know how much grace and energy the works of the Greek and Latin poets receive from the charm of versification in their original languages. If then, destitute of this advantage, exhibited in a literal version, Ossian still has power to please as a poet; and not to please only, but often to command, to transport, to melt the heart; we may safely infer, that his productions are the off-spring of true and uncommon genius; and we may boldly assign him a place among those, whose works are to last for ages.[42]

The genius of the original poet is proven by the literary powers of the translator whom he has inspired: the consequence, especially in the light of Macpherson's refusal to provide the originals, was a poem that is actually in no language at all – the English in which it is presented is only a gesture towards a language in which it will never be realised. This is perhaps why Macpherson's most important influence was through the retranslation of his text into many other translations: it is poetry as continuous translation; it is the paper currency of literature, a promissory note which can never be converted back into its 'real' equivalent and whose virtue is realisable only in the process of its various translational exchanges. That 'translational' and 'transitional' status is equally true of Blair's lectures: they may have been designed to achieve the 'translation' of Scots speakers into stylish writers of English but they also effectively projected Scottish values into the common expectations of an English-reading public. Smith's and Blair's courses in rhetoric were not simply the assimilation of English values into a Scottish context. They were also the projection of Scottish values aimed at reshaping the English culture whose own projective cultural nationalism – however 'absent mindedly'[43] – was directed at overwhelming the cultures on its boundaries.

Smith's and Blair's account of 'rhetoric and belles lettres' were to be the opening shots in a long campaign for control of 'English literature' as a key element in Britain's projection of the cultural superiority which justified its imperial acquisitions in the nineteenth century. In part as a result of its essential translatability, the poems of Ossian produced very different outcomes as they crossed the national boundaries of what, after 1801, was the United Kingdom of Britain and Ireland. In Scotland, they asserted the cultural value of the Highlands at a time when they were suffering economic and cultural disintegration and asserted, too, Scotland's right to claim that it was, unlike England, the inheritor and celebrant of a classical culture. Against Ireland, however, the Macpherson-Blair argument represented a projective nationalist claim to ownership of the cultural capital of the ancient Gaelic material. The lengthy arguments conducted by Irish historians and Celticists to prove, in opposition to Macpherson's assertions, that Ireland and not Scotland was the true home of the Ossianic poems, was shot through, as Clare O'Halloran has shown,[44] with a profound ambiguity: The northern equivalent of the 'South Sea

Bubble' that was Macpherson's cultural investment had to be punctured without producing a crash in the cultural capital of the ancient Gaelic sources themselves. Reassembling that cultural capital required the re-nationalising of Macpherson's recuperative efforts, a relationship ironically signalled when the society established in Dublin in 1852 to collect and publish the ancient Gaelic texts decided to adopt Macpherson's name for the ancient bard rather than the Irish one and called itself the 'Ossianic Society of Dublin'. The gesture towards dependence on Macpherson's example combined with the desire to re-establish purely Irish origins is indicative of the perceived collapse of the memory of the Irish nation:

> Irishmen have been often reproached with having no history of their country, and so far as there is a foundation for such a reproach, the blame rests with the last few generations, and most surely not with our ancestors, who from a very early period paid more attention than almost any European people to the preservation of the records of all important events connected with their fatherland.
>
> We certainly have no History of Ireland yet such as we could desire; but materials for such a work we have in great abundance, and the object of this Society is to rescue many of these, which remain scattered over the country in decaying manuscripts, from being lost, and to make them generally available to the English as well as to the Irish reader.[45]

Only by investing in the literal re-collection of the past and by re-enacting Macpherson's quest to assemble the remnants of their culture could the Irish acquire the cultural capital to build a resistant nationalism. In the aftermath of the Union of Scotland and England in 1707 and the Irish incorporation into the UK in 1801, their status as a continuing nation within the Union depended in part on establishing that their culture was actually the foundation upon which a later English culture had been built – that they represented the true native culture of the archipelago. In Wales, a parallel claim was to be made by Iolo Morganwg, whose reconstructions of early Welsh poetry in the 1790s implied a heritage dating back to before the Roman invasion – though Morganwg's sources were discovered to be as dubious as Macpherson's.[46]

The Irish repatriations of the Ossianic material and the accumulating doubts about the authenticity of Macpherson's text, meant that Scotland, too, needed rapidly to reinvest in alternative cultural capital. In the space of twenty years, the bardic mantle passed from the heroic primitive poet to his modern equivalent, the rustic Robert Burns, similarly promoted by the Edinburgh literati, and whose most emotive poetry was steeped in recollection of the nation's past,[47] and then, in the first decades of the nineteenth century, to the grand fabricator of the national past, that 'second Macpherson', Walter Scott.[48] Through Burns and Scott, Scotland redefined itself as a nation whose cultural tradition was primarily that of the Scots language, rather than that of Gaelic. In the course of the nineteenth century the Scottish Text Society, building on the work of the work of the Bannatyne Club (founded in 1823 and presided over by Sir Walter Scott) and the Maitland Club (founded in Glasgow in 1828), did for Scotland's past what the Ossianic Society aimed to do in Ireland, except that Scotland's cultural capital would now be built on the achievement of the late medieval 'Makars' and other texts in Scots from before 1707, as well as the remains of the oral tradition in Scots.[49]

Both in Scotland and in Ireland the cultural capital that had been threatened by the insubstantiality of Macpherson's Ossianic discoveries had to be redeemed and reinvested in more secure symbolic resources, but the claim of the Celtic cultures to be the foundation on which later English literature was built was to have a long lasting impact on accounts of literature in England. The most significant response was Matthew Arnold's *The Celtic Element in English Literature* (1865), regularly excoriated for its lack of knowledge of the Celtic literatures he claimed to be assessing. Arnold's work, however, has to be read alongside the crisis-of-cultural value he charted in *Culture and Anarchy*,[50] which presents the near bankruptcy of English culture, divided in class terms between the Barbarians, the Philistines and the Populace, each accumulating capital without culture. *Culture and Anarchy* struggles to find any ground for building a future English culture but, below ground, the spirit which infuses English literature with alternative possibilities is its Celtic substratum, as English literature is 'a vast obscure Cymric base with a vast visible Teutonic superstructure'.[51] The truly valuable symbolic capital of English literature has to be mined from its Celtic foundations:

> Its chord of penetrating passion and melancholy, again, its Titanism as we see it in Byron, – what other European poetry possesses that

> like the English, and where do we get it from? The Celts, with their vehement reaction against the despotism of fact, with their sensuous nature, their manifold striving, their adverse destiny, their immense calamities, the Celts are the prime authors of this vein of piercing regret and passion, – of this Titanism in poetry. A famous book. Macpherson's Ossian, carried in the last century this vein like a flood of lava through Europe . . .[52]

Arnold's purpose may be to assimilate the Celtic languages into English as the only viable language for a modern society but his transfusion of Celtic values into English culture turns English literature into a version of Macpherson's *Ossian*, the medium of an endless translation across the boundary between races and cultures. 'English' culture, for Arnold, will always be a recuperation and reactivation of its Celtic origins.

As the discipline of English literature developed in the late nineteenth century, Celtic culture continued to be presented as the cultural capital on which English literature drew for its inspiration. Henry Morley's massively ambitious *English Writers: Towards a History of English Literature* (1887), treats the name 'English' as mere historical accident: 'Let the tribe that was barely named by Tacitus, and from which not a tithe of the First English were descended, still furnish the name for our great brotherhood now spread over the world, one in affect, one in power, one in aim'.[53] Modern English culture emerges from all the cultures that have participated in the great civilising project whose outcome is the British Empire: 'We are of sundry races, but one people, within bounds of what the world calls England. A fair sketch of our literature must needs tell how there were from the beginning wits at work in Ireland, Scotland and Wales, as well as in England east of the Severn and south of the Tweed. The genius of a great nation is our theme, and it is no theme to be discussed in a provincial spirit'.[54] For Morley, English literature stands on several pillars, the most ancient of which is Celtic, as 'the story of our literature begins with the Gael; for there is preserved in Ireland a great mass of ancient copies of more ancient writings that reproduce most interesting traces of historic tale and song in the remotest epoch of our common history'.[55] The cultural capital of Gaeldom provides English literature with the earliest origins of our 'common history' in those 'fragments of old Gaelic verse . . . which belong to or are connected by remote tradition with Fionn, Oisin and the

Fenians'.[56] English is not, for Morley, simply the medium into which Gaelic culture can be translated. Nor is it the infusion of Celtic imagination into an alien tongue. English itself is the combination of Celtic, Anglo-Saxon and Norman-French roots in a language in which all are represented: 'But for early, frequent, and various contact with the race that in its half-barbarous days invented Oisin's dialogues with St Patrick and that quickened afterwards the Northmen's blood in France, Germanic England would not have produced a Shakespeare.'[57] As a consequence, Scottish literature of the medieval period is portrayed neither as a sub-English variant nor as an alien formation, but as the vital continuation of the literature of 'liberty' which is characteristic of all of British-English history: 'Our North gained vigour by a war for independence, and had, in the fifteenth century, poets and historians who led the way on to a golden time of Scottish Literature . . . Our South, at the same time, lost vigour by the blight of foreign and domestic wars that brought men into conflict . . . From Chaucer's time till the beginning of the sixteenth century our Literature of the North sweeps upward'.[58] 'English' culture can be understood only as an archipelagic phenomenon, something quite over and above the culture of those who now denominate themselves as English.[59]

Morley's uncompleted effort at a history of English literature was to be fulfilled some twenty years later in the multi-volume, multi-author *Cambridge History of English Literature*, which began to appear in 1907.[60] Despite its acknowledgement of a valuable 'celtic' transfusion, and of the contribution of Scots, the *Cambridge History* reveals a fundamental shift towards the re-establishment of an English national reading of the history of English literature, invoking as its origin 'the gleemen or minstrels who played on the harp and chanted heroic songs while the ale-mug or mead-cup was passed round, and was received much reward for their calling'.[61] The continuity of English literature is clear to the Cambridge editors from the fact that 'from those days to our own, in spite of periods of decadence, of apparent death, of great superficial change, the chief constituents of English literature – a reflective spirit, attachment to nature, a certain carelessness of "art", love of home and country and an ever present consciousness that there are things worse than death – these have, in the main, continued unaltered'.[62] And the status of English literature is attested by the fact that '*Beowulf* – romance, history and epic – is the oldest poem on a great scale, and in the grand manner, that exists in any Teutonic language. It is full of incident and good fights, simple in aim and clear in execution; its characters bear comparison with those of the *Odyssey* and, like them, linger in the memory; its style is dignified and heroic'.[63] The characteristics of *Beowulf*, in other words, are precisely those which Hugh Blair had attributed to Ossian. General acceptance of the fraudulence of Macpherson's work allowed English critics to set aside the Celtic foundations of British culture and to focus on a purely English line of development, despite the fact that this significant origin was unknown before 1799 and unavailable as a coherent text before 1815; and that its recovery was the work of an Icelandic scholar – Grímur J. Thorkelin – supported by a Danish government which was in search of the equivalent of the Ossianic origins of their own culture.[64] So intense was the drive towards a pure English source for English literature that scholars throughout the nineteenth century competed to find evidence that the events of *Beowulf* had actually taken place on English territory, making the poem the earliest representation of English history.[65]

England, Ireland, Scotland and Wales might have been partners in an imperial project that required the projection of 'English Literature' as one of the defining elements of the cultural superiority that justified the continuous extension of Empire throughout the nineteenth century, but they were also engaged in an internal struggle over the origins and the dynamics of that literature, and about the role of their national literatures within the consolidating discipline of English. Smith and Blair may be judged as the internal literary promoters of that 'expansion of England' which J. R. Seeley advocated as the justification of empire in the last decades of the nineteenth century,[66] but the debates about the origins and emphases of 'English' literature from the 1740s to the early part of the twentieth century confirm John MacKenzie's view that the British empire was by no means a homogeneous project – that the British Empire had 'failed to become truly "British", but instead had, for various reasons, helped to ensure the cultural survival of the respective ethnicities of the British metropolitan state.'[67] From a Scottish perspective, the debate over the origin and nature of English literature was a struggle to ensure that the literature taught to imperial subjects as the culture of the imperial homeland enhanced – or, at least, did not deflate – the specifically national cultural capital which Scotland had accumulated in the century after the publication of Macpherson's Ossianic poems.

III Capital Accumulation

The extension of the concept of capital to the arena of culture stems primarily from the work of Pierre Bourdieu in the 1960s and 70s, though the notion of the relevance of culture to the operations of class had been implicit in Marxist accounts of the 'false consciousness' by which a culture concealed from itself the workings of economic exploitation – an argument elaborated in Gramsci's account of 'hegemony' as the means by which a ruling class inculcated its values throughout a society in order to make its dominance apparently a matter of 'nature', and therefore something about which there could be no choice. In books such as *Reproduction: éléments pour une théorie du système d'enseignement*, written with Jean-Claude Passeron (1970), and *La Distinction. Critique sociale du jugement* (1979), Bourdieu sought to show in sociological detail how 'culture' was the means by which the French bourgeoisie passed on from parents to children their élite status, thus undermining any progress towards a meritocracy, and, indeed, blocking the economic and social progress of the working class as a class. As Bridget Fowler puts it, 'Where Marx had analysed only the inequality of the capital/labour contract, Bourdieu has shown the re-emergence of inherited distinction in the different relation to both pedagogic knowledge (cultural capital) and the area of artistic production and consumption.'[68] Bourdieu's analysis of the workings of cultural capital in France has much in common with the theorists of 'culture' among the New Left in Britain in the same period – Raymond Williams and Stewart Hall most prominently – though with the advantage, as Perry Anderson put it in the *New Left Review*, of 'access to a "reservoir" of Marxist ideas that the English Left lacked'.[69] But just as the New Left in Britain focused on the cultural analysis of England, at the expense of the other countries of the UK, so Bourdieu is concerned only with cultural capital in France. As Richard Jenkins notes,[70] Bourdieu claims that his model is 'valid beyond the particular French case and, no doubt, for every stratified society',[71] but his analysis of the operations of culture in France treats it not only as a relatively isolated cultural system but as though Bourdieu's own analyses were not part of that system. In *Raisons Pratiques* (1994), Bourdieu claimed, in the context of lecturing in Japan, that his analyses were indeed transferable:

> My entire scientific enterprise is indeed based on the belief that the deepest logic of the social world can be grasped only if one plunges into the particularity of an empirical reality, historically located and dated, but with the objective of constructing it as a 'special case of what is possible', as Bachelard puts it, that is, as an exemplary case in a finite world of possible configurations . . .[72]

An 'empirical reality, historically located and dated' can only become 'an exemplary case' if that empirical reality is already assumed to have an exemplary status – that the reason for plunging 'into the particularity' is that that particular particularity has already established its special status in the 'world of possible configurations'. Thus the apparently universalisable study of Bourdieu's *The Rules of Art*[73] is entirely focused on the particular development of French literature: but as the specifically *French* provenance of Bourdieu's analysis is never adverted to in the work itself, an apparently general statement such as,

> To understand the experience that writers and artists may have had of the new forms of domination they found themselves subjected to in the second half of the nineteenth century, and the horror of the figure of the 'bourgeois' sometimes inspired in them

can be completed as follows:

> we need to have some idea of the impact of the emergence of industrialists and businessmen of colossal fortunes (like the Talbots, the de Wendels, or the Schneiders). Fostered by the Second Empire's industrial expansion, they were self-made men, uncultured *parvenus* ready to make both the power of money and a vision of the world profoundly hostile to intellectual things triumph within the whole society.[74]

Few better examples could be found of the power of national cultural capital. The equating of historical epochs – 'the second half of the nineteenth century' – and the experience of 'writers and artists' in general with particular political contexts – the Second Empire – and particular social environments – the

Talbots, de Wendels etc. – reveals the extent to which French culture in this account itself 'owns' the paradigmatic history of Western literary culture. As cultural capital is a system of memory which needs to be invoked, exchanged and reinvested if it is to remain of value, the process of invoking, analysing, and redefining apparently universal categories in terms of a particular national tradition actually operates as a reinforcement of the cultural capital of that nation. If one need look no further for the problematics of bourgeois aesthetics than France, then France is not only 'exemplary' – it makes irrelevant the experience of all other cultures which do not achieve this status – with the result that France's relations with the countries beyond its borders, such as those of the former French empire, are treated as irrelevant to its internal structures.

Ironically, Bourdieu began his sociological work in Algeria, contrasting the values of native peoples with those of their colonisers, but in both *Distinction* and in *The Rules of Art*, France is treated as a self-contained entity, as though its values are entirely determined by its internal structures. In a further irony, the notion of 'cultural capital' has been widely adopted in postcolonial criticism to explain how people negotiate between the cultural capital of their own communities and the cultural capital which is held out to them by institutions which impose – or, after decolonisation – prolong the values of the colonising powers. Such analyses, however, simply by citing Bourdieu as their stimulus, help to increase or maintain France's cultural capital and, therefore, to re-enforce the idea of France's centrality to the culture of the modern world that is the theme of books such as Patrice Higonnet's *Paris: Capital of the World* (2002), or David Harvey's, *Paris, Capital of Modernity* (2003).[75] The implications of Bourdieu's analyses are underlined in Pascale Casanova's *The World Republic of Letters* (1999), in which she argues that writers from countries lacking in cultural capital must try to generate national capital:

> Writers engaged in a struggle on behalf of their nation must therefore build up literary resources of their own from nothing: they must construct a literary tradition out of whole cloth, a tradition with its own themes and genres that will achieve respectability for a language that, being unknown, and unvalued in the literary marketplace, will have to be immediately translated in order to find international legitimacy.[76]

This national struggle, however, will not achieve its aim unless the writers from the unread periphery are acknowledged as valuable in and to the publishing houses and the reading publics of the metropole. Casanova declares that there is a 'world republic' of letters, but it is republic hierarchically structured such that writers from the margins must submit themselves to the judgment of Paris before they can be accepted as citizens of that Republic. Paris's continuing accumulation of cultural capital gives it ultimate leverage and control over the system as a whole, and the consequence is that writers from the margins must escape from the 'national' if their work is to be acknowledged as having a 'universal' significance:

> Whereas national writers, fomenters of the first literary revolts, rely on the literary models of national tradition, international writers draw upon this transnational repertoire of literary techniques in order to escape being imprisoned in national tradition.[77]

'National tradition' is imprisoning; for those who 'reject the closing in of the nation upon itself and embrace international criteria of innovation and modernity',[78] liberation comes when they recognise that their work should not be *about* their cultural homeland but should be 'autonomous, purely literary'[79] – and conforming, therefore, to the standards of literariness that have developed in Paris as the city most endowed with literary and cultural capital. Unless work from the margins can accommodate itself to the expectations of Paris, it will never enter the Republic of Letters. The paradigmatic case, for Casanova, is Ireland, because its literary development from the 1880s to the 1920s illustrates how a literature progresses from the national – Yeats as the supporter of an Irish nationalism which successfully established an independent state – to the supra-national – Joyce, as one of the 'great heroes of literature [who] inevitably emerge only in association with the specific power of an autonomous and international literary capital'[80] – which is not, of course, the Dublin depicted in *Ulysses*, but the Paris in which *Ulysses* is published and acclaimed:

> The rupture provoked by James Joyce was the final step in the constitution of Irish literary space. Exploiting all the literary projects, experiments, and debates of the late nineteenth century, which is to say the literary capital accumulated by all those who came before

> him, Joyce invented and proclaimed an almost absolute autonomy. In this highly politicized space, and in opposition to the movement of the Irish renaissance, which, as he said in *Ulysses* threatened to become 'all too Irish,' he managed to establish an autonomous, purely literary pole, thus helping to obtain recognition for the whole of Irish literature by liberating it to some extent from political domination.[81]

That *Ulysses* is published and appreciated in Paris when unread in Dublin is, for Casanova, evidence that 'autonomous art' transcends the constraints of the nation. The Paris-based recognition of *Ulysses* was fulfilled, however, only by the work's translation into French, a translation in which Joyce himself participated but which completed the denationalization of the text, because translation into French is more than the simple replication in one language of what is written in another; it is, in effect, the 'transmutation' of the text to produce conformity with the aesthetic expectations of the centre: 'Paris, the denationalized capital of literature, denationalized texts so that they would conform to its own conception of literary art'.[82] The consequence is that, in this model, the world of literary production and appreciation is structured around 'an autonomous pole composed of those spaces that are most endowed in literary resources' and which look to Paris as 'a model and a recourse for writers claiming a position of independence', and, at the other end of the spectrum, 'relatively deprived literary spaces' whose works and judgments 'are dependent on political – typically national – authorities'.[83] Because no work that has not escaped from the limits of its national context can obtain recognition in a system which is 'devoted to literature as an activity having no need of justification beyond itself',[84] 'literary excellence' is, by definition, 'incompatible with what might be called cultural nationalism'.[85] National and nationalist writing in Ireland is visible only through Joyce's 'transcendence' of the cultural nationalism on which the Irish Literary Revival had been based, and those earlier works will be of literary value only when they too have been 'denationalized' – or, perhaps more truly, 're-nationlised' – according to the expectations of French avant-garde aesthetics.

In the Scottish context, Casanova argues that Sir Walter Scott's international reputation was established only by the fact that 'his novels were translated into French by Defauconpret as they appeared' and 'it was to these versions that they owed their immense worldwide fame'.[86] The French versions of Scott's novels were indeed the basis of some translations into other languages, but the world of letters does not have the singular and francophone structure that Casanova requires of it: Scott's 'worldwide' reputation was based not only on the impact of his works in Britain but on the pirating of his novels in North America and their dispersion throughout the Anglophone reading publics of the British Empire. Casanova's theory is not so much an analysis of the operations of cultural capital as it is an ideological defence of the power of French cultural capital. It also ignores the extent to which Scott's works benefited from the cultural capital built up by the translations of Macpherson's Ossianic poetry in the eighteenth century and their European impact through Goethe's incorporation of portions of them into his enormously popular *Sorrows of Young Werther* (*Die Leiden des jungen Werthers*) in 1774.[87] The reception of Scott's novels was also indebted to the more recent reception of Robert Burns's poetry. Macpherson and Burns had made Scotland interesting to a European readership whose expectations of Scottish writing were fulfilled by Scott's novels. Significantly, however, Scott's novels were printed and published in Edinburgh, not in London, underlining how Edinburgh had managed to maintain its independence as a publishing centre, despite the fact that many of its eighteenth-century literati had published their works through London printers.[88] It was that independence that not only inspired a continual flow of books on Scottish topics – for instance, the novels that are examined in Ian Duncan's *Scott's Shadow: the Novel in Romantic Edinburgh* (2007) – but the international prominence of the *Edinburgh Review* and of *Blackwood's Magazine*, as well as the influence of the *Encyclopaedia Britannica*, and ensured that Scottish works and Scottish concerns were projected to an international audience. In the 'world republic of letters' of the nineteenth century, Scotland was not a supplicant, waiting on recognition from Paris or London but, by the accumulated wealth of its cultural capital, able not only to claim the attention of a global readership but able to shape the cultural environment in which its writings were received.

IV A Country Abandoned

Scottish historiography since 2000 has been profoundly reshaped by our increasing knowledge of what has come to be known as the 'Scottish diaspora'. The Scottish influence in the Baltic and in Eastern Europe in the sixteenth and seventeenth centuries; the role of Scots in North America and the Caribbean in the period of the American Revolution; their prominence in the East India Company as Britain and France competed for control of India in the eighteenth century; their missionary role in Africa and in the far East, and their influential input into the development of the settler colonies in Canada, in Australia and in New Zealand, have all shifted the perspective in which Scotland's domestic history is understood.[89] Huge outward migration made Scotland one of largest exporters of people in the nineteenth and twentieth centuries as a proportion of its total population.[90] The traditional notion of a 'diaspora', however, implies a forced migration – the expulsion of the Jews from Israel, the Armenian flight from the violence of the Ottoman Empire – and although the 'Highland Clearances' can be understood as such an enforced departure from the homeland, the vast majority of Scottish migrants chose to leave their country, even if, in some cases, their departure was under the pressure of an economic environment in which they were poorer and less-well housed than people elsewhere in the UK. Other parts of Europe which suffered from mass migration were largely rural but Scotland in the nineteenth century was a well-developed industrial economy – indeed, arguably the most industrialised economy in the world in relation to the size of its population. Unlike the Irish, whose depopulation in the nineteenth century was triggered by famine, Scotland suffered no such catastrophe and, indeed, was itself a country of increasing numbers of immigrants, both from Ireland itself and from Eastern Europe. T. M. Devine sees this as the 'essential paradox' of Scotland's nineteenth-century history:

> It was one of the world's most highly successful industrial and agricultural economies after *c.* 1860 but was losing people in very large numbers rather than those countries traditionally associated with poverty, clearance, hunger and destitution.[91]

It was also a paradox of its cultural life: with all the endowments of its inheritance from the eighteenth century, nineteenth-century Scotland ought to have been a flourishing cultural community but it has generally been judged to have failed that eighteenth-century legacy. As Christopher Harvie summarises it,

> In the north, religious repression compounded with pseudo-science. Phrenology, centred among Duncan MacLaren's radical friends in Edinburgh, was no improvement on Monboddo's speculations on evolution and language; Robert Knox's *The Races of Man* (1850) was a disturbing regression. Samuel Smiles's equation of economic progress with a simple set of moral injunctions was scarcely an adequate successor to the work of Adam Smith. H. T. Buckle in 1863 condemned Edinburgh for lapsing into credulous medievalism, thanks to the deductive methods of Scots philosophy; in 1863 John Stuart Mill settled accounts with the school's last great man, Sir William Hamilton.[92]

A key reason for this cultural decline was judged to be the emigration of Scotland's intellectuals. 'During the nineteenth century', David Craig wrote in *Scottish Literature and the Scottish People* (1961), 'the country was emptied of the *majority* of its notable literary talents – men who, if they had stayed, might have thought to mediate their wisdom through the rendering of specifically Scottish experience';[93] Tom Nairn, in *The Break-up of Britain* (1977) was equally certain about the loss to Scotland of its migrant intellectuals: 'in a broad sense there is no doubt what happened: unable . . . to fulfil the "standard" nineteenth-century function of elaborating a romantic-national culture for their own people, they applied themselves with vigour to the unfortunate southerners. Our former intelligentsia lost its cohesion and unitary function (its nature *as* an elite) and the individual members poured their energies into the authentically "organic community" centred on London'.[94] The 'absent intellectuals' are the other side of the coin of Scotland's 'absent nationalism', their scattering beyond the borders of the nation contrasted with the close-knit nature of intellectual life in the previous century, which was, according to Rick Sher, 'firmly grounded in personal relationships among its leading practitioners. It functioned as a constellation of overlapping urban communities of scholars and literary figures who were joined through a multiplicity of common ties of nationality, kinship, religion, occupation, education, patronage, friendship and outlook'.[95]

That there was a significant outflow of Scottish intellectuals in the nineteenth century cannot be doubted: from James Mill and Thomas Carlyle, in the first half of the century to Edward Caird and William Wallace in the Oxford of the 1880s, Scots, by birth or by descent, played key roles in defining 'English' culture, and migrant Scottish writers from Thomas Campbell and Lord Byron at the beginning of the nineteenth century to Margaret Oliphant and J. M. Barrie in the second half made their literary careers in London. In part this reflected the increasing dominance of London in book and newspaper publishing – Scottish publishers who set up in London included John Murray and the Macmillan brothers – but the scale of migration was in part a consequence of the success of the Scottish universities. Because only Anglicans could be admitted to Oxford, Cambridge, London and Durham universities until the passing of Universities Tests Act of 1871, many English non-conformists attended Scottish universities (three generations of the Darwins were educated at Edinburgh) and because Scottish universities were comparatively inexpensive, and largely based in the urban centres, they could be afforded by a much broader proportion of the Scottish population than attended universities in England. Though the successful rise of a 'lad o' pairts' from a poor home to being a teacher or a minister might be an inflated myth, nonetheless a working printer, like William Smellie (1740–95), later founder of the *Encyclopaedia Britannica*, or a gardener like John Claudius Loudon (1783–1843), founder of *The Gardener's Encyclopaedia* and *The Gardener's Magazine*, and probably the most influential garden theorist of the age, could acquire elements of an education by paying to attend individual courses of lectures rather than taking a full degree. The consequence was that Scotland was producing more graduates and more university-educated people than the country could itself provide employment for, so that many, whether specialists like those trained in medicine or divinity, or the 'generalists' with their training in philosophy and the arts, had no choice but to make their careers outside of Scotland. For some, this would be in England but for many it would be in North America or more distant parts of the Empire. Dr Robert Burns (1789–1869), for instance, established the Glasgow Colonial

Society in 1825 to provide ministers for Scottish communities in North America, and himself migrated to lead the Free Church in Canada in the 1840s.[96] Burns was typical of evangelical Christianity's drive to sustain the national religion of Scottish communities in the Empire and to take the message of Scottish Christianity to the unenlightened across the world. A similar trajectory can be seen in the career of John Dougall (1808–86), originally from Paisley, who successfully established both in Montreal and in New York versions of Hugh Miller's newspaper *The Witness*, which had done so much to promote the evangelical cause in Scotland in the years before the Disruption of 1843.[97] Indeed, the conflicts which led to the establishment of the Free Church in 1843 might have been legally about the rights of congregations to choose their own ministers, an issue which dated back to the Patronage Act of 1711–12 and which, in re-establishing the rights of patrons that had been abolished in the 'Glorious Revolution' of 1688, was often raised as a breach of the terms of the Treaty of Union of 1707. This was, however, only the focus of a much broader debate about the 'mission' of the Church of Scotland. For the 'Moderates' who had led the Church from the 1750s to the 1830s, the Church of Scotland's primary concern was with managing and delivering its various social responsibilities in Scotland's parishes, since it effectively oversaw local education and the distribution of funds to the poor. For the Evangelicals, on the other hand, the Church had a mission to deliver Christianity – that is, Presbyterian Christianity – to all who needed it, whether the benighted Catholics of the Scottish Highlands whose lack of understanding was addressed by the Society in Scotland for the Propagation of Christian Knowledge (SSPCK), the poor of the rapidly expanding town and cities of Scotland which were not supported within the existing parish system, or Scottish communities across the British Empire and, beyond them, the non-Christian populations of the Empire. Missionary Christianity was the real fault line in the Church – after all, the Free Church in Canada which Dr Robert Burns went to join had no political reason for replicating the Disruption in Scotland. It did so for ideological reasons and it is significant that none of those who believed that Christian mission should be restricted to the national territory and who insisted that 'not Scotland, but the world is the field',[98] remained in the established Church after 1843. Salvational Scottishness produced an outpouring of missionary activity in the second half of the nineteenth century and made national heroes of missionaries such as David Livingstone (1813–73) and Mary Slessor (1848–1915), both of whom were to die in Africa,[99] but they were only the most admired of the many Scottish missionaries who left an enduring imprint across the globe. The Presbyterian Church of Korea, for instance, is a partner church of the Church of Scotland and has 2.5 million members; its early development was inspired in the 1880s by Scottish missionary John Ross, who oversaw the first translation of the New Testament into Korean.

The nineteenth-century outflow of Scots no doubt deprived the country of some who would have been among its intellectual leaders but the distinction between eighteenth- and nineteenth-century Scotland is not as clear cut as some accounts of the country's intellectual history would suggest. London was just as attractive to Scots in the eighteenth century as in the nineteenth, as witness the careers of writers such as James Thomson, David Mallet (Malloch) and Tobias Smollett,[100] or doctors such as William Smellie, James Douglas and William Hunter, all of whom became famous in England as 'man-midwives';[101] or, indeed, publishers, such as Andrew Millar or Thomas Cadell, who, as Sher points out, played a key role in the promotion of Scottish authors in London.[102] If London, in the second half of the eighteenth century, was suffering, according to John Wilkes, 'an inundation of Scotchmen, who come up and never go back again',[103] other parts of Europe were also flooded with Scots: David Hume wrote the central work of eighteenth-century Scottish philosophy, his *Treatise of Human Nature* (1739), not in Scotland but in France, where he resided in the 1730s. His biographer, E. C. Mossner, notes that he 'had occasionally thought of taking refuge in France from the persecution of Scotland and the intolerance of England', and came to think seriously about migrating there after the treatment he was accorded in 1763, when he went as secretary to the British ambassador in Paris, 'and was afforded the reception of a hero'.[104] If not a permanent migrant, Hume was certainly a spiritual migrant, in the sense that his work was as much at home in French culture as in Scotland – and much more so than it was in England. And Hume could be at home in France in part because it was home to such a large Scottish migrant community. As Mossner reminds us, 'No Scotsman of the eighteenth century had need to remain long solitary in France, for that kingdom was literally teeming with his fellow-countrymen, many of them exiles along with the royal Stuarts.'[105] While the Stuart court represented a very specific context for Scottish intellectual migration, the tradition of intellectual migration among Scots had been established at least as early as the founding of the Scots College in Paris in 1326 when it became, effectively, the first Scottish university. Subsequent Scots Colleges in France and Germany provided routes by which a variety of Scots, shut out from education for religious or political reasons, could pursue learning and, for some at least, maintain a career as a teacher, experimenter and writer. In the late sixteenth and early seventeenth centuries Scottish Catholics had founded colleges on the continent in Douai (in the Spanish Netherlands), Rome and Madrid in order that young men could be educated in the Catholic tradition when the penal laws forbade such education in Scotland. At the beginning of the eighteenth century the Scots Benedictine monastery in Regensburg was also designated a college and seminary. The Regensburg monastery was one of three Scottish Benedictine houses in Southern Germany – the others were in Würzburg and Erfurt – which were known as *Schöttenkloster* and during the period of the penal laws it is estimated that as many as 2000 Scots were educated at the colleges and *Schöttenkloster*.[106] Scottish intellectual exiles could be found in France, Germany, the Netherlands and as far afield as Russia: John Robison (1739–1805), later Professor of Mathematics at the University of Edinburgh, held the chair of mathematics in St Petersburg in the early 1770s. The tradition of these 'Scots Colleges', educating migrant Scots in Europe, was to be revived in the 1920s when Patrick Geddes (1854–1932), town-planner and ecological theorist, an intellectual migrant who had worked for many years in India and Palestine, returned to Europe to build a new Scots College in Montpellier.

The notion of a nineteenth-century Scotland as distinctly different from the eighteenth century in being emptied of its intellectuals also ignores the careers of those who left but later returned. Alexander Bain, for instance, made his major contributions to empirical psychology – *The Senses and the Intellect* (1855), *The Emotions and the Will* (1859) – while working in London, but in 1860 he was appointed to the Regius Chairs in Logic and English Literature at the University of Aberdeen, lecturing there until the 1880s and founding the journal *Mind* – which is still a leading journal in its field – in 1876. From Aberdeen, Bain continued to be engaged in the intellectual life of London – he published biographies both of James and of John Stuart Mill in 1882 – as well as enthusiastically engaging in the educational activities of the local Mechanics' Institute. Similarly, David Masson, who had been educated at the University of Aberdeen, and who had built a reputation from his many contributions and reviews in the periodical press, went to London in the 1840s and was appointed as professor of English Literature at University College in 1852, subsequently becoming the editor of *Macmillan's Magazine* from its inception in 1858. In 1865, however, he returned to Edinburgh as Professor of English Literature and it was from there that he completed his *Life of Milton* (6 vols, 1858–80). Masson's choice of returning to Scotland was followed after the First World War by no less than two professors of philosophy, Norman Kemp Smith and A. A. Bowman, who gave up chairs at Princeton for chairs in Edinburgh and Glasgow. But those who did not return did not, therefore, simply discard their relationship with Scotland: Robert Crawford draws attention to the fact that twelve of the twenty-eight professors in the early history of University College (founded 1828) and King's College (founded 1831) in London were Scots and that Blair's *Lectures on Rhetoric and Belles Lettres* was still on their curriculum in the 1820s.[107] Equally, David Masson did not regard Thomas Carlyle as having discarded his Scottish connections when he set out for London: he returned, proudly if only briefly, when, as Masson recalls in *Carlyle Personally and in His Writings* (1885), he was elected rector of the University of Edinburgh in 1866. Masson, however, was to organise a 'spiritual' return for Carlyle when a bust of the author of *Sartor Resartus, Signs of the Times* and *The French Revolution* was installed in the Wallace Monument, in its collection of portraits and busts of the great figures of Scottish history which extol 'the patriotic Scottish feeling, the sense of our nationality'.[108] Despite his years in London, Carlyle is, for Masson, the 'greatest of recent Scotsmen' who cannot but be included in 'this little Scottish Walhala',[109] because it is a monument that asserts that 'Scotland still stands where it did, immemorially Scotland, indestructibly Scotland'.[110] The monument and its representations of the most important figures in the nation's culture,

> serves the double function of reminding natives or tourists of the fact there *were* such centuries of independent Scottish history, and

> of impressing also the fact that those centuries are not forgotten yet by the Scottish people, and that the spirit and traditions from them are at work still in the changed conditions of our later time, nerving Scottish energy for adequate, and perhaps still peculiarly characteristic, co-operation with England and Ireland in the affairs of the united British body-politics and of the British Empire.[111]

For Masson, Carlyle in London remains engaged with the issues and with the moral values of his homeland. Indeed, he is the incarnation of those values in his writings:

> Always it was the *moral force* in Carlyle, the vein of peculiar spiritual and ethical teaching contained in his writings, that made him the unique man he was in the British Literature of the Victorian era. What need to try here to define this peculiar spiritual and ethical creed, or to specify its chief articles? Enough if I remind you of what you all already know of it by describing it generally as having consisted in a never-ceasing effort to resuscitate among his countrymen and others certain structural or elementary faiths of the human spirit which he conceived to have been lamentably dead or dormant in modern times . . .[112]

That 'moral force' was his inheritance from his parents' Presbyterianism; the 'spiritual and ethical creed' his challenge to the secularising effects of eighteenth-century Scottish philosophy, and its influence in nineteenth-century England; his 'elementary faiths of the human spirit' the spirited intensity, if not of the actual dogmas, of evangelicalism. It is precisely because Carlyle in London has not turned his back on his Scottish identity that makes him such an original figure in English letters.

Historians who try to measure the value – or lack of value – of nineteenth-century Scotland by pointing to the migration of its intellectuals as an 'emptying' of the national culture are making a fundamental error in conceiving of Scotland as bounded by the territory of its geographical statelessness: by the nineteenth century, the territory of Scottish culture stretched from Edinburgh to its mirror image in Dunedin; from Dunbar to Yosemite; from Heriot Row to Tahiti. It was a territory full of intellectuals and intellectual energy, busily promoting Scotland's cultural inheritance and engaged in making Scottish culture foundational to the new nations which it was helping to build.

V Xeniteian Empire

One of the eighteenth-century Scottish exiles in France was Andrew Michael Ramsay (b. 1686, and generally known as 'Chevalier Ramsay'), who lived mostly in France from 1710 until his death in 1743, and whose close connections to the exiled Jacobite court were underlined by the fact that he was briefly tutor to Charles Edward Stuart in Rome. Ramsay wrote a biography of the French thinker Fénelon (sometimes compared to Boswell's biography of Samuel Johnson) and what may be the first Scottish novel of the eighteenth century, *A New Cyropaedia, or the Travels of Cyrus*, first published in French in 1727. Chevalier Ramsay is interesting, however, because he not only achieved some literary fame in France but left behind an institutional legacy which lasts to this day. It is to Ramsay that the French form of freemasonry, known as the 'Scottish Rite', can be traced; and, in particular, to an oration given by Ramsay in 1737, in which he claimed that authentic freemasonry dated back to the Crusades, and that its aim was a universal enlightenment:

> Mankind is not essentially distinguished by tongues spoken, the clothes worn, the lands occupied or the dignities with which it is invested. The world is nothing but a huge republic, of which every nation is a family, every individual a child. Our Society was at the outset established to revive and spread these essential maxims borrowed from the nature of man. We desire to reunite men of enlightened minds, gentle manners and agreeable wit, not only by a love of the fine arts, but, much more, by the grand principles of virtue, science and religion, where the interests of the Fraternity shall become those of the whole human race . . .'[113]

Ramsay's claim to 'reunite men of enlightened minds' may be the most explicit assertion of the virtues of 'enlightenment' by any eighteenth-century Scot. That it came from the defeated Jacobite tradition, often seen as the antagonist of 'enlightenment', is indicative of how restricted has been the modern idea of 'Enlightenment' in relation to Scotland. Freemasonry, whose claim to promote 'liberty, equality, fraternity' was to be adopted by the French revolutionaries – as, indeed, they would adopt Fénelon as one of their secular saints, attributing to him a special day in the new calendar – spread rapidly in France after 1737, despite being banned by the authorities. Its roots, however, were in Scottish Jacobitism: the first three Grand Masters of French Masonry were all Jacobite exiles, including Charles Radclyffe, the Earl of Derwentwater, who was to be executed for his part in the 1745 Jacobite Rebellion.[114]

The establishment of Freemasonry in Paris in the 1720s was to have profound implications for European culture, shaping key elements of what we now think of as the 'Enlightenment'.[115] In exactly the same period, Freemasonry was also being established on an apparently different ideological foundation in London, where it was Scottish migrants who were also shaping the emergence of the so-called 'speculative' masonry that replaced the traditional 'operative' masonry of working masons. As David Stevenson has shown, the organisation of 'lodges' devoted to passing on the lore of masonic traditions that claimed to stretch back to ancient times, began in Scotland in the 1590s and early 1600s at the court of James VI, and it was a migrant Scot, James Anderson (1679–1739), the son of the secretary of the Lodge in Aberdeen, who drew up the first constitution of the masonic order for the Grand Lodge of London in 1723.[116] Migrant Scots, whether Presbyterians committed to making their way in England after the Union, or Catholics exiled in France, took masonry with them as a tradition that institutionalised their Scottish heritage in their new environments. Anderson's and Ramsay's versions of masonry might have been significantly different but both emphasised the key role of Scotland in the transmission of masonic knowledge. Anderson notes that

> The Kings of SCOTLAND very much encourag'd the *Royal Art*, from the earliest Times down to the *Union* of the Crowns, as appears by the Remains of glorious Buildings in that *ancient* Kingdom, and by the Lodges there kept up without Interruption many hundred Years, the Records and Traditions of which testify the great Respect of those Kings to this honourable Fraternity, who gave always pregnant Evidence of their Love and Loyalty, from whence sprung the old Toast among the *Scots* Masons, *viz.* GOD BLESS THE KING AND THE CRAFT.[117]

Anderson also attributes the development of masonry in England to the influence of the Scots:

> Yet the great Care that the SCOTS took of true Masonry, prov'd afterwards very useful to ENGLAND; for the learned and magnanimous Queen ELIZABETH, who encourag'd other Arts, discourag'd this; because, being a *Woman*, she could not be made a *Mason*, . . . But upon her Demise, King JAMES VI. of SCOTLAND succeeding to the Crown of ENGLAND, being a *Mason* King, reviv'd the *English* Lodges; and as he was the *First* King of GREAT BRITAIN, he was also the *First* Prince in the World that recover'd the *Roman* architecture from the Ruins of *Gothic* Ignorance.[118]

Ramsay, too, presents Scots emigrés in France as the medium for the transmission of ancient knowledge to modern times: when threatened with decay elsewhere, the Order, he suggests, 'preserved its splendour amongst those Scotsmen of whom the Kings of France confided during many centuries the safeguard of their royal persons'.[119] That these two traditions of freemasonry should be formed in the two dominant countries of Europe in the first generation after Scotland's union with England in 1707 is indicative of the ways in which Scots responded to the experience both of integration and migration. Michael Fry has suggested that 'Scots seldom severed their connection with home, or with each other: in the Americas, too, they won notoriety for their cliques and mutual self-help',[120] but the examples of Anderson and Ramsay suggest that rather than attempting to preserve Scottish values by isolating themselves from the communities in which they moved, they sought to maintain Scottish values by universalising them, and thereby gaining acceptance for them in their new environments. After 1707 Scotland was a nation which existed only in and through its institutions and this seems to have made Scots like Anderson and Ramsay sensitive to the significance of institutions as a means of maintaining and transmitting distinctive Scottish values. Their way of 'not losing or foreswearing their Scottishness', their way of being 'preoccupied with the families, communities and nation they had left behind',[121] was to construct in their places of 'exile' organisations which would continue Scottish traditions precisely by gaining acceptance for them as pathways to universal truth.

The ways in which Scots like Ramsay and Anderson, or Dr Robert Burns and John Dougall went about making themselves at home in their host-lands suggests that a term other than 'diaspora' is needed if we are not to be misled into equating Scottish experience with that of the Jews or the Armenians.[122] One suggestion is the adoption of another word, of Greek origin, to characterise Scottish migration: xeniteia. Xeniteian migrants do not arrive in their new territories as victims of forced expulsion dreaming of a return to the homeland but as masons or architects who carry with them the plan by which they will rebuild the familiar structures of their homeland in a foreign place.[123] Masonry, with its emphasis on the mason as geometer and architect, engaged in building a universal enlightenment, is perhaps an appropriate symbol of the xeniteian drive of Scottish migration. Indeed, wherever Scots settled or sojourned in the British Empire, they invariably established Masonic lodges.[124] Moreover, whether they travelled as settlers, as missionaries, as administrators or as explorers and scientists, Scots took with them a conception of civilisation based on the Reformation commitment to universal education, to the belief that, as Knox put it in *The First Book of Discipline*, 'we think it expedient, that in every notable town . . . [there] be erected a Colledge, in whiche the Arts, at least Logick and Rhethoric, together with the Tongues, be read by sufficient Maisteris, for whome honest stipends must be appointed; as also provisioun for those that be poore, and be nocht able by them selfis, nor by thair freindis, to be sustained at letteris'.[125] The distinctive educational system of Scotland, with its large number of parish schools and its geographically distributed universities, provided the model which Scots set out to replicate wherever they settled. As Sir Robert Falconer (1867–1943), president of the University of Toronto from 1906 until 1932, noted of his nineteenth-century predecessors in Canadian higher education, 'As the social conditions that prevailed in Canada were in many respects much more similar to those of Scotland than of England, the Scottish organization and methods of higher education were adapted to the needs of many portions of the country in the earlier stages of its development'.[126]

Wherever Presbyterian Scots settled in the Empire, a Church in the reformed tradition required a literate congregation, and therefore a school in which children could learn to read the bible, and schoolteachers trained to make that possible, which required colleges and universities that would provide church and school with appropriately qualified graduates. The university would, in turn, require a medical school – usually along the lines of the Edinburgh Medical School – to deal with the maladies of the imperial territories, and, the Medical School would itself require a botanic garden for training doctors in the efficacy of plant-based drugs. Thus, though the Scots had not been numerically significant migrants to North America until the second half of the eighteenth century, among the earliest of American universities were those based on Scottish models: the College of William and Mary was founded in Williamsburg in 1693 and its first president was the Reverend James Blair (1656–1743), an Episcopalian trained at Marischal College in Aberdeen. The curriculum at William and Mary was structured on Scottish lines, foregrounding moral philosophy. The University of Pennsylvania was also built on Scottish foundations – first, on the academy established by Francis Alison (1705–59) in New London, whose curriculum was based on the University of Glasgow's, with its central teaching texts being the works of Francis Hutcheson, Alison's own teacher at Glasgow; and, second, on the College of Philadelphia, whose first president was William Smith (1727–1803), an Episcopalian who had also studied at Marischal College in Aberdeen and who promoted the Scottish ideal of a broad curriculum of the arts and sciences in a pamphlet which has been described by an American historian as 'the first attempt in America to present systematic analysis of the aims and methods of higher education'.[127] Smith was also involved in the establishment of 'King's College' in New York, which, after the American Revolution, became Columbia University.

The same xeniteian drive towards educational institution-building was equally characteristic of the Scots in Canada, where John Strachan was the inspiration not only for McGill University in Montreal (1821) – which was named after the relative of Strachan's wife, Ann Wood McGill, who was encouraged by Strachan to leave his land for an educational establishment – but also for King's College (1843), which became the basis of the University of Toronto. A true xeniteian, Strachan went on to found Trinity College when King's College was absorbed into the University of Toronto in 1849.[128] Other Canadian universities were also Scottish-derived institutions: Dalhousie University was founded by the ninth Earl of Dalhousie (1770–1838) in 1818, and modelled on the University of Edinburgh where Dalhousie had been a student, though it became an effective university only in the mid-century under the direction of Thomas McCulloch (1776–1843), a graduate of the University of Glasgow; while Queen's College at Kingston was founded by the Church of Scotland in 1841, and all of its principals and most of its professors were Scots up to the 1920s.

New Zealand's universities were equally the work of xeniteian Scots: the University of Otago in Dunedin was largely a Scottish institution when it was founded in 1871: the Reverend Thomas Burns (1796–1871), nephew of the poet, who had joined the Free Church in 1843 and arrived in New Zealand in 1848, was its first Chancellor;[129] John Shand, a graduate of King's College Aberdeen its first professor of Mathematics and Natural Philosophy, and Duncan MacGregor, another Aberdeen graduate, its first professor of Mental Science. Among its most influential early appointments was James Gow Black (1835–1914), a classic 'lad o' pairts' from Perthshire who had funded his early education through labouring jobs, and reached the University of Edinburgh by way of the Moray House Training College for teachers. Black was to play a key role both in the technologies of the gold fields and in establishing technical education in New Zealand.[130] Similarly, three of the first four professors at the Victoria University of Wellington, founded in 1898, were Scots, as was its first Chancellor, James Hector (1834–1907), from Edinburgh, while the driving force behind its creation was Robert Stout (1844–1930), New Zealand's first premier, originally from Shetland.[131] The need to provide well-trained ministers for Presbyterian congregations in the Colonies inspired the establishment of many theological institutions, from the Princeton Theological Seminary in New Jersey, founded in 1812, to Knox College in Toronto, a product in 1844 of the Disruption, and Knox College in Otago, which, in 1909, incorporated an existing seminary founded by Thomas Burns. Much of this xeniteian endeavour was inspired by religion, and by the struggle between competing religious denominations to provide themselves with an institutional base in the expanding territories of the Empire. In their dealings with the 'heathen', missionaries found it necessary to build more than churches and congregations: they had to establish schools and hospitals in order to draw in those they hoped to convert. In Calcutta, Alexander Duff (1806–78) came to see a general education on Scottish lines, including science, philosophy and the arts, as fundamental to the discrediting of Indian religions, thereby making conversion to Christianity possible. He founded the Scottish Church College in Calcutta in 1830 and his example was followed in 1837 by the Madras

Christian College, founded by John Anderson (1805–55) from Galloway, while the Bombay Scottish School was established in 1847. Murray College in Sialkot, Hislop College in Nagpu and Wilson College, Bombay were all Church of Scotland foundations. The implicit 'westernisation' of India in such schools was to be carried forward by the influence of Lord Dalhousie (1812–60), among whose technological and institutional innovations when he was Governor-General (1848–56) were the founding of India's first three universities.[132] Scots missionaries were also responsible for the establishment of medical colleges and hospitals – as, for instance, at Agra[133] – and it was the medical missionary, in the person of David Livingstone, who was to become the iconic figure of Victorian imperialism. As Daniel MacGowan, an American medical missionary put it in 1842, 'The physician has access to communities and families in heathen lands as a missionary labourer, where the evangelist is not permitted to enter. He has it in his power at once, to give the distrustful heathen palpable demonstration of the benevolence of his errand'.[134] However much this appealed to the funders in the home country, in places like India and China the medical missionary was in fact being squeezed out by the large numbers of physicians attached to military or naval operations, or to commercial organisations, which extended their income through private practice. William Swan warned the Edinburgh Medical Missionary Society that it would be 'improper to send a Medical Missionary (whose services among the native population must be in general gratuitous) where a private practitioner has established himself, and must live by his profession'.[135] Many of those private practitioners were from Scottish medical schools, as the Scottish universities were producing such large numbers of medical graduates – as many as 10,000 between 1750 and 1850[136] – only a small proportion of whom could possibly obtain posts in the UK, particularly because the major London institutions would employ only those with degrees from the London Royal Colleges. Thus, of the 1,267 doctors appointed to posts in Bengal, Madras and Bombay between 1767 and 1811, fully 43 per cent (539) had been matriculated at the University of Edinburgh,[137] and when Patrick Manson, later to play a key role in the discovery of the transmission of malaria, graduated in medicine from Aberdeen in 1866, no fewer than ten of the nineteen who graduated with him left for careers in imperial organisations. This was a high but not an unusual proportion: John D. Hargreaves has calculated that of those graduating from Aberdeen 'about a quarter of arts graduates worked abroad' while 'well over a third of medical graduates did'.[138] The vastly disproportionate numbers of Scottish-trained physicians throughout the Empire meant that when new medical schools were required, they were founded on the Scottish model and often by graduates, especially, of Edinburgh: the first medical school in North America, in Philadelphia, was established by a group of American graduates of Edinburgh, which included Benjamin Rush, the only medical signatory to the Declaration of Independence.[139] Edinburgh graduates were also responsible for the establishment of the medical school at Columbia in New York in 1787, of the medical school attached to McGill University in Montreal in the 1820s, as well as at Dalhousie in the 1840s;[140] and the first five appointees at the Sydney medical school were all from Edinburgh,[141] as were the first at Otago.[142] As the botanic garden was a key adjunct to medical education – the *materia medica* lectures would often take place in the garden itself – these medical students took with them an interest in botany that turned many doctors into plant hunters – wisteria, gardenia and poinsettia are all named after graduates of the Edinburgh Medical School – and made others, like William Roxburgh in Calcutta, into founders of botanic gardens.[143] Indeed, the heart of the imperial network of botanic gardens at Kew was itself a Scottish foundation, having been established in the 1760s by John Stuart, Earl of Bute, the first Scottish Prime Minister of the United Kingdom, and was run by Scots through much of its history[144] – Sir David Prain, for instance, who took over as Director at Kew in 1905, after having been superintendent of the Calcutta Botanic Garden, was a graduate of Aberdeen.[145] The same pattern can be seen in the establishment of museums, both in terms of the role of Scottish migrants – such as David Boyle in the establishment of the Royal Ontario Museum[146] – and in the provision of models to be emulated: John MacKenzie notes that the 'museums of the Scottish universities were significant' models for Canadian museums, 'as were the Glasgow Normal Schools, civic and mechanics' institutions'.[147]

This world-wide network of interlocking, Scottish-inspired institutions gave mobile and ambitious Scots a huge advantage in establishing careers outside Scotland. When Patrick Manson began his work on the transmission of disease by mosquitoes, the two experts in the field with whom he corresponded were Thomas S. Cobbold (1828–86), graduate of the University of Edinburgh (1851) and, for some six years after graduation, curator the University Anatomical Museum, and Timothy Richard Lewis (1841–86), a graduate of Aberdeen working in the Indian Medical Service. The competition between them to establish the life-cycle of filariae (a cause of elephantisis and other diseases) and then of malarial parasites was played out between China, India, and the London-based medical societies and journals, a competition which was to be closed when Manson began to collaborate with Ronald Ross of the Indian Medical Service, whose empirical work in India would prove conclusively the truth of Manson's hypothesis about the role of the mosquito in the transmission of malaria.[148] Manson, according to his biographer, 'wanted to leave a legacy after spending nearly two decades in China' and 'to this end, he became the chief organizer of the Alice Marble Medical College and the Hong Kong Medical Society, and he served as their dean and president, respectively'.[149] On his retirement to London, he would found, in 1898, the London School of Tropical Medicine, while Ross, Indian-born and London-educated, but from a Scottish background, would not only win the Nobel prize in 1902 but go on to be Professor of Tropical Medicine at Liverpool and then Director of the Ross Institute and Hospital for Tropical Diseases in London (1926).[150] Without Manson's support, Ross would never have been given the opportunity to make his major scientific discovery; without the Scottish network, they would never have come to work with one another.

Symptomatic of the way in which this international network of Scottish institutions operated is a note of 1915 from Sir Robert Falconer, President of the University of Toronto, to his Professor of Political Economy, James Mavor, who had left Scotland for Toronto in 1896:

> I have a letter from Professor Seth, who writes as follows:
> 'I may mention that we have just given the degree of B. Phil to R. M. MacIver, Lecturer in Political Science and Sociology in the University of Aberdeen for an excellent thesis on "Community: a Sociological Study". It is really a large book presented to us in proof, and to be published by Macmillan as soon as the times are more favourable. As there is not much promotion here in this line of work, I think MacIver might be easily induced to cross the Atlantic.

> He is an Honour graduate (First Class) of Edinburgh and Oxford. I think very highly of him and had him to stay with me for the graduation. I do not know whether you are likely to have any openings of this sort, but I know you like to have names of good men.'
>
> This might be a man worth our keeping in view,

It is probable that by 'Seth' Falconer means James Seth (1860–1925), Professor of Moral Philosophy at Edinburgh, rather than his brother Andrew Seth (1856–1931), Professor of Metaphysics at Edinburgh (later known as Andrew Seth Pringle-Pattison). James had spent several years in North America, first at Dalhousie and then at Brown and Cornell universities before returning to Edinburgh in the 1890s – though his book on moral philosophy would remain a standard textbook in the USA until the 1920s – and would therefore have understood better the needs of a North American institution. Endorsement by a Seth was sufficient to lead to MacIver's appointment to the Department of Political Economy in Toronto in 1916, despite the fact that he had no formal qualifications in the discipline, having taken a philosophy degree at Edinburgh and written what is essentially a philosophical study of 'community', even if he had delivered lectures on sociology at the University of Aberdeen under the auspices of the Philosophy Department. Falconer's and Mavor's Scottish connections were, however, to prove trustworthy, as McIvor took on the running of the department after Mavor's death in 1925, and then went on to become Professor of Sociology at Columbia University and, by 1940, President of the American Sociological Association. Mavor, as his opponents never tired of pointing out, was himself without academic qualification for the post he occupied, since he was appointed as a professor in Toronto on the basis of lectures on political economy he had given at Patrick Geddes's summer schools in Edinburgh and on courses he taught at a working men's college in Glasgow. But both a xeniteian and a believer in Patrick Geddes's philosophy as to how art could transform urban life, Mavor not only set out to embellish Toronto with an art gallery (now the Art Gallery of Ontario) but also to use a Guild of Civic Art to shape the aesthetics of the city's new public buildings. On the occasion of the fiftieth anniversary of its establishment, the *Civic Guild Bulletin* noted how Mavor had been the driving force behind the Guild whose choice of 'historic scenes has given us a treasure house of precious records in murals and sculpture. Financial kings, artists, architects and poets, college heads and historians, united to prove modern Toronto's culture was founded in her pioneer days'.[151] Mavor's personal legacy was extended by that of his daughter, Dora Mavor Moore, who established Toronto's first professional theatre company which became, subsequently, the basis of the Stratford Festival. Early productions included Scottish works by J. M. Barrie but, more importantly, by Dora's cousin, Osborne Mavor, whose plays were presented under the name of James Bridie. Dora and Osborne were both engaged in establishing a new kind of community theatre – Osborne helped found the Citizens Theatre in Glasgow in 1943 – and the director of the revival of David Lyndsay's *The Thrie Estaites* at the Edinburgh Festival in 1949, Tyrone Guthrie, went on to be the director of the first Stratford Festival in 1953. Mavor, who corresponded with Patrick Geddes throughout his life, was a product of the 'generalism' which nineteenth-century Scottish university education encouraged, and the eclectic combinations of disciplines it made possible are illustrated by another Toronto professor, Daniel Wilson, who was noted for his antiquarian and archaeological researches in Scotland – his publications included *Memorials of Edinburgh in the Olden Time* (1848) and *The Archaeology and Prehistoric Annals of Scotland* (1851) – but who was appointed in 1853 as professor of History and English Literature at Toronto, and turned his hand to literary criticism, with a study of Shakespeare's *Caliban* as a prescient version of evolution, before becoming President of the newly federated University of Toronto in 1890. And illustrated, too, by the appointment in Otago of A. L. H. Dawson, an Aberdeen graduate, as both professor of English and lecturer in political economy.[152] And the global reach involved in these Scottish networks can be seen in the career of James Hector (1834–1907), who initially trained in medicine at Edinburgh, where he took lectures in botany and zoology and developed an interest in geology. He was selected in 1857 to join John Palliser's expedition to Western Canada both as surgeon and geologist. His geological work gained him a fellowship in the Royal Society of Edinburgh and the offer of the Directorship of the Geological Survey of Otago in New Zealand in 1861. As a result of his success in this role he was made Director of the Geological Survey and Colonial Museum in Wellington, New Zealand and, subsequently, head of an Institute for the spread of scientific knowledge which was later to become the Royal Society of New Zealand. He oversaw both Museum and Institute for forty years, building up the scientific infrastructure of the country not only through the Institute's published *Transactions* but by establishing the Wellington Botanic Garden, and, as we have seen, by becoming Chancellor of Victoria University.[153]

Scotland's xeniteian energy in the nineteenth century, the founding by migrant Scots of institutions that ranged from theological colleges and universities to medical schools and botanic gardens, challenges the notion of an enfeebled and retrospective culture that has been the burden of much Scottish historiography. These xeniteian Scots took with them the inheritance of eighteenth-century Scotland's intellectual advances from metaphysics to geology, the religious motivation of their Scottish theology, and the cultural inheritance of Robert Burns and Walter Scott. T. C. Smout suggests that Scotland's cultural inheritance was used, in the nineteenth century, to create the cultural equivalent of rigor mortis:

> Scott deliberately, and Burns unwittingly, thus provided the public with the nostalgic stability and sense of nationhood in the past that it sensed it was losing in the present. The result, however, was catastrophic to literature, as it twisted its head back to front – its poetry looking always to Burns and a dead language, in prose to Scott and a past society. In this frozen posture it was obliged to walk on into the nineteenth century seeing nothing of the real world about it.[154]

Xeniteian Scotland carried with it Burns and Scott as the markers of their continuing national identity but in the drive to establish Scottish-oriented institutions they were not only very much engaged in 'the real world', they also had their eyes firmly directed at the future.

VI Projective Nationalism

By the middle of the nineteenth century, Scottish churches, Scottish schools, Scottish-style universities and medical schools created what was effectively a distinct Scottish Empire within the British Empire, a Scottish empire underpinned by national rituals (Burns suppers, St Andrews day celebrations, Masonic investitures), by a shared print culture (*Edinburgh*

Review, *Blackwood's Magazine*, Scottish novels from Scott to Oliphant), and by an evolving philosophical tradition (Reid's 'Common Sense' was gradually displaced by the 'idealism' of Edward Caird, which gave no less support to both science and Christian faith). This Scottish Empire was characterised, like its missionary religion, by the fact that its institutions were not designed to segregate Scottish migrants, and allow them to build enclosed communities in which their national traditions could be preserved from contamination – as the institutions of many diasporas were – but rather were designed to establish Scottish values as the foundation from which a new culture could be built. Scottish values were projected outwards to be incorporated into the institutional structures of evolving communities across the territories of the Empire and the consciousness of this world-wide cultural role profoundly shaped Scotland's internal cultural and political dynamics. Scotland had no need of a 'resistant nationalism' precisely because it was an imperial nation engaged in projecting its national culture to the world. The historical problem of Scotland's 'absent nationalism' in the nineteenth century is a non-problem because far from lacking a nationalism, Scottish nationalism was vigorously engaged in imposing itself wherever Scots had achieved a determining or a significant role within the territory of the British Empire. Scottish nationalism did not need to assert itself within the British state because the 'world was its field', and its aim was to make Scotland the spiritual core of the imperial project. The Treaty of 1707, we might say, was not a treaty between two nations, even though those might have been the signatories to it; it was a treaty between two empires, the actually existing English empire in the Americas and the phantom Scottish empire that had failed to come into existence in Darien. Scotland joined with England in 1707 not in order to join a united sovereign state but in order to establish a Scottish empire, a Scottish empire which might be within the territory of the 'British' empire but which would project, institutionalise and embody specifically Scottish values. This Scottish imperial-nationalism does not fit within nationalist historiography because that historiography is focused on 'resistant nationalism', of the kind that emerged in Ireland in the second half of the nineteenth century, but imperial nationalism is also fundamental to the development of the nation states of Europe from the mid-eighteenth century, and Scotland was a participant in the imperial nationalism that was typical of England and France, and, in the later nineteenth century, of Germany and, increasingly, of the United States of America (USA). The fact that Scotland had acquired an empire made it entirely different as a national entity from those countries in which nationalism was the means to resist imperial domination. Scotland's nationalism was projective, not resistant, and therefore has not been identified as a nationalism by those who are focused on nationalism as fundamentally based on resistance to the imposition of an alien power. Efforts to present Scotland as 'colonised' by England – as in Michael Hechter's *Internal Colonialism: The Celtic Fringe in British National Development* (1975) – or, indeed, as willing its own cultural colonisation – as in Colin Kidd's *Subverting Scotland's Past: Scottish Whig Historians and the Creation of an Anglo-British Identity, 1689–c.1830* (1993) – and thereby failing to resist colonisation by the development of political nationalism, misread the dynamics of Scottish culture from the 1750s to the early twentieth century. Scotland did not need such a resistant nationalism because its imperial nationalism was projected outwards to allow it to demand recognition as a cultural force quite separate from that of 'Anglo-British' imperialism.

A regular focus of accounts of why Scotland failed to develop a nineteenth-century nationalism are the writings of Walter Scott: Scott's presentation of the Scottish past, it is argued, was designed to neuter that past's contemporary significance and to ease the path by which Scots could be fully integrated into the new supra-national culture of Britishness. For Tom Nairn,

> Walter Scott was the most influential literary representative of the old posture. Like many other voices of the long facing-both ways era, he learned to set off ineffectual (hence emotionally exaggerated) regret against a 'level-headed' (and all too effective) acceptance. Boring-bastard heroes were required for that job, and he was notoriously good at inventing them.[155]

If in slightly less aggressive terms, Murray Pittock offers a similar analysis:

> Although a Tory, [Scott] was of the Whig school of history, in that he believed in historical progression and irreversible trends. One of these trends, Scott decided, and underlined in his historical fiction, was that Scotland would be subsumed in the British state. In

> acting both as historian and novelist, Scott sought power over the imagination, while implying that the validity of this power rested on historical fact. This in itself was a brilliant fiction. Scott reinforced the idea that had surfaced at the time of the Union negotiations: that Scotland as an entity was doomed, and was possessed only of a past and not a future. The ideal medium in which to demonstrate this thesis was that of Jacobitism, the politically defeated creed which had served as the major vehicle for eighteenth-century nationalism. Scott made use of it in his fiction for precisely that reason: its defeat could be conveniently conflated with the defeat of Scotland as a whole. The past was to be buried with the full battle honours of Montrose, Claverhouse, and Charles Edward Stuart. But buried Scott was determined it must be.[156]

In this interpretation, Scott is the creator and enforcer of a dual identity conception of Scottishness, in which the past is Scottish but the future is British, and that British future has nothing to do with the Scottish past – a past that can only be recalled if safely insulated from having any effect on the future: Scots had to accept that 'Scottish history was over, and that the only suitable manner of recollecting it was elegiacally'.[157]

Whatever Scott might have intended by his literary works, Scott himself, as Graeme Morton suggested in *Unionist Nationalism* (1999), became an icon of Scottish self-definition in the nineteenth century: the important fact was not what Scott had intended but the fact that he had made Scotland not only recognisable but important in British, European and imperial culture. The work of Scott, as of Burns, was used not to insist on Scotland's incorporation into a British nationality but to validate Scotland's continuing national existence:

> When we talk of Scottish nationalism in this period [1840s and 50s], including the formation of the National Association for the Vindication of Scottish Rights in the 1850s, we would be mistaken to use our twentieth-century eyes and look only for expressions of anti-Unionism and demands for a Scottish nation-state . . . [A]t its fundamentals, Scottish nationalism in the first half of the nineteenth century was all about an independent Scottish nation locked into both the Union with England and the wider 'civilised' world.[158]

In Morton's account, nationalism continues to exist within the Union and in support of the Union: nationalism expresses itself in demands that the Treaty of Union be honoured by the Westminster government and that Scotland be accepted as an equal partner within that Union. But Morton's focus on the Union prevents his acknowledging the role of Empire in Scotland's nineteenth-century 'nationalism': he draws attention, for instance, to the 1859 celebrations of the Burns centenary and quotes from an address to the Glasgow event:

> there was a time, a century ago, when our nationality was endangered, when Scotland had been converted into that battlefield 'where those who conquer do not win, and they must lose who gain' – (Loud cheers) – the nation felt that a stranger was in the land, and his cold hand was laid on its heart. Ay, at that time there was a danger, not for our national, but for our mental independence, for a feeling sprung up in the south hostile to our progress; but in spite of all jealousies and antipathies, Scotland marched on England, not in any military way, but in the less dazzling march of mind and of intelligence; this march was preceded by Robert Burns.[159]

This version of Burns, as the advance guard of Scotland's cultural assertion of itself in England, was conceivable, however, only because of Burns's acceptance both in the Empire and in the 'spiritual empire' of the USA: as Ann Rigney and Leith Davis have demonstrated,[160] the worldwide celebration of Burns's centenary linked Scottish communities – and Scottish-inspired communities – throughout the world. Far from having been absorbed into a homogeneous Britishness, Scottishness asserted its national distinctiveness from Chicago to Sydney, even if that Scottishness could claim the universal solidarity of 'a man's a man for a' that': the letter which invited worldwide participation in the 1859 celebration declared the possibility of an alternative 'union' to the political union of the UK:

> To Scotsmen and Scotswomen everywhere – and to their posterity in the generations to come – this Centenary Celebration will, if universal, prove not only a source of the greatest delight but a lasting bond of union between the inhabitants of Caledonia and those of every country and clime who sincerely adopt as their creed – 'A man's a man for a' that.'[161]

The 'bond of union' was the bond of a shared Scottishness which could be represented as a commitment both to the local and to the universal; as Rigney notes, the 1859 Burns celebrations represent the self-conscious constitution of an 'anglophone' empire combining the cultural power of the UK and the USA, but made possible only because of the bridge of Scottish values: 'Very ironically, in view of the fact that Burns mainly wrote in the Scots dialect and not in standard English, his work ended up providing a common focus for globally dispersed English-language communities'.[162] Rigney notes that James Ballantine's *Chronicle of the Hundredth Birthday of Robert Burns*, published in May 1859, records

> 872 celebratory events that had taken place in city halls, corn exchanges, local meeting halls, hotels, and private houses on January 25 earlier that year. Flanked by a flurry of centenary publications, there were more than 600 of such meetings in Scotland. The others were spread across the British Isles, the United States, and the colonies, especially Canada and Australia . . .[163]

This record of the events to celebrate Burns, though vast, is far from complete but what it testifies to is a Burnsian Empire – 'speechmakers elsewhere also evoked the wonder of the event itself and the fact that it linked Edinburgh, Aberdeen and Belfast with the Australian bush, the banks of the Zambesi, the burning plains of India, the frozen plains of northern Canada, and so on'[164] – which was to be further consolidated as a Scottish empire by the similarly extensive celebrations of the hundredth anniversary of Scott's birth in 1871. Through the celebration of its writers, Scotland projected itself to a worldwide audience as a distinct, and still largely independent, cultural entity – the originator of an empire which was not limited by political or economic boundaries. This was an 'imperial nationalism' rather than a 'unionist nationalism' – its focus was on asserting and consolidating Scottish values across the globe and claiming for those Scottish values a universal validity that made everywhere and anywhere an appropriate location for the celebration of Scottishness.

VII Xeniteian Culture

Institutions based on Scottish models, and populated by many migrant Scots, provided the routes by which Scottish ideas could be transmitted across the globe to reshape the intellectual landscape as effectively as the transport of plants was reshaping the physical landscape both in the Scottish homeland and its migrants' host-lands. In the very period, therefore, when, according to the standard view, Scottish intellectual life was in decline in Scotland, Scottish ideas were achieving their greatest world-wide influence. Even the events which were to bring about the end of the 'First British Empire' were to be the means of consolidating Scottish influence in America and of continuing Scotland's spiritual empire in the USA. In pre-Revolutionary Philadelphia, William Smith, provost of the Academy and College of Pennsylvania was also 'grand chaplain' to the St John's Lodge in Philadelphia, one of whose members – and later Grand Master of the Philadelphia Lodges – was Benjamin Franklin. Franklin's partner in his printing business was David Hall, recommended by London-based Scottish publisher William Strahan, with whom Hall continued to work closely, acting as the Scottish publisher's American agent. Among Strahan's titles were Adam Smith's *An Inquiry into the Nature and Causes of the Wealth of Nations* (1776), William Robertson's *The History of America* (1777) and Hugh Blair's *Lectures on Rhetoric and Belles Lettres* (1783), all titles which would become standard texts in North American universities in the following half-century. It was Franklin who encouraged Benjamin Rush to study medicine in Edinburgh (thereby helping establish the Philadelphia medical school) and Rush was to become William Smith's personal physician. Hall was printer of the membership lists and regulations of the St Andrew's Society of Philadelphia, founded in 1747, and of which William Smith became a member in 1754. Like the freemasons, the St Andrew's Society had been established as a fraternal benevolent society, and its members included many Scottish sea captains trading between Scotland, the West Indies and North America, as well Philadelphia-based Scots such as Robert Smith, born in Dalkeith, and designer, in 1754, of the tower of the Christ Church building at the junction of 2nd and Market Streets.[165] Five members of the St Andrew's Society of Philadelphia were signatories to the Declaration of Independence – James Wilson, George Ross, Philip Livingston, John Witherspoon and Thomas McKean[166] – all of whom would have been known to William Smith, and Smith's fellow Freemasons, Benjamin Franklin, Benjamin Rush and Thomas Jefferson. This nexus of Scottish educational, institutional and societal connections was, according to Garry Wills, to lead to the ideas of eighteenth-century Scottish thinkers having a profound influence in shaping the new institutions of the USA. The Declaration of Independence itself was, according to Wills, fundamentally influenced by Jefferson's understanding of the philosophies of Hutcheson and Reid, as conveyed by William Small, his tutor at William and Mary. Of Small (1734–75), an Aberdeen graduate, Jefferson wrote that 'it was my good fortune, and what possibly fixed the destinies of my life, that Dr William Small of Scotland was then Professor of Mathematics, a man profound in all the usual branches of science, with the happy talent of communication, correct and gentlemanly manners, and an enlarged and liberal mind'.[167] Small provided Jefferson with a direct link to Scotland's eighteenth-century intelligentsia:

> Reid's important text [*Inquiry Into the Human Mind*] might well have been on Jefferson's list of select books even without this connection [to Small]; but the gossip of Aberdeen, relayed to him by his principal witness to intellectual life abroad, must have made him greet the book with special interest when it was published in 1764 (the year Small returned to Aberdeen). In the same way, Jefferson felt a personal connection with Small's classmate, James Macpherson – enough to embolden him to write to Macpherson's brother in Edinburgh, asking for copies of original Ossian manuscripts.[168] Jefferson had met that brother, Charles, in Virginia, and James Macpherson himself had visited America in 1764–66, on business for the central colonial administration.[169]

Though Scots – even prominent Jacobite supporters like Flora MacDonald – were largely loyalist during the American Revolution, Scottish ideas helped the creators of the new state define the nature of their project and the institutions by which it should be governed. James Wilson who was, along with James Madison, the principal architect of the Federal Constitution in 1787, had been a student at St Andrews and formed his political principles on the philosophy of Thomas Reid: 'This philosophy', he wrote, 'will teach us that first principles are in themselves apparent; that to make nothing self-evident is to take away all possibility of knowing anything; that without first principles there be neither reason nor reasoning . . . Consequently, all sound reasoning must rest ultimately on the principles of common sense'.[170] Madison, in turn, was one of the first graduates of John Witherspoon's tenure as President at the College of New Jersey: Witherspoon (1723–94), originally from Haddington, educated at Edinburgh and an evangelical minister opposed to the 'Moderates' who then dominated the Church in Scotland, arrived in New Jersey in 1768 – in part at the invitation of Benjamin Rush, who had met him in Scotland.[171] Witherspoon built the College of New Jersey into the leading university of the post-Revolutionary period, making moral philosophy – the moral philosophy of Hutcheson and Reid – into the central discipline for the training of future leaders of the new society. Witherspoon's own manual of moral philosophy was to be adopted widely and paved the way for the centrality of the ideas of Hutcheson, Reid and, later, Dugald Stewart in American colleges. Jefferson, who had met Dugald Stewart in Paris in 1788, much later wrote to congratulate him on his *Philosophy of the Human Mind* having 'become the text book of most of our colleges and academies'.[172] By the mid-nineteenth century, Scottish Common Sense had been taken up and developed by American thinkers such as Francis Wayland (1796–1865) and Noah Porter (1811–92), and had brought about what one historian of American philosophy described as 'a significant revolution in the very idea of what constitutes philosophy as well as instruction',[173] as well as inspiring enough textbooks to stock a decent-sized library.[174] The influence of Scottish rhetoric was just as pronounced: Blair's *Lectures on Rhetoric and Belles Lettres* (1783) was adopted as a text at Yale as early as 1785 and at Harvard in 1799,[175] and Andrew Hook lists its use at Rhode Island College, Columbia, Pennsylvania, North Carolina, Middlebury, Amherst, Hamilton and Wesleyan.[176] Meanwhile, at Harvard, Daniel Tyrrel Channing, appointed to the Boylston Chair of Rhetoric and Oratory in 1819, applied the theories of Smith and Blair in using literary criticism as a key component in a general education.[177] It would appear that since Scottish ideas were embedded in the founding documents of the USA, their development in the institutions of higher education was fundamental to the new society's self-understanding.

The history of Princeton illustrates the scope and longevity of this Scottish philosophical empire, as Witherspoon's influence would be reinforced in the nineteenth century by the Presidency of James McCosh, who arrived exactly a hundred years after Witherspoon in 1868. McCosh (1811–94) was born in Ayrshire, educated at the University of Edinburgh, and subsequently became professor of logic at Queen's University Belfast. Like Witherspoon, he was of the evangelical wing of the Scottish Church but found his métier in raising funds for the rebuilding of a College that had been devastated in the Civil War. As much in his homeland as in his host-land, his success as an administrator was matched by his influence as a philosopher, as his major achievement was an account of *The Scottish Philosophy*, published in 1875, which both outlined the national history of philosophy in Scotland and proposed the Scottish tradition as the basis for a new and properly American philosophy:

> I am represented as being of the Scottish school of philosophy. I am not ashamed of my country, certainly not of my country's philosophy. I was trained in it. I adhere to it in one important principle: I believe that the truths of mental philosophy are to be discovered by a careful observation and induction of what passes in the mind. Not that our observation and induction gives them their authority; they have their authority in themselves; but it is thus we discover them . . . So I call my philosophy Realism, and by help of a few obvious distinctions I hope to establish it. America has as yet no special philosophy of its own. I long to see it have such. This must be taken directly from the study of the mind, and not from Germany or any other source. My ambition is to aid a little in the foundation of an American philosophy which, as a philosophy of facts, will be found to be consistent with a sound theology.[178]

For over a century Princeton – both the University and the Princeton Theological Seminary – was to be a beacon for how Scottish thought could provide a basis for the enlightenment of American civil society, and both Norman Kemp Smith and Archibald Allen Bowman were to be heads of the Philosophy Department before their return to Scotland.

Scottish philosophy was no less important in the rest of the settler empire. In Canada, the curriculum at Queen's in Kingston in the 1850s and 60s, under James George, a graduate of St Andrews, was based on the *Physiology of the Human Mind* and *Lectures on the Philosophy of the Human Mind* by Thomas Brown (1778–1820), Dugald Stewart's successor at Edinburgh, while the curriculum devised by John Clark Murray, who was appointed to McGill in 1872, involved the reading in the second year of volume I of Dugald Stewart's

Outlines, in the third year of volume II, while in the fourth year they studied Murray's own *Outlines of Sir William Hamilton's Philosophy*.[179] At Dalhousie, too, the emphasis was on Reid, Stewart and Hamilton. According to A. B. McKillop, the 'decades of the 1850s and 1860s marked the peak of the influence of the Scottish Common Sense philosophy upon the Anglo-Canadian mind. Virtually all professors of philosophy at English-speaking universities had been educated within the Common Sense tradition. Textbooks based on the Scottish philosophy continued to be used, university examination on the thought of the founders of the school continued to be given, at one institution as late as 1890'.[180] The success of Common Sense in such societies lay in its ability to combine a traditional belief in God with an equally strong commitment to the advancements of science, and, in addition, to combine a commitment to human beings as fundamentally social creatures with a belief in a very personal relationship to God. A notion of progressive history which gave purpose to the building of a new society was thus linked to a natural theology in which God was revealing himself progressively through the extension of scientific knowledge. As Daniel Wilson urged in his President's address to the Canadian Institute in 1860, the researcher is involved 'in that glorious advancement of knowledge by which God, who has revealed himself in his world, is making ever new revelations of himself in his works; and having made known to us Him who is the wisdom and power of God, through whom we have the assurance of life and immortality in the gospel of his grace, is anew, in the great volume of nature, adding evidence of man's immortality by revelations of the inexhaustible wonders of that creation . . .'[181] When the high-tide of the influence of Common Sense had passed – largely under the impact of the Darwinian challenge to its natural theology – the high-tide of Scottish influence had not passed, for Common Sense was replaced by the evolutionary spirituality of the Scottish Idealists, especially the brothers Caird, Edward (1835–1908), professor at Glasgow and, later, Oxford, and John (1820–98), professor of Divinity and then Principal at Glasgow University. When, to previous supporters like Clark Murray, it became clear that 'Reid's thinking never represents the speculative toil of a philosophic intellect, but merely the refined opinions of ordinary intelligence',[182] it was to Caird's development of Kant and Hegel that appeal was made as the real foundation for a modern philosophy. Philosophy was to find its voice in Canada through the work of John Watson (1847–1939), Caird's student from the University of Glasgow, who arrived at Queen's, Kingston in 1872 and who was to become the presiding influence in Canadian intellectual life until the First World War. He returned to Scotland to give the Gifford lectures of 1910–12, which were published as the two-volume *Interpretation of Religious Experience* (1912).[183]

In Australia, on the other hand, philosophy only became established in time to adopt Scottish Idealism: at Sydney University, the Challis Chair in Mental and Moral Philosophy was held from 1890 to 1921 by Francis Anderson (1858–1941), another product of Caird's Glasgow. Caird's successor in Glasgow, Henry Jones (1852–1922), visited Sydney in 1910, to deliver lectures on 'Idealism as a Practical Creed', and was hosted by Sydney Scots who included Mungo MacCallum, Professor of Modern Literature since 1886 and Alexander Mackie, the first Principal of Sydney Teachers' College in 1906 and Professor of Education in 1910.[184] Philosophy at Sydney was to be transformed, however, by a second Anderson, John Anderson (1893–1962), who arrived to replace the first in the Challis Chair in 1927. A student of Jones's at Glasgow and briefly a member of the University of Edinburgh Philosophy department, Anderson established himself as the dominant figure of Australian philosophy, whose influence was exerted primarily through his contributions to the *Australasian Journal of Psychology and Philosophy* which, according to Anthony Quinton, 'became almost the house organ of the Andersonian school'.[185] Anderson rejected the 'idealism' of his Glasgow teachers and adopted a radical realism which insisted that there was no difference in kinds of knowledge and 'that all knowledge involves observation of matter of fact'.[186] Anderson became a heroic figure to many of his students for his support of workers' rights (he was aligned with, though not a member of, the Communist Party) and for his resistance to University attempts to limit debate on political matters. His appointments were generally of former students who worked within his own conception of philosophy, so that 'Sydney philosophy' came to be identified with Anderson's methodology and to be identified with a distinctively Australian contribution to modern philosophy, one which was carried forward by students of Anderson such as J. A. Passmore, J. D. Mackie (who took Andersonian ideas to Otago in New Zealand), Eugene Kamenka and David Armstrong.

The impact of Scottish philosophy, Scottish medicine, Scottish political economy and Scottish literary writing was to be amplified by the ongoing impact of Scottish publishing. The Edinburgh journals, *Edinburgh Review* and *Blackwood's Magazine*, continued into the twentieth century and their form was imitated throughout the English-speaking world: London-based Scottish publisher John Murray launched the *Quarterly Review* in 1809, and it was eventually edited by Walter Scott's son-in-law and biographer, John Gibson Lockhart; *The North American Review* was founded in Boston in 1815; *Frazer's Magazine* first appeared 1830, and it was in its pages that Thomas Carlyle's *Sartor Resartus* was presented in 1833, while *Macmillan's Magazine* was first published in 1859, with David Masson as its editor. These magazines were not only standard reading matter throughout the Empire and across the English-speaking world – pirated editions of *Edinburgh Review* were published in major American cities[187] – but they were the vehicles by which the new disciplines developing from the works of eighteenth-century Scottish thinkers were promoted to an international public: thus the pioneering work on rhetoric by Adam Smith and Hugh Blair in the 1740s and 50s became the foundation of the new style of literary criticism promoted in the *Edinburgh Review* by Francis Jeffrey (1773–1850), while the political economy of Smith and Hume was carried forward in the same journal by its economics editor John Ramsay McCulloch (1789–1864).[188] It has been estimated that, at their peak, the two Edinburgh journals each had an international readership of over 100,000,[189] and that in the 1820s the *Edinburgh Review* was selling four thousand copies per issue in North America, as much as any American publication.[190] Equally, as the nineteenth century witnessed an increasingly rapid extension of all kinds of new knowledge, the successive editions of the *Encyclopaedia Britannica* became recognised as the publication in which the most recent advances were summarised for a non-specialist audience. In the Ninth Edition (1875–89), James Clerk Maxwell's article on 'Atom' announced the advent of the new physics of energy; John Nicol's 'American Literature' was the first acknowledgment of a separate national literature in North America; James Ward's much-lauded article on 'Psychology' decisively separated psychology from philosophy, and J. G. Frazer's analysis of totems and taboos was to set the course of anthropology (and psychology) for a generation. William Robertson Smith's article on the

'Bible', which argued the case for reading the Biblical text as a historical document, proved too challenging to the Free Church of which Robertson Smith was a minister and he was put on trial for heresy and ousted from his professorship in the Free Church College in Aberdeen, an outcome which proved to be of long term benefit to the *Encyclopaedia Britannica* when he took over as editor in 1887.

The international reach of the Edinburgh journals, and their London and imperial imitators, mirrored the generalist conception of culture which was embedded in the Scottish university system: as David Finkelstein has suggested, the journals 'drew for initial inspiration on longstanding eighteenth-century traditions of Scottish debate on philosophy, politics, economics, evolution and revolution, while consistently upholding the superiority of the Scottish educational and legal systems'.[191] They both promoted and benefited from the success of Burns and Scott, whose international reputations transformed Scotland into a place which resonated with literary associations,[192] and provided European and American publishers not only with the opportunity to sell translations and pirated editions of the works of Scottish authors but encouraged imitations by local writers – Fenimore Cooper was immediately hailed as the 'American Scott' on the publication of *The Spy* in 1821 and William Kirby as the 'Scott of Canada' for his *The Golden Dog* in 1877.[193] Scots vernacular became a familiar part of the educated reading-public's literary resources throughout the Anglophone world, as the celebrations of Burns's centenary in 1859 demonstrated.

The international scope of these Scottish connections and the insistent demand for Scottish materials – Sir James Mackintosh, Scottish judge in Bombay, wrote to his wife, shortly after her departure for Britain, that he had 'read since my separation from you, the 28th and 29th numbers of the *Edinburgh Review*'[194] – meant that Scottish publishers came increasingly to be concerned with satisfying the demands of imperial audiences. In 1843 John Murray initiated a series under the title of 'Colonial and Home Library' designed to sell reprints of their back catalogue in India. The venture failed but the idea was to be taken up by the other major London-based Scottish publishing house, founded by the brothers Daniel and Alexander Macmillan in 1843. By the 1860s they had begun to develop a substantial Indian customer base for educational and recreational reading, and in the 1870s began to publish a series designed specifically for an Anglophone Indian public, both primers in English style – P. C. Sircar's *Books of Reading*, containing literary selections and commentaries, sold over five million copies – and cheap editions of novels and travel books which were sometimes published in India before they were published in the UK. By 1901, according to Priya Joshi, over 80 per cent of Macmillan's total foreign sales came from the Indian market, exceeding even the sales from the firm's New York branch'.[195] Macmillan was able to establish a dominant position in the Indian market for many years, despite competition from a wide range of other British publishers, and their imprint provided an effective route by which popular Scottish authors such as William Black reached imperial audiences. If Macmillan's operation in India was run from London to suit the needs of the Orient, in Australia the firm of Angus and Robertson played exactly the opposite role, encouraging local talent and developing a self-consciously 'national' literature. Robertson had been trained in Glasgow in the James MacLehose company, and applied in Sydney the techniques which had given MacLehose such a strong base in its home territory. Their books were largely by Australian writers or on Australian topics and they remained the major developer of Australian writers from their foundation in the 1880s until the later 1980s, when it was absorbed by HarperCollins, itself the product of a takeover of a once powerful Scottish company by an American rival.[196]

Angus and Robertson are an excellent example of how Scottish xeniteians applied their skills to the building of new national cultures in migrant communities. And, of course, wherever they went these xeniteians took with them their sports, football to Latin America in the late nineteenth century – Alexander Watson Hutton, the man acknowledged as 'the father of Argentinian football', was born in Glasgow and went to Argentina as a school teacher[197] – and curling to Canada, where the first club was formed in Montreal in 1807. And, of course, wherever they went they took Highland Games,[198] a tradition stretching back to the era of the Wars of independence but codified in the early nineteenth century in time to be translated across the globe by xeniteians keen to advertise the athletic and musical skills they brought to their new environments. And there was golf: early golf clubs appear to have been combined with masonic lodges and to have spread along the international channels that Masonry made possible. The earliest club in England was the Blackheath Golf Club where the players, according to a newspaper report of 1787, 'were upward of thirty gentlemen of the London Scots Society',[199] and through their Masonic connections to the East India Company, golf was established at Calcutta as early as 1829.[200] Although there is evidence of the implements of golf being shipped to North America as early as the 1740s, it was in the last decades of the nineteenth century and the first of the twentieth that golf took off in the USA, with large numbers of Scottish golfers and apprentices lured to North America to build and maintain new courses. There are, across the globe, now more than half a million[201] places devoted to imitating the landscape of Scotland and encouraging people to follow in the footsteps of Scotland's xeniteian empire.

VIII All that is Original and Characteristic

The editorial 'On the Proposed National Monument at Edinburgh' in *Blackwood's Magazine* of July 1819, reflected on the nature of the relations between Scotland, England and Ireland in the context of the expanded Union of 1801. 'It is indispensible', it argued

> that each nation should preserve the remembrance of its own distinct origin, and look to the glory of *its own people*, with an anxious and peculiar care . . . It is quite right that the Scotch should glory with their aged sovereign in the name of Britain: and that, when considered with reference to foreign states, Britain should exhibit an united whole, intent only upon upholding and extending the glory of that empire which her united forces have formed. But it is equally indisputable that her ancient metropolis should not degenerate into a provincial town; and that an independent nation, once the rival of England, should remember, with pride, the peculiar glories by which her people have been distinguished. Without this, the whole good effects of the rivalry of the two nations will be entirely lost, and the genius of her different people, in place of emulating and improving each other, will be drawn into the centre where all that is original and characteristic will be lost . . .[202]

A 'National Monument', the editorial argued, would contribute to maintaining Scottish distinctiveness. Standard accounts of Scotland in the nineteenth century, and, indeed, the failed project of the National Monument itself – 'Scotland's Disgrace' – might seem to suggest that the writer's worst fears of provincialisation had been realised but, on the other hand, the power across the globe of institutions founded on Scottish models, and the influence of Scottish ideas and Scottish writings in so many different territories, might, by the end of the nineteenth century, have suggested that the country had indeed established 'a dominion over the minds of men' at least as effective as the military and political power which kept the empire together. Building on its outstanding eighteenth-century achievements, Scotland's 'empire of intellect' had given the nation a truly global significance.

None of the Scottish intellectuals holding chairs in universities from British Columbia to Otago, however, even in disciplines like English literature, political economy, sociology or psychology, which had distinct roots in Scotland's eighteenth-century thought, would have thought of themselves as the inheritors of a 'Scottish Enlightenment' – for the simple reason that there was no concept of any such historical event. There is no mention of 'Enlightenment' in James McCosh's account of Scottish philosophy in 1875 and none in *Scottish Philosophy in its National Development* by Henry Laurie (1837–1922), published in 1902 when Laurie had already been Professor of Mental and Moral Philosophy at Melbourne for over fifteen years. McCosh's failure to identify what has now become so universally acknowledged – Scotland's 'Enlightenment' – should lead us to question the historical model which sees a 'Scottish Enlightenment' culture flowing forth from Scotland to reshape cultures elsewhere in a haemorrhage which leaves the homeland enfeebled. In philosophy itself, so often taken to be the centrepiece of Scottish cultural distinction, McCosh's account of the national past is written from a xeniteian perspective and with a xeniteian ambition. A Scottish past is being constructed to fit with the values and ideals of some, at least, of the country's migrants in their new homelands. For McCosh, the tradition of Scottish philosophy was the tradition of resistance to Hume and his atheistic scepticism, and McCosh's account of Scottish philosophy was designed to demonstrate both the falsity of Hume's philosophy – a task he undertook more extensively in his book *The Agnosticism of Hume and Huxley* (1884) – and its dangers for an America just entering the business of constructing a national philosophy.

McCosh's 'realism' was designed to prove that 'Agnosticism never can become the creed of the great body of any people',[203] and to point the way forward to a religiously empowered philosophy and a religiously motivated imperial mission.

When McCosh's version of Scottish philosophy came to be displaced it was a result of the work of one of his successors at Princeton, Norman Kemp Smith, a St Andrews graduate who, in the year before taking up his position at Princeton, had published in the journal *Mind*, two essays in which he argued for a view of Hume very different from McCosh's: Kemp Smith's Hume was not the sceptic whom McCosh needed to cast out but rather a thinker who held a 'purely naturalistic conception of human nature', one in which 'the thorough subordination of reason to feeling and instinct is the determining factor'.[204] This Hume would no longer be the atheistic antagonist he had been taken to be by Reid and Beattie, or the 'subjective idealist' of the Kantian tradition, for whom 'nothing exists but subjective mental states':[205]

> Only when we have recognised the important functions which Hume ascribes to feeling and instinct, and the highly complex emotions and propensities which he is willing to regard as ultimate and unanalysable, are we in a position to do justice to his new, and very original, conception of the nature and conditions of experience. Hume may, indeed, be regarded, even more truly than Kant, as the father of all those subsequent philosophies that are based on an opposition between thought and feeling, truth and validity, actuality and worth.[206]

This new Hume is no longer the outsider to Scottish philosophy that he was for McCosh, and when Kemp Smith returned to Scotland in 1919 and took up his work on Hume again, he completed Hume's re-integration into the Scottish tradition by demonstrating, in his *The Philosophy of David Hume*, not finally published until 1941, how Hume's central conceptions were built on the work of Francis Hutcheson. That integration of Hume into the Scottish tradition made it possible to envisage Hume, a leader of European 'enlightenment', as a participant in a distinct 'Scottish Enlightenment', a conceptual framework which achieved institutional embodiment not in Scotland but at Cambridge in the 1960s, in Duncan Forbes's course on 'Hume, Smith and the Scottish Enlightenment'.[207]

The very possibility of envisaging 'the Scottish Enlightenment' is, in other words, a product of Scottish migrations, both in terms of people and ideas. And it was not in Scotland that the concept of the Scottish Enlightenment first began to accumulate value as cultural capital but in North America, where, as McCosh had predicted, the works of the Scottish school were studied as the foundation of America's own social and political sciences.[208] The 'Scottish Enlightenment' did not send out its intellectuals to populate the world – rather, Scottish ideas swept around the world and returned to remake Scotland's past into an Enlightenment[209] – although, in the process, side-lining that other Scotland, the 'romantic' Scotland of Macpherson's Ossian, of Burns and of the Waverley novels, which had itself been sustained in large measure by the commitment to it of Scotland's migrants. The Scottish Enlightenment was not an origin but an outcome, an outcome of the long sustained interaction of Scotland and its cultural empire and the rethinking by Scottish intellectuals of the nature of the cultural capital they had inherited from their homeland.

Notes

1. Minto, G. E., *Proposals For Carrying on Certain Public Works in the City of Edinburgh* (Edinburgh: Paul Harris Publishing, [1752] 1982), p. 5.
2. Ibid. p. 24.
3. Ibid. pp. 33–4.
4. Ibid. p. 32.
5. Ibid. p. 25.
6. Ibid. p. 29.
7. Campbell, R. H., A. S. Skinner and W. B. Todd (eds), Adam Smith, *An Inquiry into the Nature and Causes of the Wealth of Nations* (Oxford: Clarendon Press, 1976), p. 426.
8. 'On the Proposed National Monument in Edinburgh', *Blackwood's Magazine* 5 July 1819, pp. 379–85.
9. Smollett, T., *The Expedition of Humphry Clinker* (Harmondsworth: Penguin, [1771] 1967), p. 269.
10. Gaskill, H. (ed.), *The Poems of Ossian and Related Works* (Edinburgh: Edinburgh University Press, 1996), p. 357.
11. Ibid. p. 346.
12. Ibid. p. 349.
13. Smollett, *The Expedition of Humphry Clinker*, p. 277.

14. 'The Publisher to the Reader', *Watson's Choice Collection of Comic and Serious Scots Poems* (Glasgow, [1706–11] 1869), Part 1.
15. Pittock, M., 'Historiography', in Alexander Broadie (ed.), *The Cambridge Companion to the Scottish Enlightenment* (Cambridge: Cambridge University Press, 2003), p, 264.
16. Oz-Salzberger F., (ed.), Adam Ferguson, *An Essay on Civil Society* (Cambridge: Cambridge University Press, 1995), p. 215.
17. Ibid. p. 215.
18. Ibid. p. 214.
19. Pittock, M., 'Plaiding the Invention of Scotland', in Brown, I. (ed.), *From Tartan to Tartanry: Scottish Culture, History and Myth* (Edinburgh: Edinburgh University Press, 2010), pp. 40–1.
20. Lockhart, J. G, *Memoirs of Sir Walter Scott* (Edinburgh: Adan and Charles Black, 1869), Vol. VII, p. 49. Lockhart notes that 'With all respect and admiration for the noble and generous qualities which our countrymen of the Highland clans have so often exhibited, it was difficult to forget that they had always constituted a small and always unimportant part of the Scottish population; and when one reflected how miserably their numbers had of late years been reduced in consequence of the selfish and hard-hearted policy of their landlords, it almost seemed as if there was a cruel mockery in giving so much prominence to their pretensions'.
21. Royle, T., 'From David Stewart to Andy Stewart: the Invention and Re-invention of the Scottish soldier', in Brown I. (ed.), *From Tartan to Tartanry: Scottish Culture, History and Myth*, (Edinburgh: Edinburgh University Press, 2010), p. 53.
22. Masson, D., *Memories of Two Cities* (Edinburgh and London: Oliphant, Anderson and Ferrier, 1911), p. 26.
23. Gellner, E., *Nations and Nationalism* (Oxford: Blackwell, 1983); Hobsbawm E., *Nations and Nationalism since 1780* (Cambridge: Cambridge University Press, 1990); Anderson, B., *Imagined Communities: Reflections on the Origin and Spread of Nationalism* (London: Verso, 1983); Smith, A., *The Ethnic Origins of Nations* (Oxford: Blackwell, 1986); Smith, A., *Myths and Memories of the Nation* (Oxford: Oxford University Press, 1999); Hutchinson, J., *The Dynamics of Cultural Nationalism; the Gaelic Revival and the Creation of the Irish Nation State* (London: Allen & Unwin, 1987).
24. Gellner, E., *Thought and Change* (London: Weidenfeld & Nicolson, 1964), p. 68. This became the basis of Gellner, E., *Nations and Nationalism* (Oxford: Blackwell, [1983] 2006), p. 55 – which underlines that 'Nationalism is not what it seems, and above all not what it seems to itself'. For the application

of the 'modernist' view of the nation see Hobsbawm E. and T. Rangers (eds), *The Invention of Tradition* (Cambridge: Cambridge University Press, 1983), and particularly chapter 2, Trevor-Roper, H., 'The invention of tradition: the Highland tradition of Scotland'), *The Invention of Tradition*, pp. 15–42.

25. Armstrong, J., *Nations before Nationalism* (Chapel Hill, NC: University of North Carolina Press, 1992), p. 4.
26. Smith, A. D., *Nationalism and Modernism: a critical survey of recent theories of nations and nationalism* (London: Routledge, 1998), p. 181.
27. Devine T. M. (ed.), *Scotland and the Union 1707–2007* (Edinburgh: Edinburgh University Press, 2008); Watt, D., *The Price of Scotland: Darien, Union and the Wealth of Nations* (Edinburgh: Luath Press, 2007); Whatley, C. A., *The Scots and the Union* (Edinburgh: Edinburgh University Press, 2007); Fry, M., *The Union: England, Scotland and the Treaty of 1707* (Edinburgh: Birlinn Ltd, 2007); Kidd, C., *Union and Unionisms: Political Thought in Scotland, 1500–2000* (Cambridge: Cambridge University Press, 2008).
28. Brown, G., *My Scotland, Our Britain* (London: Simon & Schuster, 2014), p. 19.
29. Bottomore, T. B. and M. Rubel (eds), *Karl Marx: Selected Writings in Sociology and Social Philosophy* (Harmondsworth: Penguin, 1963), p. 157.
30. Ibid. p. 146.
31. Ngugi wa Thiong'o, *Decolonising the Mind: The Politics of Language in African Literature* (London: James Currey, 1986), p. 16.
32. Ibid. p. 16.
33. Jameson, F., *The Cultural Turn: Selected Writings on the Postmodern, 1983–1998* (London: Verso, 1998), p. 161.
34. Said, E., *Culture and Imperialism* (London: Chatto & Windus, 1993), p. 8.
35. Bhabha, H. K., *The Location of Culture* (London: Routledge, 1994), p. 172.
36. Nairn, T., *Faces of Nationalism: Janus Revisited* (London: Verso, 1997).
37. Gordon, W. T. (ed.), Marshall McLuhan, *Understanding Media: The Extensions of Man, critical edition* (Corte Madera, CA: Gingko Press, [1964] 2003), p. 40.
38. Anderson, B., *Imagined Communities: Reflections on the Origin and Spread of Nationalism* (London: Verso [1983] 1991), p. 44.
39. Ibid. p. 116.
40. Smith was succeeded in Edinburgh as lecturer in Rhetoric and Belles Lettres by Robert Watson, who was subsequently

appointed at St Andrews University in 1756 as professor of Logic, Rhetoric and Metaphysics.

41. Crawford, R., *Devolving English Literature* (Oxford: Clarendon Press, 1992), p. 42.
42. Blair, H., 'A Critical Dissertation on the Poems of Ossian', in Gaskell H. (ed.), *The Poems of Ossian and Related Works* (Edinburgh: Edinburgh University Press, 1996), p. 399.
43. Porter, B., *The Absent-Minded Imperialists: Empire, Society, and Culture in Britain* (Oxford: Oxford University Press, 2006).
44. O'Halloran, C., 'Irish Re-creations of the Gaelic Past: the Challenge of Macpherson's Ossian', *Past and Present*, 124 August 1989, pp. 69–94; O'Halloran, C., 'Ownership of the past: antiquarian debate and ethnic identity in Scotland and Ireland' in Connolly, S. J., R. A. Houston and R. J. Morris (eds), *Conflict, Identity and Economic Development: Ireland and Scotland 1600–1939* (Preston: Carnegie Publishing, 1995), pp. 135–47.
45. *Proposal of The Ossianic Society, Founded on St Patrick's Day, 1853, for the preservation and Publication of Manuscripts in the Irish Language, illustrative of the Fenian period of Irish History, &c. with Literal Translations and Notes*, p. 1; Somerville-Woodward, R., 'The Ossianic Society 1853–1863', available at <http://www.ucd.ie/pages/99/articles/somewood.html> (last accessed 11 July 2017).
46. See Jenkins, G. H., *A Rattleskull Genius: The Many Faces of Iolo Morganwg* (Cardiff: University of Wales Press, 2005).
47. As Marilyn Butler has noted, 'Burns is the first of our cultural nationalists, through his brilliantly-imagined construction of modern Scotland. In drawing together a nation, he both anticipates Scott and outdoes him', Butler, M., 'Burns and Politics', in Crawford R. (ed.), *Robert Burns and Cultural Authority* (Edinburgh: Edinburgh University Press, 1997), pp. 86–112, at 111.
48. Sir Walter ironically attributes this to himself in the 'Dedicatory Epistle' to *Ivanhoe* (Oxford: Oxford University Press, 1996), p. 14.
49. The Scottish Text Society was founded in 1882; the first article of its constitution was, 'That the name of the Society shall be the Scottish Text Society for the Publication of Works illustrative of the Scottish Language, Literature and History prior to the Union', quoted by Alexander Law, *The Scottish Text Society 1882–1982* (Edinburgh: The Scottish Text Society, 1982), p. 1.
50. Wilson, J. D. (ed.), *Matthew Arnold, Culture and Anarchy* (Cambridge: Cambridge University Press, [1869] 1935).

51. Arnold, M., *The Study of Celtic Literature* (London: John Murray, [1866] 1912), p. 127.
52. Ibid. p. 127.
53. Morley, H., *English Writers: an attempt towards a history of English Literature* (London: Cassell and Company Limited, 1887), Vol. I, p. 164.
54. Ibid. p. 164.
55. Ibid. p. 165.
56. Ibid. p. 180.
57. Ibid. pp. 189–90.
58. Morley, *English Writers*, Vol. VI, p. 1.
59. Morley's argument might be seen as a prefiguration of Colley, L., *Britons* (New Haven: Yale University Press, 1992); and also of Kerrigan, J. *Archipelagic English: Literature, History and Politics 1603–1707* (Oxford: Oxford University Press, 2008).
60. Ward, A. W. and A. R. Waller (eds), *The Cambridge History of English Literature* (Cambridge: Cambridge University Press, 1907).
61. Ibid. p. 3.
62. Ibid. p. 1.
63. Ibid. pp. 3–4.
64. See Morley, *English Writers*, Vol. 1, p. 311ff, for a nineteenth-century sceptical view of the value of *Beowulf*.
65. Ibid. pp. 326–7: 'The latest theory that assigns an English origin to Beowulf is that of a very genial scholar, who has often put freshness of thought into old English studies, the Rev. John Earle, professor of Anglo-Saxon in the University of Oxford' [*Times,* 30 September and 29 October 1885].
66. Seeley, J. R., *The Expansion of England* (London: Macmillan, 1883).
67. MacKenzie, J. M. and T. M. Devine (eds), *Scotland and the British Empire* (Oxford: Oxford University Press, 2011), 'Introduction', p. 9.
68. Fowler, B., *Pierre Bourdieu and Cultural Theory: Critical Investigations* (London: Sage, 1997), p. 174.
69. Quoted in Hewison, R., *Culture and Consensus: England, art and politics since 1940* (London: Methuen, 1997), p. 157.
70. Jenkins, R., *Pierre Bourdieu* (London: Routledge, 1992), p. 148.
71. Bourdieu, P., *Distinction: a social critique of the judgement of taste,* trans. Richard Nice (London: Routledge and Kegan Paul, 1984), p. xii.
72. Bourdieu, P., *Practical Reason: On the Theory of Action*, trans. Randall Johnson (Cambridge: Polity, 1998), p. 2; first published in France in 1994 as *Raisons Pratiques* (Paris: Éditions du Seuil, 1994).

73. Bourdieu, P., *The Rules of Art: Genesis and Structure of the Literary Field*, trans. Susan Emanuel (Cambridge: Polity Press, 1996).
74. Ibid. p. 48.
75. Higonnet, P., *Paris: Capital of the World*, trans. Arthur Goldhammer (Cambridge, MA: Harvard University Press, 2002); Harvey, D., *Paris, Capital of Modernity* (London: Routledge, 2003).
76. Casanova, P., *The World Republic of Letters*, trans. M. B. DeBevoise (Cambridge, MA: Harvard University Press, [1999] 2004), p. 275.
77. Ibid. p. 327.
78. Ibid. p. 280.
79. Ibid. p. 315.
80. Ibid. p. 109.
81. Ibid. p. 315.
82. Ibid. p. 155.
83. Ibid. p. 108.
84. Ibid. p. 85.
85. Ibid. p. 149.
86. Ibid. p. 146.
87. Gaskill, H., 'Introduction', *Translation and Literature; Versions of Ossian: Receptions, Responses, Translations*, 22:3 November 2013, pp. 293–301.
88. Sher, R., *Enlightenment & the Book: Scottish authors & their publishers in eighteenth-century Britain, Ireland, & America* (Chicago: University of Chicago Press, 2006).
89. The origin of this reconstruction of Scotland's past may have been John M. MacKenzie's inaugural lecture, 'Scotland and the Empire' at the University of Lancaster, in 1992: it was a theme taken up by: Fry, M., *The Scottish Empire* (Edinburgh: Birlinn, 2001); by Devine, T. M., *Scotland's Empire 1600–1815* (London: Penguin, 2003); and in MacKenzie, J. M. and T. M. Devine (eds), *Scotland and the British Empire* (Oxford: Oxford University Press, 2011).
90. Devine, T. M., *To the Ends of the Earth: Scotland's Global Diaspora 1750–2010* (London: Allen Lane, 2011), p. 271.
91. Devine, T. M., *The Scottish Nation 1700–2000* (London: Penguin, 1999), p. 469.
92. Harvie, C., *Scotland and Nationalism: Scottish Society and Politics 1707–1994* (London: Routledge, 1994), p. 93.
93. Craig, D., *Scottish Literature and the Scottish People: Character and Influence* (London: Chatto & Windus, 1961), p. 276.
94. Nairn, T., *The Break-up of Britain: Crisis and Neo-Nationalism* (London: Verso, 1981), p. 124.

95. Sher, R. B., *The Enlightenment & the Book*, p. 147.
96. *Dictionary of Canadian Biography*, available at <http://www.biographi.ca>, Burns, Robert (last accessed 26 October 2012).
97. *Dictionary of Canadian Biography*, available at <http://www.biographi.ca>, Dougall, John (last accessed 26 October 2012).
98. Murison, B. C., 'The Disruption and the Colonies of Scottish Settlement' in Brown S. J. and M. Fry (eds), *Scotland in the Age of the Disruption* (Edinburgh: Edinburgh University Press, 1993).
99. Breitenbach, E., *Empire and Scottish Society: The Impact of Foreign Missions at Home, c. 1790 to c. 1914* (Edinburgh: Edinburgh University Press, 2009), especially Ch. 5.
100. Scott, M. J., 'James Thomson and the Anglo-Scots', in Andrew Hook (ed.), *The History of Scottish Literature, Volume 2, 1660–1800* (Aberdeen: Aberdeen University Press, 1987), pp. 81–101.
101. Willocks, J., 'Scottish Man-Midwives in 18th Century London', in Dow, D. A. (ed.), *The Influence of Scottish Medicine: An historical assessment of its international impact* (Carnforth: Parthenon, 1988), pp. 43–62.
102. Sher, R.B., *The Enlightenment & the Book: Scottish Authors and their Publishers in Eighteenth-Century Britain, Ireland and America*, Chapter 4, 'Forging the London–Edinburgh Publishing Axis', pp. 265–326.
103. Hill, G. B., (ed.), *Boswell's Life of Johnson*, revised by L. F. Powell, 6 vols (Oxford: Oxford University Press, 1934–64), Vol. 3, pp. 77–8.
104. Mossner, E. C., *The Life of David Hume* (Edinburgh: Nelson, 1954), p. 441.
105. Ibid. p. 93.
106. McInally, T., 'George Gordon: the Man who Refuted Aristotle', *Journal of Scottish Thought*, 2:1 2009, pp. 127–137.
107. Crawford, R., *The Scottish Invention of English Literature* (Cambridge: Cambridge University Press, 1998), pp. 185–88.
108. Masson, D., *Carlyle: the address delivered by David Masson, LL.D. on unveiling a bust of Thomas Carlyle in the Wallace Monument* (Glasgow: Carter and Pratt, Printers, 1891), p. 25.
109. Ibid. p. 29.
110. Ibid. p. 26.
111. Ibid. p. 27.
112. Ibid. pp. 17–18.
113. Available at <http://www_freemason_freemasonry_.com/ramsay_biography_oration.html> (last accessed 30 October 2010).

114. Baigent, M. and R. Leigh, *The Temple and the Lodge* (London: Cape, 1998; 1989), p. 253ff.
115. Jacob, M. C., *The Radical Enlightenment: Pantheists, Freemason and Republicans* (London: Allen & Unwin, 1981).
116. Stevenson, D., *The Origins of Freemasonry: Scotland's Century, 1590–1710* (Cambridge: Cambridge University Press, 1988), p. 231.
117. Benjamin Franklin edition of *The Constitutions of the Free-Masons* (1734), electronic edition, Libraries at University Nebraska-Lincoln, available at <http://digitalcommons.unl.edu/libraryscience/25/> p. 34; (last accessed 30 October 2010).
118. Ibid. p. 35.
119. McGregor, M. I., 'A Biographical Sketch of Chevalier Andrew Michael Ramsay, including a full transcript of his oration of 1737', available at <http://www.freemasons-freemasonry.com/ramsay_biography_oration.html> (last accessed 30 October 2010).
120. Fry, M., 'A Commercial Empire', in Devine, T. M. and J. R. Young (eds), *Eighteenth Century Scotland: New Perspectives* (East Linton: Tuckwell, 1999), p. 63.
121. Ibid. p. 63.
122. For the problematic identification of Scottish migrants as a 'disapora', see Basu, P., *Highland Homecomings: Genealogy and Heritage Tourism in the Scottish Diaspora* (New York: Routledge, 2007).
123. I have adopted this term from Rozen, M. (ed.), *Homelands and Diasporas: Greeks, Jews and Their Migration* (London: I. B. Tauris, 2008), p. 57ff.
124. Harland-Jacobs, J. L., *Builders of Empire: Freemasonry and British Imperialism 1717–1927* (Chapel Hill, NC: University of North Carolina Press, 2007).
125. Laing, D. (ed.), *Works of John Knox* (Edinburgh: Printed for the Bannatyne Club, 1895), Vol. 2, p. 210.
126. Falconer, R., 'Scottish Influence in the Higher Education of Canada', *Proceedings and Transactions of the Royal Society of Canada*, Third Series, Vol. XXI (1927), sect II, 7–20 at 14.
127. Turnbull, A., 'Scotland and America', in Daiches, D., P. Jones and J. Jones (eds), *The Scottish Enlightenment* (Edinburgh: Edinburgh University Press, 1986), p. 140.
128. *Dictionary of Canadian Biography Online*, available at <http://www.biographi.ca/>, Strachan, John; (last accessed 28 October 2010).
129. Brooking, T., 'Burns, Thomas', *Dictionary of New Zealand Biography* (Wellington, New Zealand: Allen & Unwin and Department of Internal Affairs, 1990), p. 58; also available at <https://teara.govt.nz/en/biographies>.

130. Fenby, D. V., 'Hector, James', *Dictionary of New Zealand Biography* (Wellington, New Zealand: Allen & Unwin and Department of Internal Affairs, 1990), p. 183; also available at <https://teara.govt.nz/en/biographies>.
131. Barrowman, R., *Victoria University of Wellington 1899–1999: A History* (Victoria University Press: Wellington, 1999), pp. 11–30; available at the New Zealand Electronic Text Centre, <http://nzetc.victoria.ac.nz/tm/scholarly/name-121602.html>.
132. Fry, M., *The Scottish Empire* (Edinburgh: Birlinn, 2001), p. 207.
133. Ebenezer, M., 'Modern Reformed Ecumenism in India', *World Reformed Fellowship*, available at <http://www.wrfnet.org/c/portal/layout?p_l_id=PUB.1.13&p_p_id=62_INSTANCE_XnIU> (last accessed 15 October 2010).
134. MacGowan, D. J., *Claims of the Missionary Enterprise on the Medical Profession* (William Osborn: New York, 1842), p. 13; quoted in Haynes, D. M., *Imperial Medicine: Patrick Manson and the Conquest of Tropical Disease* (Philadelphia: University of Pennsylvania Press, 2001), p. 22.
135. Haynes, *Imperial Medicine*, p. 24.
136. Girdwood, R. H., 'The Influence of Scotland on North American Medicine', in Dow D. A. (ed.), *The Influence of Scottish Medicine: an historical assessment of its international impact* (Carnforth: Parthenon, 1988), p. 39.
137. Rosner, L., *Students and Apprentices: Medical Education at Edinburgh University, 1760–1810*, PhD Johns Hopkins University, 1986, p. 353.
138. Hargreaves, J. D., *Academe and Empire: Some Overseas Connections of Aberdeen University 1860-1970* (Aberdeen University Press, Aberdeen, 1994), p. 7.
139. Girdwood, R. H., 'The Influence of Scotland on North American Medicine', in Dow, D. A. (ed.), *The Influence of Scottish Medicine*, p. 40.
140. Ibid. pp. 40–1.
141. 'The History of the Sydney Medical School', available at <http://sydney.edu.au/medicine/about-the-school/history.php> (last accessed 12 October 2010).
142. Sir Hercus, C. and Sir G. Bell, *The Otago Medical School under the First Three Deans* (Edinburgh: E. & S. Livingstone, 1964), pp. 10–13.
143. Robinson, T., *William Roxburgh: The Founding Father of Indian Botany* (Chichester: Phillimore, 2008).
144. Craig, C., *Intending Scotland: Explorations in Scottish Culture since the Enlightenment* (Edinburgh: Edinburgh University Press, 2009), pp. 77–144.
145. Hargreaves, *Academe and Empire*, p. 65; Prain had been pre-

ceded at Calcutta by another Aberdeen graduate, George King, who held the post from 1871 until 1898, and was succeeded by two more Aberdeen graduates, Andrew Gage and Charles Calder.
146. MacKenzie, J. M., *Museums and Empire: Natural History, Human Cultures and Colonial Identities* (Manchester: Manchester University Press, 2009), pp. 33–40.
147. Ibid. p. 39.
148. Haynes, *Imperial Medicine*, pp. 104–24.
149. Ibid. p. 82.
150. Ibid. pp. 29–56, pp. 85–124.
151. 'The Toronto Guild of Civic Arts', Extract from Civic Guild Bulletins, 1901–1912, Thomas Fisher Rare Book Library, University of Toronto, James Mavor Papers, Box 56a, item 34.
152. Hargreaves, *Academe and Empire*, p. 55.
153. Dell, R. K., 'James Hector', *Dictionary of New Zealand Biography*, available at <http://www.dnzb.govt.nz/dnzb> (last accessed 28 October 2010).
154. Smout, T. C., *A History of the Scottish People 1560–1830* (London: Collins/Fontana, 1969), p. 469.
155. Nairn, T., *After Britain: New Labour and the Return of Scotland* (London: Granta, 2000), p. 230.
156. Pittock, M., *The Invention of Scotland: The Stuart Myth and the Scottish Identity, 1638 to the Present* (London: Routledge, 1991), p. 88.
157. Ibid. p. 54.
158. Morton, G., *Unionist-Nationalism: Governing Urban Scotland, 1830–1860* (East Linton: Tuckwell, 1999), p. 172.
159. Morton, *Unionist Nationalism*, p. 175.
160. Rigney, A., 'Embodied Communities: Commemorating Robert Burns, 1859', *Representations*, 115:1 Summer 2011, pp. 71–101; Davis, L., 'The Robert Burns 1859 Centenary: Mapping Transatlantic (Dis)location', in Aker, S., L. Davis and H. F. Nelson (eds), *Robert Burns and Transatlantic Culture* (Farnham: Ashgate, 2012), pp. 187–205.
161. Rigney, A., 'Embodied Communities: Commemorating Robert Burns, 1859', *Representations*, 115:1 Summer 2011, p. 72.
162. Ibid. p. 92.
163. Ibid. p. 71.
164. Ibid. p. 74.
165. The St Andrew's Society of Philadelphia, available at <http://www.standrewsociety.org/index2.htm> (last accessed 15 October, 2010).
166. Ibid.
167. Quoted in Turnbull, A., 'Scotland and America', Daiches, D., P. Jones and J. Jones (eds), in *The Scottish Enlightenment*

(Edinburgh: Edinburgh University Press, 1986), p. 139, from Thomas Jefferson, *Autobiography*.
168. Boyd, J. P. (ed.), *The Papers of Thomas Jefferson* (Princeton: Princeton University Press, 1950), Vol. 1, p. 96. Jefferson wrote to Charles McPherson in 1773 to inquire if he were related to James, 'to whom the world is so much indebted for the collection, arrangement and elegant translation, of Ossian's poems. These pieces have been, and will I think during my life continue to be to me, the source of daily and exalted pleasure. The tender, and the sublime emotions of the mind were never before so finely wrought up by human hand. I am not ashamed to own that I think this rude bard of the North the greatest Poet that has ever existed'.
169. Wills, G., *Inventing America: Jefferson's Declaration of Independence* (New York: Doubleday, 1978), p. 183.
170. McCluskey, J. R., *The Works of James Wilson* (Cambridge, MA: Belknap Press of Harvard University, 1967), Vol. I, p. 213.
171. For an alternative account of Witherspoon's departure from Scotland, see Crawford, R., *The Lost World of John Witherspoon* (Aberdeen: Aberdeen University Press, 2014).
172. 'From Thomas Jefferson to Dugald Stewart, 26 April 1824', available at <https://founders.archives.gov/documents/Jefferson/98-01-02-4219> (last accessed 1 July 2017). Jefferson was writing to solicit Stewart's help in identifying candidates who could be appointed to the newly established University of Virginia.
173. Schneider, H. W., *A History of American Philosophy* (New York: Columbia University Press, 1946), p. 238.
174. Schneider, *History of American Philosophy*, pp. 233–45; and Bryson, G., 'The Emergence of the Social Sciences from Moral Philosophy', *International Journal of Ethics*, XLII April 1932, pp. 304–23.
175. Horner, W. B., 'Introduction', in Gaillet, L. L. (ed.), *Scottish Rhetoric and its Influences* (Mahwah, NJ: Hermagoras Press, 1998), p. 3.
176. Hook, A., *Scotland and America: A Study of Cultural Relations* (Glasgow: Blackie, 1975), p. 76.
177. Court, F. E., 'Scottish Literary Teaching in North America', in Crawford R., (ed.), *The Scottish Invention of English Literature* (Cambridge: Cambridge University Press, 1998), p. 153.
178. McCosh, J., *Incidents of my Life in Three Countries*, typescript, Princeton University Library, Mudd LD4605.M3 A3, pp. 183–4.
179. McKillop, A. B., *A Disciplined Intelligence: Critical Inquiry and Canadian Thought in the Victorian Era* (Montreal: McGill-Queen's University Press, 1979), p. 33.

180. Ibid. pp. 52–3.
181. 'President's address', *Canadian Journal,* ser. 2, vi March 1860, p. 120; quoted in McKillop, *A Disciplined Intelligence*, p. 95.
182. Murray, J. C., 'The Scottish Philosophy', *Macmillan's Magazine*, xxxix December 1876, p. 121.
183. Trott, E. A., 'John Watson', *The Canadian Encyclopedia*, available at <http://www.thecanadianencyclopedia.com/index.cfm?PgNm=TCE&Params=A1ARTA0008483> (last accessed 20 October 2010).
184. Kennedy, B., *A Passion to Oppose: John Anderson, Philosopher* (Melbourne: Melbourne University Press, 1995), p. 74. Jones's lectures were published as *Idealism as a Practical Creed: being the lectures on philosophy and modern life delivered before the University of Sydney* (Glasgow: J. MacLehose and Sons, 1909).
185. Quinton, A., 'Foreword', A. J. Baker, *Australian Realism: The Systematic Philosophy of John Anderson* (Cambridge: Cambridge University Press, 1986), p. xi.
186. Ibid. p. 19.
187. Shattock, J., 'Reviews and Monthlies', in Bell B. (ed.), *History of the Book in Scotland*, Volume 3, *Ambitions and Industry 1800–1880* (Edinburgh: Edinburgh University Press, 2007), p. 347; Hook, A., *Scotland and America*, p. 94.
188. A review of his work in the *North American Review* in 1827, noted that 'the basis of his work is the 'Wealth of Nations', which he often quotes verbatim for several pages', *North American Review, Vol. 24–5*, available at <http://digital.library.cornell.edu/n/nora/nora.html>, 56:113 (last accessed 20 October 2010).
189. Shattock, J., 'Reviews and Monthlies', in Bell, B. (ed.), *History of the Book in Scotland*, Volume. 3, p. 347.
190. Hook, *Scotland and America*, p. 94.
191. Ibid. pp. 202–3.
192. Hook, *Scotland and America*, Ch. 5, pp. 116–173.
193. Black, F. A., 'Bookseller to the World: North America', in Bell, B. (ed.), *Edinburgh History of the Book in Scotland,* Volume 3, *Ambitions and Industry 1800–1880*, p. 450.
194. Mackintosh, R. J. (ed.), *Memoirs of the Life of the Right Honourable Sir James Mackintosh*, 2 vols (London: Edward Moxon, 1835), Vol. II, p. 23.
195. Joshi, P., 'Trading Places: the Novel, the Colonial Library, and India', in Abhijit Gupta and Swapan Chakravorty, *Print Areas: Book History in India* (Delhi: Permanent Black, 2004), pp. 17–64 at p. 42.
196. Alison, J., 'Publishers and Editors: Angus & Robertson, 1888–1945', in Lyons, M. and J. Arnold (eds), *A History of the Book*

in Australia: A National Culture in a Colonised Market (St Lucia, Queensland, 2001), pp. 27–36.

197. Available at <http://www.scotsman.com/sport/argentine-football-returns-to-roots-of-its-scottish-founder-1-1146916> (last accessed 20 January 2017).
198. For the history of curling in Canada, see <http://www.curling.ca/about-the-sport-of-curling/the-history-of-curling> (last accessed 20 January 2017).
199. Stirk, D., *Golf: History and Tradition* (Ludlow: Excellent Press, 1998), p. 40.
200. Ibid. p. 42.
201. Available at <http://www.scottishgolfhistory.org/news/how-many-golf-holes-are-there-in-the-world/> (last accessed 13 July 2017).
202. 'On the Proposed National Monument at Edinburgh', *Blackwood's Edinburgh Magazine*, Vol. V, No. XXVIII (July 1819), p. 379.
203. McCosh, J., *The Agnosticism of Hume and Huxley, with a notice of the Scottish School* (New York: Scribner's, 1884), p. 55.
204. Smith, N., 'The Naturalism of Hume (1)', *Mind*, new series, 54 (April, 1905), p. 11.
205. Ibid. p. 11.
206. Smith, N., 'The Naturalism of Hume (2)', *Mind*, new series, 55 (July, 1905), p. 346.
207. For an account of Forbes's course see John Robertson, available at <http://sas-space.sas.ac.uk/4408/1/The_Scottish_Contribution_to_the_Enlightenment_by_John_Robertson___Institute_of_Historical_Research.pdf> (last accessed 13 July 2017).
208. The work of W. C. Lehmann, on *Adam Ferguson and the Beginnings of Modern Sociology* (1933) helped establish Scotland as an origin for US sociology.
209. Evensky, J., *Adam Smith's Moral Philosophy: A Historical and Contemporary perspective on Markets, Law, Ethics and Culture* (Cambridge: Cambridge University Press, 2005), pp. 245–8.

2 In the Race of History

1 The Darkening Enlightenment

The Scottish Enlightenment is a term which has, in recent times, been accorded an almost entirely positive status in Scottish discourse – representing the country's contribution to the advancement of reason, to the development of science, to the understanding of human nature and the workings of human societies and, indeed, to the foundation of modernity.[1] But while historians and philosophers have, with increasing relish, charted the achievements of 'Enlightenment' in Scotland, thinkers in other disciplines have, over many decades and with increasing vehemence, sought to characterise the Enlightenment as the source of the evils which blight the modern world. As early as the 1930s, Edmund Husserl perceived the problems of the contemporary 'Crisis of European Sciences' as the ineluctable outcome of falsehoods generated by the Enlightenment's substitution of nature as it is experienced by human beings with a nature in which 'true-being-in-itself' is entirely 'mathematical'.[2] In the 1940s, for Theodor Adorno and Max Horkheimer, the world created by the Enlightenment is a 'mass deception', a prelude to a reduction of humanity to 'helpless victims' in a 'society alienated from itself'.[3] In the 1950s, C. Wright Mills argued that the political ideals 'born of the Enlightenment' had become redundant in world where 'increased rationality may not be assumed to make for increased reason'.[4] In the 1960s, Jürgen Habermas's defence of the 'uncompleted project of Enlightenment' was met with hostility by a whole range of emerging 'poststructuralist' and 'postmodern' theorists for whom Nietzsche's analysis of truth-claims as mere rhetoric, and his celebration of the unavoidable multiplicity of meanings, were invitations to replace the search for a singular certainty with a joyful provisionality. From a Scottish perspective, the case was put most incisively by Alasdair MacIntyre in *After Virtue* (1981), in which he praised Nietzsche's 'historic achievement' of revealing that 'what purported to be appeals to objectivity were in fact expressions of subjective will',[5] thus revealing why the modern world is the outcome 'of the failure of the Enlightenment project'.[6] MacIntyre traces the sources of this failure to the overthrow of Aristotelian conceptions of morality initiated by the scientific revolution of the seventeenth century and conceptualised in accounts of reason by the philosophies of the eighteenth: 'Reason is calculative; it can assess truths of fact and mathematical relations but nothing more. In the realm of practice therefore it can speak only of means. About ends it must be silent'.[7] In attempting to create a 'science of man', the Scottish Enlightenment thinkers, according to MacIntyre, reduced humanity from a species governed by an 'ought' to a species which had to accept merely what 'is': 'What Hume identifies as the standpoint of universal human nature turns out in fact to be that of the prejudices of the Hanoverian ruling elite'.[8]

Among those prejudices, it appears, is race. As Colin Kidd frames the issue in *The Forging of Races: Race and Scripture in the Protestant Atlantic World, 1600–2000* (2006):

> The Enlightenment, it has been suggested, bore the unmistakable imprint of white supremacy. Some figures, such as David Hume . . . who achieved notoriety during the Enlightenment for their religious heterodoxy have now obtained a new kind of notoriety in recent decades for having endorsed the proposition that blacks were mentally inferior to whites. While all racist statements are abhorrent, any racist statement which wins the imprimatur of a figure hitherto securely ensconced in the canon of philosophical greatness needs to be exposed and refuted. Furthermore, the very existence of this sort of statement automatically calls into question the vaunted wisdom of Hume as well as his very status within the canon.[9]

The basis of the Enlightenment's racialism – if not racism – was, according to Kidd, its scepticism about the 'monogenetic' account of the origins of humanity provided by the biblical account in 'Genesis'. If all human beings are the offspring of one original pair, then all, whatever their surface differences, are of the same kind. That the Biblical account would be deemed inadequate to explain the diversity of human beings encountered in the great expansion of the European world from the beginning of the sixteenth century was, according to David Hume's kinsman, Henry Home (Lord Kames), inevitable: 'Kames speculated that a "local creation" of the aboriginal race appeared to be an "unavoidable" conclusion from the evidence. Kames found that "every rational conjecture" pointed towards "a separate creation"'[10] and therefore to multiple origins. 'The biblical account of the origins of mankind from a single pair of humans struck him as incompatible with the facts of biology and geography'.[11] Despite attempting to align the 'facts of biology and geography' with the Bible by envisaging Babel as a second Fall, one which scattered mankind to different parts of the globe where climatic conditions reduced them to the condition of 'savages',[12] Kames's name, according to Kidd, became 'a byword for polygenesis in the later Enlightenment'.[13]

Whether David Hume agreed with the polygenetic or the climatic account of human differences, the now apparently notorious footnote in his essay 'Of national characters' has been read as evidence of his belief in a fundamental difference between the capabilities of white-skinned and black-skinned peoples. While acknowledging the ways in which peoples could change character over time – 'we may observe that our ancestors, a few centuries ago, were sunk into the most abject superstition, last century they were inflamed with the most furious enthusiasm, and are now settled into the most cool indifference'[14] – Hume suggested that 'there is some reason to think, that all the nations, which live beyond the polar circles or between the tropics, are inferior to the rest of the species',[15] a view given further articulation in the footnote, which begins: 'I am apt to suspect the negroes to be naturally inferior to the whites. There scarcely ever was a civilized nation of that complexion, nor even any individual eminent either in action or speculation'.[16] For critics like Emmanuel Chukwudi Eze,[17] this is symptomatic of modern racism's foundations in the Enlightenment, a racism equally evident in the works of other major philosophers of the period, such as Immanuel Kant: what it indicates, at the very least, is how easily the stadial theory of human progress, which implied that all societies will journey through the same stages from primitive hunting or simple pastoral farming to modern commercial societies, could be inverted to become a theory of the progress of some and the impossibility of progress for others – the 'primitive', rather than being the starting point of a journey that will eventually be made by all, becomes the category of those who have, because of innate inability, failed to start upon the race of historical progress. As Hume's footnote would have it, 'there are NEGRO slaves dispersed all over EUROPE, of whom none ever discovered any symptom of ingenuity; though low people, without education, will start up amongst us, and distinguish themselves in every profession'.[18] The supposedly progressive history of the human race comes to be defined by the nature of the races who constitute human history.

The significance of Hume's footnote is shaped by the fact that his philosophy claimed to be more than just another speculative system based on 'extravagant hypothesis',[19] but was, as the original title page of his *A Treatise of Human Nature* announced, 'an attempt to introduce the experimental method of reasoning into moral subjects', and to provide all knowledge with a proper foundation in the understanding of the nature of man:

> 'Tis evident, that all the sciences have a relation, greater or less, to human nature; and that however wide any of them may seem to run from it, they still return back by one passage or another. Even *Mathematics, Natural Philosophy, and Natural Religion*, are in some measure dependent on the science of MAN; since they lie under the cognizance of men, and are judged by their powers and faculties . . . There is no question of importance, whose decision is not compriz'd in the science of man; and there is none, which can be decided with any certainty before we become acquainted with that science.[20]

The 'certainty' that Hume sought was the kind that had been revealed by Newtonian physics; his study of the workings of the mind would show 'the principles of union or cohesion among our simple ideas', and 'a kind of ATTRACTION, which in the mental world will be found to have as extraordinary effects as in the natural'.[21] Hume's philosophy would bring order to the human world in the same way that Newton's 'gravity' brought order to the physical world. But if this is the case, is a theory of 'race' necessary to it – and if so, will it be a racist theory?

The issue has been given added impetus by the apparently belated discovery that Scotland's rapid economic progress in the latter part of the eighteenth century was in fact powered by the profits of businesses which were dependent on 'chattel slavery' for their very existence.[22] The evidence that very few ships leaving Scottish ports were directly engaged in the slave trade, and the public declarations in 'the cause of the poor Africans'[23] by some of the lesser figures of the Scottish Enlightenment, such as James Beattie, have been taken as evidence that Scotland had not benefited from the slave trade and had, in fact, played a prominent role in the campaign for its abolition: 'A country that was about 10 per cent of the British population contributed at times about a third of the petitions to Parliament advocating abolition of the slave trade'.[24] It appears, however, that Scots were not only significantly involved in the business of slave ships running out of Liverpool, London and Bristol, but that they represented a substantial proportion of those managing plantations in certain parts of the West Indies. Eric Graham quotes Edward Long, the first historian of Jamaica, to the effect that 'Jamaica indeed is greatly indebted to North Britain as very near one third of the [white] inhabitants are either natives of that country or descendants from those who were'.[25] Scotland's 'amnesia' about its involvement in slavery,[26] and the commercial benefit it garnered from slavery, is the economic equivalent of its failure to recognise the apparent racism of David Hume, the leading figure of its Enlightenment. Even if Adam Smith argued that slavery was, in actuality, an inefficient use of economic resources and an unsustainable mode of production, Scots were deeply implicated in the slave economies of North America and the West Indies, and their own economic progress in the latter part of the eighteenth century – built as it was on the import of tobacco, sugar and cotton, all crops for which delivery to Scottish ports was made possible by slavery – established the foundation for their later economic development and the country's rapid industrialisation. 'Scottish intellectual attack on slavery', T. M. Devine suggests, 'seemed in the short run mainly insulated from the actual practice of countless Scots in the sugar plantations and the African trade'.[27]

Scotland's Enlightenment, like its economy, had its feet sunk deep in the moral morass of slavery: Tobias Smollett, proclaimer of eighteenth-century Edinburgh as a 'hot-bed of genius', arranges for his protagonist in *Roderick Random* to achieve a final uplift in his fortunes, and to marry the woman of his dreams, after travelling under his uncle's captaincy as a surgeon on a ship which carries 'four hundred of negroes'[28] to South America, where they could 'have put off five times the number at our own price'.[29] Only by participation in the slave trade will Random be able to escape from the insecurities that have plagued his life, a participation to which he gives almost no thought – it is simply trade – but which haunts modern conceptions of the virtues of the Enlightenment in Scotland. That the nation's greatest poet was himself haunted by the life he might have lived – or the death to which he might have succumbed – had his plan to emigrate to Jamaica in order to escape his failures as an Ayrshire farmer not been prevented by the unexpected success of the Kilmarnock edition of his poems, is clear from his letter to Dr Moore of 2 August 1787: ''twas a delicious idea that I would be called a clever fellow, even though it should never reach my ears a poor Negro-driver, or perhaps a victim to that inhospitable clime, and gone to the world of Spirits!' [30]

II The Machinery of Race

In 1829, Thomas Carlyle, then still resident in a cottage in Craigenputtock in Dumfriesshire and three years before his move to Cheyne Walk in London, published in the *Edinburgh Review* an essay entitled 'Signs of the Times', which was to become one of the most influential analyses of the new age of industrialism in Britain. The essay declared that Carlyle's generation not only lived in the 'Age of Machinery',[31] but had become obsessed by the fact that there were only mechanical truths: the mental machinery of the age presupposed that, 'except the external, there are no true sciences . . . that, in short, what cannot be investigated and understood mechanically, cannot be understood at all'.[32] Nevertheless, Carlyle held out the hope 'that Mechanism is not always to be our hard taskmaster, but one day to be our pliant all-ministering servant: that a new and brighter spiritual era is slowly evolving itself for all men'.[33] That hope was to be dashed by what Carlyle saw as the 'anti-spiritual' development of Victorian society in the period between the First and Second Reform acts of 1832 and 1867, its commitment not only to ever more tawdry – '*Cheap and*

Nasty'[34] – mechanical production, but to ever more hypocritical ideologies of 'freedom' and 'equality': in the future, Carlyle prophesied, people will be under

> Divine commandment *to vote* ('Manhood Suffrage,' – Horsehood, Doghood ditto not yet treated of); universal 'glorious liberty' (to Sons of the Devil in overwhelming majority, as would appear); count of Heads the God-appointed way in this Universe, all other ways Devil-appointed; in one brief word, which includes whatever of palpable incredulity and delirious absurdity, universally believed, can be uttered or imagined on these points, 'the equality of men', any man equal to any other; Quashee Nigger to Socrates or Shakespeare; Judas Iscariot to Jesus Christ; – and Bedlam and Gehenna equal to the New Jerusalem, shall we say?[35]

The 'Quashee Nigger' invoked in comparison with the great figures of Western (white) European culture had become notorious from Carlyle's earlier writings – his 'Occasional Discourse on the Negro Question' of 1849[36] and its revised version *Occasional Discourse on the Nigger Question* of 1853.[37] There 'Quashee' had been invoked as the type of the negro after the emancipation that followed on the abolition of slavery in the West Indies in 1833–4, an abolition instigated – according to Carlyle – by the Christian sentimentalists of Exeter Hall and paid for by the British government in compensation to the slave owners:

> Exeter Hall, my philanthropic friends, has had its way in this matter. The twenty millions, a mere trifle, despatched with a single dash of the pen, are paid; and, far over the sea, we have a few black persons rendered extremely 'free' indeed. Sitting yonder, with their beautiful muzzles up to the ears in pumpkins, imbibing sweet pulps and juices; the grinder and incisor teeth ready for every new work, and the pumpkins cheap as grass in those rich climates; while the sugar crops rot round them, uncut, because labour cannot be hired, so cheap are the pumpkins; and at home, we are but required to rasp from the breakfast loaves of our own English labourers, some slight 'differential sugar duties,' and lend a poor half million, or a few more millions, now and then, to keep that beautiful state of matters going on. A state of matters lovely to contemplate, in these emancipated epochs of the human mind, which has earned us, not only the praises of Exeter Hall, and loud, long-eared halleluiahs of

> laudatory psalmody from the friends of freedom everywhere, but lasting favour (it is hoped) from the Heavenly Powers themselves; – and which may, at least, justly appeal to the Heavenly Powers, and ask them, If ever, in terrestrial procedure, they saw the match of it! Certainly, in the past history of the human species, it has no parallel; nor, one hopes, will it have in the future.[38]

'Quashee' becomes the personification of a post-emancipation slave culture in which work as well as slavery has been abolished, and in which the economy of the West Indies ceases to deliver benefits to the homeland:

> If Quashee will not honestly aid in bringing out those sugars, cinnamons, and nobler products of the West India islands, for the benefit of all mankind, then, I say, neither will the powers permit Quashee to continue growing pumpkins there for his own lazy benefit, but will sheer him out, by and by, like a lazy gourd overshadowing rich ground – him, and all that partake with him – perhaps in a very terrible manner. For, under favour of Exeter Hall, the 'terrible manner' is not yet quite extinct with the destinies in this universe; nor will it quite cease, I apprehend, for soft-sawder or philanthropic stump-oratory, now, or henceforth. No! the gods wish, besides pumpkins, that spices and valuable products be grown in their West Indies; thus much they have declared in so making the West Indies; infinitely more they wish – that manful, industrious men occupy their West Indies, not indolent, two-legged cattle, however 'happy' over their abundant pumpkins![39]

Carlyle might have rejected much of the intellectual inheritance of his eighteenth-century predecessors, but he retained a staunch belief that races had been created to fulfil their appropriate roles in the world:

> Essentially the Nigger Question was one of the smallest [in the late American War]; and in itself did not much concern mankind in the present time of struggles and hurries. One always rather likes the Nigger; evidently a poor blockhead with good dispositions, with affections, attachments, – with a turn for Nigger Melodies, and the like: – he is the only Savage of all the coloured races that doesn't die out on sight of the White Man; but can actually live beside him, and work and increase and be merry. The Almighty Maker has appointed him to be a Servant.[40]

The roles of the races are written into the structure of creation, which is why Carlyle's later writings always identify both himself and his audience as 'English': the English represent the aristocracy of race, despite the headlong rush of the English people in the nineteenth century to overthrow aristocracy in favour of democracy and, thereby, according to Carlyle, to overthrow their own dominant place in the world's history. But Carlyle's 'racism' is only one of three different versions that Carlyle develops in analysing the individual's relationship with broader communal identities. First, there is a 'national' identity which is a matter of cultural inheritance from a specific local set of circumstances: thus Walter Scott is not simply the product of individual genius but genius shaped by a national religion:

> Nobody who knows Scotland and Scott can doubt but that Presbyterianism too had a vast share in the making of him. A country where the entire people is, or has once has been, laid hold of, filled to the heart with an intimate religious idea, has 'made a step from which it cannot retrograde.' Thought, conscience, the sense that man is denizen of the Universe, creature of an Eternity, has penetrated to the remotest cottage, to the simplest heart.[41]

This is Carlyle's account of the nationality that informs his own vision of the world – the sense derived from Scottish religion of humanity as peculiarly a 'creature of an Eternity'; the sense, as he puts it in *The French Revolution*, of 'what wonders lie in every Day, – had we the sight, as happily we have not, to decipher it: for is not every meanest Day "the conflux of two Eternities"'.[42] Second, there is the sense of a racial identity which underlies historical experience: thus the history of England ought to be 'a kind of BIBLE' because 'England too (equally with any Judah whatsoever) has a History that is Divine; an Eternal Providence presiding over every step of it';[43] this is the England with which a Scot can identify as it is the fulfilment of the Scottish sense of living at the 'conflux of two Eternities' and of two 'nationalities' which share the same language. And, third, there is the contemporary nation with its effort to negotiate between its domestic politics and its imperial place in the world, a nation which ought to be fulfilling – but is actually failing – the meaning of its national identity and national mission – a failure which is all the more evident to a Scot who understands, as the English by and large do not, what England's national mission ought to be in the light of Eternity. England, to Carlyle, is a primordial continuity created by Eternity which, like its rivers, is being destroyed by laissez-faire modernity: it is in the name of an England with a spiritual meaning that transcends the history of a mere nation that Carlyle speaks out against the 'cash-nexus', against unbridled capitalism, against the unrestrained abuse of the nation's inheritance:

> . . . the Rivers and running Streams of England; primordial elements of this our poor Birthland, face-features of it, created by Heaven itself: Is Industry free to tumble out whatever horror of refuse it may have arrived at into the nearest crystal brook? Regardless of God and men and little fishes. Is Free Industry to convert all our rivers into Acherontic sewers; England generally into a roaring sooty smith's forge?[44]

Carlyle would not be the last Scot in the nineteenth century to take his personal and religious philosophy to be represented by and, potentially, fulfilled in, the England to which his writings were addressed. The England which had failed Carlyle was the England which he had made in the image of own his Scottish Presbyterian inheritance – a modern Westminster Confession that allowed him, like the Covenanters, to see England as the fulfilment of a Union reshaped to conform to Scottish values, an England in which traditional values of order and custom would resist the tide of modern anarchy.

The complexities and crosscurrents of the relations between Scotland, England, Empire and Eternity that are revealed in the writings of Carlyle were to be given an assertively racial configuration in the work of Carlyle's near-contemporary Robert Knox – they were born within two years of each other in the 1790s – who became famous both as the doctor who received corpses from the grave-robbers Burke and Hare and also, later in the century, for his theories of race. If Knox (1793–1862) is one of the descendants of the Scottish Enlightenment, then the answer to whether the Enlightenment was racist has to be 'yes'. Knox, like Hume, was attempting to bring the principles of Newton into what he considered to be fundamental to all other forms of knowledge – the developmental history of the human body. What Knox describes as 'transcendental anatomy' brings to the biological world the 'great law of unity of the organization' that Newton had revealed in the physical world; indeed,

Knox believed the discoveries of 'transcendental anatomy' had already been glimpsed by Newton:

> Newton seemed to think that there existed only one kind of matter; he was amongst the earliest to announce the doctrine of unity of the organization. His vast mind foresaw the truth, to be afterwards more fully brought out: Divine mind! In advance of his age by a century at least'.[45]

The understanding of the world that the application of Newtonian principles produced was one in which,

> Human history cannot be a mere chapter of accidents. The fate of nations cannot always be regulated by chance; its literature, science, art, wealth, religion, language laws, and morals, cannot surely be the result of merely accidental circumstances. If any one insists with me that a Negro or a Tasmanian accidentally born in England becomes thereby an Englishman, I yield the point; but should he further insist that he, the said Negro or Tasmanian, may become also a Saxon or Scandinavian, I must contend against so ludicrous an error. With me, race, or hereditary descent, is everything; it stamps the man.[46]

The wealth of the nation is in fact its racial inheritance and Knox's *The Races of Men* of 1850 argues that race and only race is the permanent reality of human history: nations and empires are, by contrast, merely passing accidents. To understand the development of world history as Knox conceives it, one has to understand the characteristics of the different races of the world, and what such an understanding of race reveals is that it is the Saxon race that will shape humanity's future: 'No race interests us so much as the Saxon . . . He is about to be the dominant race on the earth; a section of the race, the Anglo-Saxon, has for nearly a century been all-powerful on the ocean'.[47] The Saxon is 'destined some day to rule the world'.[48] Knox would have agreed with his influential contemporaries in the United States, Josiah Nott and George Glidden, that, 'human progress has arisen mainly from the war of races' because 'all the great impulses which have been given to it from time to time have been the results of conquests and colonizations'.[49]

Significantly, however, Knox's race theory, though based on a secular scientific world-view, was not built on a foundation of polygenesis, the view that Colin Kidd sees as fundamental to biblically-based racism.[50] The key evidence which, for Knox, proved polygenesis false, and which had been established as early as the 1820s by the work of the French natural historian Étienne Geoffroy and his Scottish correspondent Robert Edmond Grant (who had been Darwin's tutor at the University of Edinburgh),[51] lay in the development of the embryo, which revealed that 'in the structure of one animal all the forms are included',[52] 'that the fully-developed, or grown-up brute forms of birds and fishes, of reptiles and mammals, are represented in the organic structures of the human embryo',[53] with the result that throughout the living world there is 'but one living, principle, one animal, one eternal law'.[54] This fundamental unity – 'Mankind is of one family, one origin. In every embryo is the type of all races of men'[55] – did not prevent humanity being divided into separate 'types' or 'species', constituting different races, any more than the similarities of their embryos meant that there were no distinctions between human beings and other mammals. The unity of mankind meant that individuals of different types could inter-breed, but the distinction of the types meant that the offspring of such relationships would either themselves be infertile or would revert to the pure type of one of their parents. The hybrid, he insisted, was a deformation which, like any other individual deformation, would not be passed on to the next generation. Nor did the unity of mankind prevent the types of human beings from being necessarily at war with each other, for in the struggle of life 'destroy and live, spare and perish, is the stern law of man's destiny':[56] 'might is the sole right', and, like the beasts who have been hunted to extinction following the migrations of European peoples, native peoples must give way before the Saxons, for 'now the aim of the Saxon man is the extermination of the dark races of men – the aborigines – the men of the desert and of the forest'.[57]

Because nation and race in the modern world do not share the same geographical spaces, nations and their empires are, for Knox, not only inherently unstable but involved in inevitable internal as well as external conflicts. In Scotland, Knox found the perfect evidence for the influence of race on history, for Scotland, like Ireland, was a country divided between Saxon and Celt: it was 'the Caledonian Celtic race, not Scotland, fell at Culloden, never more to rise; the Boyne was the Waterloo of Celtic Ireland'.[58] Such defeats were inevitable because of the inferiority of the Celts to their Saxon neighbours:

> 700 years of absolute possession has not advanced by a single step the amalgamation of the Irish Celt with the Saxon English; the Cymri of Wales remain as they were: the Caledonian still lingers in diminished numbers, but unaltered, on the wild shores of his lochs and friths, scraping a miserable subsistence from the narrow patch of soil left him by the stern climate of his native land . . . [C]arry him to Canada, *he is still the same* . . .[59]

Saxon racial superiority will, in the end, drive out the Celts of Britain and Ireland, since 'the strong will always grasp at the property and lands of the weak';[60] it is important to note, however, that though Knox, like many nineteenth-century Scots, wanted to identify himself as 'Saxon', this was not the same as the assimilation to the 'Englishness' to which so many Scots then aspired – 'we English', Thomas Carlyle unblushingly declared, 'had the honour of producing' Shakespeare.[61] For Knox, there were four races on the British Isles,[62] the Celts, the Saxons, the Normans and, dominant in the south of England – but nonetheless inferior – the Belgians.[63] The territory of the Saxons was northern England and southern Scotland, which is why, for Knox, Scotland, as a nation, had no real existence; Saxon and Celt confront each other in Scotland as incompatible neighbours, because 'each race has its own form of civilization, as it has its own language and arts'.[64] Knox's conclusion was, therefore, that 'the Caledonian Celt of *Scotland* appears a race as distinct from the Lowland Saxon of the same country, as any two races can possibly be: as negro from American; Hottentot from Caffre; Esquimaux from Saxon'.[65]

It was a conclusion which echoes – indeed, may be an actual recollection of – what Walter Scott had written in Chapter 44 of *Waverley*, in describing the response of the citizens of Edinburgh to the arrival of Bonnie Prince Charlie's Highland army during the 1745 Jacobite rebellion:

> So little was the condition of the Highlands known at that late period that the character and appearance of their population, while thus sallying forth as military adventurers, conveyed to the South-Country Lowlanders as much surprise as if an invasion of African Negroes or Esquimaux Indians had issued forth from the northern mountains of their own native country.[66]

The Celt was as alien to Scottish lowlanders as were the peoples then being incorporated into the Empire in Canada and Jamaica.

The racial hierarchy that Scott's description implied was no passing fancy in his view of the world, for the opposition of Saxon to Celt had also been the burden of his 'The Lady of the Lake' (1810), which presents late-medieval Scotland as divided between its 'Saxon' rulers and its aboriginal Celtic peoples;

> The Gael beheld him grim the while,
> And answer'd with disdainful smile, –
> 'Saxon, from yonder mountain high,
> I mark'd thee send delighted eye,
> Far to the south and east, where lay,
> Extended in succession gay,
> Deep waving fields and pastures green,
> With gentle slopes and groves between: –
> These fertile plains, that soften'd vale,
> Were once the birthright of the Gael;
> The stranger came with iron hand,
> And from our fathers reft the land.
> Where dwell we now! See, rudely swell,
> Crag over crag, and fell o'er fell.[67]

The defeated Gaels have retreated before the advancing Saxons and ceded them the fertile territory over which they now rule. Scott uses the term 'Saxon', but in Knox's account this Saxon – who is James V in disguise – is in fact a Norman, descendant of one of those who came to Britain with William the Conqueror, and the condition of the original Saxons of Britain is, according to Knox, little different from that of the Celts:

> I was, I think, the first, or, amongst the first, to point out to the reading world the antagonism of the present Norman government of England to her presumed Saxon population. From 'the elements of race,' advocated by me as a leading feature – *the leading feature* in human thoughts and actions, the deduction was direct. No right-thinking person could avoid coming to the conclusion, that, in the present dynasty and aristocracy of Britain, the descendants of William and his Norman robbers had a perfect representative. What the sword enabled him to do, the sham constitution of England qualifies the present dynasty to attempt.[68]

Knox's claim to primacy was vastly overstated: the argument for a continuing Norman domination over a fundamentally

Saxon population had evolved steadily through the seventeenth century in resistance to the Stewart monarchs and for many nineteenth-century Scottish historians, what distinguished Scotland from England was that Scotland was truly Saxon, never having had a significant Norman aristocracy imposed on it.[69] This Saxon identification had become a key part of the development of eighteenth-century literature, as poets began to use the techniques of what they saw to be native literary forms – ballads, and accentual rather than syllabic verse – to restore a 'native' Anglo-Saxon culture.[70]

Walter Scott's early ballad-collecting was part of this effort to take modern literature back to the nation's ethnic foundations, but the work of Scott's which most emphatically presented British history as founded on racial oppositions was *Ivanhoe*, published in 1819. As Michael Banton has noted,[71] *Ivanhoe* is one of the earliest works to use the word 'race' with the implications that it came to acquire later in the nineteenth century: for Scott, Norman and Saxon are distinct 'races' who are deeply conscious of 'the great national distinctions' between them. The racial theme of the novel is underlined by the subplot of the Jew, Isaac, and his daughter, Rebecca, who is told by her Norman abducter that 'no race knows so well as thine own tribes how to submit to the time'.[72] Race is character. The world of *Ivanhoe* is segregated on racial lines because of the need 'to maintain a line of separation betwixt the descendants of the victor Norman and the vanquished Saxons'.[73] The possible crossing of races is dramatised by the Jewess Rebecca's relationship with the Saxon Ivanhoe, who is saved from death by her medical skills and who in turn saves her from being burned at the stake as a witch, but Ivanhoe, descendant of Saxon kings, will marry Rowena, 'a fair Saxon',[74] maintaining the purity of the Saxon race, even if, thereafter, the 'recollection of Rebecca's beauty and magnanimity' recurred to him 'more frequently than the fair descendant of Alfred might altogether have approved'.[75] Walter Scott, it would seem, is one of the links that binds Hume to Knox in a tradition of intensifying racial discriminations.

III Old Worlds in New

Ivanhoe Elementary School is situated in the Silver Lake area, five miles from downtown Los Angeles, California, an early centre of the film industry and an area full of Scottish names, especially names from Walter Scott novels – Rowena and Kenilworth, for instance. The original naming of the district as 'Ivanhoe' was in the 1830s by Hugo Reid (1809–52), one of the earliest anglophone landowners in Southern California and later, in 1849, one of the delegates at the constitutional convention which prepared the way for California's entry into the United States.[76] It is said that Reid, who grew up in Cardross in Dumbartonshire, thought the rolling green hills of Southern California were like the hills of his native Scotland – which probably meant he first arrived during California's two-week winter wet season. Climatic disjunction is, however, not the least of the ironies in the naming of the district of 'Ivanhoe'. For a start, 'Ivanhoe' was in fact the first of Scott's novels not to be set, at least in part, in Scotland: it is the novel with which he set out to prove that he was not constrained to remain forever within the limits of those 'Scottish manners, Scottish dialect, and Scottish characters of note . . . with which the author was most intimately and familiarly acquainted'.[77] To apply the name 'Ivanhoe' as an emblem of California's Scottishness was, therefore, in one sense, profoundly misplaced: 'Ivanhoe' is the symbol of Scott's departure from Scottishness. On the other hand, it may have had an unconscious appropriateness, as Scott's effort to 'colonise' the English novel was symptomatic of the ways in which the arrival of a Scot like Reid was a harbinger of the anglophone colonisation of California, then still a dominion of Mexico, which had itself achieved its independence from Spain in 1821. *Ivanhoe*, a novel about the aftermath of conquest and the processes of colonisation, might indeed reflect the world into which California was about to be incorporated in the mid-nineteenth century.

At the very time, however, when Hugo Reid was imposing his 'Scottish' names on the Californian landscape, on the other side of the American republic, Scott – and especially *Ivanhoe* – was also extraordinarily popular, for the novel's theme of racial difference made it a favourite text of the ante-bellum slave states of the American South, where re-enactments of the jousting tournaments in *Ivanhoe* became popular public spectacles, designed to reinforce the South's sense of itself as an aristocratic and chivalric society.[78] The *Richmond Enquirer* in September 1845 noted a recent 'Tournament of Knights' at Fauquier White Sulphur Springs where 'the costumes and skill of the riders and knightly horsemen will rival any previous display of the kind, and do honour to those days of Chivalry', and where the knights took their names from *Ivanhoe*.[79] This celebration of medieval aristocratic manners was part of a complex race mythology by which Southerners justified both their slaveholding and their superiority to the puritans of the Northern States: 'As part of the defense of the institution of chattel slavery, they proclaimed the superiority of the white race over the black race. And as part of a defense against Northern attacks on the barbarity of southern culture, they advocated a racial myth that demonstrated to the region's satisfaction the superiority of a southern American race over a separately descended northern American race'.[80] For the Southern theorists of race, the people of the South were the descendants of aristocratic Normans, while the Northerners were the descendants of the defeated Saxons. In the 1850s, according to Ritchie Devon Watson Jr, during the decade of Knox's major influence on race theory,

> the leaders of Dixie's political and journalistic establishments would begin feverishly concocting the myth of the South's aristocratic and chivalric Norman racial inheritance, and it would imagine this newly minted Norman race to be in a fight for survival with an implacable foe: a northern Saxon race descended from the middling commercial and yeoman classes of England and imbued with deeply imprinted racial qualities of Puritan self-righteousness and intolerance that made peaceful co-existence and mutual accommodation within a national framework impossible.[81]

Such an identification between the South and the novels of Walter Scott produced yet another irony in Ivanhoe, California, for Hugo Reid became a landowner there through his marriage to a Native American woman of the Gabrieleno tribe, whose four children from her first marriage to a Californian Native American he adopted, as well as having by her two further children of his own. Ivanhoe, California, was the context for precisely the kind of miscegenation that the narrative of *Ivanhoe* resisted, a resistance that underpinned its appeal to the race mythologies of the Southern States. Hugo Reid would go on to be a defender of the rights of the native peoples of California – though he failed to get those rights secured in the California constitution – and a documenter, in a series of letters published in the *Los Angeles Star*, of their customs and traditions.[82] In a further irony, it was California's entry into the Union in 1850 as a 'free state' – that is, one in which slaveholding was not permitted – that meant the Southern States could no longer muster a majority against their Northern critics, and that led to the increasingly vociferous demands for secession which were a prelude to the Civil War.[83]

Scott's text is thus profoundly implicated in the development of race theory in the nineteenth century, but Scott's text is not necessarily as racist as some readings of it would suggest,[84] because despite the racial oppositions which, for Scott, characterised the post-Conquest period in England, the outcome is a fusion of the two peoples through the emergence of a language which combines both of their traditions:

> 'the necessary intercourse between the lords of the soil, and those oppressed inferior beings by whom that soil was cultivated, occasioned the gradual formation of a dialect, compounded betwixt the French and the Anglo-Saxon, in which they could render themselves mutually intelligible to each other; and from this necessity arose by degrees the structure of our present English language, in which the speech of the victors and the vanquished have been so happily blended together; and which has since been so richly improved by importations from the classical languages, and from those spoken by the southern nations of Europe'.[85]

A linguistic 'nationality' is established by the emergence of an English language which transcends the racial differences by which the nation, after conquest, is divided: the English people exist by the erasure of racial distinctions made possible by a shared language, a model which is equally appropriate to the emergence of a 'British' nation in the eighteenth century, equally bound together by the shared medium of the English language. A primitive racial antagonism is thus turned into a progressive cultural unity, which was precisely the aim of Hugo Reid's account of the Native Americans of Southern California: his own children were, after all, the inheritors not only of Scottish and Native American traditions, but of the Spanish culture to which both Reid and his wife had become integrated before their marriage – originally named Bartolomea, his wife had become Doña Victoria on becoming a Mexican citizen; Reid himself had to become a Catholic in order to marry her, and chose the name Perfecto, and much of his correspondence, even with other Anglophones, was conducted in Spanish and inscribed as from 'Don Perfecto'.

Ivanhoe provided Reid with a model not of racial separation but of racial integration; *Ivanhoe* is an appropriate (con)text for Reid's life story because what the novel presents is the story of how the conquerors and the conquered can gradually become one people. Ivanhoe himself is the descendant of pure Saxons but he has learned the manners and the technological advantages of the Normans: he is, quite literally, dressed as a Norman, and is addressed as a Norman, even by his own father, and will regain power in the territory which his people have lost because he is able to act – both in the sense of 'undertake' and in the sense of 'perform' – like a Norman. The freedoms of which the Saxons have been deprived can be saved only for the future by adopting – and adapting – the cultural traditions of their conquerors. The 'Norman yoke' of the British aristocracy has not been overthrown by revolution, but has been dissolved by cultural assimilation.

That Scott's novel could be read in such radically different ways in the South and in the West of the United States reveals the profoundly ambiguous nature of the historical novel that Scott had launched on the world with the publication of *Waverley* in 1814, an ambiguity captured by Georg Lukács's ground breaking *The Historical Novel*, a study of Scott's influence on the development of the European novel which was originally written in the 1930s but was first published in English in 1962. Lukács pointed to two very different emphases about the nature of history that could be traced in Scott's novels. On the one hand, there was the stadial conception of historical progress which Scott had inherited from Smith and Hume and which – importantly for Lukács, a Marxist – had been taken up by Marx: ". . . in the field of theory and historiography only historical materialism is capable of intellectually unearthing this basis in history, of showing what the childhood of mankind was really like. But what in Morgan, Marx and Engels was worked out and proved with theoretical and historical clarity, lives, moves and has its being poetically in the best historical novels of Scott'.[86] Whatever Scott's personal politics, Scott's works underwrite the truths of a rationally explicable history that foretells a future in which human progress will have escaped from barbarity into an ever more integrated world of commercial cosmopolitanism. On the other hand, what Scott's novels also revealed for Lukács was the 'endless field of ruin, wrecked existences, wrecked or wasted heroic, human endeavour, broken social formations etc. which were the necessary preconditions of the end result'; Scott's achievement lay in his ability to 'portray objectively the ruination of past social formations, despite all his human sympathy for, and artistic sensitivity, to the splendid, heroic qualities which they contained . . . he saw at one and the same time their outstanding qualities and the historical necessity of their decline'.[87] History as the inevitability of progress is balanced against history as the inevitability of tragic loss: history as 'improvement', leading to the civility of the present, is also the history of 'ruination', of cultural, linguistic and national pasts that have been reduced to rubble to make progress possible. This ambiguity in Scott was not simply a matter of the romantic imposition of novelistic 'glamour' on the materials of the past provided by history; rather, it underlined what eighteenth-century Scottish history excluded from its narrative in order that it could constitute itself as the part of the 'science of man', and therefore as the study of progress. Hume's *The History of England* is effectively premised on his essay on miracles, which appears as section x of his *Enquiry Concerning Human Understanding* (first published in 1748):

> It is no miracle that a man, seemingly in good health, should die on a sudden: because such a kind of death, though more unusual than any other, has yet frequently been observed to happen. But it is a miracle, that a dead man should come to life; because that has never been observed in any age or country. There must, therefore, be a uniform experience against every miraculous event, otherwise the event would not merit that appellation. And as a uniform experience amounts to a proof, there is here a direct and full *proof*, from the nature of the fact, against the existence of any miracle . . .[88]

A serious history can be written only on the presumption that the events it recounts are not the product of miraculous interventions in the order of nature; or, rather, that when such miraculous interventions appear in the historical record they can be accounted as the projections of a human psyche which distorts and misunderstands the events by which it is confronted:

> When we peruse the first histories of all nations, we are apt to imagine ourselves transported into some new world; where the whole frame

> of nature is disjointed, and every element performs its operation in a different manner, from what it does at present. Battles, revolutions, pestilence, famine and death, are never the effect of those natural causes which we experience. Prodigies, omens, oracles, judgments, quite obscure the few natural events, that are intermingled with them. But as the former grow thinner every page, in proportion as we advance nearer the enlightened ages, we soon learn, that there is nothing mysterious or supernatural in the case, but that all proceeds from the usual propensity of mankind towards the marvellous, and that, though this inclination may at intervals receive a check from sense and learning, it can never be thoroughly extirpated from human nature.[89]

'History' presupposes that the past, whatever its inhabitants might have believed, was not shaped by spiritual forces no longer accepted in modern experience; such events simply testify to the psychological deformity of a primitive stage of human development. The discipline of history, in its explanations of the past, is founded on its conformity with the values and beliefs of an 'advanced', commercial, scientific culture and only those things which 'make sense' in such a culture can be allowed as explanations of the past: things which seemed sensible to earlier cultures – 'prodigies, omens, oracles' – cannot be used to explain the past except as the delusions which prevented people from understanding the real nature of their own circumstances and the real sources and implications of their own actions. The historical novel, on the other hand, even when it assumes that such a view of 'history' is correct, takes seriously the experiential assumptions of earlier epochs and presents its characters as living within and accepting the values of those conceptions of the world that would now be regarded as entirely false. The territory of the historical novel is not the territory of history – 'It is not our purpose to intrude on the province of history'[90] Scott notes at the beginning of Chapter 27 of *Waverley* – but the territory of what is excluded from history's account of the past – belief in the supernatural, belief in forces now regarded as without foundation in reality, belief in virtues which have been declared redundant by modernity. The historical novel, unlike history itself, is able to give equal weight both to the 'delusions' which govern people's actions and to the realities which those delusions conceal from them. *Waverley* dramatizes this conflict at the moment when Edward Waverley, the English-born protagonist but dressed as a Highlander and preparing to act like a Highlander, realises how delusional is his commitment to the Stuart cause:

> It was at that instant, that, looking around him, he saw the wild dress and appearance of his Highland associates, heard their whispers in an uncouth and unknown language, looked upon his dress, so unlike that which he had worn from his infancy, and wished to awake from what seemed at the moment a dream, strange, horrible, and unnatural.[91]

The historical novel as a medium of progressive history operates by revealing the delusions which govern human actions, delusions from which, Scott assumes, his readers, as creatures of modernity, have escaped. There is nothing, however, to prevent readers so identifying with those delusions as to re-assert their truth; indeed, many of Scott's plots, as in the case of *Waverley* itself, are structured around a figure of modernity who is tempted to identify themselves with and to give credence to the delusions of an earlier stage of history. The plot of *Ivanhoe* could point forward to a world in which the mixed racial inheritance of Hugo Reid's family would be irrelevant, or it could be read as revealing the underlying and continuing racial oppositions on which modern Anglophone civilisation was founded.

This double direction of Scott's construction of the historical novel meant that its power lay not in its dramatisation of the past as it was recovered in the medium of history but in its ability to challenge the underlying assumptions of secular history: people who, in every week of their lives, celebrated the miraculous birth and resurrection of Christ were necessarily committed to events which could have no place in Hume's secular conception of history. History can 'explain' the spread of Christianity in the first centuries of the modern era but it can only 'explain away' the miracle on which Christianity is founded, as that foundation assumes the intervention of the divine to redirect and reshape the narrative of history. The Christianity which constituted Scots' perception of their own place in the universe, and shaped the thinking of many of its leading intellectuals in the eighteenth century, was founded on the belief that there were events for which history – in Hume's sense – could give no explanation. The historical novel, in its willingness to accept the power of 'prodigies, omens, oracles', is not a subservient version of historical narration but its antithesis: a form which gives voice to that which cannot speak in the secular narration of history. Scott's invention of the 'historical novel' is, in effect, the invention of the 'anti-historical' novel, a form which challenges the very nature of history, thus pre-empting those philosophical accounts of the writing of history, from Nietzsche's *On the Use and Abuse of History for Life* (1874) to Hayden White's *Metahistory* (1973), which insist that history is not a neutral medium for recording what we know of the past, but a rhetorical means by which to shape the narrative of the past according to values of the present. The power of the historical novel lies in its ability to reveal, resist and disrupt the ways in which 'history' has emplotted the past – the ways in which 'history' cannot help, however inadvertently, but falsify the past which it claims to represent.

IV The Enduring Past

In 1826, in flight from the consequences of his bankruptcy, Scott attended in Paris a performance of Rossini's *Rob Roy*. Scott's novels had already been on stage in Scotland since 1816: indeed, the final act of George IV's visit to Edinburgh in 1822 was a performance of *Rob Roy* where the King was accompanied by the as-yet-unannounced author to behold the sources of his own kilted persona. Scott's works adapted for the stage were so important to Scottish national consciousness that Barbara Bell has described them as the backbone of a specifically National Drama that lasted until the late nineteenth century.[92] Equally, of course, it was as much through theatre, whether dramatic or operatic, as through his novels that Scott helped shape European romantic nationalism. The theatricality of Scott's novels that made them so easily translatable to the stage was no accident: as Peter Garside's excavation of the origins of *Waverley* has revealed,[93] Scott's novelistic career was initially inspired by a theatrical work – Joanna Baillie's *The Family Legend*. Garside dates the writing of the early chapters of *Waverley* to 1810, the year in which Scott became one of the trustees of the Theatre Royal in Edinburgh and promoted, as the main Scottish element of its first year's productions, Joanna Baillie's play about a fifteenth-century blood feud on the island of Mull. The theatrical Highlands which Scott helped to design – he took an active interest in the accuracy of the Highland costumes – and which he actively advertised – he wrote to all the chiefs of the Highland clans, inviting them to attend the first night to make it a 'great Scottish occasion'[94] – were to shape not only the content but the style of Scott's first novel. The extravagant stage construction of the adaptations of Scott novels later in the century – including, for instance, a 'real waterfall' in their elaborate scenery[95] – were simply the repatriation to the stage of the theatrical scene-setting – 'Here, like one of those lovely forms which decorate the landscapes of Poussin, Waverley found Flora'[96] – through which Waverley first encounters the Highlands. Scott's characters are presented not as actors in history, but as actors upon the stage of history, a stage on which, as they are only too well aware, they have to put on their best performance. So, for instance, in *Quentin Durward*, Louis performs the part of a king rather than being it, and what Quentin sees in the privacy of his chamber is a man who 'exhibited all the fatigue of a celebrated actor, when he has finished the exhausting representation of some favourite character'.[97] The spectacular construction of Scott's fiction inspired performativity in a double sense: it encouraged transference from printed page to the mimicry of staged representation but, equally, it encouraged transference from acting on stage to the acting out of roles previously prepared by fictional narrative: thus Scott's characters were taken out of their original settings in novels and turned into dramatic set-pieces, or were gathered together in pageants (as for his centenary), or were reassembled as in the sculptures of the Scott monument. Scott's novels were not there simply to be consumed as reading matter: they were there to be enacted, and *re*-enacted – in imagination, on stage, and in reality, and it was this innate transferability that made them so potent both in the culture and politics of romantic nationalism and in the transmission of Scottish culture in the nineteenth century.

There is a moment in *Kenilworth* that reveals Scott's self-consciousness about the enactment of history and its narrative relationship to the present. When Queen Elizabeth arrives at Kenilworth Castle she is entertained by a masque, which figures 'four separate bands' of masquers, 'each representing one of the various nations by which England had at different times been occupied':

> The aboriginal Britons, who first entered, were ushered in by two ancient Druids, whose hoary hair was crowned with a chaplet of oak, and who bore in their hands branches of mistletoe . . . their legs, arms and the upper part of their bodies, being sheathed in flesh-coloured silk, on which were traced in grotesque lines representations of the heavenly bodies, and of animals and other terrestrial objects, gave them the lively appearance of our painted ancestors, whose freedom was first entrenched upon by the Romans.
>
> The sons of Rome, who came to civilize as well as conquer, were next produced before the princely assembly . . . The Roman eagles were borne before them by two standard-bearers, who recited a hymn to Mars, and the classical warriors followed with the grave and haughty step of men who aspired at universal conquest.
>
> The third quadrille represented the Saxons, clad in their bear-skins which they had brought with them from the German forests, and bearing in their hand the redoubtable battle-axes which made such havoc among the natives of Britain . . .
>
> Last came the knightly Normans, in their mail shirts and hoods of steel, with all the panoply of chivalry.[98]

The 'stages' of English history appear successively on the theatrical stage but then perform an intricate dance which sets them in interaction, providing the spectators with 'a very pleasant spectacle' in which 'the various bands, preserving regularity and amid motions which seemed to be totally irregular, mixed together, and then disengaging themselves, resumed each to their own original rank'. Asked to decide which is the 'pre-eminent stock, from which the present natives, the happy subjects of that angelical Princess, derived their lineage', Elizabeth responds by accepting the simultaneous presence of all the stages of the past in her contemporary England, since 'the Englishman had from the ancient Briton his bold and tameless spirit of freedom, – from the Roman his disciplined courage in war, with his love of letters and civilizations in time of peace, – from the Saxon his wise and equitable laws, – and from the chivalrous Norman his love of honour and courtesy, with his generous desire for glory'.[99] Scott dramatises on stage the pageant of a history which is precisely the opposite of the stadial history to which Hume and Smith were committed – to history as the erasure of each stage of the nation by the one which inevitably replaces it. Instead, Scott presents history as a process of the continuous reclamation of earlier stages of the national narrative rather than one of wreckage and disruption.

Kenilworth, as a novel that plays fast and loose with real history, might seem to be an archetypal version of the nation as a dark illusion – as an 'imagined' community that is founded, as in the 'modernist' theories of the nation of Gellner, Hobsbawm and Anderson, on nothing more than a 'fiction'. In the introduction to *Ivanhoe*, however, Scott tells us that the idea of his novel came from 'the ingenious and unfortunate Logan's tragedy of Runnamede, in which, about the same period of history, the author had seen the Saxon and Norman barons opposed to each other on different sides of the stage'.[100] On stage, the two 'nations' are set in confrontation with one another, despite the fact that 'history was violated' by such an opposition. What the opposition reveals, however, is 'the existence of two races in the same country, the vanquished distinguished by their plain, homely, blunt manners, and the free spirit infused by their ancient institutions and laws; the victors, by the high spirit of military fame, personal adventure, and whatever could distinguish them from the Flower of Chivalry'.[101] The nation, in other words, is not a unity – it is not a matter of one conquering people replacing another, or, indeed, of a hybridisation of cultures into a new totality. Nations are neither the erasure of the stages of the past nor the construction of a unity – imagined or otherwise – in the present: they are a space in which the values and virtues of various pasts continue to be played out through the debates and conflicts of the present. The various pasts of the nation remain as potential positions in a contemporary debate about the present and future values and actions of the nation. On stage, the successive temporality of history is transformed into a simultaneous presence in which past principles are re-enacted in a performance that may be prelude to their re-performance in the real events of the future. The nation is not a stage – in the sense of the last in a sequence which has transcended and replaced its predecessors – but a stage as a space of representation, preserving within its boundaries certain cultural possibilities, some of which at least are always available as roles to be taken up by those who are actors in current events. We act in history in part by performing and re-performing the possible roles provided for us by the drama of our national pasts.

It was such a performative restaging of history that was dramatised in the streets of Edinburgh in 1822. For Trevor-

Roper, George IV's visit might constitute a 'farce' but the theatrical implication of his terminology underlines that the events of 1822 are not an accidental political sideline to Scott's novelistic career. The power of Scott's fictions lies in the fact that they take seriously their own status as prologues-to-performance and this continuity of the performative is indicated by the fact that Scott employed the director of Baillie's *The Family Legend* in 1810, the theatrical producer Daniel Terry, for the spectacular staging of the pageant of 1822. Terry, whose various theatrical ventures Scott underwrote financially until his bankruptcy in 1825, provided a public dramatisation of the king of the United Kingdom as a figure out of one of Scott's novels. As Lockhart put it, revealing the depths of Scott's implication with theatre, 'high and low were in the humour, not only to applaud, but each, according to his station, to take a share in what might really be described as a sort of grand terryfication of the Holyrood chapters in Waverley'.[102] Scott and Terry created a political theatre in which a Hanoverian English monarch could appear upon the stage of Edinburgh to act the part of a Stuart King. One way of seeing this is Anderson's, as fiction seeping into and undermining reality; alternatively, however, we can see it as art providing symbolic structures that allow people to perform – and through performance to reshape – the roles to which they are called in their real social relations. When George IV performed the role of a Scottish king in Scotland he became a Scottish king in Scotland and Scotland's national identity – Scottish national difference, which had been under threat since the Union of 1707 – was given the seal of royal approval. The constitutional status of Scotland within the Act of Union, including the legal commitment to the maintenance of its separate institutional status, was reinforced by the monarch's symbolic Scottish identity – to perform that identity (in however fictionalised a form) was to underline the institutional reality of Scotland's separate and distinctive civil society.

The 'terryfication' of 1822 is usually taken as an index of how Scott's Unionist politics turns the Scottish past into mere nostalgia, irrelevant to the modern British State to which he gave his active allegiance. As Katie Trumpener puts it, in relation to *Guy Mannering*, Scott's novel 'commemorates in order to forget, politicizes the memory problem only to subjectivize it, and retrieves the problem of empire in order to relegate it to the realm of infantile memory'.[103] For Trumpener, Scott's novels predict a postcolonial politics and literature in which cultural nationalism 'survives because it learns to separate cultural distinctiveness from the memory of political autonomy and can therefore be accommodated within the imperial framework',[104] but Scott's novels, like the events of 1822, were to be a crucial part of the resistance to Scotland's incorporation into a single, unitary British state: the staged incorporation of the different stages of the English nation in *Kenilworth* is a model of how the different nations of the United Kingdom can be integrated into the same contemporary performance without losing the particular identities of their individual pasts. Scott's 'unionism' was also a resistant nationalism, one of the elements by which the country could then assert its own projective nationalism to the British Empire.

The paradoxical effect of this interaction of past, present and future is attested by an article in *Blackwood's Edinburgh Magazine* which Ann Rigney quotes in her analysis of the Scott centenary of 1871:

> Could we go back to that Scotland of 1771, into which a new Scott was born . . . how strangely different we would find it! The people we should meet . . . would remember the '45, and still feel in their hearts some remnant of that thrill of doubt and fear and hope which must have run through the island before the ill-fated prince turned on his way to London. But in their recollections there would have been no Vich-Ian-Vohr, no Evan Dhu, no Flora . . . What a strange, what an incredible difference! No Highland emigration could so depopulate those dearest hills and glens as they are depopulated by this mere imagination. A hundred years ago they were bare and naked – nay, they were not, except to here and there a wandering hasty passenger ('Century', 1871).[105]

The Highlands are repopulated by the characters of Scott's imagination in defiance of the history which is depopulating them: whatever Scott's own Unionist politics, his works keep alive a distinctive Scottish past which insists – as he himself discovered in responding to the issue of the possible banning of Scottish banknotes in the *Letters of Malachi Malagrowther* (1826)[106] – on the continuing modern integrity of the nation. Scott's Unionism was supported by a nationalism which insisted that Scotland had not disappeared from history, post-1707 – that its rights to continuing existence were inscribed in the

Treaty, and that the memory of the independent Scotland on which those rights were based was inscribed in his works. The Scotland remembered by Hugo Reid's naming of Ivanhoe and its Scott-inspired street-names was a continuing and not merely a historical entity. Its evocation of Scott and Scotland was not a sentimental gesture to the past but the foundation on which the values of a new society could be built – in Reid's case, the values of racial and linguistic equality between aboriginal peoples and the recently-arrived but politically dominant migrants. Scott's memories of a national Scotland were inscribed in the landscapes of empire not as the mere recollection of a dead past, but as the assertion of values that could be translated not only across space but also across time.

V At the Boundary of History

In 1872, James Clerk Maxwell published in his study *Theory of Heat* a version of the 'mind experiment' he had been discussing with his correspondents since 1867, a mind experiment that was named by William Thomson, Lord Kelvin, as 'Maxwell's demon' because it was so potentially disruptive of the laws of physics as Kelvin and Peter Guthrie Tait had developed them in their *Treatise on Natural Philosophy*, itself published 1867. Maxwell's 'demon' is a molecular-sized creature who sits between two containers of gases. The temperature of the gases is a function of the velocity of the particles which they contain, but in any gas there will be particles which are faster (hotter) or slower (colder) than the overall average. The 'demon' operates a shutter which allows particles to pass between the two containers but allows only the fastest (i.e. the hottest) from the cooler container and the slowest (i.e. the coolest) from the warmer container to be exchanged. As a consequence, heat (the average speed of particles) 'flows' from the cooler to the warmer chamber, reversing the expectations of the second law of thermodynamics that a loss of energy (cooling) is the inevitable outcome of all physical activity. The significance of this imaginary experiment was that it challenged the ultimate destiny of the universe as envisaged by thermodynamics, a science which had first been named in Scotland and had been the driving force of new conceptions of the physical universe since the 1840s. Thomson, who taught at The University of Glasgow, and Tait, who taught at the University of Edinburgh, believed they had overthrown the Newtonian physics of 'force' with a new physics of 'energy', one in which matter is understood not as fixed objects interacting through the effects of gravity but as energy flowing into or fusing into different forms as it is heated or cooled. In energy physics matter is not only dynamic – that is, it is characterised by movement – but it is in constant transformation: the same energy can take many forms. In any transformation of matter, however, some energy is dissipated into the environment – the energy required to boil water could not all be collected and used in the steam which drove an engine – which meant that in the long run the energy which made our existing universe possible would be evenly distributed across space, making activity of any kind, impossible. As David Masson described it in his *Recent British Philosophy* (1867):

> By a process which has been named the Equilibration of Forces, and which is slowly going on, it seems to be foreseen that a period will come when all the energy locked up in the solar system, and sustaining whatever of motion or life there is in it, will be exhausted . . . and all its parts through all their present variousness will be stiffened or resolved, as regards each other, in a defunct and featureless community of rest and death . . . [Farther, Science] yet sees no other end but that all the immeasurable entanglement of all the starry systems shall also run itself together at last in an indistinguishable equilibrium of ruin.[107]

To many Victorians, this was far more threatening than the implications of Darwinism, which could be interpreted as justifying the struggle towards a better and more successful future. But thermodynamics suggested that all such efforts were doomed to succumb to a universal exhaustion: neither 'history' nor 'race' could guarantee survival in the 'equilibrium of ruin' that was the conclusion of energy physics.

Maxwell's 'demon', however, suggested that the 'laws' of physics were not inevitable constraints but, rather, statistical probabilities in a universe that was more disorderly than Thomson and Tait's science could have expected, so that the seemingly inevitable cooling of the universe might, if only by random accident, indeed be reversible. In effect, Maxwell's 'demon' pointed to a boundary line where the expected nature of reality was overturned and where apparently orderly progress underwent a sudden and radical reversal. The 'demon' was to have long afterlife both in physics and in communications theory but the 'demon' is itself the after-echo of narratives deeply embedded in Scottish culture, and which had been the subject of many of the 'revivals' in the eighteenth and nineteenth centuries. Such narratives focused on a figure who stands on – or, in the case of Burns's Tam O' Shanter, rides across – the boundary line between the world of time, which has become the world of secular history, and the world of the supernatural, or of the religious world of resurrection. If *Waverley* seemed to present Scott as the novelist of historical process and historical progress, *Guy Mannering*, published early in 1815, pointed in a very different direction, a direction revealed in an early encounter between Guy Mannering, Oxford-educated visitor to Scotland, and 'Dominie Sampson', as to the validity of astrology:

> 'Truly,' said Sampson, 'I opine with Sir Isaac Newton, Knight, and umwhile master of his Majesty's mint, that the (pretended) science of astrology is altogether vain, frivolous, and unsatisfactory.' And here he reposed his oracular jaws.
>
> 'Really,' resumed the traveller. 'I am very sorry to see a gentlemen of your learning and gravity labouring under such a strange blindness and delusion. Will you place the brief, the modern, and, as I may say, the vernacular name of Isaac Newton in opposition to the grave and sonorous authorities of Dariot, Bonatus, Ptolemy, Haly, Ketler, Dieterick . . . Do not Christians and Heathens, and Jews and Gentiles, and poets and philosophers, unite in allowing the starry influences!'[108]

The conversation is a joke at the expense of Sampson by his much better educated interlocutor, but Mannering's pretence of a commitment to astrology will come back to haunt him as his predictions of the future turn out not only to be true but to confirm the supernatural insights of the novel's wild gypsy, Meg Merrilies. Meg's racial background ensures that she remains an outsider to contemporary society but it is she, nonetheless, who holds the key by which events in imperial India can be linked to those a generation earlier in Scotland. Meg will be the means by which an orderly relation of cause (the young Harry Bertram's disappearance) and effect (the return of the so-called Captain Brown from India) will be re-established in the narrative, as well as the means by which Bertram will be able to secure his family inheritance, but her role requires an apparently supernatural – not to say demonic – capacity for intervening in and re-directing the events of the narrative. She is the symbol of an ancient and primitive insight into the world which is entirely at odds with modern secular history – watching her, Mannering 'could not help feeling that her figure, her employment, and her situation conveyed the exact impression of an ancient sybil';[109] she disrupts modernity with the return of the 'supernatural',[110] appearing to the other characters 'as if emerging out of the earth',[111] and travelling with a superhuman power: 'There was something frightful and unearthly, as it were, in the rapid and undeviating course which she pursued'.[112] Meg haunts the narrative of *Guy Mannering* as the 'other' of secular history, as that which secular history ought to have banished but without which the order of contemporary society will be disputed and disrupted. Secular history, it appears, depends on the continued operation of those supernatural forces which it claims to have abolished. The demonic Meg makes possible the reversal of the criminal order by which the present has been constituted, allowing a past injustice to be undone and a lost identity – Bertram's concealed within Brown's – to be recovered. *Guy Mannering* prefigures the many later Scott plots in which characters will cross the boundary of secular history to encounter that which lies – 'Merri-lies', we might say – beyond it; indeed, to reveal that progressive, secular history is actually founded on and continues to depend upon that which it believed to have been erased from the present and safely locked into the past.

Scott's 'anti-historical' novels prefigured much of nineteenth-century Scotland's cultural concerns, in its exploration of the boundary between history and what lay beyond history. Scottish intellectuals' engagement was not with the history of a rapidly changing modern Scotland but with the remains of, or the return of, an a-historical or an anti-historical force which history had failed to subdue: from the resurrection of the devil in James Hogg's *The Private Memoirs and Confessions of a Justified Sinner* (1824) to the supernatural of Margaret Oliphant's 'The Library Window' (1896); from George MacDonald's *Phantastes* of 1848 – a story based on the implications of energy physics – to Stevenson's *Strange Case of Dr Jekyll and Mr Hyde* in 1886 – a story equally based on the entropic view of the universe suggested by Thomson and Tait – Scottish writers, thinkers and artists were engaged in defining how history related to what lay beyond or outside of the territory it claimed. From the epochal perspectives of Charles Lyell's *Principles of Geology* (1830–3), which revealed how insignificant was the timescale to which secular history was committed, to Robert Chambers's *Vestiges of the Natural History of Creation* (1844), which pre-empted much of the account of evolution that Charles Darwin was to make public a decade and a half later in his *On the Origin of Species by Means of Natural Selection* (1859), Scottish thinkers revealed the power of forces which history could not withstand. By the end of the century, in J. G. Frazer's anthropology, the forces of the primitive and the pre-historical are not just part of the distant past of modern humanity, or the distant margins of imperial expansion, but remained at the very heart of civilisation itself: Frazer claimed, of his *Golden Bough*, that 'it is not our business here to consider what bearing the permanent existence of such a solid layer of savagery beneath the surface of society' might mean for the human future, but he goes on to insist on precisely the threat that savagery poses:

> The dispassionate observer, whose studies have led him to plumb its depths, can hardly regard it otherwise than as a standing menace to civilisation. We seem to move on a thin crust which may at any moment be rent by the subterranean forces slumbering below. From time to time a hollow murmur underground or a sudden spirt of flame into the air tells of what is going on beneath our feet.[113]

The anti-historical underlies the historical and may be much more powerful and more enduring than the potential for historical progress implied in stadial conceptions of history: instead of consigning savagery to the past, the lesson of history is that it is 'continual menace', an inevitable accompaniment to the progress of civilisation.

VI Race and History

Race remained an influential category of Scottish thought through the nineteenth and into the twentieth century. Scots were assimilated to Saxons in order to justify their role in Empire, Celts were castigated for their racial inadequacies; Lowland Scots were singled out by Francis Galton for the size of their brains, Catholic Irish were regarded as a threat to the purity of the nation's bloodstock as well as the national religion; the 'Celtic' offered an alternative to the modern industrial society of Anglo-Saxonism even if, as in the case of 'Fiona MacLeod', the Celtic was assumed to be itself on the edge of extinction. These racial accounts of human difference might have been based on entirely false presuppositions, but what they represented was resistance to the account of human history as the necessary incorporation of people into the stadial sequence that made modern commercial society the necessary end point of human progress, and that made history itself the necessary context within which human lives and human societies had to be understood. Theories of race were one of the ways in which Scotland resisted the tyranny of 'history' as the only relevant category within which human experience could be understood.

In Kidd's *The Forging of Races*, the falsity of such notions of race is founded on an antithesis between 'objective science' and 'myth', or between 'superficially objective science' (i.e. false science) and a 'cultural creativity' that endlessly generates new 'fantasia' rather than real knowledge,[114] fantasia which are 'the product not of nature but of the imagination'.[115] Kidd had hoped to show that, because all human beings are the descendants of Adam and Eve, there could be no Biblical justification for theories of racial difference, but what he discovers is that the 'human imagination is equally capable of interpreting the Christian scriptures in a racialist as in an anti-racialist manner'.[116] The use of the term 'imagination' is here designed to protect 'reason', 'science' and 'logic' from contamination by such fantasies, but this is an opposition which is unsustainable: all scientific 'truths' may turn out to be mere imaginings, including the 'truth' that there are no such things as races. At every stage of its development 'science' has been haunted by the desire that its imaginings will find justification in its correspondence with some transcendentally justified truth, but the opposition that Kidd invokes between a conception of race that 'belongs not so much to the realm of objective biology as to the quite distinct realm of human subjectivity',[117] assumes that 'objective biology' has no dependence on 'human subjectivity', despite the fact that we know that all agreed scientific 'truths' depend on shared methods of validation which are the outcome of agreement between human subjects, and, therefore, an outcome of human subjectivity. Equally, Kidd believes that 'the Bible says nothing about race, and functions, in this respect, merely as a screen on which its so-called interpreters project their racial attitudes, fears, and fantasies',[118] but it is impossible to distinguish between what a text means and what its interpreters infer from it: all texts are a 'screen' that depend – like *Ivanhoe* – on the interpretive context in which it is situated. We may have rules about how texts ought to be interpreted but those rules cannot ever be 'objective' – they are simply mutually supportive subjectivities framed within institutional networks that affirm how subjective assertions and arguments are to be tested and given validation. The science of race is, in this sense, no different from the science of 'phlogiston' or of 'aether', which were both at one time believed to be necessary to the explanation of the world as then understood but which were later discovered to be redundant: they were not 'pseudo-science' or 'fantasy science' but scientifically agreed parts of a supposedly 'objective' world which turned out not to exist. Kidd confuses the lack of objectivity of the 'science of race' with his own moral outrage at the racism which that science was designed to support: but 'race' will not disappear because we find the 'true' way of reading the Bible as anti-racist or because we find that biological 'evidence is so cross-grained that arbitrariness is intrinsic to any system of racial classification':[119] all scientific knowledge depends on classifications that are, in the end, arbitrary, and all interpretation, whether of text or of nature, is caught in a hermeneutics in which our foundational assumptions will predetermine our outcomes – until, that is, we reach the boundary point at which we encounter the demon which forces us to rethink those foundational assumptions. What Kidd traces *in extenso* is not fantasy science – the mere projection of prejudice on to the screen of reality – but a science that is being tested and found wanting and revised or discarded; it becomes 'fantasy' in the eyes of those who believe that they have been 'enlightened' by the revelation of a later and an alternative truth, but all truths, whether of science or textual interpretation, are subject to the possibility that they will become fantasies to future generations. Maxwell's 'demon' was a threat to his contemporary explorers in energy physics precisely because it dramatized the possibility of such a turning point. The problem is dramatized in the ambiguity of Kidd's title – does 'forge' mean forgery, as in a false or unreal version, or does it mean 'forged', as hot metal beaten on an anvil is reshaped into a horseshoe: if the former is a fiction, is the latter a new addition to reality? That ambiguity encapsulates a doubleness from which neither science nor any interpretive human activity can escape. It was with this doubleness, the doubleness of trying to account both for the secular history of progress and for those forces which intrude from beyond its borders, forces which interrupt, intervene in and disrupt the processes of that history, that many of the works of nineteenth-century Scottish culture were engaged in charting. Scotland, the most rapidly industrialising and urbanising country in Europe, was also a culture obsessed with the disruption of order, whether in religion (the founding of the Free Church), in history (Carlyle's 'Shooting Niagara'), in science (Maxwell's 'Demon') or in literature (*Dr Jekyll and Mr Hyde*). Nineteenth-century Scotland refused to accept its eighteenth-century inheritance of the virtues of stadial history.

In one of Robert Louis Stevenson's early stories, *The Merry Men* (1882), a student of the famous Scottish historian and proponent of the stadial account of human progress, William Robertson, uncovers manuscripts that suggest a galleon of the Spanish Armada had sunk in the bay of an island on the West Coast of Scotland where he spends his summers. Returning there, he discovers unsettling evidence that his uncle, Gordon Darnaway, has not only been stocking his house with goods looted from ships which have run aground on the island, but that he may even have murdered survivors of those shipwrecks to do so. The student also encounters a group of sailors whose leader, he believes, had presented himself to Professor Robertson as a Spanish historian tracking the route of the ships of the Armada, but who is actually in search of the galleon's undiscovered store of gold. The narrative of a search for the truth of history is a disguise for an entirely different purpose. Visiting the island, this group of sailors is overtaken by a sudden storm and though they make it back to their ship, the ship itself has no chance of escape from the dangerous waters around the island and is wrecked on the 'Merry Men', a series of reefs lying just below the surface of the sea. Darnaway revels in the power of the 'Merry Men' and takes ecstatic pleasure in watching the ship being wrecked and all of its sailors drowned: 'Eh man,' he continued, touching me on the sleeve, 'it's a braw nicht for a shipwreck!'.[120] The sailors who have come to recover the treasure trove of history, discover that they are subject to far more powerful forces than the history which they hope to exploit. In the aftermath of the destruction of the ship, and Darnaway's guilty joy in the destructive power of nature, which he takes to be a reflection of the destructive implications of his own Calvinist theology, it is discovered that one of the landing party had been left behind, and appears suddenly out of the hull of the sunken ship from which Darnaway had salvaged the furnishings of his house, and one of whose sailors he has killed:

> The form of a man stood upright on the cabin-hutch of the wrecked ship; his back was towards us; he appeared to be scanning the offing with shaded eyes, and his figure was relieved to its full height, which was plainly very great, against the sea and sky. I have said a thousand times that I am not superstitious, but at that moment, with my mind running upon death and sin, the unexpected appearance of a stranger on that sea-girt, solitary island filled me with a surprise that bordered on terror. It seemed scarce possible that any human soul should have come ashore alive in such a sea as had raged last night.[121]

The man, it turns out, is black: to the narrator he is probably a slave but acts 'like a fallen king':[122] 'if he were a slave, as I supposed, I could not but judge he must have fallen from some high place in his own country'.[123] The black man stands at the boundary of two different histories: the history of his own country, in which he is king-like, and the history of slavery in the European empires, in which he is abandoned on the Scottish coast as being of no value; but he also represents, to Darnaway, a different boundary line – that in which the Devil has come to claim him for his sins: the outcome is a race along the beach, with Darnaway being pursued by the black man, who is trying to save him from his madness:

> The pursuer still ran, the chase still sped before him screaming; they avoided the grave, and skimmed close past the timbers of the wreck; and still my kinsman did not pause, but dashed straight into the surf; and the black, now almost within reach, still followed swiftly behind him . . . There was never a sharper ending. On that steep beach they were beyond their depth at a bound; neither could swim; the black rose once for a moment with a throttling cry; and the current had them, racing seaward . . .[124]

The white Calvinist and the black but kingly slave are bound together in a race in which neither can communicate to the other their purposes or their fears: they are an emblem of the ironies of stadial history and are consumed together as a result of an encounter which takes place on the boundary of the a-historical, a sea across which men navigate but over which they have no control – an energy which, from the perspective of nature, seems 'merry' but which, from a human perspective, is tragic.

Notes

1. Herman, A., *The Scottish Enlightenment: The Scots' Invention of the Modern World* (London: Fourth Estate, 2001).
2. Husserl, E., *The Crisis of European Sciences and Transcendental Phenomenology*, trans. David Carr (Evanston: Northwestern University Press, 1970), Part II, h, p. 48.
3. Adorno, T. and M. Horkheimer, *Dialectic of Enlightenment* (London: Verso, [1944] 1979), pp. 120, 131, 121.
4. Mills, C. W., *The Sociological Imagination* (Harmondsworth: Penguin, [1959] 1983), p. 184.
5. MacIntyre, A., *After Virtue: A Study in Moral Theory* (London: Duckworth, [1981] 1985), p. 113.
6. Ibid. p. 62.
7. Ibid. p. 54.
8. Ibid. p. 231.
9. Kidd, C., *The Forging of Races: Race and Scripture in the Protestant Atlantic World, 1600–2000* (Cambridge: Cambridge University Press, 2006), p. 80.
10. Ibid. p. 96.
11. Ibid. p. 96
12. Ibid. p. 98.
13. Ibid. p. 99.
14. Miller, E. F. (ed.), David Hume, *Essays: Moral, Political and Literary*, 3rd edn (Indianapolis: Liberty Fund, [1748] 1985;), p. 206.
15. Ibid. p. 207.
16. Ibid. p. 208.
17. Eze, E. C., *Race and the Enlightenment: A Reader* (Oxford: Blackwell, 1997).
18. Miller (ed.), David Hume, *Essays*, p. 208.
19. Selby-Bigge, L. A. (ed.), David Hume, *A Treatise of Human Nature* (Oxford: Clarendon Press, 1888), xviii.
20. Ibid. p. xix.

21. Ibid. p. 13.
22. Devine, T. M., 'Did Slavery Make Scotia Great? A Question Revisited', in Devine T. M. (ed.), *Recovering Scotland's Slavery Past: The Caribbean Connection* (Edinburgh: Edinburgh University Press, 2015), pp. 225–38. Devine concludes that 'the strategic connection between the Atlantic slave-based economies and Scotland's Great Leap Forward before 1830 . . . was arguably a potent one, especially in relation to raw material supply for cotton manufacturing, vigorous expansion of new and larger markets, and large-scale capital transfers to industry and agriculture'; p. 238.
23. Devine, T. M., *Scotland's Empire 1600–1815* (London: Allen Lane, 2003), p. 247.
24. Devine, *Recovering Scotland's Slavery Past*, p. xiii.
25. Graham, E. J., 'The Scots Penetration of the Jamaican Plantation Business', in Devine T. M., (ed.), *Recovering Scotland's Slavery Past*, p. 82.
26. Sassi, C., 'Acts of (Un)Willed Amnesia: Dis/appearing Figuration of the Caribbean in Post-Union Scottish Literature', in Covi, G., J. Anim-Addo, V. Pollard and C. Sassi (eds), *Caribbean Scottish Relations: Colonial and Contemporary Inscriptions in History, Language and Literature* (London: Mungo Publishing, 2007), pp. 131–98.
27. Devine, *Scotland's Empire*, p. 247.
28. Smollett, T., *Roderick Random* (London: Everyman, 1927), p. 403.
29. Ibid. p. 403.
30. Robert Burns, letter to Dr Moore, 2 August 1787; Roy, G. R. (ed.), *The Letters of Robert Burns* (Oxford: Clarendon Press, 1985), Vol. 1, p. 144.
31. Carlyle, T., 'Signs of the Times', Thomas Carlyle, *Critical and Miscellaneous Essays*, Vol. III (London: Chapman and Hall, 1889), p. 317.
32. Ibid. p. 324.
33. Ibid. p. 341.
34. Carlyle, T., 'Shooting Niagara: And After?', *Critical and Miscellaneous Essays*, Vol. III, pp. 590, 616.
35. Carlyle, 'Signs of the Times', Thomas Carlyle, *Critical and Miscellaneous Essays*, p. 591.
36. Carlyle, T., 'Occasional Discourse on the Negro Question', *Fraser's Magazine for Town and Country* (London, Vol. XL, February 1849), pp. 670–679.
37. Carlyle, T., *Occasional Discourse on the Nigger Question* (London: Thomas Bosworth, 1853).
38. Carlyle, T., 'Occasional Discourse on the Negro Question',

Fraser's Magazine for Town and Country Vol. XL, February 1849, pp. 529–30.

39. Ibid. pp. 533–4.
40. Carlyle, 'Shooting Niagara: And After?', *Critical and Miscellaneous Essays*, Vol. III, p. 592.
41. Carlyle, T., 'Sir Walter Scott', *Critical and Miscellaneous Essays*, Vol. III, p. 419.
42. Fielding, K. J. and D. Sorensen (eds), Thomas Carlyle, *The French Revolution* (Oxford: Oxford University Press, 1989), p. 141.
43. Carlyle, 'Shooting Niagara', *Critical and Miscellaneous Essays*, Vol. III, p. 610.
44. Ibid. p. 626.
45. Knox, R., *The Races of Men: A Fragment* (London: Henry Renshaw, 1850), p. 33.
46. Ibid. pp. 12–13.
47. Ibid. p. 15.
48. Ibid. p. 16.
49. Nott, J. C. and G. Robinson Gliddon *et al.*, *Types of Mankind* (Philadelphia: Lippincot, Grambo & Co., 1854), p. 53.
50. Many intellectual historians have misunderstood Knox's arguments and assimilated him to the polygenist account of human origins; see, for instance, John Sutherland's account of him in: Sutherland, J., *The Life of Walter Scott* (London: Blackwell, 1995), p. 229.
51. Desmond, A. J., *The Politics of Evolution: Morphology, Medicine, and Reform in Radical London* (Chicago: University of Chicago Press, 1989).
52. Knox, *Races of Men*, pp. 296–7; Knox is quoting from Geoffroy.
53. Ibid. p. 29.
54. Ibid. pp. 296–7; Knox is quoting from Geoffroy.
55. Ibid. p. 297.
56. Ibid. p. 307.
57. Ibid. p. 314.
58. Ibid. p. 15.
59. Ibid. p. 18.
60. Ibid. p. 43.
61. Carlyle, T., 'The Hero as Poet. Dante; Shakespeare', *On Heroes and Hero-Worship and the Heroic in History* (London: Chapman and Hall, [1841]; 1897), p. 161.
62. Knox suggests that in his own time there are only three 'races', presumably on the basis that the Normans were no longer of 'sufficient numerical strength to maintain, if not political power and unity, at least their integrity as a race distinct from others, in sufficient numbers to resist the aggressive action of the admix-

ture of race by intermarriage; to neutralize, to a great extent, such intermarriages, and to render that admixture comparatively unimportant', even if they continued, as an aristocracy, to exert significant power over the country; *Races of Men,* p. 12.

63. Knox, *Races of Men*, p. 48.
64. Ibid. p. 57.
65. Ibid. p. 14.
66. Hook A. (ed.), Sir Walter Scott, *Waverley* (Harmondsworth: Penguin, [1814] 1972), p. 324.
67. Scott, W., 'Lady of the Lake', Canto V, VII, Robert Ford (ed.), *The Poetical Works of Sir Walter Scott* (London & Glasgow, nd; c. 1863), p. 247.
68. Ibid. p. 247.
69. Burton, J. H., *The Scot Abroad* (Edinburgh: William Blackwood and Sons, 1864), pp. 5–6: '[After the Norman invasion] England became Normanised, while Scotland not only retained her old Teutonic character, but became a place of refuge for the Saxon fugitives. The remnants of Harold's family – the only royal guard of England – came among the other fugitives to Scotland, and took up their position there as an exiled court awaiting their restoration.
70. Doyle, Laura, 'The Racial Sublime', in Richardson A. and S. Hofkosh (eds), *Romanticism, Race and Imperial Culture 1780–1834* (Bloomington: Indiana University Press, 1996), pp. 15–23.
71. Banton, M., *Racial Theories* (Cambridge: Cambridge University Press, 1987), p. 13: 'It is probable that no single book or event did more to introduce the word race into popular use than Scott's historical romance'. See also Banton, M., *The Idea of Race* (London: Tavistock, 1977), p. 15.
72. Duncan I. (ed.), Sir Walter Scott, *Ivanhoe* (Oxford: Oxford University Press, [1819] 1996), p. 428.
73. Ibid. p. 27.
74. Ibid. p. 502.
75. Ibid. p. 502.
76. For the details of Reid's life, see Dakin, S. B., *Scotch Paisano in Old Los Angeles: Hugo Reid's Life in California, 1832–1852, derived from his correspondence* (Berkeley: University of California Press, [1938] 1978); for Silver Lakes, see <http://www.silverlake.org/about_silverlake/aboutSL_frmset.htm> (last accessed 20 October 2010).
77. Duncan (ed.), Scott, *Ivanhoe*, p. 3.
78. Rigney, A., 'Re-Enacting *Ivanhoe*', *The Afterlives of Walter Scott: Memory on the Move* (Oxford: Oxford University Press, 2012), pp. 106–126.
79. Watson, Jr, R. D., *Normans and Saxons: Southern Race*

Mythology and the Intellectual History of the American Civil War (Baton Rouge: Louisiana State University Press, 2008), p. 47.

80. Ibid. p. 33.
81. Ibid. pp. 17–18.
82. Reid's letters form an Appendix to Susan Bryant Dakin's *Scotch Paisano in Old Los Angeles*, p. 195ff.
83. Watson, *Normans and Saxons*, p. 25.
84. Sutherland, *The Life of Walter Scott*, 1995, p. 230: Sutherland notes that 'The most objectionable form of racism given currency by *Ivanhoe* is anti-semitism'.
85. Duncan (ed.), Scott, *Ivanhoe*, p. 27.
86. Lukács, G., *The Historical Novel*, trans. Hannah and Stanley Mitchell (London: Merlin, [1962] 1989), p. 56.
87. Lukács, *The Historical Novel*, pp. 54–5.
88. Selby-Bigge, L. A. (ed.), David Hume, *Enquiries Concerning the Human Understanding and Concerning the Principles of Morals* (Oxford: Clarendon Press, 1902), p. 115.
89. Ibid. p. 119.
90. Hook (ed.), Scott, *Waverley*, p. 389.
91. Ibid. p. 333.
92. Bell, B., 'The Nineteenth Century', in Findlay, B. (ed.), *A History of Scottish Theatre* (Edinburgh: Edinburgh University Press, 1998), p. 144.
93. Garside, P., 'Popular Fiction and National Tale: the Hidden Origins of Sir Walter Scott's Waverley', *Nineteenth Century Literature*, 46:1 June 1991, pp. 30–53.
94. Sutherland, *The Life of Walter Scott*, p. 156.
95. Bell, 'The Nineteenth Century', *A History of Scottish Theatre,* p. 169.
96. Hook (ed.), Scott, *Waverley*, p. 177.
97. Alexander, J. H., and G. A. M. Wood (eds), Walter Scott, *Quentin Durward* (Edinburgh: Edinburgh University Press, 2001), p. 129.
98. Alexander, J. H. (ed.), Walter Scott, *Kenilworth* (Harmondsworth: Penguin, 1999), p. 349: The performativity of Scott's sense of history in this novel is a point made by Alexander in his 'Introduction': '*Kenilworth* is just as perceptive in its understanding of the way in which the whole of Elizabethan society, not just individuals, fashions itself through performance' (p. xiv).
99. Alexander (ed.), Scott, *Kenilworth*, pp. 350–1.
100. Duncan (ed.), Scott, *Ivanhoe*, p. 5.
101. Ibid. pp. 5–6.
102. Lockhart, J. G., *Memoirs of Sir Walter Scott* (Edinburgh: Adam and Charles Black, 1869), Vol. 7, pp. 49–50.

103. Trumpener, K., *Bardic Nationalism: The Romantic Novel and the British Empire* (Princeton: Princeton University Press, 1997), p. 191.
104. Ibid. pp. 246–7.
105. Leerssen, J. and A. Rigney, *Commemorating Writers in Nineteenth-Century Europe: Nation-Building and Centenary Fever* (Basingstoke: Palgrave Macmillan, 2014), p. 65.
106. Scott, P. H. (ed.), Sir Walter Scott, *The Letters of Malachi Malagrowther* (Edinburgh: William Blackwood, [1826] 1981).
107. Masson, D., *Recent British Philosophy*, 2nd edn (London: Macmillan, [1865] 1867), pp. 151–2.
108. Garside, P. (ed.), Walter Scott, *Guy Mannering* (Edinburgh: Edinburgh University Press, 1999), p. 16.
109. Ibid. p. 23.
110. Ibid. p. 43: 'her tall figure, relieved against the clear blue sky, seemed almost of supernatural stature'.
111. Ibid. p. 324.
112. Ibid. p. 326.
113. Frazer, J. G., *The Golden Bough* (London: Macmillan, 1922; one-volume edition), p. 56.
114. Kidd, *The Forging of Races*, p. 7.
115. Ibid. p. 9.
116. Ibid. p. 271.
117. Ibid. p. 18.
118. Ibid. p. 3.
119. Ibid. p. 7.
120. Stevenson, R. L., *Markheim, Jekyll and the Merry Men: Shorter Scottish Fiction* (Edinburgh: Canongate, 1995), pp. 187–8.
121. Ibid., p. 199.
122. Ibid. p. 201.
123. Ibid. p. 201.
124. Ibid. p. 207.

3 Living Memory: Nostalgia, Necromancy and Nostophobia

I The Arts of Memory

The revivalism by which Scotland maintained a sense of its own distinctive culture after 1707 made the understanding of memory crucial to its eighteenth-century philosophies. Indeed, it was David Hume's account of memory in his *Treatise of Human Nature* that assured Thomas Reid that a sceptical philosophy would always be self-defeating. For Hume, the difference between a remembered experience and an imagined experience, both of which were derived from the 'impressions' imposed on consciousness by our immediate interaction with the world, was a matter of the 'force and vivacity' by which they were characterised:

> For tho' it be a peculiar property of the memory to preserve the original order and position of its ideas, while the imagination transposes and changes them, as it pleases; yet this difference is not sufficient to distinguish them in their operation, or make us know the one from the other; it being impossible to recal the past impressions, in order to compare them with our present ideas, and see whether their arrangement be exactly similar. Since therefore the memory is known, neither by the order of its *complex* ideas, nor the nature of its *simple* ones; it follows that the difference betwixt it and the imagination lies in its superior force and vivacity. A man may indulge his fancy in feigning any past scene of adventures; nor would there be any possibility of distinguishing this from a remembrance of a like kind, were not the ideas of the imagination fainter and more obscure.[1]

Memories retain some of the 'force and vivacity' of their original impressions – that 'force' deriving from the fact that they are imprinted vividly upon us as soon as we encounter the world we assume to be external to ourselves – whereas imagined objects and events will be feebler. Memories, however, may decay to such an extent that they are 'taken for an idea of the imagination: so, on the other hand, an idea of imagination may acquire such a force and vivacity, as to pass for an idea of the memory, and counterfeit its effects on the belief and judgment'.[2] The boundary line between memory and imagination has no certainty or fixity to it. It was this lack of a strict boundary that Reid could not accept:

> Now, I would gladly know of this author, how one degree of vivacity fixes the existence of the object to the present moment; another carries it back to time past; a third, taking a contrary direction, carries it into futurity; and a fourth carries it out of existence altogether. Suppose, for instance, that I see the sun rising out of the sea. I remember to have seen him rise yesterday: I believe he will rise to-morrow near the same place; I can likewise imagine him rising in that place, without any belief at all. Now, according to this sceptical hypothesis, this perception, this memory, this foreknowledge, and this imagination, are all the same idea, diversified only by different degrees of vivacity.[3]

For Reid it was the 'belief' that accompanies an idea which gives us a degree of certainty in distinguishing present experience from past memories and from future expectations or imaginings, and those beliefs are part of our fundamental constitution:

> Such original and natural judgments are, therefore, a part of that furniture which Nature has given to the human understanding. They are the inspiration of the Almighty, no less than our notions or simple apprehensions. They serve to direct us in the common affairs of life, where our reasoning faculty would leave us in the dark. They are part of our constitution: and all the discoveries of our reason are grounded upon them. They make up what is called *the common sense of mankind*; and what is manifestly contrary to any of those first principles, is what we call *absurd*.[4]

As Norman Kemp Smith suggests in his discussion of these passages, Reid had failed to grasp how close Hume's argument was to his own, and that for Hume what distinguished memory from imagination is 'that we are conscious in memory that the order of ideas is determined for and not by us'.[5] Reid's real target, however, was not Hume's account of the relation of memory and imagination, but what underlay that account – Hume's insistence that all mental experience was governed by the 'association of ideas', and was therefore reducible to three fundamental principles, 'resemblance, contiguity in time and space, and cause and effect'.[6] For Hume the 'association of ideas' represented 'a kind of ATTRACTION, which in the mental world will be found to have as extraordinary effects as in the natural',[7] making the association of ideas the equivalent in 'the mental world' of the 'gravity' which had allowed Newton to transform our understanding of the physical world: 'association' is the psychological equivalent of gravity, the power by which the phenomena of consciousness are organised and held together. For Hume, regular and repeated association between our ideas gives rise to our expectation that a cause will be followed by its effect, but this is no more than a psychological phenomenon; it does not justify belief in any 'necessary connexion'[8] between a cause and its effect:

> The efficacy or energy of causes is neither plac'd in the causes themselves, nor in the deity, nor in the concurrence of these two principles; but belongs entirely to the soul, which considers the union of two or more objects in all past instances. 'Tis here that the real power of causes is plac'd . . .[9]

For Reid, acceptance of Hume's conception of association undermined the law-abiding nature of God's world:

> For, if we express it in plain English, it is a prescience that things which he hath found conjoined in time past will be conjoined in time to come. And this prescience is not the effect of reasoning, but of an original principle of human nature . . . There must be many accidental conjunctions of things, as well as natural connections: and the former are apt to be mistaken for the latter.[10]

There are psychological connections which we may mistake for natural connections, but not all connections are, for Reid, as they are for Hume, psychological. Hume's account makes causality entirely dependent on memory – only because I remember *x* being followed by *y* can I anticipate that this conjunction will recur – and, despite Reid's protests, Hume's account was to have profound consequences in the development of later conceptions of the workings of the mind: Hume's principle of 'association' was to be the ground on which empirical psychology developed, from Hartley's *Observations on Man, His Frame, His Duty and His Expectations* (1749), through James Mill's *Analysis of the Phenomena of the Human Mind* (1829) to Alexander Bain's *The Senses and the Intellect* (1855) and *The Emotions and the Will* (1859). The area of investigation in which Hume's theory of association first flourished, however, was in the theory of 'taste', in the understanding of what, in the eighteenth century, were understood as experiences of the 'beautiful' and the 'sublime', and which, in modern terminology, are generally described as the 'aesthetic'. By the time of Archibald Alison's *Essays on the Nature and Principles of Taste*, first published in 1790, Hume's theory of 'association' – which, for Reid, was the foundation of scepticism – has become the encompassing explanation for all aesthetic experience, even for a clergyman like Alison:

> When any object, either of sublimity or beauty, is presented to the mind, I believe every man is conscious of a train of thought being immediately awakened in his imagination, analogous to the character or expression of the original object. The simple perception of the object, we frequently find, is insufficient to excite these emotions, unless, according to common expression, our imagination is seized, and our fancy busied in the pursuit of all those trains of thought, which are allied to this character or expression.[11]

Hume's associationist account of the mind was successful, in part, because it helped explain how a response of 'taste' is different from any other kind of experience: in an aesthetic response the mind is released from its practical considerations and, in a state of 'reverie', traces a stream of associated memories whose unimpeded passage through the mind is constitutive of the experience of beauty or sublimity. Each successful work of art will be the occasion for a train of associations unique to a particular individual, and the intensity of that individual's experience will depend on the memory resources that can be released and sustained in a connected chain, which is why those with the richest memories – often, therefore, the most educated – will have the most powerful aesthetic experiences. The work of art so experienced will itself then become an addition to the wealth of memory resources on which an individual can call, thus further enriching any future aesthetic experience. Association not only explains how, to one observer, a landscape is simply a place of utility for grazing animals or for growing crops, while to another it is a scene of beauty, it also accounts for how two observers may both attribute 'beauty' to the same object and yet have very different individual experiences of it, and make very different judgments as to how beautiful it is. Alison's theory is often treated as though it were an endpoint which would be made redundant by Romantic notions of the 'creative imagination', but in fact associationist accounts dominated much nineteenth-century thinking about art and continued to shape what artists and writers hoped to achieve by their works until well into the twentieth century.[12]

One of the earliest applications of associationist principles to a work of literature is to be found in Hugh Blair's *A Critical Dissertation on the Poems of Ossian*, first published in 1763, in which Blair implied that Ossian's – or Macpherson's – poetic method was fundamentally associational:

> Very often two objects are brought together in a simile, though they resemble one another, strictly speaking, in nothing, only because they raise in the mind a train of similar, and what may be called, concordant ideas; so that the remembrance of the one, when recalled, serves to quicken and heighten the impression made by the other.[13]

And Blair points out something in the Ossianic poems that would become the foundation of theories such as Alison's:

> Such analogies and associations of ideas as these, are highly pleasing to the fancy. They give the opportunity for introducing many a fine poetical picture. They diversify the scene: they aggrandize the subject; they keep the imagination awake and sprightly. For as the judgment is principally exercised in distinguishing objects, and remarking the differences among those which seem like; so the highest amusement of the imagination is to trace likeness and agreements among those which seem different.[14]

Blair here deploys three of the most important consequences of associationist aesthetics: firstly, the aesthetic experience depends on the activity of the perceiving mind as it generates new trains of association on the basis of identifying likenesses in the poet's imagery; secondly, the resource required for this activity is a well-stocked memory, because the more memories that are aroused the greater the mental activity and therefore the more intense the aesthetic experience; and, thirdly, aesthetic experience is characterised by what Francis Hutcheson had described as 'uniformity amidst variety'[15] – a variety of associations held together by a single unifying emotion.

These associationist principles were, of course, assumed to be universally true of the art of all times, but once they are identified they begin to influence the ways in which art is structured, and to foreground those effects which offer the largest stimulus to memory. Macpherson's *Fragments of Ancient Poetry* offered its readers characters and scenes that had, unlike classical literature, no pre-existing associations: readers' minds had to be, in Alison's words, 'busied in the pursuit of all those trains of thought, which are allied to this character or expression'; the very limitedness of a 'fragment' offered the opportunity for releasing unexpected associations:

> The manner of composition bears all the marks of the greatest antiquity. No artful transitions, nor full and extended connection of parts; such as we find among the poets of later times, when order and regularity of composition were more studied and known; but a style always rapid and vehement, in narration concise even to abruptness, and leaving several circumstances to be supplied by the reader's imagination.[16]

Even when Macpherson published the more connected narrative of *Fingal*, the style displayed the same rapid, vehement abruptness, the same sudden digressions – as, for instance, in Book VI, when the action suddenly switches to the story of Trenmor, 'great grandfather to Fingal'.[17] Was this style in the nature of primitive poetry, as Blair suggests, or was it, rather, the product of Macpherson's time at the University of Aberdeen, where one of his teachers was Alexander Gerard, the first Scottish thinker after Hume to apply Hume's conception of the mind to the understanding of 'taste'? In *An Essay on Taste* (1759), Gerard quotes Hume's *Treatise* as part of his discussion of the sublime and concludes that,

> The sentiments of taste depend very much on *association*. So far as they proceed from this, *custom* must augment them, as custom, by adding a new principle of union, renders the connection more intimate, and introduces the related ideas more quickly and forcibly. Custom likewise begets new associations, and enables works of taste to suggest ideas which were not *originally* connected with them: and what a surprizing intenseness, the association of ideas, originally foreign, bestows on our perceptions, both pleasurable and painful, is obvious in too many instances to require being enlarged on.[18]

Macpherson's style is not just a rendering of how ancient Gaelic poetry is structured but also a deliberate exploitation of the ways in which Gerard and Blair understood poetry to work in the context of an associationist conception of the mind. Macpherson had created works which could invoke the new eighteenth-century conception of the nature and workings of 'taste', one in which, as Gerard puts it,

> Sublimity of style arises, not so much from the sound of the words, though that doubtless may have some influence, as from the nature of the ideas, which we are accustomed to annex to them, and the character of the persons, among whom they are in most common use. This too is the origin of the grandeur we ascribe to objects high and elevated in place; of the veneration, with which we regard things in any direction distant; and of the superior admiration excited by things remote in time; especially in antiquity or past duration.[19]

That which is 'distant' and 'remote in time' is more productive of associations and therefore more aesthetically interesting, so that Macpherson's insistence on the 'ancientness' of the poetry he is translating is, at least in part, an invitation to the associational activity of his readers. To underline the relation between temporal distance and aesthetic effect, Gerard specifically cites Hume's analysis of our sense of the 'elevated', whether in nature or in society, as running in parallel with our experience of gravity: 'we feel a difficulty in mounting, and pass not without a kind of reluctance from the inferior to that which is situated above it; as if our ideas acquired a kind of gravity from their objects'.[20] This 'sense of difficulty' is even greater in relation to time: 'a considerable distance in time produces a greater veneration for the distant objects than a like removal in space', because, as Hume frames it:

> The imagination moves with more difficulty in passing from one portion of time to another, than is the transition thro' the parts of space; and that because space or extension appears united to our senses, while time or succession is always broken or divided . . . The mind, elevated by the vastness of its object, is still further elevated by the difficulty of the conception; and being oblig'd every moment to renew its efforts in the transition from one part of time to another, feels a more vigorous and sublime disposition, than in a transition thro' the parts of space, where the ideas flow along with easiness and facility.[21]

Distance in time fractures the ease with which events can be associated with one another, but by doing so forces the mind into greater efforts to establish those associations, efforts which, in turn, increase the intensity of the aesthetic experience.[22] The ancientness of Macpherson's Ossianic poems corresponds with Gerard's new poetics of sublimity, a poetics which also requires that the responsive reader must have

> such a *sensibility of heart*, as fits a man for being easily moved, and for readily catching, as by infection, any passion, that a work is fitted to excite. The souls of men are far from being alike susceptible of impressions of this kind. A hard hearted man can be a spectator of very great distress, without feeling any emotion: A man of cruel temper has a malignant joy in producing misery. On the other hand, many are composed of so delicate materials, that the smallest uneasiness of their fellow creatures excites their pity.[23]

Ossianic poetry is situated at such a temporal and cultural distance from the modern reader that the associational process is fragmented, and the mind must strive to overcome the gaps which resist a continuously connected chain of associations, but in doing so the mind is forced to focus on those fundamental emotions – the '*sensibility of heart*' – which are the common basis of 'human nature' in all the ages. The peculiar effectiveness of Ossianic poetry is that it challenges the modern reader with the difference of its associational context and, at the same time, confirms the universality of the emotions which underpin our associational expectations.

Associationist accounts of aesthetic experience were always, however, poised on the edge of an abyss – the abyss of the loss of those memories which make a natural scene or an object of art the focus of an aesthetic experience. Without an appropriate set of memories to initiate and sustain a train of association, a mountain would be simply a piece of geology, a painting would be no more than oil on canvas. If an audience has lost the capacity to make a work of art the source of its exploration of its own remembered experiences, then both nature and art will become a meaningless blank. It is this threat that Francis Jeffrey pointed out in 1811, in his review of the second edition of Alison's work, when he noted of Scott's description of Loch Katrine that 'the particular train of images, by the help of which [our] general impressions may be moulded into distinct objects of emotion, is evidently altogether loose and undetermined, and must depend on the taste, dispositions and information of every different beholder'.[24] Associationism made aesthetic experience profoundly private and personal – beauty depended entirely on each individual's personal memory resources. Loss or decay of the memories that could interact with a particular aesthetic object would negate the aesthetic experience, returning the object to being simply a material fact of no aesthetic significance. In its insistence on the significance of memory to aesthetic experience and in its trepidation about the possible erasure of the memories on which aesthetic experience depended, the associationist aesthetic was a very precise enactment of the dilemmas of post-Union Scotland – a country whose very existence depended on the maintenance of the memories which made its past aesthetically and historically significant but which was continually threatened by the displacement of those memories by an alternative English memory complex which would make it impossible to respond to the Scottish past and render it a blank emptiness.

The expiring Ossian, the 'last of his race', cut off from community and communication because he has no surviving children to whom he can transmit his memories, dramatises the finality of such cultural obliteration and the subsequent amnesia which will nullify its aesthetic potential:

> No more shalt thou rise, O my son, to partake of the feast of Cromla. Soon will thy tomb be hid, and the grass grow rank on thy grave. The sons of the feeble shall pass over it, and shall not know that the mighty lie there.[25]

But as the supposedly third century Ossian predicts an unremembering future in which he and his race will be forgotten, the eighteenth-century James Macpherson reverses the process and makes the forgotten memorable again. In *The Last of the Race*, Fiona Stafford takes Macpherson's Ossianic poems as an instance of the drama of being the last, a drama in which 'the death of the last bard has a finality which is hard to reject':[26]

> In the literature of the last bard, there is no real attempt to cross the boundary between the primitive and the civilized, and the bard must remain with his race, preserved at an earlier stage of society. The poetry is in part a fictitious memorial to the lost race, protecting the last man in an ideal world which could never be destroyed since it had already vanished.[27]

The point of Macpherson's poetry, however, is that the last bard has not vanished: he has returned, and his memories are at home again in another age. The 'Celtomania' that Macpherson's Ossianic poems initiated was not the product of Macpherson's turning his back on modernity and retreating into the romantic mists of a forgotten history: he adopted the most original modern conception of the 'science of man', with its stadial account of historical progress, and used the new psychology that underpinned Hume's analysis of the mind to elaborate an aesthetics of memory that would make the past of his people valuable again in the present. Even if his claims for the authenticity of the original poems were untrue, they were cast in a form that was designed to achieve the sublimity that the mind experiences in overcoming the strangeness and the lack of easy progression that Hume describes as characteristic of our sense of the past. In form, therefore, the poems are like the ghosts of the past that Ossian gives voice to – the continual recall and re-appearance in the present of that which has, apparently, been lost to the past. Stafford's account of the 'last bard' is only half true, for the last man is not the end of the story as long as the story can be recovered and restated, creating a new and living memory in an entirely different world: as long as the poetry can generate new associations, the last bard will survive in the memories of modern readers. Macpherson's Ossianic poetry is the first of many associationist works that both dramatize and defy the threat of oblivion, melancholically grieving over a past that has been forgotten but in so doing finding a way to raise those lost memories to new and vigorous life.

It was a trope which Walter Scott was to deploy in his first major poem, 'The Lay of the Last Minstrel' (1802), which presents us with a Border equivalent of Macpherson's bard:

The harp, his sole remaining joy,
Was carried by an orphan boy.
The last of all the bards was he,
Who sang of Border chivalry,
For, welladay! their date was fled,
His tuneful brethren all were dead.

Given a final opportunity to perform, however, the minstrel seizes it:

But when he caught the measure wild
The old man raised his face, and smiled,
And lighten'd up his faded eye,
With all a poet's ecstasy!
In varying cadence, soft or strong,
He swept the sounding chords along:
The present scene, the future lot,
His toils, his wants, were all forgot:
Cold diffidence, and age's frost,
In the full tide of song were lost;
Each blank in faithless memory void,
The poet's glowing thought supplied.[28]

The poem resurrects the Minstrel from a former time and presents him as the agent for the resurrection of an even older and more forgotten time, but the 'blank in faithless memory' is, of course, reversed by the poem itself, which turns the ephemerality of the Minstrel's voice into the permanence of print, and returns to present immediacy what seemed to have been consigned to oblivion. Memory becomes, in Hume's terms, a new and immediate impression – like the impress of moveable type on paper – and gives vitality again to what had apparently faded from consciousness. The bard and his audience, long dead, are both living memories, defying forgetfulness.

II Nostalgia

Liz Lochhead's *Mary Queen of Scots Got her Head Chopped Off* (1987) opens with a monologue by 'La Corbie', a choric commentator on the historical events which the play recounts:

> LA CORBIE: Country: Scotland. Whit like is it?
> It's a peatbog, it's a daurk forest.
> It's a cauldron o' lye, a saltpan or a coal mine.
> If you're gey lucky it's a bricht bere meadow or a park o' kye.
> Or mibbe . . . it's a field o' stanes
> It's a tenement or a merchant's ha'.
> It's a hure hoose or a humble cot. Princes Street or Paddy's Merkit.
> It's a fistfu' o' fish or a puckle o' oatmeal.
> It's a queen's banquet o' roast meats and junkets.
> It depends. It depends . . . Ah dinna ken whit like your Scotland is.
> Here's mines.
> National flower: the thistle.
> National pastime: nostalgia.
> National weather: smirr, haar, drizzle, snow.
> National burd: the crow, the corbie, le corbeau, moi![29]

What Scotland is 'depends' on which language is used to define it: 'La Corbie' is, like the subject of the play, Scoto-French – or Franco-Scottish – just as the weather is divided between terms distinctively Scots – 'smirr, haar' – or shared with standard English – 'drizzle, snow' – or, like 'burd', poised between the two. The 'national pastime', however, is invoked by a word coined from Greek – *nostos* meaning home and *algia* meaning pain – by the Swiss physician Johannes Hofer in the late seventeenth century to identify the condition of extreme homesickness that he discovered among Swiss mercenaries fighting on behalf of other peoples' cultures: its symptoms were 'despondency, melancholia, excessive emotion, including profound bouts of weeping, refusal of food and a wasting away which sometimes ended in attempts at suicide.'[30] Nostalgia is the sickness of those for whom 'pastime' is an unreachable home, making it impossible to connect memory with actuality; it is a sickness in which memory overwhelms immediate reality, making the sufferer incapable of dealing with the world of the present. Nostalgia was a recognised medical condition throughout the eighteenth and nineteenth centuries: the *Edinburgh Medical and Physical Dictionary* of 1799, for instance, gives the following description:

> NOSTALGIA, a vehement desire for revisiting one's home. This is a genus of disease in the class locales and order dysorexia . . . characterised by impatience when absent from one's native home, a vehement desire to return, attended with gloom and melancholy, loss of appetite, and want of sleep. Dr Cullen says, this is to be reckoned a species of melancholy; and unless it be indulged, it very commonly proves not only incurable but even fatal.[31]

It was a disease assumed to be physical rather than merely psychological: Dominique Jean Larrey, Napoleon's physician, examined the brains of those who had died of it to show that they had suffered inflammation of the brain, while, in the Civil War in the United States, 'nostalgia' was listed on printed medical reports alongside pneumonia as a cause of death.[32] Scotland was as much a country of mercenary soldiers in the sixteenth and seventeenth centuries as Hofer's Swiss – according to the calculation of Steve Murdoch and Alexia Grosjean, some 50,000 Scots served as mercenaries in European armies during the Thirty Years War[33] – and therefore as likely to suffer from the consequences of nostalgia. And given the scale of Scottish emigration in the nineteenth and twentieth centuries, both those who departed and those who remained might have suffered from a sense of isolation from their former associates that would result in the symptoms of 'nostalgia', particularly as that term came to signify, in the nineteenth century, not a spatial but a temporal separation. As 'nostalgia' gradually disappeared from the medical textbooks as a physical condition, it migrated to become a psychological feature of modern life – the ache of the desire for a lost past to which one could never return. Indeed, it has become the subject of much sociological and medical analysis in recent decades, in part because it has been recognised as an affect which can be of value in the marketplace: radio stations are devoted to musical nostalgia, adverts associate contemporary products with an idealised past, the heritage industry markets the past as a justification for a nostalgic vacation which will bring people to spend money in places like Scotland.[34] 'Nostalgia' which was, originally, the disease of separation from the homeland has become the justification, in marketing strategies such as the Scottish Government's *Year of Homecoming* in 2009, of a return to the homeland. 'National pastime: nostalgia' summarises what many have believed to be the pathological condition of modern Scotland, an obsession with the sentimental recollection of the past as an evasion of the actualities of the present. The fact that Burns's 'Auld Lang Syne' has become the international anthem that marks the dismissal to the past of the year in which we have been living is perhaps indicative of how deeply 'nostalgia' is inscribed in Scotland's national consciousness. Through Burns's reworking of a traditional Scottish song, a nation's nostalgia has become the world's, but the world's nostalgia, we might say, passes as the New Year takes over from the old, while the nation's nostalgia is, apparently, without end. Francis Jeffrey, in an early response to Burns's work, while insisting that Scots was not 'a provincial dialect – the vehicle only of rustic vulgarity and rude local humour' – and that it is 'the language of a whole country, long an independent kingdom', focused on the fact that Scots speech had a particular significance to Scots who had, through education, adopted standard English as their normal medium of communication:

> [Scots] is still recollected even by them as the familiar language of their childhood and of those who were the earliest objects of their love and veneration. It is connected, in their imagination, not only with that olden time which is uniformly conceived as more pure, lofty and simple than the present, but also with all the soft and bright colours of remembered childhood and domestic affection. All its phrases conjure up images of schoolday innocence, and sports, and friendships which have no pattern in succeeding years.[35]

Burns's language, for English-speaking Scots, evokes a childhood world which was 'more pure, lofty and simple than the present' and brings back the memories of our earliest 'domestic affection': Scots is the language of a past which can be recalled only to underline how radically we have been shut out from the intimacies and the relationships to which it gestures. This particular linguistic experience may, however, only be indicative of a more general problem: modern studies of nostalgia suggest that nostalgia is peculiarly the emotion produced by living in linear history, which makes the recall of the past necessarily an experience of irretrievable loss. Societies which live in a cyclic or redemptive conception of time will never experience nostalgia, because for them the past will either be recapitulated or recovered in the forward progress of time. For those who live in linear history, however, remembrance is necessarily fused with the sense of ultimate loss: if, as Walter Scott suggests in his 'Postscript' to *Waverley*, 'there is no European nation which, within the course of half a century, or little more, has undergone so complete a change as the kingdom of Scotland',[36] and if that rapidity of progress was understood in terms of the theory of stadial history, with its inevitable displacement of one stage of history by another, Scotland becomes not only a likely sufferer from nostalgia but one in which, as with Hofer's Swiss soldiers, memory will overwhelm its capacity to deal with the present. The long-term influence of what came to be known as the 'Kailyard school' of Scottish literature – deriving from the work of J. M. Barrie, Ian MacLaren and S. R. Crockett in the 1890s – is taken, in its focus on small town and rural communities in an age of mass urbanisation – to be symptomatic of Scottish culture's evasion of the present and indulgence in the past, its reduction of the eighteenth-century's engagement with conceptions of a universal history to a perspective in which one could see no further than the boundaries of a provincial parish. Nostalgia, based on childhood memory, was necessarily a retreat to the local, and the fear that this was endemic to Scottish culture haunted even those who were establishing the institutional structures of devolved government in the 1990s: Andrew Nash recounts, for instance, how, in 1998, Donald Dewar, then Secretary of State for Scotland and preparing for the establishment of a devolved parliament, suggested that a 'devolved structure for Scottish radio and television might lead to the production of "Kailyard" broadcasting'.[37] Devolution was a threat as well as a promise. But recent medical, sociological and psychological studies of nostalgia have suggested that its nineteenth-century implication of a terminal retreat from the present were misconceived: nostalgia has emerged from recent research not as an escape from the present to the past, but a means by which the past can be used to redirect the energies of the self towards the future: nostalgia can be future-oriented rather than past-oriented.

The complexity of relationships of past, present and future in what we have traditionally described as 'nostalgia' can be seen vividly in the works of the progenitor of the 'Kailyard' school, J. M. Barrie. Barrie's first book of stories about the village of Thrums – a fictional version of his home town of Kirriemuir – was titled *Auld Licht Idylls* (1888) and the title gestures to Barrie's belief – derived from the lectures of David Masson – that literature can never be a representation of reality but is necessarily bound by the conventions of genre. *Auld Licht Idylls*, however, deploys the genre of the 'idyll' – implying a rustic world of peace and contentment – to represent a world of poverty, early industrialism, and conflictual religion, the 'auld lichts' being one of the earliest groups to secede from the Church of Scotland. Barrie uses his own memories of his mother's stories about her childhood community not to take us into the comfortable world of the idyll, but into a deeply uncomfortable world where Darwinian theories of evolution collide with traditional Christianity, where weavers working from home are being displaced by larger, mechanised forms of production, and where the wry humour with which Barrie invites his readers to regard his characters is regularly punctured to reveal that the reader's response is entirely inappropriate to the tragic circumstances in which the characters are trapped: 'When they were not starving themselves to support a pastor the Auld Lichts were saving up for a stipend. They retired with compressed lips to their looms, and weaved and weaved till they weaved another minister'.[38] The weaver community of Thrums lives on the edge of starvation, on the edge of extinction – the name itself implies that it is already a leftover industry, since the 'thrums' are the threads left behind when the body of the woven cloth has been removed – and lives on only in the memory of the schoolteacher who, like the last of his race, recounts its communal past in order to give some substance to a personal past which now has no place in a continuing community. Barrie's 'idylls', in effect, reverse the process of 'revivalism': instead of bringing the past back into the present as a living reality capable of interacting with and reconfiguring the world of the future, it revives the past only to evoke the pathos of how utterly irrelevant its beliefs and its sufferings have been made by the progress of the modern world. It is a world in which the word 'nostalgia' no longer applies to the past-directed gaze of the narrator or the reader but to the future-directed gaze of the characters: they are nostalgic for a homeland which they have not yet found but which they believe themselves always to be on the verge of creating – they 'weaved and weaved till they weaved another minister'. Barrie's texts reach backwards into the past only to reveal a past striving towards a future which we know the characters will never come to inhabit: they are redundant to the history-to-come and the conflict between recollected past and unfulfilled future is what produces the pathos of his stories. We are not being invited to indulge in the past as an escape from the present: we are being invited to see in the past a striving after an unfulfillable future, and therefore to envisage our own present strivings as ones which will, in due course, be subject to the same reversal.

Barrie's self-consciousness about the relationship between art and memory are clear in *Sentimental Tommy* (1896), a novel which reshapes Barrie's own biography, as a child enchanted by the stories told to him by his mother, into the character of Tommy, whose mother tells her children stories of the Thrums from which she is now in exile in London, having abandoned her fiancé for an apparently more powerful and more glamorous man who turns out to be dissolute and impoverished. From London she writes letters to former friends in Thrums to say how wealthily she now lives, when in fact she and her children live in desperate poverty, and her fictionalisation of her London life in those letters is mirrored by her son's imaginative investment in retelling her stories about Thrums, as though it were an ideal community by which the London in which he actually lives should be censured. After the death of his mother, however, Tommy and his sister are taken back to Thrums to be looked after by the lover whom his mother had abandoned, and find, instead of the town of their imagining, a place meagre and unappealing. The children have a 'home' with the man who still mourns the loss of their mother, and has never, therefore, had a home of his own, but they are effectively 'homeless' by having lost the imagined Thrums which had been their 'homeland' in London. They are the children of nostalgia but *Sentimental Tommy* dramatizes the particular homelessness of modern Scotland as the homelessness of everyone who is born into the modern world:

> It might be said of these two boys that Shovel knew everything but Tommy knew other things, and as the other things are best worth hearing Shovel liked to listen to them, even when they were about Thrums, as usually they were. The very first time Tommy told him of the wondrous spot, Shovel had drawn a great breath and said, thoughtfully:

'I allers knowed as there were sich a beauty place, but I didn't jest know its name.'

'How could yer know?' Tommy asked jealously.

'I ain't sure,' said Shovel, 'p'raps I dreamed on it.'

'That's it,' Tommy cried. 'I tell yer, everybody dreams on it!' and Tommy was right; everybody dreams of it, though not all call it Thrums.[39]

Thrums is, for Barrie, the personal version of the home which every inhabitant of the modern world dreams can be recovered from the past but which, if recovered, would prove to be no less satisfying than the modernity they already inhabit. The 'idyll' is less than idyllic, for there is no past to which we can escape that is not already full of the discontents of modernity. Whatever might be said of other writers associated with the Kailyard school, Barrie's version of it is far from being a flight from the present to the past but is, rather, a dramatisation of why such a flight should be both appealing and impossible.

Scotland's construction of itself in the eighteenth and early nineteenth centuries as founded on memory intersects with the onset of modernity, and its transformation of human beings' relationship with their past, to produce at least three different kinds of nostalgia that claim Scotland as the *nostos* after which they yearn, and which we need to differentiate if we are to understand the kinds of nostalgia to which they gave rise.

Firstly, for those living in Scotland, there is the nostalgia caused by the historical rupture of the Union of 1707: whether you were a Jacobite or a Unionist, in post-1707 Scotland, the past was another and a different country, which could be regretted, celebrated or denigrated, but which could be approached only in terms of the radical discontinuity of the past's relationship with the present. This version of nostalgia was given its archetypal form by Allan Ramsay's *The Gentle Shepherd* (1725), in which the pastoral setting recalls the classical arcadia of an unfallen world, but which locates that arcadia in the immediate aftermath of the restoration of the Stuart monarchy in 1660, when Sir William Worthy is able to return to the estate from which he had fled after Cromwell's annexation of Scotland in the 1640s:

Seeing's believing, Glaud, and I have seen
Hab, that abroad has with our Master been;

Our brave good Master, wha right wisely fled,
And left a fair estate, to save his head:
Because ye ken fou well he bravely chose
To stand his liege's friend with great Montrose.
Now Cromwell's gane to Nick; and ane ca'd Monk
Has play'd the Rumple a right slee begunk,
Restor'd King Charles, and ilka thing's in tune:
And Habby says, we'll see Sir William soon.

The return which Worthy makes is spatial – he has been in exile on the continent – but leads to the recovery of the son whom he had to abandon when he fled, a son who has been brought up believing himself to be the offspring of the peasant family in whose care he had been placed but who, after the discovery of his 'gentle' birth, will in turn discover that his lower class lover is also his cousin, another child hidden for safety among the peasantry but beneath her peasant dress concealing an aristocratic lineage. Worthy's return thus takes on a temporal dimension as the characters are returned to the 'real' identities of which they had been deprived at birth. The temporal return to the homeland in 1660 takes on a particular significance when viewed from the perspective of the play's initial audience in the 1720s, for the 'homeland' to which the play returns its audience is the homeland that had been lost as a result of 'Glorious Revolution' of 1688 and the exile of the Stuart monarchs. The play uses the genre of arcadian comedy as a means of underlining how different is the new Scotland from a pre-Union country in which there was harmony not only between nature and humanity but between aristocracy and peasantry. Before Union the country was united in a way that it cannot be post-Union. By its celebration of the virtues of the Stuart past, however, the play is also preparing the ground for the events of 1745, and for the Stuarts' attempted recapture of the monarchy from which they had been ousted. The 'nostalgia' of *The Gentle Shepherd* is thus a 'future oriented' nostalgia and would remain so even after 1746, because its celebration of agricultural productivity and the harmony of an agrarian economy chimed with the underlying impetus of Adam Smith's *The Wealth of Nations*, which, as David McNally has argued, is based not on the defence of commercial or industrial capitalism, but on the promotion of agrarian capitalism as the foundation of a beneficent society.[40] *The Gentle Shepherd* asserts the virtues of an ordered agrarian society not just as a nostalgic recollection of a better world in the past, but as the basis of a better world in the future. The ongoing contemporary relevance of Ramsay's 'opera' – its form merging traditional Scottish folksong with themes from classical pastoral – is evident not only in the fact that it remained part of the repertoire of theatre companies throughout the eighteenth century – Janet Sorenson suggests there were over 160 productions in Scotland, England and America[41] – but that it was republished in North America at least seven times between 1750 and 1813.[42] At various periods of the eighteenth century, *The Gentle Shepherd* could represent an agrarian ideal that would challenge the Union itself – only the return of Stuarts will bring back health to the country, still a real possibility in the 1720s – or could express disquiet, if not revulsion, from the increasingly commercialised world of a Scotland where the traditional relations of class were being disrupted by agricultural 'improvement' – which generally meant the clearing of people from their land – and by the introduction of new industrial structures, like the domestic weaving trade, the last days of which are depicted in Barrie's stories of Thrums. 'Nostalgia' is here a mode of critique of modernity, because the world it evokes is still, socially and politically, a possible future which, by an acceptance of the values it endorses, can be reconstituted as a future continuation of that cultural past. 'Nostalgia' is not passive resignation in the recollection of the past but an active attempt to impress the pattern of the past on the future. Of course, with the passage of time that future-oriented possibility becomes less feasible and the play returns to being an arcadian dream that can exist only as a literary possibility, but a literary possibility which still has a future orientation through the ways in which its language provides resources for future poetry in Scots.

Secondly, there are Scotland's xeniteian migrants who, even as they determinedly reconstruct the institutions of their homeland, need to test their continued commitment to its values by an imaginative return to the homeland whose values guide their activities. The Scottish past, ritualised in Burns Suppers and St Andrew's Day celebrations, allow people to enact their sense of a shared heritage of values by recalling a place which, however distant in both space and time, is brought back to life as symbolic of those shared values: the associations generated by memory bind the participants as associates in a communal endeavour. For nineteenth-century xeniteians, the central poem of the Burns canon was 'The Cotter's Saturday Night', because of its direct proclamation of the values underpinning Scotland's distinctive emigrant mission: 'From Scenes like these, old SCOTIA'S grandeur springs.'[43] The poem's celebration of work – 'The toil-worn COTTER frae his labour goes/*This night* his weekly moil is at an end'; of family life – 'With joy unfeign'd, *brothers* and *sisters* meet'; and of the inheritance of a literate religion – 'The sire turns o'er, wi' patriarchal grace/ The big *ha'-Bible*, ance his *Father's* pride'[44] – were elements of the national life that could be mapped on to lives in very different places and times. It is nostalgia not as a regression from the present to the past but as a call to arms to make the future worthy of the national past:

> O THOU! Who poured the *patriotic tide*,
>   That streamed thro' WALLACE'S undaunted heart
> . . .
> O never, never SCOTIA'S realm desert;
>   But still the *Patriot*, and the *Patriot-bard*
> In bright succession raise, her *Ornament* and *Guard*!

The nation lives through the patriotism that celebrates – and is prepared to repeat – the nation's heroic struggle for independence, as well as in the activities of the 'patriot-bards' who keep the memory of that past alive through each succeeding generation. The continuity of bardic poetry and its annual performance maintains the wealth of memory that makes the nation of continuing value to those who are the inheritors of its past, and ensures that their construction of the future is still in conformity with the fundamental values of that past.

Thirdly, there is the nostalgia for a Scotland which was the 'heartland' of romanticism – homeland to Ossianic epic and the historical novel and to a folk culture which inspired the collecting of folk literature throughout Europe. Instead of being the subject of nostalgia, Scotland is here the object of other peoples' nostalgia, as though it could represent a 'home' for those who feel homeless in their own environments. This starts as early as 1774 with Goethe's *Die Leiden des jungen Werthers*, and Werther's discovery, in the letter of 12 October, of Ossian:

> Ossian has ousted Homer from my heart. What a world that exalted soul leads me into! To wander across the heath in the pale moon-

> light, with the gale howling and spirits of his forefathers in the vaporous mists! To hear amidst the roar of a forest torrent the faint moans of the spirits in their mountainside caves, and the laments of that mortally stricken maiden weeping over the four mossy, grassed-over stones that mark the grave of the noble warrior who was her lover! And then to find him, that grey-haired bard, wandering on the vast heath, seeking the places his forefathers knew, and then, ah! finding their tombstones, and raising his eyes in lament to the sweet star of evening as it sinks in the waves of the rolling sea. And times gone by are relived in the hero's soul . . .[45]

Ossian's world of loss and memory becomes an alternative homeland to Werther, who is spurned in his own society and who fails to win Lotte from her bourgeois marriage to Albert: homeless in Germany, he and Lotte find the image of their own unfulfillable desires in his translations of Ossian: 'They could sense their own wretchedness in the fates of the noble heroes, they sensed it together, and shed tears in harmony'.[46] Romantic Scotland offers itself as an alternative home to those whose imaginings are unfulfillable in their own homelands.

Since the eighteenth century, Scotland, as the potential fulfilment of other peoples' nostalgia, has lived in a constant tension between Scotland as the impress on Scots of the Scotland in which they actually live and the Scotland which is the memory with which the country is identified in others' imaginings. Of course, this is a nostalgia to which Scots themselves gave rise when they accommodated the country's Gaelic past into its modern articulation of itself, and when it adopted the style of Scottish military dress as a code for its continuing difference in the Union, but it is a nostalgia which has been made available not only to those who – as in the upsurge of Highland games in North America in the 1980s – see themselves as in need of an 'ethnic' differentiation in the hyphenated world of modern multiculturalism, but to anyone in need of a past 'homeland' whose loss has to be mourned as the cost of the passage to modernity. Scotland can fulfil this role only because of the powerful impression that Scottish culture made in the nineteenth century on the emergent world of modernity and as a symbol of the regret for a lost world which that modernity made inevitable. That unavailing regret is enacted in the many translations of Burns's 'My Heart's in the Highlands', a song which dramatizes distance and separation in both space and time:

Farewell to the Highlands, farewell to the North,
The birthplace of Valour, the country of Worth:
Wherever I wander, wherever I rove,
The hills of the Highlands for ever I love. –

My heart's in the Highlands, my heart is not here;
My heart's in the Highlands, a chasing the deer
Chasing the wild deer, and following the roe;
My heart's in the Highlands, wherever I go. –

Farewell to the mountains high cover'd with snow;
Farewell to the Straths and green valleys below:
Farewell to the forests and wild-hanging woods;
Farewell to the torrents and loud-pouring floods. –

My heart's in the Highlands &c.[47]

The *Bibliography of Scottish Literature in Translation*[48] lists over ninety translations of this song in almost every major European language (there are many versions in German, in Italian and in Polish) but, more significantly, in many 'minor' languages (including Latvian, Lithuanian, Belarusian, Bulgarian, Czech, Slovak, and Serbo-Croat). The poem's articulation of a sense of continued belonging to a homeland – 'My heart's in the Highlands' – and of ongoing commitment to its values – 'The birthplace of Valour, the country of Worth' – is juxtaposed with the inevitability of a displacement – 'Wherever I wander, wherever I rove' – that will mean that that 'heartland' can now exist only as memory – 'Farewell . . . Farewell . . . Farewell'. This is a literary version of 'nostalgia' in Hofer's original construction of the term, and the success of such Scottish writing in the late eighteenth and early nineteenth centuries makes Scotland itself the 'homeland' of a readerly nostalgia not for one's own national past, but for a country that represents the past as readers in an alienated modern world would wish it to be – noble, heroic, rich in emotions from military courage to personal affection. Scotland becomes, in effect, a 'heartland' of literary memory, a past to which there can never be a return in reality because it is a place which can exist only in the imagination of a present which no longer has a home in the world.

The Scotland as the 'nostalgia-of-the-other' is often rendered in terms of so-called 'Highlandism' – the projection of a Highland culture as the 'essence' of the modern country, despite the fact that most Scots live, as Paul Basu notes, 'in towns and cities of the Central Belt and whose landscape is one of urban renewal and industrial decay, commuter trains and motorways, housing estates and retail parks'[49] rather than in Highland bens and glens. But this is an opposition which is too easily invoked: most Scots live in places where hills and mountains shape the visible landscape, whether in Edinburgh with its backdrop of the Pentland Hills and the immediate upsurge of Arthur's Seat and Salisbury Crags, or Glasgow, with its prospects of the Cathkin Braes and, on a clear day, Ben Lomond, or even Aberdeen, with its hinterland of the Grampians. Lowland Scotland is not now separate from but always in immediate juxtaposition to its Highlands, which are, in any case, not very high: as: Nan Shepherd puts it in *The Living Mountain*, published in 1977, 'one does not look upward to spectacular peaks but downward from the peaks to spectacular chasms'.[50] The country's visual identity is its mountains: 'on a clear day one looks without any sense of strain from Morven in Caithness to the Lammermuirs, and out past Ben Nevis to Morar'.[51] The attempt to separate Lowland from Highland Scotland ignores the extent to which many Lowland Scots are the descendants of Highlanders, and how many Lowland Scots, like Nan Shapherd, made the country's mountains the focus of their spiritual aspirations. 'Highlandism' is not simply the ersatz adoption of a stereotypical version of Scottish culture which is entirely unconnected with the reality of modern Scottish life: the Highlands are both the geographical and the historical backdrop with which 'Lowland' Scottish culture interacts. As Walter Scott notes in *Guy Mannering*, Scotland is embraced by Highlands: 'It may not be unnecessary', he says in a footnote, 'to tell southern readers that the mountainous country in the southwestern borders of Scotland is call Hĭeland, though totally different from the much more mountainous and more extensive district of the north, usually accented Hĭelands'.[52] Highlandism comes in many forms, and if some of them invoke a 'dead end' nostalgia, such as Diana Gabaldon's 'Outlander' series or the groups across modern Europe who play at being Scottish by taking part in Highland games and performing in pipe bands (as charted by David Hesse in *Warrior Dreams*),[53] for others the Highlands are the place in which it is possible to encounter what Nan Shepherd described as '*feyness*', an emotion which 'intensifies life to the point of glory'.[54] If the Scottish tourist industry markets Scotland as a 'homeland' to those in search of an 'other-to-modernity', that does not negate the fact that Scotland is, indeed, a homeland to which memory can return not as a nostalgia which is a refusal of modernity, but as the nostalgia which is the recollection of values by which the future ought to be shaped.

III Necromancy

Lurking in Allan Ramsay's *Evergreen* was a poem entitled 'The Vision', which he claimed had been 'compylit in Latin be a most lernit Clerk in Tyme of our Hairship and Oppression, anno 1300, and translatit in 1524', and which is attributed to 'Ar. Scot.' – a name which might have implied the sixteenth-century Scottish poet, Alexander Scott, but which in fact concealed 'Allan Ramsay Scotus', using the events of Scotland's suffering under the oppression of Edward I as an allegory of its suffering under the Hanoverians. Ramsay's creation of an 'original' ancient poem revealed how easily the editorial effort of reconstituting the body of the nation's literature could turn into the creative replenishment of the nation's past with modern productions. The past thus became infused with the future, the future shadowed by a past whose reality is uncertain: the literary editor as gatekeeper between the past and the present was also an aspirant poet recreating the past in his own image. Walter Scott was not above such reshaping of the past as he collected the poetry that went into his *Minstrelsy of the Scottish Border* (1802–03), but in *Marmion* published in 1808, he did exactly the opposite by interleaving his romance of the Scottish defeat at Flodden with letters to his friends that comment on the ways in which they have helped contribute to his creation; he thus underlines how much his version of the past – 'Mine is a tale of Flodden Field, /And not a history'[55] – is based on boyhood reading, on shared interest in the literature of romance and the search for antiquarian remains. Scott's letters underline the modernity of the interests from which his tale arises. In the 'Introduction to Canto Fifth', for instance, the address to Edinburgh begins in its architectural transformation –

> So thou, fair City! Disarrayed
> Of battled wall, and rampart's aid,
> As stately seem'st, but lovelier far
> Than in that panoply of war[56]

– Scott emphasises how distinctly different is the past from the present, but the letter ends in the assertion of the city's continuing spiritual purpose as a place committed to ancient loyalties:

Destined in every age to be
Refuge of injured royalty;
Since first, when conquering York arose,
To Henry meek she gave repose,
Till late, with wonder, grief and awe,
Great Bourbon's relics, sad she saw.[57]

Whatever continuity Edinburgh represents, recent 'historical' events and personal memories underline the distance between Scott's 'tale' of 'all the pomp of chivalry'[58] and the contemporary world in which it is written. The 'tale', however, is symptomatic of literature's ability to project upon the past an awareness of the future that, had it taken place in the time in which the tale is set, could only have been the result of supernatural forces: as James's army musters in Edinburgh there appears at Edinburgh Cross –

A vision, passing Nature's law,
Strange, wild, and dimly seen,
Figures that seem'd to rise and die,
Gibber and sign, advance and fly[59]

– a vision out of which comes an 'awful summons' that lists the names of those who will, on the following day, die on Flodden Field. The summons is possible, of course, only because the names of those who actually died are known to history, but that knowledge of the past becomes an apparent foreknowledge of the future in the world of the romance:

Each chief of birth and fame,
Of Lowland, Highland, Border, Isle,
Fore-doom'd to Flodden's carnage pile,
Was cited there by name[60]

The past is transfused with the knowledge of a later time as though it had, in the past, been given a preternatural insight into the future. In the introduction to the sixth canto, Scott addresses fellow collector of antiquities and 'ancient mystery',[61] Richard

Heber, and cites a peasant tale of the castle of Franchément in which two characters, one a demonic huntsman, the other a 'necromantic priest', struggle to unlock a huge treasure chest:

> It is a hundred years at least,
> Since 'twixt them first the strife begun,
> And neither yet has lost nor won.
> And oft the Conjuror's words will make
> The stubborn Demon groan and quake:
> And oft the bands of iron break,
> Or bursts one lock, that still amain,
> Fast as 'tis open'd, shuts again.[62]

The conflict mimics the struggle between history and the supernatural for the treasure chest of the past, but also dramatizes the impossibility of a conclusion to that struggle, as however 'secular' in its account of the past history might seek to be, it can recover the past only through the values of the present, and reshapes by its own knowledge of what was an unknown future to the people of the past the account it gives of their intentions and actions: the dead are raised from their graves to speak in modern voices. The supernatural myths by which ancient chronicles account for human actions –

> Such general superstition may
> Excuse for old Pitscottie say;
> Whose gossip history has given
> My song the messenger from Heaven,
> That warns, in Lithgow, Scotland's King[63]

– are no less mythical than the magic by which the historian calls up the past to make it speak: all history, as an art of memory, is engaged in an endless struggle with necromancy, for when the dead speak, in whose voice do they tell their story?

It was this tension which led Scott to begin to surround his historical narratives with multiple narrators – himself, of course, the invisible Wizard of the North but, in a novel like *Old Mortality*, with a series of live and dead narrative voices. As John Sutherland describes it, in *Old Mortality*

> The author of *Waverley* has disguised himself . . . as Jedediah Cleishbotham, a pedantic schoolteacher. Cleishbotham, however,

> is merely the conduit, transcribing the literary remains of Peter Pattieson. Pattieson, although a thoroughly literary (and strangely doomed) figure is not, however, the author. He has recorded stories taken from a fanatic and vagrant haunter of Scottish churchyards, Robert Paterson. And, if one thinks about it, Paterson himself must have had the story of Henry Morton from somebody who had it from, probably, Cuddie Headrigg.[64]

Pattieson's attempted revival of the memory of late seventeenth-century conflict between government forces and the rebellious Covenanters is counteracted by the fact that he is himself now dead, and interred in an old burial ground which he has chosen for his last resting place because of its associations with the Covenanters, some of whom, killed by government troops, had been interred there in graves the remembrance of which was kept alive by the local peasantry: 'although the moss has been collected on the most modern of these humble tombs during four generations of mankind, the memory of some of those who sleep beneath them is still held in reverend remembrance':[65]

> The peasantry continued to attach to the tombs of those victims of prelacy an honour which they do not render to more splendid mausoleums; and when they point them out to their sons, and narrate the fate of the sufferers, usually conclude, by exhorting them to be ready, should times call for it, to resist to the death, in the cause of civil and religious liberty, like their brave forefathers.[66]

The novel opens not only with a scene of 'reverend remembrance' which now includes remembrance of the putative author, as Cleishbotham has raised a stone on the grave of Pattieson that he too may be remembered, but with a scene in which remembrance is being refreshed by Old Mortality himself, a stonemason who has made it his life's work to clean and renew the graves of the Covenanters. The passage to the events of the past is possible only because, on the one hand, of the renewal of the associations of places such as this burial ground through the oral communications of the peasantry, and, on the other hand, by the active commemoration that is the re-engraving of the headstones that mark where the victims of government violence were buried. Only repeated acts of commemoration can keep open the passage from the present to the past but those acts of commemoration are not neutral: they are made possible by the political insistence of those who wish to keep alive their belief that it is their right to 'resist' state authority, if necessary 'to the death, in the cause of civil and religious liberty'. Motivated memory keeps the past alive and prevents its being buried beyond recollection – it also, therefore, keeps alive the possibility that, like Pattieson's text, it can rise from the grave to speak again to the present. This, in a sense, was what was to happen to Scott when the Reverend Thomas McCrie famously challenged him over the depiction of the Covenanters in *Old Mortality*,[67] as having degraded those fighting for liberty by representing them as ignorant fanatics and 'homicidal maniacs':[68] In the novel itself, Henry Morton, having become the prisoner of those Covenanters and having been condemned to death, finds himself

> among these pale-eyed and ferocious zealots, whose hardened brows were soon to be bent, not merely with indifference, but with triumph, upon his execution – without a friend to speak a kindly word, or give a look either of sympathy or encouragement, – awaiting till the sword destined to slay him crept out of the scabbard gradually, and as it were by straw-breadths, and condemned to drink the bitterness drop by drop . . .[69]

Morton, however, is saved by the sudden arrival of Claverhouse and his troops, and survives because he is 'buried' under the body of one his captors – 'the whig who stood next to Morton received a shot as he was rising, stumbling against the prisoner, whom he bore down with his weight, and lay stretched above him a dying man.'[70] He is thus allowed to 'arise' from death – he 'was speedily raised and in the arms of the faithful Cuddie, who blubbered for joy when he found that the blood with which his master was covered had not flowed from his own veins'[71] – but this 'resurrection' turns out to be but the prologue to another resurrection – that of the Covenanter Mucklewrath – who has lain wounded but concealed in the apartment where Morton and Claverhouse converse:

> His face, where it was not covered with bloodstreaks, was ghastly pale, for the hand of death was on him. He bent upon Claverhouse eyes, in which the grey light of insanity still twinkled, though just about to flit for ever, and exclaimed, with his usual wildness of ejaculation, 'Wilt thou trust in this bow and in thy spear, and in

> thy steed and in thy banner . . . I summon thee, John Grahame, to appear before the tribunal of God, to answer for this innocent blood, and the seas besides which thou hast shed.'[72]

The past which has, supposedly, been killed off, rises again not only to challenge the present but to predict the future: 'Morton was much shocked as this extraordinary scene, and the prophecy of the dying man, which tallied so strangely with the wish which Claverhouse had just expressed; and he often thought of it afterwards when that wish seemed to be accomplished'.[73] Necromancy allows the dead to rise again to prophesy the future of the living and to assert the values of the defeated against the tyranny of those by whom they have been suppressed. McCrie may have been correct about Scott's own ideological opposition to the values of the Covenanters, as disrupters of traditional loyalty, but he failed to recognise the extent to which Scott's art, on the side of memory and against forgetfulness, resurrected in the present the very forces that he feared in the past. Memory is a double-edged sword: it can consign the past to a burial ground where the past returns only as a train of melancholy reflections, or it can recall the past as though it is a living present and a call to action. Of the figure of Old Mortality, we are told: 'One would almost have supposed he must have been their contemporary, and have actually beheld the passages which he related, so much had he identified his feelings and opinions with theirs, and so much had his narratives the minute circumstantiality of an eye-witness.'[74] The past has not died: Old Mortality's narration makes it seem a living part of the present, and his act of commemoration is a preparation for the virtues of the past to be resurrected and re-enacted in the present.

If nostalgia draws us from the present towards immersing ourselves in the past, necromancy brings the past disruptively into the present: the past returns in defiance of the orderly progress of history.[75] James Hogg's *Private Memoirs and Confessions of a Justified Sinner*, first published in 1824, performs this act of historical recuperation both in terms of its own narrative, which resurrects Robert Wringhim's 'confession' from his eighteenth-century grave to stalk its uncomprehending nineteenth-century 'editor', but also by its own textual history, as it was a novel 'resurrected' in the aftermath of the Second World War as a commentary on a modernity in which diabolic evil had returned to haunt a world that believed it had consigned such evil to a past from which it could never return. As Wringhim's grave gives up both his undecomposed body and his composed text – 'I will now seal up my little book, and conceal it, and cursed be he who tries to alter or amend!'[76] – the present finds itself confronted by its necromantic past. So potent has been this return of the past to haunt the present that it has, itself, become a haunting presence in recent Scottish literature, its structure adopted and redeployed in novels such as Emma Tennant's *The Bad Sister* (1978), Iain Banks's *Complicity* (1993) and Alasdair Gray's *Poor Things* (1992). Hogg's *Confessions*, so long regarded as of no literary value, has come to be seen as the defining text of a culture in which the past, once assumed to be dead, has necromantically risen to reassert itself in the present. The revival of Hogg's text has gone along with the revival of Walter Scott: consigned to literary irrelevance by critics such as F. R. Leavis – in *The Great Tradition* (1948) Scott is described in a footnote as 'primarily a kind of inspired folk-lorist, qualified to have done in fiction something analogous to the ballad-opera'[77] – the critical perception of Scott's works changed not only with Georg Lukács's *The Historical Novel* in 1962 but, from an entirely different perspective, with the work of Canadian critic Northrop Frye, for whom literature should not be judged in terms of its ability to represent 'reality', but by its ability to call up the archetypal structures of the unconscious: 'the essential difference between novel and romance lies in the conception of characterization. The romancer does not attempt to create "real people" so much as stylized figures which expand into psychological archetypes'.[78] For Frye, 'most "historical novels" are romances',[79] and to read romances as though they were intended to represent reality is simply a category mistake. From Frye's theorising, Scott emerged not as an old-fashioned, failed realist but as a fabulator whose work, as Jerome McGann insisted in 1999, was, in its adoption of various metafictional techniques and ironic combinations of contradictory genres, prescient of postmodernism.[80]

This alternative Scott – not the Scott of progressive history but the Scott of the archetypal memories that return to disrupt our present – was one that Alan Massie dramatised in *The Ragged Lion* (1994). Massie's Scott is a man haunted by the ghost of a boy from a poor family with whom he had fought as a child and whom he knew only as 'Green Breeks', but who represented for him an ideal of primitive nobility. Massie's novel claims to be a memoir written by Scott, a copy of which Scott's son had presented to a noble family in Italy, a family with whom Massie had become acquainted when he was teaching English there.[81] Massie's text, however, is constructed to make Scott the voice of later nineteenth-century writers: like Jekyll in the latter stages of Stevenson's novel, Scott fears that he is 'possessed of another spirit, another incomprehensible being' and is so afraid of himself that, on waking, he 'seized a glass from the table by my bed and scrutinized my face . . . [t]o see that I was the same man, wearing the same face, as had gone to bed;'[82] and, like J. G. Frazer, he believes the 'primitive' to be always present in us:

> I employ the word 'primitive', not as my friend Francis Jeffrey and his troop of Whig reviewers might employ it: to denote a condition from which the progress of civilization has to set us free: but rather as something inescapable, something that is of our necessary and enduring essence.[83]

By allowing Scott to become the necromantic voice of nineteenth-century Scotland's cultural future, Massie implies how much those voices – as Robert Crawford has argued in *Devolving English Literature*[84] – were themselves dependent on Scott. Stevenson's and Frazer's texts are haunted by Scott and the Scott of the memoir in Massie's novel is retrospectively haunted by their writings. Necromancy turns past into future, future into past in an exchange which defies Whig notions of linear progress.

Another contemporary Scottish writer haunted by Scott is James Robertson. In his doctoral thesis on *The Construction and Expression of Scottish Patriotism in the Works of Walter Scott* (1989), Robertson argued that Scott had constructed a specifically Scottish patriotism that could exist only in the past so that it would not conflict with the British patriotism of a Scotland now committed to Union. Scott had made Scottish history famous by, effectively, bringing it to an end, confining it to the era when 'passion', rather than 'prudential reason', ruled men's actions. But the ghosts of Scott's novels still haunt modern Scotland and Robertson's novels. *The Fanatic* (2000) juxtaposes events in Scotland in 1997, in the run up to the Labour Party's victory of that year in the Westminster elections, with events in the 1670s when James Mitchel is tried and executed for the attempted assassination of Archbishop Sharp, betrayer of the principles of the Scottish Covenant. Sharp's ultimate assassination is, of course, part of the plot of *Old Mortality* and the use of the 'boot' as an implement of torture is presented in both novels. The two periods of *The Fanatic* are linked by Andrew Carlin, a former history student so ghostlike in appearance that he is asked to perform in a 'ghost tour' of Edinburgh's Old Town, playing Major Weir, an associate of Mitchel's who was executed for incest and diabolism in 1670. Carlin becomes obsessed with understanding Mitchel, and doing research on the period, uncovers 'a secret book' supposedly written by one John Lauder, who was also obsessed by Mitchel's fanaticism, and the book brings Carlin so close to the events of the past he feels as though 'It's like the past isna past. It's right there happenin in front o me'.[85] Before Carlin can finish Lauder's book, however, both the book and the librarian who provided it disappear, leaving no record of their existence. Carlin is the medium for a necromantic return of the past, in defiance of Scott's strategy of making it redundant: Carlin is a ghost who 'looks like he's been wandering around there for centuries trying to find a way out'[86] but in fact allows the past to return in all its raw brutality. The consequences of reading Scott are also played out in Robertson's *Gideon Mack* (2006) in which the central character reads Scott's novels both in defiance of the expectations of his own times – it is the 1960s, he should be listening to the Beatles – and in defiance of his father, a minister of the Kirk who has long since been convinced by McCrie's arguments against Scott's presentation of the Covenanters and, therefore, of the falsity of Scott's fiction. Father and son replay the debate about historical fiction's relationship to reality, a debate which is given a very different turn when Gideon finds in his father's library a copy of Robert Kirk's *Secret Commonwealth of Elves, Fauns and Fairies*, with its accounts of supernatural encounters with creatures who exist somewhere between humans and angels. Gideon begins to live his life as the ghostly performance of various characters in fiction: thus when he has to deliver a sermon to achieve appointment as a minister, he models himself on Chris Guthrie's second husband, Robert Colquhoun, out of Lewis Grassic Gibbon's *A Scots Quair*, a book he had 'recently finished reading'[87] Gideon's subsequent appointment proves that living as literature makes him one of the elect, released from the burden of choosing as himself. The rest of the narrative takes him further into events that mimic scenes in literature

– a meeting with the devil, for instance, in an underground cave that echoes the meeting of Burley and Balfour in *Old Mortality*. In the end, Gideon will set off for Ben Alder, one of the locations in Stevenson's *Kidnapped*, leaving behind the manuscript of his life story, which, like Kirk's, tells of his encounters with the supernatural and the diabolic. In Carlin and Gideon, Robertson dramatizes how the historical moment of the present is haunted by the literature of the past, which returns to its characters so vividly as to reshape the present on a model of the past. As Robertson puts it in his introduction to his collection of *Scottish Ghost Stories* (1996), 'I am . . . highly sceptical of that kind of absolute certainty which categorically denies there can be any such thing as a ghost', it nonetheless may be 'that reason and science are not the keys to every locked door; it may be that our ancestors had access to doors now locked and bolted to all but a few of us.'[88] In fact those doors are ones that the Scottish novel of recent times has been continuously exploring by invoking necromancy as a challenge to secular modernity.

IV Nostophobia

Scotland's xeniteian empire did not survive the First World War and the aftermath of economic depression in Scotland that lasted from the early 1920s until the beginning of the Second World War. The British Empire may have faded only in the decades after the Second World War, and might have continued to use Scottish iconography – a kilted piper played down the Union Jack when Britain handed Hong Kong back to the Chinese – as the appropriate medium for an elegiac sense of loss; Scotland, homeland of memory, was the doorway through which the British Empire was ushered into the past. The dissolution of the Scottish empire, however, was not just a consequence of the erosion of the country's vitality by the 100,000 deaths it suffered in the First World War, nor of the collapse of many of the industries which had been essential to that war but were ill-prepared for the peace, but because the core areas of the Scottish empire in Canada, Australia and New Zealand, and even, perhaps, in the parts of India and Africa where Scottish culture had a particular hold, had, through their participation in the War, begun to assert their own independent national identities and to discover the meaning and value of their own national traditions. A

Scot like the philosopher John Anderson in Australia would no longer represent the continuation of Scottish philosophy as part of Scotland's spiritual empire but would instead be the founder of a new national philosophy, able to assert its own distinctive values. The consequence in Scotland was a radical undermining of the culture that had supported the nation's imperial mission: the established Church and the Free Church were reunited in 1928 but it was a union which implicitly acknowledged the failure of their efforts to create a worldwide Scottish mission. The culture of Scotland's nineteenth-century empire became, almost overnight, a failed culture, a false culture, an illusion which had deceived the nation about its own significance in the world. Burns and Scott were, suddenly, not an index of Scottish superiority but an index of Scotland's inferiority – alternative versions of the 'fake' culture which had been constructed and then dissipated by Macpherson's Ossianic poetry.

One cannot doubt the energy with which Scottish artists of the 1920s went about the business of producing new kinds of poetry (Hugh MacDiarmid, Edwin Muir), new kinds of novel (Neil Gunn, Nan Shepherd), new styles in theatre (Joe Corrie, James Bridie) and energetic new forms of art (F. C. B. Cadell, Anne Redpath), but their creative activities took place in a context in which the Scottish past was increasingly seen as of no relevance to Scotland's future. For Hugh MacDiarmid, for instance, the rebirth of the nation required the erasure of what had passed for Scotland's national culture since the Reformation: Scotland had to go back to its pre-Reformation religion, culture and language – 'Back to Dunbar' – in order to find an idiom that had not been corrupted by the Anglicisation introduced into Scotland by the King James bible, and by the anglocentric cultural values of the literati of the eighteenth century. MacDiarmid listed 'anglophobia' as one of his interests in his entry in *Who's Who*, but much more significant in terms of the development of Scottish culture was his rejection of the homeland which he had inherited from nineteenth-century Scotland, his rejection of its cities, its bourgeoisie and its culture in favour of the re-creation of a Scotland which could, in defiance of the country's actual history, become the continuation of the Scotland of the Wars of Independence and of the flourishing culture to which they gave rise.

The homeland to which xeniteian Scotland had been committed and from which it had drawn its values was, suddenly, an emptiness – the illusory imitation of a culture rather than the real thing. The so-called 'Scottish Renaissance' became, in effect, the gravedigger of the Scottish past, devaluing the cultural capital which the country had built up through the eighteenth and nineteenth centuries. MacDiarmid, writing in praise of Edwin Muir (at the stage when he and Muir were still allies in the Renaissance movement), declared that the 'majority of Scottish writers during the past hundred years have been entirely destitute of intellectual equipment adequate to work at international calibre, or even national calibre comparatively considered'; the historical extent of this failure, however, is then expanded to include every writer back to the Makars of the fifteenth century:

> Scotland has consequently become insular and has 'fidged fu' fain' on the strength of work that reflected only its national degeneracy and its intellectual inferiority to every other European country. The majority of the Scottish writers held most in esteem by contemporary Scots were (or are) too 'unconscious' even to experience the sense of frustration. They were too completely destitute of artistic integrity. It is in this that Muir is so significantly differentiated from the great majority, if not all, of his predecessors back to the time of the Auld Makars both as a critic and creative artist.[89]

The whole Scottish tradition is blighted with the same disease, a disease which goes back to the Reformation, because 'if the religious and political courses to which we have been committed have not come between us and the realisation of our finest potentialities, it is impossible to account for our comparative sterility'.[90] The blight means that even when MacDiarmid praises Burns as 'the most powerful lyrical poet the world has ever seen', it is only in order to emphasise how Scotland itself distorted and repressed that genius:

> It is in keeping with the cultural history of Scotland that such a Pegasus should have had to work in double harness with the clumsiest of carthorses, that Burns's wonderful power of song should have been so prosaically shackled, that his unique gift should have had to manifest itself behind such an irrelevant array of trite platitudinisation. And it is in keeping too with the cultural history of Scotland that even yet he should be most esteemed for the orthodox externalities of his work, for all that is irrelevant to, most opaque

> to, and most disfiguring of his genius rather than for the essence of that genius in itself.[91]

Rather than being the expressive voice of Scottish culture, Burns is its tragic victim – a promethean talent tied down by the inadequacies of the culture that he happens to inhabit:

> The tragedy of Burns is that he was a great poet who lived in an age and under circumstances hopelessly uncongenial to the exercise of his art and that, as a consequence, he was prevented from penetrating to an intellectual plane in keeping with his lyrical genius. There is an unspanned gulf between his matter and his manner, between his calibre as a poet and the kind of poetry to which he was for the most part restricted by his want of cultivation, between his powers and the work he actually produced and the influence that work has had.[92]

This, from 1926, was to be reinforced by Edwin Muir's influential analysis of Walter Scott in *Scott and Scotland* of 1936:

> . . . men of Scott's enormous genius have rarely Scott's faults; they may have others but not these particular ones; and so I was forced to account for the hiatus in Scott's endowment by considering the environment in which he lived, by invoking the fact – if the reader will agree it is one — that he spent most of his days in a hiatus, in a country, that is to say which was neither a nation nor a province, and had, instead of a centre, a blank, an Edinburgh, in the middle of it. But this Nothing in which Scott wrote was not merely a spatial one; it was a temporal Nothing as well, dotted with a few disconnected figures arranged at abrupt intervals: Henryson, Dunbar, Allan Ramsay and Burns, with a rude buttress of ballads and folk songs to shore them up and keep them from falling.[93]

In other words, the writers of the Scottish Renaissance movement demoted within or excluded from their pantheon of Scottish culture, the very Scottish writers who not only attempted to utilise the folk tradition that was 'undeniably one of the finest in the world' but who, despite the accusations of their 'intellectual inferiority to every other European country', had had, in fact, the greatest influence on European literature.

MacDiarmid and Muir's inter-war onslaught on the Scottish past was to provide the context for many of the most influential analyses of Scottish culture in the period after the Second World War. Thus, despite the fact that he saw himself as being in opposition to the poetic aims of the Scottish Renaissance, David Craig adopts precisely MacDiarmid's and Muir's rejection of the value of Burns and of Scott in his *Scottish Literature and the Scottish People*, published in 1961:

> This glorification of Scotland's 'Golden Age' does not explain the cultural impasse which followed: the use of the native language became embarrassed, poetry ran shallow and dried up, the novel was provincial from the start, many of the most original minds emigrated. Hence the historian is left calling Victorian culture in Scotland '*strangely* rootless', whereas a more critical sense of the eighteenth century would have seen that some sort of disintegration was already visible even in the best Scots poetry and in the way the language was being used.[94]

Craig's study is a study of the decline of Scottish culture as it moves from the integrated popular culture that the Reformation destroyed, through the narrowing achievements of the eighteenth-century literàti to the work of Burns and Scott, each major figure representing, despite individual successes, a further symptom of the disintegrative environment in which they worked. The end-point of such narratives is always the death of Scottish culture, or its arrival at a condition in which it is, in Muir's words, in 'a sort of limbo, half within the world of life and half outside it'. Craig's essay first appeared in MacDiarmid's journal *The Voice of Scotland* and, in 1945, following the announcement of a festival in Edinburgh to help in the reconstruction of Europe, and to which 'every distinguished composer and executant might be attracted', MacDiarmid responded in his journal by suggesting that such an occasion would only 'emphasize the absence of their peers in Scotland itself and the better the programmes the more ghastly would yawn the abyss between them and the utter inability of the Scottish people to assimilate and profit by anything of the sort, let alone be stimulated even to try to produce anything of comparable worth on their own part'.[95] Even though 'Scottish internationalism' is to be preferred to and asserted against 'English insularity', the value of the Scottish tradition is minimal: 'Literary critics in Scotland have always been as rare as snakes in Iceland – that's one of the reasons for our creative poverty'.[96] The irony of MacDiarmid's position was that its attempted re-rooting of Scotland in the creative achievements of the late medieval period was in large measure possible only because of the efforts of eighteenth- and nineteenth-century scholars such as John Jamieson (1759–1838) whose *Etymological Dictionary of the Scottish Language* (1808) provided MacDiarmid with much of the Scots in his poetry, or David Laing (1793–1878), who first edited the poems of William Dunbar in 1834. Without the efforts of those generations of Scottish scholars living in periods which MacDiarmid dismissed as irrelevant to Scotland's cultural development, his return to the language of the Makars would have been impossible.

A term for this profoundly negative reading of the Scottish past is required, and, it could be suggested, that the appropriate term is the antithesis of nostalgia, one which we might designate, following a suggestion of Fred Davis's, as 'nostophobia',[97] an emotional revulsion from the homeland. In 1968, Edwin Morgan was one of the editorial advisers to the newly launched *Scottish International* magazine and its second issue published 'The Flowers of Scotland', a poem later included in the *Penguin Modern Poets* volume that Morgan shared with Norman MacCaig and Liz Lochhead and which set out clearly the failings of his native land:

> Yes, it is too cold in Scotland for flower people; in any case who would be handed a thistle?
> What are our flowers? Locked swings and private rivers – and the island of Staffa for sale in the open market, which no one questions or thinks strange – and lads o' pairts that run to London and Buffalo without a backward look while their elders say
> Who'd blame them –
> and bonny fechters kneedeep in dead ducks with all the thrawn intentness of the incorrigible professional Scot –
> and a Kirk Assembly that excels itself in the bad old rhetoric and tries to stamp out every glow of charity and change, most wrong when it thinks most loudly it is most right –[98]

Thirteen verse paragraphs of the ailments of Scotland are contrasted with the powerlessness of those who resist its repressions: 'and dissidence crying in the wilderness to a moor of boulders and two ospreys'. The editorial of that issue of *Scottish*

International declares that 'Much of what we struggle against is summed up by Edwin Morgan's poem on the facing page'.[99]

Though Morgan carefully distanced himself from those – the poets of so-called 'second wave' of the Renaissance – who thought that only poetry in Scots could carry forward MacDiarmid's achievements, 'nostophobia' was a distinctive thread in the magazine to which he was editorial advisor. In an 'Open Letter to Archie Hind', for instance, published in *Scottish International* in October 1971, John Lloyd challenged Hind's support for the workers of the Upper Clyde Shipbuilders, and of his desire to identify himself with the 'authenticity' of working men:

> The cutting edge is the guilt Scots often appear to feel that they are writers/artists/intellectuals at all, and not part of the nitty gritty of boots and shovel, pick and piece-bag. It's as though they develop a mental castration fear. Having dared to develop the mental organ until it stands up above those of his fellows, the one thing the Scot wants to do is to disguise it, in case someone takes a chop at it.[100]

By contrast, Lloyd explained how,

> . . . I like living in London much of the time. It was in London that I learned various pleasures like, for example, LSD (the drug), wearing my hair long, that I began to gain a measure of sexual freedom and feel a gradual loosening of the tightness of my own inhibitions. Now all these things could have happened in Govan, perhaps, but in London it was easier . . .[101]

Scotland is the place where intellectuals are mentally castrated, London where they are sexually liberated. Eighteen months later, the April 1973 edition of the magazine advertised a forthcoming conference on 'What Kind of Scotland?' but the issue was introduced by a piece of 'reportage' which underlined the effect of arriving in Scotland from the metropolitan London that Lloyd had evoked:

> Step straight from the middle-class ghetto – well-dressed, well-mannered children, Saturday morning coffee in Louis's *patisserie*, Sunday lunchtime drinks in the *Horse and Groom* – into Glasgow now, and the effect is . . . well, shattering is not too strong a word. Surely it wasn't as bad four or five years ago? On my way to stay with friends near Drymen, I drove through Glasgow at night, just

> as the pubs were skailing. A dying place, murdered by neglect. Crumbling peeling stonework, boarded-up shops, slogans sprayed everywhere. Children clustered aimlessly on street corners. I stopped twice at phone boxes, both vandalised, the floors covered in spew and piss. I couldn't believe it . . .[102]

The journey towards the debate about 'What kind of Scotland?' begins in nostophobia; little wonder that the nostophobic haunts its discussions: 'The relevance of what was being said about fear, guilt and lack of confidence was sharp and tangible to this kind of Scottish audience'.[103] John Herdman's report on the conference in the May-June-July 1973 issue of *Scottish International* begins by recounting psychiatrist Aaron Eesterson's idea that 'people are often driven mad directly by the behaviour towards them of members of their own families', and muses on how, for the audience, this must have raised the question of 'how far the tensions of a small, cramped national society like that of Scotland, not dissimilar to a family in many ways, may help to induce various kinds of corporate madness in the Scottish people'.[104] Scotland – an insanitary, insane place.

The political and historic ironies of the situation are caught in an 'Open Letter' from Tom Nairn, who challenges 'the romantic-nationalist' conception of the nation and notes 'How unpropitious the terrain has always been in Scotland for such imagined "nationalist phases", whether in music or anything else! And hence the true nationalist's irrepressible gloom in our land . . .'[105] – a gloom that is evidenced by a quote from Morgan's 'The Flowers of Scotland'. Nairn has, however, his own nostophobic conception of Scotland as a culture in which past failure gives it a strange kind of advantage over the failings of other countries like England and France:

> It was natural, inevitable, that the great age of European nationalism triumphant (1848–1945) should have produced such responses everywhere in Europe, even in those marginal areas which did not and could not 'make it' like the bigger states. Nor is it surprising that the ideology lives on into the days of the Common Market. However, I believe that attention to 'what is really there' shows that the long winding road was never in fact traversable by the Scots. Their major cultural talent is the shortcut. *Not* having 'roots' of the requisite kind has been their chief advantage in life, at least during modern times. It is why they were so important in the brief

> era of cosmopolitanism before nationalist cultures were entrenched everywhere; and also why they have put up such a desperately poor performance during the age of *Nationalstaat* itself. It was not their element – nor is it ever likely to be now.[106]

Scotland's advantage in the modern world is the failure of its national and nationalist culture: those who succeeded in creating a nineteenth-century nationalism are now the sclerotic leftovers of a historical epoch of no contemporary relevance. Failure may be the basis of modern Scottish culture, but it failed earlier and differently than England or France – and that is its only hope. Nairn projects a future in which Scots could be the new 'wandering Jews' of Europe, dislocated from their national homeland and so able to escape from the (inevitably) disabling effects of national identity:

> The cultural nationalist invariably sees a fruitful culture as rooted in an internal wealth and psychological development: in the inner depths of the national personality's *Id*, as it were. For him it's roots or nothing. Outside them there is nothing but (I quote again from your editorial of No. 1) 'a colourless or promiscuous internationalism . . . to nobody's advantage'. But this antithesis itself belongs to the universe of nationalism (as does its corollary, the primary commonplace of the past age, that an achieved nationalism is the necessary precondition of 'true' internationalism) . . . Europe's new 'Jews' are far more likely to be . . . delinquents from the outer edge: cultural nomads from the barrens, so to speak . . .[107]

A new 'chosen people' of the post-nationalist world, the Scots will be able to assert their European significance precisely to the extent that they escape from, rather than commit to, 'the national personality's *Id*': recognising that their national – or, at least, their nationalist – failure ('not having "roots" of the requisite kind has been their chief advantage in life')[108] will liberate Scots to become the true new Europeans, inheritors of an Enlightenment which was built on 'our critical ability to rise above a relatively weak national inheritance in a manner at once intellectual and universal in its aim',[109] and allow us to fulfil the agenda set by the first issue of *Scottish International*, which insisted that Scots must escape 'a self-conscious cultural nationalism . . . leading to bad habits of stereotyped thinking and unwillingness to look at the situation as it really is'.[110]

'Looking at the situation as it really is', and in negation of its previously nostalgic representations, is always the claim of the nostophobe: nostalgia conceals, nostophobia reveals. What such accounts fail to recognise, however, is how ingrained 'nostophobia' had been in twentieth-century Scottish culture. The nostophobe always presents his or her realisation of the bleak reality of Scottish culture as a radical breakthrough, as the recovery of sanity in a world of 'pathological' illusion, but nostophobes never acknowledge that their own responses are the expression of a pattern just as powerful – and just as baleful – as the one they want to overthrow. If, as is often claimed, nineteenth-century Scotland was the country of nostalgia, then for most of the twentieth century Scotland has been the country of nostophobia. Far from being the minority opposition in modern Scottish culture, nostophobia was, in fact, the ideology of much of the cultural 'establishment'.

IV Prisoners of War

J. M. Barrie's stories were a popular resort for early filmmakers: when Katharine Hepburn starred in *The Little Minister* in 1934 it had already been made twice in the United States of America (the two films competing in 1922),[111] and when the director of *Brigadoon*, Vincente Minnelli, was in search of a Scottish location for his film but could find none in Scotland that looked sufficiently Scottish, it was probably because he had in mind the lavish set that was built for *The Little Minister*, a set so expensive that it was retained and re-used for Laurel and Hardy's *Bonnie Scotland* in 1935. *The Little Minister* was to set the pattern for much filmic representation of Scotland – a place set back in time or on the margins of modernity, a community made up of quirky and eccentric individuals where apparently supernatural, or, at least, inexplicable occurrences interrupt or redirect the ordinary flow of events. Outsiders are magically transformed by their encounter with this world as they discover that the past has virtues lost to their more modern societies. The irony of such encounters is repeated in the formal properties of film, dependent as it is on the infrastructure of modernity – lighting, cameras, make-up, a mass audience – and yet used to subvert the values of that modernity. The audience, as in Barrie's stories, is invited in to share the values of an alternative form of community which they can themselves no longer enjoy, only to be reminded as the lights go up that what they have been experiencing is an unfulfillable nostalgia. It was a structure most fully enacted in Alexander MacKendrick's *Whisky Galore!* (1949), based on the novel by Compton Mackenzie (an Englishman who had adopted a Scottish identity), and Bill Forsyth's *Local Hero* (1983), which was a self-conscious modernisation of Mackenzie's story: both depended on having as the film's central character an outsider – the English army officer in *Whisky Galore!*, the American businessman in *Local Hero* – who is enchanted – and outmanoeuvred – by the community into which he has been parachuted. Such films construct Scotland as the *nostos* of value systems which pre-date modernity, systems apparently made redundant by modernity but which can, in art, be re-encountered with a fulfilling sense of home-coming.

If such films are instances of Scotland as the international home of nostalgia, two Scottish-based films of the 1970s and 80s return to the root meaning of the term among Hofer's Swiss soldiers: Bill Douglas's *My Childhood* (1972) and Michael Radford's version of the Jessie Kesson novel, *Another Time, Another Place* (1983) are films that build their narratives around the interaction between people in a local Scottish community and soldiers who are prisoners of war. This intersection of the plotlines is telling in part because the two directors' careers could not have been more different. Douglas's film was produced with funding from the British Film Institute, having previously been turned down for Scottish funding because it did not project a sufficiently positive image of the country. It turned into a trilogy – *My Ain Folk* and *My Way Home* were produced in 1973 and 1978 – whose reputation is in inverse proportion to the budget of less than £40,000 on which they were made. Indeed, the 'Trilogy' has taken on an almost legendary status as one of Britain's truly innovative cinema creations and it was indicative of a turn by British directors towards a European arthouse tradition of cinema-making of which *Another Time, Another Place*, winner of a whole series of European prizes, is one of the major outcomes. Radford, born in India to an English father and an Austrian mother, had only a brief period of acclimatisation to Scottish culture as a teacher in a college in Edinburgh, but a television film of Jessie Kesson's *The White Bird Passes*, made for BBC Scotland in 1980, led to the plan for a larger-scale adaptation of one of Kesson's other works. *Another Time, Another Place* was to be the beginning of a very successful international career for Radford, including films such as *1984* and *Il Postino*, while Douglas, before his early death in 1991, produced only one full-length film, *Comrades*, in 1984.

Both *My Childhood* and *Another Time, Another Place* look back to the Second World War and have as their protagonist a character who develops a relationship with prisoners of war working on the land. In *My Childhood*, a German prisoner of war, Helmut, befriends Jamie, who is one of two brothers deserted by their parents and living in abject poverty with their grandmother in a desolate and run-down Scottish coalmining town. For Jamie, Helmut, one of the 'enemy' (as is underlined by a scene in an air-raid shelter), has become a surrogate for the father who has abandoned him, and together they read a children's book and begin to learn each other's languages. Helmut's inevitable departure leaves Jamie bereft: while the prisoner of war can return home, Jamie is already at home but has no home, and, in the final sequence, leaps on to a coal wagon that gradually carries him beyond the boundaries of the village and out of shot. In *Another Time, Another Place*, the central character, Janie, is a 'young woman' (as she is called throughout the novel), who is married to a dour farmer some fifteen years her senior and on whose farm are quartered Italian prisoners of war. She is fascinated by their very different culture, full, as it seems to her, of a sensual responsiveness to life that is entirely absent from her own. When she becomes romantically and sexually involved with them, it is at terrible cost to them all.

For the prisoners of war in *My Childhood* and *Another Time, Another Place* rural Scotland is no idyllic escape from modernity. *My Childhood*, shot in black and white, reduces the landscape to a featureless flatness, like the suspended lives of the prisoners whose labour, under the eye of a soldier with a gun, is punishment, while the colour of *Another Time, Another Place* is used to emphasise how colourless is the landscape – as bleak in its monotony as the work that has to be done on the farm. In both, what the prisoners of war ironically underline is how much greater is their freedom than the people of the community among whom they temporarily live: they have a home to which, one day, they will return, whereas the Scots are trapped in an imprisonment that is apparently without end. As Jessie Kesson's novel puts it:

> Times like these, the young woman felt imprisoned within the circumference of the field. Trapped by the monotony of work that wearied the body and dulled the mind. Rome had been taken. Allies had landed in Normandy, she'd heard that on the wireless. 'News' that had caused great excitement in the bothy, crowded with friends, gesticulating in wild debate. Loud voices in dispute. Names falling casually from their tongues, out of books from her school-room days. The Alban Hills, The Tibrus . . . 'O Tibrus, Father Tibrus. To whom the Romans pray . . .' Even in her schooldays those names had sounded unreal. Outdistanced by centuries, from another time. Another place.[112]

The 'young woman' is the real prisoner, the 'servant of circumstances'.[113] Her brief relationship with one of the prisoners will confirm the sensual poverty of the world in which she lives, just as Jamie's relationship with Helmut will confirm the material and spiritual poverty of the 'family' in which he is growing up. Both films succeed in evading the nostalgia for a return to an idealised, rural Scotland by seeing Scotland in the light of the real nostalgia of prisoners of war who ache to return to their homelands. Nostalgia, for them, is possible precisely because they come from places rich in culture, rich in colour. No such nostalgia is possible for the Scots, whose memories are, like Janie's, only of a lost world they were once introduced to in school, or, like Jamie, of a life of exclusion and rejection. Hofer's description of the symptoms of nostalgia are in fact the symptoms of the Scots who are already at home: Jamie's grandmothers both waste away in the course of the film in bouts of weeping and melancholia; his mother, incarcerated in an institution, hides under the sheets when Jamie goes to see her, refusing contact with the world, and she, too, wastes away. In the children's 'home' to which he is sent, Jamie himself refuses food and his 'despondency' and 'melancholia' are such that he agrees to be taken back by his father despite his awareness that there is no home for him to return to. The original meaning of nostalgia is here – it is a disease which has come to inflict a civilian population 'on the home front', where 'home' represents just as profound a separation from a sustaining community as being at war did for Hofer's Swiss soldiers. In these films, the desire of the Scottish characters to escape from their 'imprisonment' may be just as powerful as it is for the prisoners of war but they have no place to return to. They are displaced persons for whom nostalgia can have no object. In *Another Time, Another Place*, the Italian prisoners of war make themselves at home, creating their own shrine in the bothy where they live; the 'young woman', at home, can find home only indirectly – and briefly – in them. Janie's desire is for that other time, that other place that is home to them.

Whatever its roots in Bill Douglas's personal experience, *My Childhood* and its sequels have been read not simply as the account of the life of one extremely unfortunate family but as an iconic overturning of the nostalgic representation of the nation. In a volume intended to honour Douglas's achievement, *Bill Douglas: A Lanternist's Account*,[114] Andrew O'Hagan's essay, 'Homing', seeks to locate the significance of his own childhood through Douglas's work:

> I thought of how my own growing awareness of small-town life had been given a painstaking visual language in the films of Bill Douglas. It was an awareness of broken promises and crumbling illusions – both inside my home and outside, in the shambolic 'ideal corporate living space' that was the Scottish new town. Scotland, my own imagined community, had produced an artist who mocked the quixotic posturing of a bogus national identity – exploding the tired, iron platitudes of family loyalty, couthy neighbours and yer ain fireside . . .[115]

In Douglas's films the 'flickering shadow-play of great cinematic art'[116] is capable not only of reshaping our sense of Scottish film but has 'the capacity to break with our traditional sense of nationhood'.[117] Scotland, the nation, is not a place about which to be nostalgic: 'Scotland's search for a noble identity, as ever, means nothing more than the ceremonial waving of a blank banner and collective aversion of eyes from prevailing, indigenous social injustice'.[118] 'Home', for O'Hagan – and, he assumes, for Douglas – is a place which one has to discover by travelling in 'the opposite direction from the religious pieties and cultural prejudices' which represent 'the traditional values and supposed certainties of his Scottish roots'.[119] 'Will I never get out of this place?' Janie keens in *Another Time, Another Place*.

Framing, in their dates of production, the referendum of 1979, these films also frame the terms of the debate by which Scottish culture was defined in that period: on one side was the nostalgic indulgence of 'Scotch myths' – what came to be known as 'Tartanry and Kailyard' – and on the other side a 'realism' which could force its audience to acknowledge Scotland as a place of exploitation, suffering and repression. As Joyce McMillan puts it:

> The standard iconography of working-class community life, in Scotland as elsewhere in the industrialised world, is all to do with compensatory virtues of warmth and solidarity, with the innate decency and the family values that, in legend, kept the home fires burning and the doorsteps gleaming white even in the toughest times; with the sense that 'we', the workers, were more caring people, for all our poverty. It takes a brave man to drive a coach and horses of bitter memory through all that.[120]

The power of Douglas's work lies in its ability to unravel the myths by which Scotland conceals itself from itself, or, as O'Hagan puts it, in its 'critical assault on the cultural tradition that draws much of its force from the Kailyard'.[121] Douglas's films with their absent, careless fathers, no less than *Another Time, Another Place*'s presentation of 'the young woman' trapped in the power of an apparently infertile patriarchy, can thus be seen to 'explode effectively the fanciful mythology which has long held sway in romantic tales of Scottish childhood, family and community'.[122] The abused child and the repressed wife, living in the constrictions of a poverty both material and spiritual, refute Burns's belief in a community where, 'With joy unfeign'd, *brothers* and *sisters* meet,/And each for other's welfare kindly speirs', and treat with irony his plea that 'Heaven' may 'their simple lives prevent/From luxury's contagion'.[123] Poverty in these films cannot be the basis for communality or for spirituality: such virtues can be encountered only through the people classified by the nation as the 'enemy', prisoners of war nostalgic for another place.

The debates from which Scottish film criticism emerged in the 1970s were ones in which criticism saw its function as resistance to the falsehoods apparently endemic to whatever might constitute the tradition of Scottish film – what Colin McArthur dubbed the 'Scottish Discursive Unconscious'[124] – and by the effort to identify and encourage films which, like Douglas's and Radford's, could be read as negations of those traditions. This, however, was not simply an argument about 'Scottish film culture' but about the influence of Scottish culture on film: the source of the problem for Scottish films was in the national culture itself rather than in the specific conditions under which films were made in Scotland. As Colin McArthur puts it,

> The Scottish Discursive Unconscious has been constructed over several centuries, its key architects including James 'Ossian' Macpherson, Sir Walter Scott, Felix Mendelssohn, Queen Victoria, Sir Edwin Landseer and Sir Harry Lauder. Within it a dream Scotland emerges which is highland, wild, 'feminine', close to nature and which has, above all, the capacity to enchant and transform the stranger . . .[125]

It is not film which is the problem but film's inheritance of over two hundred years of Scottish misrepresentation, a misrepresentation which 'has come to suffuse every sign system: literature, music, easel painting, photography, advertising, right down to film and television in our own day'.[126] It is not film-in-Scotland which is the problem but Scotland-in-film, the whole development of its history and its culture: 'the dire outcome is that, when Scots set out to produce images of their own country, Tartanry and Kailyard exercise a magnetic pull on them, irrespective of what they may wish to do or what they think they are doing'.[127] Importantly, this is not simply the condition of any small country in the era of industrialization and imperial expansion: Scotland's problem is that it is not normal, and, as a consequence, its development was, in the words of Tom Nairn, 'one which naturally appears as "neurosis" in relation to standard models of development'.[128] Xeniteian Scots may happily celebrate Scottish culture while they get on with building their new nationalities, but Scots at home are, in effect, prisoners of war, trapped in a repressive world from which, like actual prisoners of war, it is legally required that one tries to escape.

Douglas's trilogy did not arrive, in other words, simply as a filmic challenge to the nostalgic traditions of film-making about Scotland but as a filmic fulfilment of the long-established nostophobia of much of the Scottish intelligentsia. Thus Jamie's liberation in Part Three of the trilogy comes in Egypt, when he is shut up in an army camp – when he has become the equivalent of those prisoners of war with whom, as a boy, he had consorted. Of course, nostalgia for him is impossible – he has no home to mourn – and so he has to learn the value of 'home' from someone else's nostalgia, from his friend Robert's nostalgia for England. 'Home' is written across Robert's calendar on the day when their tour of duty is due to end and as they prepare to leave Robert invites Jamie to visit him. The film concludes with a long-held image of a rich orchard in bloom, the place to which Robert invites Jamie to 'look us up; you can call it home'. The orchard home is the absolute antithesis of the treeless landscapes of the Egyptian desert in which they have met, a desert which also metaphorically replicates the infertile territory in which Jamie has grown up. Through Jamie's soldiering, in his deployment far from home, Douglas effectively backtracks into the origins of the word 'nostalgia' but allows Jamie – like generations of Scottish intellectuals – to acquire his nostalgia at second hand, nostalgia for a culture whose past has the real 'cultivated ethos'.

Indeed, Douglas's trilogy, despite all the plaudits about its 'realism', runs on the most conventional of narrative lines about working-class life: a boy or a young man with a special talent – think of *This Sporting Life*, *Kes*, *Billy Elliot*, or even *The Full Monty* – allows the film to explore a working class environment while insisting on the individual's ability to transcend it. It is a transcendence, however, which is either temporary – the protagonist is drawn, inevitably and tragically, back into the limitations of the community from which he has sought escape – or, if permanent, simply emphasises how rare and arbitrary such escapes must be. Douglas plays a skilful game with this narrative: Jamie is allowed to tell his family and to tell Robert that he hopes to be an artist or a film director, and the head of the 'home' to which he is sent tells his father he ought to be sent to art school, but unlike the protagonists of these other films we never see him actually engaged in activity which will lead to this conclusion. His life, therefore, is presented as being bleakly empty of creative activity, while Douglas's own was in fact the reverse: his obsession with film was not only sufficient to get him regularly into the local cinemas but to inspire him to send off drawings to Hollywood film studios in the hope of getting a job. No such efforts divert Jamie from his inner torment. The absence of such creative activity in what we see of Jamie's life allows him to seem trapped within the determining boundaries of his working-class experience: his assertion that he wants to be an artist or film director remains, at the level of plot, merely utopian – except, of course, that the film itself is its realisation.

In other words, the 'realism' of Douglas's trilogy is selectively unrealistic; it is through the suppression of the real events of Douglas's own life that it generates its iconic, nostophobic power. There is a moment, however, at the beginning of the second part of the trilogy when the black and white of the rest of the film is suddenly displaced by colour – the colour of a film of 'Lassie' with a backdrop of American pastoral by which the boy's upturned face is mesmerised. The film immediately cuts, of course, to the contrastingly bleak and colourless world of the coal mining town, but it points to what Douglas himself acknowledged in his essay on 'Palace of Dreams': 'For as long as I can remember I always liked the pictures. As a boy I spent so much time in cinemas, a friend suggested I take my bed with me. I would have, had it been possible. That was my real home, my happiest place when I was lucky enough to be there. Outside, whether in the village or the city, whether I was seven or seventeen, it always seemed to be raining or grey and my heart would sink to despairing depths. I hated reality'.[129] 'Home' is, in effect, the world of film: it is the world of film itself for which Jamie/Douglas are nostalgic, and which drives their nostophobia towards their actual home.

Because the theory of film has been developed largely from and in relation to the major centres in which film production is possible, we take too little account of the extent to which film, in the first half of the twentieth century, quite literally displaced and made redundant the traditions of local popular culture. In the music halls which the cinemas replaced, even touring companies would incorporate material specifically tailored to its local audience, or would incorporate local performers. The music hall's mode of address was interactive: film, as Adorno and Horkheimer disenchantedly pointed out, was not only consumed passively but was designed to encourage passivity: 'all the other films and products of the entertainment industry which they have seen have taught them what to expect: they react automatically. The might of industrial society is lodged in men's minds'.[130] The effect, they believed, was one in which 'the whole world is made to pass through the filter of the culture industry. The old experience of the movie-goer, who sees the world outside as an extension of the film he has just left (because the latter is intent upon reproducing the world of everyday perceptions), is now the producer's guideline ... Real life is becoming indistinguishable from the movies'.[131] This may have been the case in Frankfurt, Berlin, Paris or in the Los Angeles where Adorno and Horkheimer had taken refuge during the Second World War and where *The Dialectic of Enlightenment* was written, but movies had the absolutely opposite effect in places which had no access to the scale of audience and the scale of industrial production necessary for making them. Instead of 'real life becoming indistinguishable from the movies', the movies represented a 'real' life which rendered the actuality of local culture empty, insignificant, and unrealisable within the creative processes of modernity. Life had to imitate the elsewhere of the movies – as John Byrne's *Slab Boys* (1978) and his television series *Tutti Frutti* (1987) comedically insisted – if there was to be a continuity between film culture and local culture. Douglas, sitting down to create a film after he graduated from film school, could not attempt costume drama or adaptations of contemporary novels because of the cost: the restrictions of the medium for which he was writing forced him to write about his childhood: 'strangely enough, my trilogy is not about a dream world, but about the real landscape I had wanted so badly to escape from'.[132] Except, of course, it is not the real landscape but the nostophobic recollection of that landscape as refracted through its absence from the world of film, through its estrangement from the filmic world, through its creator's and protagonist's nostalgia to be at home in the world of film. The form of film, in its mid-twentieth-century technological development, insisted that local culture could be represented only as a nostalgic place lost in time or as its nostophobic antithesis, a place for which no nostalgia is possible.

That the narrative of Scottish films is driven by modes of escapism – whether the escapism of the fantasy narratives of *Whisky Galore!* or *Local Hero* or the escapism of the 'realistic' films which show someone, like Jamie, escaping his destructive environment – is not a commentary upon Scotland but a commentary on the nature of film itself in the first fifty years of its development. Film is an inherently nostalgic medium: even the most 'realistic' of movies frames a time which, through time, becomes 'another time, another place', and the possible location of a lost emotional homeland. Film made its audiences, like Jamie and Janie, homeless at home, nostalgic for that other time, that other place of the film itself.

Walter Scott, despite the criticism heaped on him for creating a national nostalgia, never allowed his readers to forget that they were *readers* and that the purpose of their reading was founded on the pleasure of illusion, on what Sandy Stranger, in Muriel Spark's *The Prime of Miss Jean Brodie*, calls 'The Transfiguration of the Commonplace'. It is such a transfiguration of the commonplace that Douglas's trilogy achieves – a transfiguration just as magical, and just as distant from representational realism, as the films – like *Whisky Galore!* or *Local Hero* – to which it has been regularly opposed. Nostophobia is no escape from nostalgia: it is the product of that profound nostalgia for film itself which was produced by the first wave of globalised mass entertainment: as Andrew O'Hagan nostalgically recalls, a Scottish childhood was one in which 'I stretched out on the grass chewing my hands, reading about the lives of American movie stars in large-format colour books', one in which 'I lost myself in Harpo's laugh, Lombard's crash, or Marilyn's fatal affairs with the Kennedys'.[133] Nostophobia is not an escape from national nostalgia: it begins and ends in identification with someone else's nostalgia.

Notes

1. Selby-Bigge, L. A. (ed.), David Hume, *A Treatise of Human Nature* (Oxford: Clarendon Press, 1888), p. 85.
2. Ibid. p. 86.
3. Beansblossom, R. E. and K. Lehrer, *Thomas Reid's Inquiry and Essays* (Indianapolis: Hackett Publishing, 1983), p. 99.
4. Ibid. p. 118.
5. Smith, N. K., *The Philosophy of David Hume: A Critical Study of its Origins and Central Doctrines* (London: Macmillan, 1941), p. 236.
6. Selby-Bigge (ed), Hume, *A Treatise of Human Nature*, p. 11.
7. Ibid. pp. 12–13.
8. Ibid. p. 88.
9. Ibid. p. 166. See also Locke, J., *An Essay Concerning Human Understanding, The Works of John Locke in Nine Volumes*, 12th edn (London, 1824), Part 1, Ch. XXXIII, 5, p. 419; available at <http://oll.libertyfund.org/titles/761> (last accessed 27 October 2015). For Locke, association is the accidental uniting of ideas in the mind as a result of custom or education, producing disruptive 'gangs' which cannot be policed by reason; for Hume, on the other hand, 'reason is, and ought only to be the slave of the passions'.

10. Beansblossom and Lehrer (eds), *Reid's Inquiry and Essays*, p. 102.
11. Alison, A., *Essays on the Nature and Principles of Taste*, 2nd edn (Edinburgh: Bell and Bradfute, 1811), Essay 1, pp. 4–5.
12. Craig, C., *Associationism and the Literary Imagination: From the Phantasmal Chaos* (Edinburgh: Edinburgh University Press, 2007).
13. Gaskill, H. (ed.), *The Poems of Ossian and Related Works* (Edinburgh: Edinburgh University Press, 1996), p. 382.
14. Ibid. p. 383.
15. Downie, R. S. (ed.), Francis Hutcheson, *Philosophical Writings*, 'Treatise 1; An Inquiry Concerning Beauty, Order, Harmony, Design' (London: J. M. Dent, 1994), p. 15.
16. Gaskill (ed.), *The Poems of Ossian*, p. 354.
17. Ibid. p. 98.
18. Gerard, A., *An Essay on Taste* (London: printed for A. Millar in the *Strand*, A. Kincaid and J. Bell in *Edinburgh*, with three dissertations on same subject by Mr. De Voltaire, Mr. D'Alembert, Mr. De Montesquieu, 1759; Scolar Press reprint, 1971), Part II, Sect IV, 'Of the sensibility of taste', p. 112.
19. Ibid. p. 21.
20. Selby-Bigge (ed), Hume, *Treatise of Human Nature*, Bk II, Part III, Sect. viii, p. 435.
21. Ibid. p. 436.
22. See Gaskill, H., 'Herder, Ossian and the Celtic', in Brown T. (ed.), *Celticism* (Leiden: Rodopi, 1996), pp. 257–72, for the responses in France and Germany to the 'asyndetic abruptness of folk-poetry' and the new appreciation of the 'loose and broken manner' of ancient Greek poetry, especially Pindar; p. 261.
23. Gerard, *An Essay on Taste*, p. 86.
24. Jeffrey, F., 'Essays on the Nature and Principles of Taste by Archibald Alison', *Edinburgh Review*, Vol. XVIII, No. XXXV, May 1811, pp. 1–45, at p. 23.
25. Gaskill (ed.), *Poems of Ossian*, 'Fingal', p. 103.
26. Stafford, F., *The Last of The Race: The Growth of a Myth from Milton to Darwin* (Oxford: Clarendon Press, 1994), p. 94.
27. Ibid. p. 93.
28. Ford, R. (ed.), *The Works of Sir Walter Scott* (London & Glasgow, nd), p. 3.
29. Craig, C. and R. Stevenson (eds), *Twentieth-Century Scottish Drama* (Edinburgh: Canongate, 2001), p. 467.
30. Davis, F., *Yearning for Yesterday: A Sociology of Nostalgia* (London: Collier Macmillan, 1979), p. 1.
31. Quoted in Dickinson, H. and M. Erben, *Nostalgia and Auto/*

Biography: considering the past in the present (Nottingham: Auto/Biography Study Group, 2016), p. 6.
32. Freeman, D., *The South to Prosperity: an Introduction to the Writings of Confederate History* (New York: Scribner's, 1939), p. 4.
33. Murdoch, S. and A. Grosjean, *Alexander Leslie and the Scottish Generals of the Thirty Years War, 1618–1648* (London: Pickering and Chatto, 2014).
34. Routledge, C., *Nostalgia: A Psychological Resource* (London: Routledge, 2016).
35. Jeffrey, F., 'Robert Burns' (January 1809), *Contributions to the Edinburgh Review* (London: Longman, Brown, Green and Longmans, 1853), p. 429–30.
36. Hook, A., Sir Walter Scott, *Waverley* (Harmondsworth: Penguin, 1792), p. 492.
37. Nash, A., 'The Kailyard: Problem or Illusion?', Manning, S. (ed.), *Edinburgh History of Scottish Literature, Volume 2, Enlightenment, Britain and Empire (1707–1918)*, (Edinburgh: Edinburgh University Press, 2007), p. 317.
38. Barrie, J. M., *The Works of J. M. Barrie, Auld Licht Idylls* (London: Hodder and Stoughton, 1888), p. 69.
39. Barrie, J. M., *Sentimental Tommy* (London: Cassell and Company, 1896), pp. 25–6.
40. McNally, D., *Political Economy and the Rise of Capitalism: A Reinterpretation* (Berkeley: University of California Press, 1988).
41. Sorenson, J., 'Folk Songs, Ballads, Popular Drama and Sermons', in Manning, S. (ed.), *The Edinburgh History of Scottish Literature* Volume 2, *Enlightenment, Britain and Empire (1707–1918)* (Edinburgh: Edinburgh University Press, 2007), p. 137.
42. Hook, A., *Scotland and America: A Study of Cultural Relations* (Glasgow: Blackie, 1975), p. 117.
43. Noble, A. and P. S. Hogg (eds) *The Canongate Burns* (Edinburgh: Canongate, 2001), p. 91.
44. Ibid, pp. 89–90.
45. Goethe, J. W. von, *The Sorrows of Young Werther*, trans. Michael Hulse (London: Penguin, 1989), p. 95.
46. Ibid. p. 125.
47. Nobel and Hogg (eds), *Canongate Burns*, pp. 335–6.
48. Available at <http://www.nls.uk/catalogues/boslit> (last accessed 21 March 2017).
49. Basu, P., *Highland Homecomings: Genealogy and Heritage Tourism in the Scottish Diaspora* (New York: Routledge, 2007), pp. 67–8.

50. Shepherd, N., *The Grampian Quartet* (Edinburgh: Canongate, 1996), *The Living Mountain*, p. 1.
51. Ibid. p.2.
52. Garside, P. (ed.), Walter Scott, *Guy Mannering* (Edinburgh: Edinburgh University Press, 1999), p. 517.
53. Hesse, D., *Warrior Dreams: playing Scotsmen in mainland Europe, 1945 – 2010*, Edinburgh University PhD, available at <https://www.era.lib.ed.ac.uk/handle/1842/5971> (last accessed at 18 February 2017).
54. Shepherd, *Grampian Quartet*, *The Living Mountain*, p. 5.
55. Ford, R. (ed.), *The Poetical Works of Sir Walter Scott* (London and Glasgow: nd, *c.* 1863), p. 103, Canto V, XXXIV.
56. Ibid. p. 103, Canto V, 'Introduction', p. 89.
57. Ibid. p. 90.
58. Ibid. p. 90.
59. Ibid. p. 99, Canto V, XXV.
60. Ibid. p. 99, Canto V, XXVI.
61. Ibid. p. 103, Canto VI
62. Ibid. p.105.
63. Ibid. p. 105.
64. Sutherland, J., *The Life of Walter Scott: A Critical Biography* (Oxford: Blackwell, 1995), p. 198.
65. Mack, D. (ed.), Walter Scott, *The Tale of Old Mortality* (Edinburgh: Edinburgh University Press, 1993), p. 7.
66. Ibid. p. 7.
67. Thomas McCrie published his review of *Old Mortality* in the *Christian Instructor* in 1817; it is included in his son Thomas's edition of his father's *Miscellaneous Writings, Chiefly Historical* (Edinburgh: John Johnstone, 1841).
68. Sutherland, *Life of Walter Scott*, p. 200.
69. Mack (ed.), Walter Scott, *The Tale of Old Mortality*, p. 264.
70. Ibid. p. 265.
71. Ibid. p. 265.
72. Ibid. p. 268.
73. Ibid. p. 269.
74. Ibid. p. 11.
75. This accords with Catherine Jones's argument in *Literary Memory: Scott's Waverley Novels and the Psychology of Narrative* (Lewisburg: Bucknell University Press, 2003), that 'one dimension of the Waverley novels is their presentation of a breakdown of narrative order' in which 'fragmentary memory is the narrative realization in form, allegory or theme of historical trauma', that trauma being provoked by a realisation that history does not progress but 'repeats itself' (pp. 131–2).
76. Carey, J. (ed). James Hogg, *The Private Memoirs and Confessions*

of a Justified Sinner (Oxford: Oxford University Press, 1970), p. 240.
77. Leavis, F. R., *The Great Tradition: George Eliot, Henry James, Joseph Conrad* (London: Chatto & Windus), p. 5.
78. Frye, N., *Anatomy of Criticism: Four Essays* (Princeton: Princeton University Press, 1957), p. 304.
79. Ibid. p. 307
80. Jerome McGann, lecture to the biannual Walter Scott conference, Eugene Oregon 2001; published as 'Walter Scott's Romantic postmodernity' in Davis, Duncan and Sorensen (eds), *The Borders of Romanticism* (Cambridge: Cambridge University Press, 2004), pp. 113–30.
81. Timothy C. Baker in *Contemporary Scottish Gothic: Mourning, Authenticity, and Tradition* (London: Palgrave, 2014), has demonstrated how regularly modern Scottish novels redeploy the Gothic trope of the found manuscript (Chapters 2 and 3).
82. Massie, A., *The Ragged Lion* (London: Hodder and Stoughton, [1994] 1995), p. 88.
83. Ibid. p. 4.
84. Crawford, R., *Devolving English Literature* (Oxford: Clarendon, 1992), pp. 156–75.
85. Robertson, J., *The Fanatic* (London: Fourth Estate, 2000), p. 52.
86. Ibid. p. 49.
87. Robertson, J., *The Testament of Gideon Mack* (London: Penguin, 2006), p. 135.
88. Robertson, J. (ed.), *Scottish Ghost Stories* (London: Warner Books, 1996), p. ix.
89. MacDiarmid, H., *Contemporary Scottish Studies* (Edinburgh: Scottish Educational Journal, n.d.), p. 31
90. Ibid. p. 32.
91. Ibid. p. 114.
92. Ibid. p. 114.
93. Muir, E., *Scott and Scotland* (London: Routledge, 1936), pp. 11–12.
94. Craig, D., *Scottish Literature and the Scottish People, 1680–1830* (London: Chatto & Windus, 1961), p. 13.
95. MacDiarmid, H., 'Editorial', *The Voice of Scotland*, Vol. II, No. 2, December 1945, p. 29.
96. MacDiarmid, H., 'Editorial', *The Voice of Scotland*, Vol VI, No. 3 October 1965, p.3; MacDiarmid, H. 'Editorial', *The Voice of Scotland*, Vol. VI, No. 4, January 1956, p. 3.
97. Davis, F., *Yearning for Yesterday: A Sociology of Nostalgia* (London: Collier Macmillan, 1979), p. 14.

98. Morgan, E., *Collected Poems 1949–1987* (Manchester: Carcanet, 1990), p. 203.
99. 'Change and the need for more change', *Scottish International*, No. 2 April 1968, p. 2.
100. Lloyd, J., 'Open Letter to Archie Hind', *Scottish International*, October 1971, p. 17 (this issue does not have a volume number).
101. Ibid. p. 17.
102. Possum, 'News Review: Who Will Kill the Commission', *Scottish International*, Vol. 6, No. 4, April, 1973, p. 3.
103. Hardman, J., 'What Kind of Scotland: Documentary: A View of the Conference', *Scottish International*, Vol. 6, No. 6, May–June–July, 1973, p. 11.
104. Ibid. p. 11.
105. Nairn, T., 'Culture and Nationalism: An Open Letter from Tom Nairn', *Scottish International*, Vol 6, No. 4, April, 1973, p. 7.
106. Ibid. p. 8.
107. Ibid. p. 7.
108. Ibid. p. 8.
109. Ibid. p. 7.
110. Quoted, Tom Nairn, 'Open Letter', *Scottish International*, April 1973, p. 7.
111. Available at <http://www.imdb.com/title/tt0012398/> and <http://www.imdb.com/title/tt0013318/> (last accessed 6 July 2017).
112. Kesson, J., *Another Time, Another Place* (Edinburgh: B. & W., [1983] 1993), p. 101.
113. Ibid. p. 115.
114. Dick, E., A. Noble and D. Petrie (eds), *Bill Douglas: A Lanternist's Account* (London: BFI, 1993).
115. Ibid. p. 206.
116. Ibid. p. 206.
117. Ibid. p. 206.
118. Ibid. p. 212.
119. Ibid. p. 213.
120. Dick, Noble and Petrie (eds), 'Women in the Bill Douglas Trilogy', *Bill Douglas: A Lanternist's Account* p. 220.
121. Dick, Noble and Petrie (eds), 'Homing', *Bill Douglas: A Lanternist's Account*, p. 210.
122. Ibid. p. 207.
123. Ibid. p. 92.
124. McArthur, C., *Brigadoon, Braveheart, and the Scots: Distortions of Scotland in Hollywood Cinema* (London: I. B. Tauris, 2003). p. 8ff.
125. Ibid. p. 12.
126. Ibid. p. 12.

127. McArthur, C., *The Cinema Image of Scotland* (London: Tate Gallery, 1986), p. 8.
128. Nairn, T., *The Break-up of Britain: Crisis and Neo-Nationalism* (London, 1981: Verso, 1977), p. 153.
129. Available at <https://www.bdcmuseum.org.uk/about/palace-of-dreams-the-making-of-a-film-maker/> (last accessed 1 September 2017).
130. Adorno, T. and M. Horkheimer, 'The Culture Industry', *Dialectic of Enlightenment* (London: Verso, 1979; 1944), p. 126.
131. Ibid. p. 126.
132. Ibid. p. 126.
133. Dick, Noble and Petrie (eds), *Bill Douglas: A Lanternist's Account*, p. 205.

4 Theoxenia: Openings to the Gods

I Recuperations

In the early 1950s, London publishers Routledge had been contracted to publish a study of nineteenth-century Scottish philosophy by George Elder Davie; they asked, however, if he could add an introductory chapter outlining the institutional context in which Scottish philosophy had developed. That chapter, nearly a decade later, became *The Democratic Intellect*,[1] a book-length study of how Scottish philosophy first resisted and then capitulated to intellectual specialisation. The book to which *The Democratic Intellect* is a prologue was not finally published until 2001, under the title of *The Scotch Metaphysics: A Century of Enlightenment in Scotland*. *The Scotch Metaphysics*, thus paradoxically both an earlier and a later book than *The Democratic Intellect*, was focused on a very technical exposition of how Scottish philosophers had attempted to validate our fundamental belief in the reality of an external world by showing that the senses, and particularly the senses of sight and touch, compensate for each other's limitations, and how, from our experience of particular objects, we manage to develop abstract ideas. According to Davie, the reason that this constitutes a particularly 'Scotch metaphysics' is that there is

> . . . a certain continuity between the work of the quartet of nineteenth-century philosophers I examine, namely Stewart, Brown, Hamilton and Ferrier, and that of the eighteenth-century quartet composed of Hutcheson, Hume, Reid and Smith. The title serves

> to mark off the debates of these eighteenth and nineteenth-century Scottish philosophers from the debates engaged in by philosophers in England and Ireland. It distinguishes a set of philosophical problems that have less affinity with the latter than with questions being treated then and to be treated later by philosophers on the continent of Europe.[2]

The continuity of this tradition is made possible and intensified by the ways in which nineteenth-century Scottish philosophers devote much of their intellectual energy to reviewing and promoting their eighteenth-century predecessors: in Dugald Stewart's case through his biographical essays on Adam Smith, William Robertson and Thomas Reid, and the account in his *Dissertation Exhibiting the Progress of Metaphysical, Ethical and Political Philosophy, since the Revival of Letters in Europe*, of 'The Metaphysical Philosophy of Scotland';[3] in Brown's case through his defence of Hume's theory of causality in his *Observations on the Nature and Tendency of the Doctrines of Mr Hume, concerning the relation of cause and effect* (Edinburgh, 1806); and in Hamilton's case by his edition of Reid's works (1849), with its enormous apparatus of supplementary arguments intended to validate and extend Reid's philosophical positions.

For Davie, this continuity of metaphysical interests establishes them as participants in a philosophical debate which forms part of a distinctive national culture. *The Democratic Intellect* has become an icon of the ongoing assertion of Scottish difference but in fact the story that Davie told was one of the erasure of that difference, of a Scottish philosophical tradition ground down between the forces, within its own national boundaries, of religious division, and, from outwith its borders, by the pressures of Anglicisation and the gradual integration of Scotland's universities to English norms. It is a book torn between celebration of the achievements of a generalism that resulted from philosophy's central place in the Scottish university curriculum and a despairing acknowledgment of the country's inability to build on that heritage: increasingly, in Davie's view, philosophy would itself become a specialism, a specialism in which development would be directed by English rather than Scottish arguments – in the early twentieth century by Moore and Russell, later by Austin and Ryle. For Davie, J. F. Ferrier was the last of the line of the 'Scotch metaphysics', and in his abandonment of

Common Sense he prefigured the nation's abandonment of its cultural traditions:

> The Scottish Universities, in their anxiety to accommodate themselves to the expansive epoch of Durbars and Jubilees, had suddenly turned their backs on the long procession of characteristic personalities, whose memory had hitherto always inspired the continuing adventure of the democratic intellect. An all-embracing oblivion engulfed the heroes of Scottish learning since Renaissance-Reformation times, and the same neglect which overwhelmed mid-Victorians like Sir William Hamilton and Principal Forbes and Dr. Melvin equally blotted out their eighteenth-century equivalents like Thomas Reid and Colin Maclaurin and Thomas Ruddiman. Thus at the very time when other neighbouring countries were becoming increasingly 'history-minded', the Scots were losing their sense of the past, and their leading institutions, including the Universities, were emphatically resolved – to use a catch phrase fashionable in Scotland of the early twentieth century – 'no longer to be prisoners of their own history'.[4]

Like a philosophical 'Old Mortality' that keeps the memory of the national philosophy alive while brooding over the symbols of its death, *The Democratic Intellect* is deeply shaped by the nostophobia of mid-twentieth-century Scotland. But simply by recording the influence of nineteenth-century Scottish philosophy it kept open the possibility of finding a new relevance for that philosophy at some point in the future, and with the emergence of the notion of the Scottish Enlightenment not only did the work of Hume and Smith acquire a new centrality to the Western philosophical tradition, but the Common Sense tradition initiated by Reid, and apparently abandoned by Scottish philosophy in the latter part of the nineteenth century, became again a relevant part of modern philosophical debate.

Davie's perspective on the history of Scottish philosophy was, however, to be significantly extended by Alexander Broadie's researches into medieval Scottish philosophy in books such as *The Circle of John Mair* (1985) and *The Shadow of Scotus: Philosophy and Faith in Pre-Reformation Scotland* (1995). What Broadie's work revealed was that the eighteenth century was not a unique period of Scottish philosophical achievement and that there were distinct continuities in the thought of earlier and later Scottish philosophers: 'There is no doubt', Broadie wrote in his *The Tradition of Scottish Philosophy* (1990), 'that it is possible to trace a line of philosophical influence from Mair's circle to the philosophers of the Scottish Enlightenment'.[5] The Enlightenment, often presented as the outcome of English influence in Scotland after the Union, could be seen in an alternative historical perspective which brought together two apparently separate periods of Scottish intellectual life as a possibly continuous tradition, one which Broadie was later to trace in detail in his *History of Scottish Philosophy* (2009).[6] In the introduction to that book Broadie notes that even although he was a student of George Elder Davie in the 1960s, only Hume featured in his education, no mention being made of any other Scottish philosopher: the amnesia Davie had identified as overwhelming the Scottish philosophical tradition in the latter part of the nineteenth century was maintained even in the philosophy department of which he was a member in the 1960s. Indeed, Davie himself revised his version of events with the publication of *The Crisis of the Democratic Intellect* in 1986, in which he argued that a series of accidents resulting from the efforts of the recently formed Scottish Education Department to integrate the universities into their newly planned secondary school system allowed philosophy to recover its place in the university curriculum; as a result not only did philosophy regain some of its previous status, but by 'reversing the anti-intellectual currents which, throughout the rest of Britain, were cutting philosophy off from the other subjects and were getting it to withdraw into itself in a self-complacent exclusiveness', philosophy 'began to reforge its broken links with the sciences, human as well as natural'.[7] The death of the generalist tradition of Scottish philosophy might therefore have been postponed but it was merely delayed: with the expansion of the universities after the Second World War, English philosophy swamped Scottish universities and eradicated its traditions, promoting the notion that 'philosophy was the handmaiden of the sciences and not [as Scottish thinkers argued] their metaphysical critic'.[8] Even those Scottish thinkers who maintained the tradition of 'speculative metaphysics'[9] that had been abandoned in England, were, in the end, defeated by the very spirit they were resisting, for when the philosophies of those who maintained the Scottish tradition, such as Kemp Smith and John Anderson

> fail to achieve a full and systematic development, and peter out in hesitations, silences, and loose ends, it is because, in working

> out their positions as professional philosophers, they are too much affected by the separatist spirit of which Russell, indeed, was the chief proponent in Britain, but which made its mark on a whole generation of thinkers, whatever their positions.[10]

The death of Scottish philosophy may have been a slow one, stretching from the Disruption of 1843 to the Robbins Committee on Higher Education in 1963, but it was a death nonetheless. Philosophy in Scotland no longer recognised 'the Scotch Metaphysic' as relevant to the discipline that it professed. Ironically, Davie's deep-seated pessimism about Scottish traditions, characteristic of the nostophobia of his generation, was about to be reversed as research into the origins and consequences of the Scottish Enlightenment became a worldwide enterprise that brought scholars from many countries to Edinburgh, Glasgow and Aberdeen to study the Scottish philosophical tradition. The philosophy departments in Scottish universities might no longer be interested in Scottish philosophy – indeed, one might argue they were no longer interested in *philosophy* as it had traditionally been conceived – but Scottish philosophy proved to be of profound interest to historians of many other disciplines in a recuperation which was to be characteristic of many areas of Scottish culture between the first referendum on the establishment of a Scottish government in 1979 and the second in 1997.

One of the features of Davie's account of Scottish thought in *The Democratic Intellect*, was the deep commitment of Scottish philosophy to the work of Isaac Newton. Not only had the Scottish universities been the first to teach Newton's theories in the 1690s, Scots such as David Gregory (1659–1708), John Keill (1671–1721) and Colin Maclaurin (1698–1746), had been amongst Newton's closest associates and supporters,[11] and the Newtonianism they did much to establish came to be regarded as crucial to the Scottish intellectual tradition. It was a tradition in which the poet James Thomson was trained at Edinburgh University and informed his poem 'The Seasons' which, through its several revisions between 1726 and 1746, did much to reshape the eighteenth century's conception of the natural world. In his 'Poem Sacred to the Memory of Isaac Newton', Thomson had declared:

> O unprofuse magnificence divine!
> O *Wisdom* truly perfect! thus to call

> From a few causes such a scheme of things,
> Effects so various, beautiful, and great,
> An universe complete! and O belov'd
> Of Heaven! whose well-purg'd penetrative eye,
> The mystic veil transpiercing, inly scann'd
> The rising, moving, wide-establish'd frame.

Thomson's assumption that Newton, by revealing the laws of the universe, had made himself at one with the 'divine', was one of the theological underpinnings of Scottish Common Sense philosophy's attempt to combine science and Christian belief. Consequently, the defence of Scotland's independent intellectual tradition in the 1830s turned in part on the issue of the Scottish universities continued support for Newton's mathematics as against 'the great Continental movement, originally Cartesian and Leibnitzian, which by this time had become naturalised in Cambridge'.[12] A key figure in these debates was Sir David Brewster (1781–1868), whose commitment to Newton was such that he produced two biographies, each designed to challenge suggestions that Newton's mind had sometimes been less than 'divine'.

The first, *The Life of Sir Isaac Newton*, published in 1831, was written to refute a French account of Newton by Jean-Baptiste Biot, which suggested that Newton had suffered some kind of mental breakdown in 1692–3, a breakdown which had permanently affected his intellectual capabilities.[13] In the context of Scottish philosophy's integration of Newton's physics with his theology this was a serious charge, as Biot regarded Newton's theology as the product of his intellectual enfeeblement. Brewster, who was amongst the first to have access to Newton's correspondence, insisted on both his continuing intellectual powers and the coherence of his theology with his physics:

> During this period of bodily indisposition, his mind, though in a state of nervous irritability, and disturbed by want of rest, was capable of putting forth its highest powers. At the request of Dr Wallis he drew up an example of one of his propositions on the quadrature of curves in second fluxions. He composed, at the desire of Dr Bentley, his profound and beautiful letters on the existence of the Deity.[14]

For Brewster, Newton's pre-eminence in mathematical physics was a guarantor of the validity of the Christianity to which both of them were committed:

> If such, then, is the character of the Christian faith, we need not be surprised that it was embraced and expounded by such a genius as Sir Isaac Newton. Cherishing its doctrines, and leaning on its promises, he felt it his duty, as it was his pleasure, to apply to it that intellectual strength which had successfully surmounted the difficulties of the material universe . . . [T]he investigation of the sacred mysteries, while it prepared his own mind for its final destiny, was calculated to promote the spiritual interests of thousands. This noble impulse he did not hesitate to obey, and by thus uniting philosophy with religion, he dissolved the league which genius had formed with skepticism, and added to the cloud of witnesses the brightest name of ancient or of modern times.[15]

In his first biography, Brewster gave short shrift to another suggestion that might have sullied Newton's reputation – that he had been steeped in alchemical lore and had been an active alchemist. Although he had found some evidence of notes on alchemical subjects in Newton's handwriting, Brewster treated them as an offshoot of Newton's researches into 'chymical subjects' relating to 'fire, flame and electric attractions'.[16] By the time of his second biography, however, Brewster had become acquainted with previously unresearched papers held by the family of Lord Portsmouth, a collateral descendant of Newton's. In these, Brewster discovered that Newton had pored over the writings of, and taken copious notes from, alchemical 'philosophers', studying them with as much intensity as he had studied the text of the Bible. Given that these were texts and activities 'commencing in fraud and terminating in mysticism', Brewster could find no excuse for Newton's efforts to master alchemy:

> In so far as Newton's inquiries were limited to the transmutation and multiplication of metals, and even to the discovery of the universal tincture, we may find some apology for his researches; but we cannot understand how a mind of such power, and so nobly occupied with the abstractions of geometry, and the study of the material world, could stoop to be even the copyist of the most contemptible alchemical poetry, and the annotator of a work, the obvious production of a fool and a knave.[17]

The Newton who had brought light and enlightenment to the world was a Newton who was also lost in a darkness which the biographer could put down only to 'the mental epidemics of a past age'.[18]

As we now know, however, the real extent of Newton's involvement in alchemy was much greater than even Brewster imagined – Newton's notes have been reckoned to amount to more than a million words.[19] In 1936 the papers which Brewster had looked into came up for auction, after having been refused by the University of Cambridge because they were of no scientific interest. About half were acquired by John Maynard Keynes, who decided, after reviewing them, that 'Newton was not the first of the age of reason. He was the last of the magicians, the last of the Babylonians and Sumerians, the last great mind which looked out on the visible and intellectual world with the same eyes as those who began to build our intellectual inheritance rather less than 10,000 years ago'.[20] The Enlightenment account of Newton as the founder of a rationalist science which would be pursued by all those interested in discovering the truths of the universe – d'Alembert's article on the *Histoire des sciences* in the *Encyclopédie* announces that Newton had given 'philosophy a form which apparently it is to keep'[21] – is contradicted by Newton's own scripts, which reveal him to be committed not to a knowledge which progresses from darkness into light by cutting itself free from the past, but to the recovery of an esoteric body of knowledge which had been known to the ancients. As Piyo Rattansi has argued, Newton 'in his secret thoughts held a vision of history which would very much have astonished the *philosophes*':

> It reduced all he had discovered to a rediscovery of scientific truths well known to some of the great thinkers of the ancient world. One of the few public hints of this attitude was conveyed in a letter which Newton's young *protégé*, the Swiss mathematician Nicolas Fatio de Dullier, wrote some five years after the publication of the *Principia*. For a brief time Fatio had been entrusted with preparing a second edition of the *Principia*. In 1692 he wrote to the great Dutch physicist and Cartesian, Christian Huygens, that Newton had discovered that all the chief propositions of the *Principia* had been known to such ancients as Pythagoras and Plato, although these worthies had turned them into a '*great mystery*'.[22]

Newton toyed with incorporating his historical researches into new editions of the *Principia*, but left only hints; David Gregory, however, in his Newtonian account of *Elements of Astronomy, Physical and Geometrical* (first published in Latin in 1702) was more forthcoming:

> . . . the famous Theorem about the proportion whereby Gravity decreases in receding from the Sun was not unknown at least to *Pythagoras*. This indeed seems to be that which he and his followers would signify to us by the Harmony of the Spheres: That is, they feign'd *Apollo* playing upon an Harp of seven Strings, by which Symbol, as it is abundantly evident from *Pliny, Macrobius* and *Cenforinus*, they meant the Sun in Conjunction with the seven Planets, for they made him the leader of the Septenary Chorus, and Moderator of Nature; and thought that by his Attractive force he acted upon the Planets (and called it Jupiter's Prison, because it is by this Force that he retains and keeps them in their Orbits . . .)[23]

The new astronomy based on the calculations of the effects of gravity is not a modern revelation but ancient truth resurrected.

It was only a year after David Gregory's assertion of this Newtonianism of the ancients that Newton became President of the Royal Society. According to Richard Westfall, Newton had by that time ceased to engage with alchemy: his final notes on the subject date from the mid-1690s, and the only alchemical books in his library published later than 1700 are ones gifted to him.[24] By 1703, it might be thought, Newton had ceased to be the 'alchemical Newton' and had become the Newton of rational modernity, but the very organisation over which he presided had itself been founded by a firm believer both in alchemy and in the secret continuation of ancient truth into the modern world – Sir Robert Moray (1608–73), friend of Richelieu and of Charles II, and the first man inducted into freemasonry on English soil (while he was acting as quarter-master general to the army of the Covenanters, then encamped at Newcastle). Moray, born in Perthshire, was the driving force behind the establishment of the Royal Society and it was by Moray's persuasion that Charles II granted the Society its Royal charter. According to historians of masonry, the success of the Royal Society was based not only on the fact that many of its original members were masons, but that Moray informed the Society with the procedures of the Masonic Lodges – election of the Master (President), no discussion of politics or religion, commitment to equality and fraternity.[25] Scottish Masonic tradition, with its assumption of an ancient wisdom continually renewed through the induction of its aspirants, was incorporated into the foundations of the world's first state organisation devoted to the pursuit of new scientific knowledge. Newton, as President of the Royal Society, was as supported by Scots and by Scottish traditions as powerfully as he had been as the author of the *Principia*, and in the nineteenth century even Brewster's discovery of the alchemical notes did not reduce his status: linking Newton with Boyle and Locke, Brewster concluded that, 'The ambition neither of wealth nor of praise prompted their studies, and we may safely say that a love of truth alone, a desire to make new discoveries in chemistry, and a wish to test the extraordinary pretensions of their predecessors and their contemporaries, were the only motives by which they were actuated'.[26]

There is a certain irony to the fact that Brewster felt the need to write two biographies of Newton, as his most famous contribution to science was the invention, in 1849, of the 'stereoscope', the means by which two images, when looked at through a pair of lenses, seem to become not only one but three-dimensional. Brewster's two accounts of Newton are founded on different bodies of evidence, evidence which might justify a radically different image of its subject. But what unites them is Brewster's continuing belief in the harmony of science and theology that is demonstrated in the life and thought of Newton: 'If Sir Isaac Newton had not been distinguished as a mathematician and a natural philosopher, he would have enjoyed a high reputation as a theologian'.[27] Such harmony between Newtonian science and spiritual truth had, however, come to be regarded with suspicion by romantic poets: as William Blake put it in an epistolary poem addressed to Thomas Butts,

> May God us keep
> From Single vision & Newton's sleep!

It is a thought which is given visual form in a print of 1795, which represents Newton bent over a pair of compasses, with his back turned to the natural world, and which is titled 'Newton: Personification of Man Limited by Reason'. That image was to be taken up by Scottish artist Eduardo Paolozzi in a 1989 sculpture – named 'Master of the Universe' – which sits at the entrance to the Scottish National Gallery of Modern Art (Two) and which reshapes Blake's version of Newton's body into a mechanical structure which, rather than being a living organism, looks as though it has been bolted together from pieces of metal. The sculpture, in a much grander version installed in 1995, now decorates the space outside the British Library in London, but its prominent location is representative not only of the achievements of Scottish art in the last decades of the twentieth century but also of the recuperation of a central element in eighteenth- and nineteenth-century Scottish thought: Paolozzi's statue is a homage not only to William Blake but also a tribute to Davie's account of Newton's role in Scottish thought.

Sir David Brewster, however, has himself been the focus of a significant recuperation of the Scottish past: in 2009 Scottish artist Calum Colvin mounted an exhibition entitled 'Natural Magic|Natural Magic' which celebrated Brewster's *Letters on Natural Magic* of 1832, in which he discusses the apparently magical effects that can be achieved by various kinds of optical illusions. Colvin's artworks were designed to illustrate the ways in which Brewster's stereoscopy could be used as a recuperative technique in relation to Scottish culture: thus the exhibition contained not only a portrait of Brewster himself but portraits of Robert Burns and of Lord Byron, as well as images of those involved in the development of stereoscopy together with a portrait of the artist which alludes to a portrait of his Scottish precursor, Hugh Lyon Playfair.[28] Colvin's exhibition produced innovative modern art by exploiting nineteenth-century Scottish scientific discoveries and used those discoveries to create stereoscopic images of the Scottish culture to which they belonged. Colvin's experiments in stereoscopy were also experiments in historical double vision, combining the Scottish present and Scottish past as though in a stereoscopic lens. This technical recuperation of the Scottish past continued a fundamental theme of Colvin's work in which the stereotypical images of Scottishness were re-imagined through the digital possibilities of modern media. Thus the exhibition entitled *Ossian Fragments of Ancient Poetry*, which was mounted at the Scottish National Portrait Gallery in 2002, reconceptualised the Ossianic bard as a standing stone or sculpture which, through the series of images, gradually decays until the features of the Bard disappear – or, if one walked the exhibition in the opposite direction, till the features come back into focus;[29] similarly, the Burnsiana exhibition of 2013[30] mixes the clichés of Scotland's cultural life with a celebration of the Bard's enduring relevance.

In Colvin's art the Scottish past, both literary and scientific, is recuperated through the most modern technologies as an ongoing contribution to the Scottish present. It effectively develops in visual form the argument of Davie's *The Democratic Intellect*, in which Sir David Brewster is presented as a key figure in the debate about how modern scientific knowledge could continue to be developed 'against the background of Scotch metaphysics'.[31]

II The Art of the Possible

In 1982, Polygon decided to republish Edwin Muir's *Scott and Scotland: the Predicament of the Scottish Writer*, with a new introduction by Allan Massie. Muir's book had first appeared in 1936 but Francis Russell Hart, an American literary critic who had published a study of *Scott's Novels* in 1966, with the subtitle *The Plotting of Historic Survival*, concluded his 1978 study of *The Scottish Novel*, by suggesting that 'there is still much truth in Edwin Muir's gloomy diagnosis of the novel in Scotland',[32] a view with which Massie concurred, not only in his introduction to the re-issue of Muir's book but in his review of Hart's in the *London Magazine*, in which he suggested that Hart had identified the 'real problem which nobody in Scotland had answered satisfactorily. How do you write about a second-hand society?' In the aftermath of the Referendum of 1979, the 'plotting of historic survival' seemed as difficult for the novel as for the nation.

And yet the rise of nationalism offered Massie the opportunity of an apparently historic event in Scotland itself, and in *One Night in Winter*, published in 1984,[33] Massie presented Fraser Donnelly as the putative leader of a Scottish nationalist movement which he claims will bring about 'a real revolution, a revolution of consciousness, a revolution of morals', one that will allow Scots to escape 'the auld Scotland of kirk and kailyard' and produce a country 'that's free and rich too'.[34] What Donnelly actually surrounds himself with, however, is not a modern political machine of the kind that the SNP had been building in the 1960s and 70s and that had gained them 11 Westminster seats in 1974, but 'a Court'[35] as full of intrigue and sexual corruption as any in Renaissance Italy. That archaic social structure is, however, only the gateway to even more atavistic emotion: 'sometimes you have to go back in time to make the next leap'[36] he tells one of his courtiers, Jimmy, who later explains its significance:

> As for what he meant by a' that going back in time, well, he'd been doing an awfy lot of reading – that surprises you, that Fraser's a great reader, it shouldna – about old religions, the Ancient Greek Mysteries, and he'd got haud of the notion that they offered the sort of transcendental experience you needed for real sexual liberation.[37]

In Fraser Donnelly, nationalism is figured as a retreat from modernity and a return to primitivism, as the invitation to the dark gods of the ancient religions – the 'Greek Mysteries' – to engulf civilisation. Fraser Donnelly travels to the Mediterranean in the hope of an encounter with those gods, re-enacting in practice the explorations of the primitive that J. G. Frazer had undertaken as he traced, in the successive versions of *The Golden Bough* published between 1890 and 1916, the meaning of magic and religion in the history of early humanity. To the ancient Greeks hospitality to strangers had been a moral imperative because one never knew when such strangers might be the gods in disguise, come to take stock of the mortals whose lives they oversaw: theoxenia, hospitality to strangers, was a pragmatic insurance against a surprise violation of the order of the universe. The gods that Donnelly seeks do not, however, come back as kindly strangers but as the destructive release of primitive violence. For Donnelly, 'any pagan ceremony must be intended to liberate the Life-Force' and he therefore seeks in Crete a place where ancient ceremonies might still survive; to those who travel with him,

> It was impossible not to feel that Fraser had given them something of profound reminiscent appeal; that the Buick had carried them like a chariot across the gulfs of history, back to the dawn, to a time when the bonding of flesh and spirit was natural to man, before sense was dulled by moral convention, to a time when the primal moving forces of the world acted directly on tingling nerves.[38]

Nationalism is, for Massie – a Conservative commentator both in Edinburgh and in London newspapers – a release of archaic energy that may seem to be creative but proves – as it does for Donnelly – to be profoundly destructive both of self and of society.

Massie's *One Night in Winter*, narrated by middle-aged Dallas Graham, looking back from his life in London to the year in which he graduated from Cambridge and returned to his family home in Scotland, is structured so as to juxtapose the early days of the upsurge of Scottish nationalism with the world left by its apparent foundering in the aftermath of the first devolution referendum of 1979. What is revealed by Fraser Donnelly's search for liberation, and his eventual murder by his wife Lorna, is a Scotland which cannot be liberated or regenerated by political action, as Donnelly himself is allowed to state: 'Scotland's a douce, canny shy place. The mair it's a failure, and by God it's a failure, the mair loth it is to turn to anything new'.[39] All efforts at transformation founder in a culture whose capital city has 'the atmosphere of the undertaker's parlour',[40] whose bars 'were in the kingdom of limbo, the never-never land of those lost girls and boys who had been caught half-way out of their prams',[41] whose efforts at modernization showed 'the poverty of imagination . . . of a denatured and broken culture',[42] and whose only intensity is a round of golf – 'that was the limit of the man's capacity for passion. It was the limit of the country's'.[43] Donnelly will be killed as much by Scotland as by Lorna, since her nature is so shaped by the country: 'Lorna's damnable timidity, her inability to choose, her damn fatalism; that was Scots. She was in love with defeat, with a Fate that had singled her out as a victim. It's in the air there. It chokes you'.[44] As one old relative tells Dallas:

> Let Scotland be as independent as they wish, it will not alter the fact that there's little . . . to keep talent here . . . You won't stay in Scotland, Dallas. For all the protestations of clowns like Mr Gregory and men of exuberant but ill-directed will like Fraser, Scotland will grow ever less Scottish and ever less stimulating; we live in a withered culture. Sounds of energy are the energy of the death-rattle.[45]

Dallas will indeed go off to London – 'nothing would be real till he was back in London . . . the real train was back on the rails'[46] – but he will carry with him his country's capacity for defeat, its nostophobic rejection of its own history. An instinctive Jacobite with a 'dislike of the Modern Age',[47] Dallas will become a failed novelist, able to write only by narrating again the disturbing events that led to Fraser Donnelly's death and that reveal how hollow is the nation which shaped both protagonist and narrator. Dallas's final journey away from Scotland becomes emblematic of the nation itself:

> We drove south, devouring miles in a thin rain. Dropping through the grey-black wet of Dundee to the bridge across the river, fog shrouded us; the coast of Fife could not be seen. Miles later, at the next firth, we hung suspended, motionless in jammed traffic, over a river that could not be known to exist. I felt life thrown into reverse.[48]

Modern Scotland is a land suspended, in a state of stasis, a place of endless repetition. Scotland, it appeared, was a place resistant to any art that needed the propulsion of significant historical events; it is a dilemma that James Robertson dramatized in his novel *And the Land Lay Still* (2010), in which a member of an audience at a literary reading asks an author why 'he set his books in Italy, France America and England, but not in Scotland':

> The writer stroked his chin. Because nothing happens here. The centres of activity, the places where decisions are made, where politics and personalities and power collide are elsewhere. London, New York, Paris, Rome. Anywhere but this quiet backwater. Delightful to live in but nothing to write about.[49]

This in itself recuperates a much-quoted exchange between Duncan Thaw and his friend Kenneth McAlpin in Alasdair's Gray's *Lanark*

> 'Glasgow is a magnificent city,' said McAlpin, 'Why do we hardly ever notice that?' 'Because nobody imagines living here . . . think of Florence, Paris, London, New York. Nobody visiting them for the first time is a stranger because he's already visited them in paintings, novels, history books and films. But if a city hasn't been used by an artist not even the inhabitants live there imaginatively . . . Imaginatively, Glasgow exists as a music-hall song and a few bad novels . . .'[50]

Glasgow, Thaw concludes, 'never got into the history books, except as a statistic'[51] and could disappear without anyone noticing or caring: it is, like the Scotland of which it is a part, an unreal and unrealisable place.

That was why, perhaps, so many of the country's best artistic talents had gone into exile – Helen Adam in San Francisco; Alexander Trocchi in New York; Muriel Spark first to London, then New York and then Tuscany; Kenneth White to France; Alastair Reid to Spain and South America; Alan Sharp, abandoning the promising trilogy that had been initiated by *A Green Tree in Gedde* in 1965, left to become a script writer in Los Angeles; not to mention all those who, like James Kennaway or Bill Douglas or the 'two Roberts', the artists MacBride and Colquhoun, had decamped to London.

The stasis of Scotland became a motif of Scottish novels in the years after 1979: in Gray's *Lanark*, the central character arrives by train in the city of Unthank having forgotten his past life and names himself after a picture on the railway compartment wall; in Iain Banks's *The Bridge* (1986) the central character is in a coma after a car crash on the Forth Road Bridge, his life being imaginarily continued on an endless version of the Forth Rail Bridge; in Janice Galloway's *The Trick is to Keep Breathing* (1989), the protagonist has been reduced to non-existence by society's refusal to acknowledge her place in her dead lover's life:

> 1. The Rev Dogsbody had chosen this service to perform a miracle
> 2. He'd run time backwards, cleansed, absolved and got rid of the ground-in stain.
> 3. And the stain was me.
>
> I didn't exist. The miracle had wiped me out.[52]

A. L. Kennedy's *So I am Glad* (1995) is narrated by a character whose 'peace and calmness is, in fact, empty space'[53] and Roy Strang in Irvine Welsh's *Marabou Stork Nightmares* (1996) survives 'down here in the comforts of my vegetative state, inside my secret world'.[54] Scotland is in a state of amnesia – is a state in amnesia.

For Francis Russell Hart the problem of the modern Scottish novel was focused on the case of Muriel Spark (1918–2006): noting that only *The Prime of Miss Jean Brodie* is actually set in Scotland, he asks 'Can the most eminent living novelist nurtured by Scotland be recognized, then, in her eminence, in her eccentricity, as a Scottish novelist?'[55] Alan Massie himself had written a short critical book on Spark in which he presented her as a novelist in the tradition of 'Waugh, Firbank, Henry Green and Powell, who have attempted to understand the world by cultivating detachment',[56] a list which would seem to constitute a very English tradition of the modern novel that would put the country's 'most eminent' novelist on the outside of any definition of the 'Scottish novel'. Hart and Massie, however, had only about the first half of Spark's oeuvre to consider, but in 1979 she published her fifteenth novel, entitled *Territorial Rights*, set in modern Venice, in which a group of characters – all exiles – struggle to control the power that the past has to disrupt the present. At the centre of the plot is the body of Victor Pancev, a Bulgarian executed towards the end of the Second World War, whose corpse was cut in two so that each half could be buried separately and his grave(s) tended by two sisters both of whom had been his lovers. It is the image of a Europe torn apart by American and Soviet 'great powers' which competes for ownership of its past. But running through the narrative is an intrusive voice from another past much closer to Spark's original home:

> Anthea fell asleep in her chair. She did not dream of the book but of her grandmother from Scotland who used to chant to her:
> For her I'll dare the billow's roar,
> For her I'll trace a distant shore,
> That Indian wealth may lustre throw
> Around my Highland lassie, O.[57]

It is as though the folk voice of Scotland becomes a ghostly disruption of modernity, offering a choric reflection on the novel's action. That voice is allowed the last word in the penultimate chapter before the novel officiously tidies up and packs away all its puppets: 'the pennie's the jewel that beautifies a'', it ironically chants.[58] Confronted by a world of chaotic international corruption, in which only material values count, Spark implicitly asserts, through Scottish balladry, her own territorial rights – the right to refuse simply to imitate the narrative of the modern world. It is, for Spark, modernity as a whole which is a 'second hand world', one which the novelist can approach only by a radical subversion of the realist tradition that would give primacy to the narrative trajectory of modernity. It is a strategy she had used in *The Ballad of Peckham Rye* (1960) in which Dougal Douglas is a Scottish devil set loose in London, and in *Hothouse by the East River* (1973), in which J. M. Barrie's *Peter Pan* becomes the intertextual commentary upon the action of a novel set in a purgatorial New York, and which she was to use later in *The Takeover* (1976), which takes place in Nemi, the setting of the opening of J. G. Frazer's *Golden Bough*, and again in *Symposium* (1990), in which Margaret Murchie and her Uncle Magnus are carriers of the apparently magical powers invoked by old Scottish ballads:

> Magnus lowered his voice. 'Who do you have', he said, 'but me? Out of my misfortune, out of my affliction I prognosticate and foreshadow. My divine affliction is your only guide. Remember the ballad:
>
> As I went down the water side
> None but my foe to be my guide
> None but my foe to be my guide[59]

Scottish traditions form a thread of opposition to the 'realities' of the modern world, a resistant and subversive attitude to realism that had been evident from the beginning of Spark's novel-writing career but which is explored most intensively in her second novel, *Robinson* (1958). It is a novel to which Massie, like many others who have written about Spark, gives hardly any consideration but it is key to the aesthetics that guides her subsequent fiction.

Robinson is a story about three survivors of an air crash on a small island in the Atlantic which is inhabited only by a religious recluse named Robinson and a young boy whom he is looking after. Everything in *Robinson* is disconcertingly doubled, so Robinson the man shares his name with the island, also called Robinson, just as the central character, January Marlow has a first name which implies Janus, the god of doors who points in opposite directions, and shares her second name with Conrad's narrator in *The Heart of Darkness*. Likely to be trapped on the island for many weeks until a boat arrives with supplies, January finds herself confusing Robinson and the other two survivors of the plane crash with the members of her own family back in London, as though she can 'read' her present only in terms of her past. Equally, the events of the novel are subject to much dubiety, as January claims they are reconstructed from a diary she kept during her time on the island but of which the novel gives us only occasional – and unconfirmable – specimens, and because the island itself, we are told, has subsequently disappeared owing to a volcanic convulsion. Most critics have dismissed the novel as a failed experiment written when Spark was trying to find a way forward from the radical innovations of her first novel, *The Comforters* of 1957. But in the same year that *The Comforters* was published, another book appeared in which a character called 'Robinson' featured prominently – Ian Watt's influential study of the *The Rise of the Novel*,[60] which argued that the novel in English is rooted in the work of Defoe, and that its founding statement is *Robinson Crusoe*, a work which establishes the novel as the genre of 'formal realism',[61] in which language is 'much more referential . . . than in other literary forms',[62] and in which 'the character is to be regarded as though he were a particular person and not a type'.[63] This new literary form is shaped by the forces of an economic individualism directed away from the past and towards the future – 'it posits a whole society mainly governed by the idea of every individual's intrinsic independence . . . from that multifarious allegiance to past modes of thought and action denoted by the word "tradition"';[64] such economic individualism derives directly from Protestantism – 'if there is one element which all forms of Protestantism have in common it is the replacement of the rule of the Church as the mediator between man and God by another view of religion in which it is the individual who is entrusted with the primary responsibility for his own spiritual direction'.[65] The formal origins of the novel are in 'the autobiographical memoir which was the most immediate and widespread literary expression of the introspective tendency of Puritanism'.[66] Thus the 'works of Defoe are the supreme illustration in the novel of the connexion between the democratic individualism of Puritanism and the objective representation of the world of everyday reality and all those who inhabit it',[67] and, equally, of the 'tendency to secularization which was rooted in material progress',[68] a progress by which economic individualism judged its spiritual achievements, for material success was a sign of belonging to the elect. Crusoe's island 'offers the fullest opportunity for him to realize three associated tendencies of modern civilization – absolute economic, social and intellectual freedom for the individual'.[69]

If Watt's analysis is correct about the meaning of the novel as a form, it is a form which can be of no value to a writer who has just denied the inheritance of the Reformation to embrace the 'tradition' of Catholicism: Watt, for instance, cites Georg Lukács on the fact that the novel 'is the epic of a world forsaken by God'.[70] Nor, indeed, can the novel in this form be of any value to a woman writer, as the tradition which Watt outlines is insistently male – 'Studies in Defoe, Richardson, Fielding' is his subtitle – and women in Defoe's fiction, we are told, 'have only one important role to play, and that is economic'.[71] If this is the nature of the medium that is the novel, it is a medium impossible for a female writer inspired by Catholicism: idling in Robinson's library, January 'cast around for a novel' and happens to open an eighteenth-century edition of *Tom Jones* at the page in which Sophia's 'agonies . . . rather augmented than impaired her beauty; for her tears added brightness to her eyes, and her breasts rose higher with her sighs',[72] a male construction of the female heroine as love object very different from Spark's analysis of a writer such as Emily Brontë, whose personality 'was more than human; she was some strange rugged monolithic mystic'.[73] January's lighting on the *Tom Jones* passage is her creator's gesture of defiance to a tradition which would find no place for women authors like Brontë, or like Spark, both of whose characters are resistant to traditional forms of male-female relationships, since in Brontë's work, Spark suggests, 'men and women . . . are apt to meet each other on the grounds of passionate mutual identity, which excludes sexual union'.[74] Spark's *Robinson* is designed to undermine (January has to escape pursuit through a series of underground tunnels) and then to destroy (the island of Robinson explodes) the tradition by which Watt effectively constrains the female imagination. Spark's novel is an act of refusal to be bound by a tradition that is male, Protestant, materialistic and without either God or the miraculous: *Robinson* allowed Spark to liberate herself from the traditional realist novel and to produce novels which are no longer tied to the aesthetics of the 'probable', but rather to an aesthetics in which, as the final words of *Robinson* put it, 'all things are possible'.[75] The overthrow of realism aligns Spark with the anti-realism of both Robert Louis Stevenson – who insisted in his response to Henry James that one must resist the temptation to judge the novel by its approximation to reality: 'The whole secret is that no art does "compete with life"'[76] – and J. M. Barrie, whose work, like Spark's *The Hothouse by the East River* (1973) in which *Peter Pan* appears as an intertext, is fabulatory and foregrounds the artifice of the novel: like some of the characters in *Symposium*, it is as though Spark has 'skipped the nineteenth century in our genes'[77] and gone back to the playfulness of the pre-realist tradition of the novel as initiated by Cervantes. Despite her migration and the international settings of her novels, Spark continually threads Scottish elements into her fiction as part of an anti-realist style which connects her work with her Scottish predecessors – and which also prefigures the ways in which the novelists of the 1980s and 90s will respond to the stalled history of Scotland.

In a condition of psychological trauma the Scottish novel repeats in surreal form the crisis that it has lived through: it is a place where a drug-taking dropout can be the resurrected spirit of Cyrano de Bergerac (A. L. Kennedy, *So I am Glad*, 1995);[78] where a daughter can be drugged by her father into believing she is a castrated boy (Iain Banks, *The Wasp Factory*, 1984);[79] where a Catholic cleric can attend a doctor's surgery because he has flowers blossoming from his backside (Christopher Whyte, *Euphemia MacFarrigle and the Laughing Virgin*, 1995);[80] where a journey from Edinburgh to Glasgow goes via Salerno and Vladikavkaz, in each of which the protagonist encounters the same characters he has been trying to escape in Edinburgh (James Meek, *Drivetime*, 1995);[81] and where a girl struggles to get a pizza into the oven because the dead body on the floor 'caused the usual hassles' (Alan Warner, *Morvern Callar*, 1996).[82] It is a world where reality no longer operates by the usual rules, an effect like the *Electric Brae* of Andrew Greig's novel of 1992, whose epigraph explains the phenomenon of a hill which slopes opposite to its apparent direction: 'On fine weekends the Brae can be a populous spot, frequented by cyclists struggling downhill, open-mouthed motorists saving petrol whilst they coast uphill, and by those children who amuse themselves by stotting balls then watch them run away in the wrong direction'.[83] It is a place where ordinary causality is suspended, and where alternative otherworlds become visible, as in the case of James Kelman's *The Busconductor Hines*:

> There is a crack in the pavement a few yards from the close entrance: it has a brave exterior: it is a cheery wee soul; other cracks can be shifty but not this one. Hines will refer to it as Dan in future. Hello there Dan. How's it going?[84]

Named as 'Dan' the crack in the pavement becomes addressable as a person. In Iain Banks's *Walking on Glass* (1985),[85] on the other hand, Stephen Grout believes that in the 'static' of tape recordings he can hear the engines of bombers from another world: this apparently mad belief that he has discovered 'a Leak, a tiny slip they had made which let part of reality slip through into this prison of his life',[86] becomes, however, the reality of a second narrative of a future world which has invented a technology allowing its inhabitants to enter the heads of people in the past – like Grout – and control them for their own pleasure.[87] As though in defiance of the stalled political reality in which it is trapped, Scottish literature of the 1980s and 90s drew its energy from discovering a variety of routes into alternative ontologies where the imaginary can become real, from the mind bending effects of drugs in Irvine Welsh's *Trainspotting* (1993)[88] to the body bending of Joss Moody, female impersonator of a male trumpeter in Jackie Kay's *Trumpet* (1998),[89] from the space opera epic of sci-fi games in Iain M. Banks's *The Player of Games* (1988)[90] to the laconic absurdities of Frank Kuppner's 500 chapters of *The Concussed History of Scotland* (1990), in chapter 486 of which we are told, 'But after a hundred or so empty ones had been passed, the meteorite ran alongside one which contained a cigarette packet still holding a single cigarette. What bizarre things one will find in the sky if one is only prepared to look for long enough!'[91] In the suspended animation of the real – 'its concussed history' – a dream logic takes over that allows narrative to continue in defiance of its historical condition, as in many of the contributions to Daniel O'Rourke's anthology *Dream State: The New Scottish Poets* (1994), in which Robert Crawford imagines a world in which Einstein was Glaswegian, proved by the fact that, 'As a wee boy he'd read *The Beano*'.[92] If politics cannot change the world, then art must.

Spark's resistance to the virtues of realism were to be the gateway to the alternative Scotlands of the 1980s, an effect magnified by the publication of Alasdair Gray's *Lanark* in 1981. Gray's novel had been taking shape since the 1950s and is, therefore, in a sense, parallel in its development to much of the work of Spark, but its long-delayed publication meant that it was first read in the context of the post-referendum environment, and in its epic scale and radical playfulness, in its combination of literary genres – realism, fantasy, science fiction

– and its framing of each of its four books with Gray's artwork, *Lanark* challenged the possibilities of the novel in Scotland. It sought both to analyse the nostophobic sickness of the culture in which Gray had grown up in the 1950s and 60s – sicknesses mirrored in the ill-health of its protagonist Duncan Thaw, and in his incapacity to complete the huge mural to which he has committed himself – and, by its innovations – Book Three precedes Book One, the 'Epilogue' intercedes four chapters from the end – to defy those that would believe a Scottish imagination necessarily suffers from the same constrictions as the novel's protagonist. The novel's form joyfully challenges the bleak world of deindustrialisation and psychological repression that it charts, demonstrating a vitality that breaks free of the constraints by which its characters are limited. Francis Hart had identified as one of the problems of the Scottish novel that it attempts to bear witness to 'fidelity to local truth, to the particulars of a communal place and time' while at the same time seeking 'to represent national types and whole cultural epochs', with the consequence of a 'tendency to force implication, to make the particular mean too much on too many levels'.[93] Gray does exactly this but assertively, littering the realistic sections of his novel with characters who repeat famous names out of Scottish history – Thaw's friend Kenneth McAlpin bears the name of the earliest king of the Scots – and making the fantasy sections a repetition on a different level of the events in the realistic sections – as, for instance, in the disease of 'dragonhide' in which Lanark is gradually being encased and which mimics Thaw's self-enclosed resistance to relationship with others. The realism of Books 1 and 2, which chart Thaw's growth as an unfulfilled 'portrait of the artist as a young man', is revealed to be symptomatic of a society which cannot understand what is happening to it, since realism can present a society's condition – its de-industrialisation, its constricted opportunities, its sexual repression – but cannot explain them: the explanations either lie in a past which is no longer accessible or relevant – 'His past suddenly seemed a very large, very dreary place'[94] – or in the international workings of a capitalism which are invisible in the realistic representation of the city but which can be made visible through the narrative's continuation of Thaw's life into the fantasy world of Lanark's, where Lanark can confront the sources of the power that governs the world in which Thaw is trapped: given a brief interview with Lord Monboddo, the head of the Council which is planning to consume Unthank to provide energy for other cities, Thaw discovers not only his own lack of agency but that of the leaders as well: Monboddo declares, 'Leaders are the effects, not the causes of changes. I *cannot* give prosperity to people whom my rich supporters cannot exploit'.[95]

What makes *Lanark* so distinctive, however, is not just its epic scale and its structural innovations but its recuperative intent: it is a novel whose indebtedness to previous Scottish literature is ironically displayed by its 'Index of Plagiarisms', many of which are spoofs – the entry for 'Black Angus' states 'See Macneacail, Aonghas', while the entry for 'Macneacail, Aonghas' offers 'See Nicolson, Angus' and that for 'Nicolson, Angus' invites us to 'See Black Angus'[96] – but which nonetheless point the reader to the ways in which the forgetfulness in which the novel's characters live is defied by the memory which the novel invites us to recover. So the entry on 'Archie Hind', for instance, points us to 'Epilogue, para 14' and tells us that 'The disciplines of cattle slaughter and accountancy are dramatized in the novel *The Dear Green Place*',[97] when in fact the whole career of Duncan Thaw might be seen as a version of *The Dear Green Place*'s presentation of the struggle of a man of working-class background to become a writer; similarly, the entry on the Reverend George MacDonald points us to his story *The Key* and tells us that 'the journey of Lanark and Rima across the misty plain in Chap. 33 also comes from this story, as does the death and rebirth of the hero halfway through . . . and the device of casually ageing people with speculative rapidity in a short space of print'[98] but this conceals the broader indebtedness of Book 3 to MacDonald's *Phantastes* (1858) and *Lilith* (1895), often recognised as the inspiration for much modern fantasy writing.[99] *Lanark* is a novel engaged in formally defying the amnesia and nostophobia in which its central character is trapped and therefore in defying the cultural conditions of the modern Scotland by which both author and character are shaped: the novel recuperates a Scottish past as the context by which its present ought to be invigorated and in doing so pitches the nation's past cultural wealth against the poverty of its own understanding of itself.

III Recoveries

In the late 1930s, as a result of the threat posed by Germany, the Scottish artist J. D. Fergusson (1874–1961) returned to Glasgow from France, where he had mainly lived since the first decade of the century. Fergusson, who had been the art editor of Middleton Murry's Paris-based magazine *Rhythm* before the First World War, became the art editor of a magazine entitled *Scottish Art and Letters*, published by William MacLellan, which lasted from 1944 to 1950 and was one of several journals of the postwar era dedicated to 'Scottish reconstruction', including *The New Scot*, which appeared in five volumes from 1945 to 1949 and the *Scottish Journal* (subtitled 'The Popular National Monthly'), which promoted modern Scottish art in a populist format from 1952 to 1954. Because of Fergusson's engagement with early modernist art in prewar Paris – he knew Picasso, and exhibited at venues which supported experimental art[100] – *Scottish Art and Letters* represents a key Scottish response to the nature of modernism. If Paris had been modernism's capital, it was, for Fergusson, because Paris was the capital of a Celtic culture: 'to go to Paris was the natural thing for the Scot . . . it doesn't seem to have occurred to the modern Scot that the Scottish Celt, when in France, was among his own people, the French Celts'.[101] For the first issue of *Scottish Art and Letters*, Fergusson wrote an essay on 'Art and Atavism: The Dryad', which is an autobiographical account of how he produced one of his most famous works, a wooden sculpture entitled *The Dryad* (1924). Its inspiration was a visit from Scottish artist Charles Rennie Mackintosh, who brought Fergusson 'a small flower pot with two slim intertwined twigs, two leaves near the bottom and two or three at the top' because, he said, 'it's so like you.'[102] Mackintosh's gift combined in Fergusson's recollection with the shape of a bagpipe in Glasgow's Kelvingrove Art Gallery and Museum and formed the inspiration for his sculpture, combining modernist experiment with Celtic tradition, and contemporary abstraction with those forms of Celtic – or Pictish – art which were celebrated in *Scottish Art and Letters* by George Bain in an article into which images of paintings by Fergusson and S. J. Peploe were inserted in order to underline the continuity of Celtic tradition with Scottish modernism.[103] In 'Art and Atavism' Fergusson looked back to the emergence of modernism as it was 'taken up later and systematized'[104] by the Celticist theories of Metzinger and Gleizes, who promoted the notion that Cubism was the expression of a Celtic, rather than a Latin, French culture. For Fergusson, modernist experiment is made possible only by the recovery of Celtic roots.[105]

The Celticism of *Scottish Arts and Letters* also looks back to the Celticism of Patrick Geddes's magazine *The Evergreen*, which was published for only one year in 1894, each of its four issues being linked to a particular season, but which itself looked back to Alan Ramsay's *The Ever Green* of 1724. While Ramsay's anthology was committed to the revival of pre-Union literature in Scots, Geddes's aimed at the recovery of a Celticism which would combine contemporary evolutionary science with a critique of modern industrial society, and which would seek to re-establish a more communitarian society of the kind that had existed in the pre-industrial Celtic world. Geddes's notion of Celticism was given powerful expression in the work of its leading graphic contributor, John Duncan, whose murals still grace the walls of the buildings that Geddes refurbished on Edinburgh's High Street and that were named Ramsay Garden; it also helped inspire journals such as the *Celtic Review*, which lasted from 1904 until 1916, and the *Pictish Review* of 1927–8, and it helped shape the Celtic ethos in the novels of Neil Gunn and the pan-Celticism that Hugh MacDiarmid adopted in the 1930s.

The long-term significance of Geddes's Celticism is, however, perhaps best seen in the career and work of Kenneth White, who left Scotland for France in 1968 and eventually became Professor of Poetics at the Sorbonne. White justified his own departure from Scotland as being in the tradition of the 'wandering Scot', treading in the footsteps of the many distinguished Scots, from John Mair (who taught at the Sorbonne in Paris in the early sixteenth century) and George Buchanan (Mair's student at St Andrews, who later became professor at Bordeaux, where he wrote his major works), to David Hume (who wrote his *Treatise of Human Nature* in France) and Patrick Geddes himself, who, in emulation of the original Scots College established in Paris in 1325, built a new *College des Ecossais* at Montpellier in the 1920s. Those Scottish migrants in France were themselves, however, in White's view, travelling in the footsteps of the Celtic missionaries who came from Ireland and Scotland to bring Christianity to a barbarised Europe:

> Brandan, born in Kerry, founds a monastery at Clonfert, and then when a certain Barintus tells of a trip he made to visit a disciple of his on a distant island, embarks for the Hebrides, Iceland, Brittany, and maybe farther. St Malo, St Pol, St Renan settle in Brittany. Others come to Reims, Cambrai, Soissons. There were so many of them at Péronne the place was called Perrona Scottorum.[106]

These 'scotic' wanderers were disrupters of convention – 'Their existence was extravagant, their encyclopaedic knowledge was overwhelming, their intellectual acuity was disquieting and unorthodox, and their ideas were incomprehensible, but definitely heretical';[107] they were rebels in favour of freedom – 'When Belgian abbeys on the Scarpe and the Escaut began to draw up "charts of liberty", the inspiration can be traced back to Scotic influence';[108] they were examples of the 'nomadic intellect' which refuses incorporation into the fixed structures of an existing society and seeks 'always how, against the mechanics of history, to maintain some dynamic that transcends history'.[109] If MacDiarmid needed to go 'Back to Dunbar' to find the resources for a modern Scottish poetry, White is determined to go even further back – to Pelagius, who challenged the Augustinian emphasis on original sin;[110] to the ninth-century theologian John Scot Erigena, 'one of the prime examples of the Celtic intellectual';[111] or Michael Scot,

> in the early 13th century
> an '*internationalgebildeter Mann*'
> with a mass of knowledge
> crystallising in his brain.[112]

That these Celtic and Scottish precursors all precede the formation of the nation of Scotland is significant: like many Scottish poets of the twentieth century, White regards the historical Scotland, the Scotland 'marked by Calvinism, Victorianism, and an industrial revolution',[113] as a country not only 'bruised and numb',[114] but riven by 'Anglo-Scotic schizophrenia'.[115] It is a place which, as a historical nation, is incapable of providing support for creativity: that support has to come not from the nation's history but from the place's geography, from the 'attempt to get back into the living forest, the archaic ground':[116]

> A country is that which offers resistance. The word itself says it, stemming as it does from *contra* (same thing in the German *Gegend*, region, district, which contains *gegen*, against). But in the course of time, the resistance wears down, the country gets covered with cliché and becomes couthy, or even cruddy. Alba is Scotland un-couthied, un-cruddied, re-discovered. Scotland itself after all is a colonial term, and Scotland has been over-colonised. Post-colonial Scotland means getting back down to Alba, to original landscape-mindscape, and connecting them, wordscape.[117]

The business of the Scottish poet, then, is to get beyond existing Scotland and to discover another that will be 'devoid of romantic sentimentality, Gaelic piety and Lowland reductiveness – a ground we lost long ago, which went subterranean'.[118] Getting back to the 'ground' demands, for White, both a cultural archaeology designed to find the fundamental forces of creativity that link apparently discrete cultural environments – 'Over the years, I have come to see a connexion between Celtic naturalism, Eskimo vision, Siberian shamanism, Amerindian religion and Japanese Shinto continued into Zen'[119] – and an exploration of actual territories that have resisted the 'autobahn of Western civilization',[120] as, for instance, in these first three sections of 'On Rannoch Moor':[121]

> 1.
> Here, where the glacier started
> snow hardening into ice and
> slowly moving –
> sculpting the tertiary terrain.
>
> 2.
> This morning
> (a few millennia later)
> a chill wind blowing
> on original ground.
>
> 3.
> An erratic boulder
> let it be the centre
> from it, the eye travels
> tracing the circle . . .

The 'accidental' centre – from the viewpoint of history – is the real centre for poetry, because it provides a place of vision – 'the eye travels' – from which can be discovered an 'original ground':

> 9.
> On this plateau
> has taken place
> the ultimate union
> of matter and space.

The merely historical 'unions' in which the state of Scotland has existed are irrelevant in comparison to this 'ultimate union' of which its landscape is a symbol. At this level the local and universal are one, as 'poetry signifies the transcendence of individual conscience and the introduction to a world (a cosmos, a beautiful whole in movement)'.[122] The search for this transcendence is best conducted at the margins of the defined territory of the nation: the Ayrshire coast of White's boyhood explorations; Pau, in the Pyrenees, on the borders of France and Spain and the Basque country, where he lived in the 1970s; Britanny and the Atlantic coast, where he has been settled since 1983. These are places where national culture peters out and where the messages come not from an economically-driven state but from beyond the limits of the human world:

> The sounding of the silence here
> is a *kerrak-rrok-rrok*
> pronounced by dark birds
>
> and the endless emptiness of the sky
> is filled with slowmoving cloud
> from the open ocean
>
> meditation is and is not the name for what goes on
>
> a single, sun-bright concentration
> while a thousand blue waves break on the horizon.[123]

The 'open ocean' is an opening through which it is possible to glimpse the world as it is in itself, in its 'silence', before it submits to the imposition of human meanings: to rediscover that ground it is necessary to escape the ground as defined by the nation.

Despite the disclaimer of the value of the historical nation, White's conception of the world is profoundly linked to his Scottish predecessors and, in particular, to Patrick Geddes. Geddes represents for White the generalising, totalising intellect that refuses to limit itself to the empirical and atomising tendencies of institutional forms of knowledge in the modern age. Geddes, who challenged Darwinian conceptions of evolution because they failed to acknowledge the evolutionary advantage provided by a species committed to community and to love,[124] offers White an intellectual ground not only committed to rethinking humanity's relationship with its environment but one already constructed from a Franco-Scottish interaction, as Geddes's theories developed from the work of the French sociologist and anarchist, Frederic le Play. In Geddes, White finds conceptions of an alternative trajectory for Western civilisation which foreshadows – in a way that MacDiarmid's Marxism could not – his own conception of 'geopoetics':

> Paleotechnics [industrial society] meant waste of natural resources, blighted landscapes, pandemoniac cities full of factories, offices, slums and stunted human lives. Neotechnics meant the use of non-polluting energy and the attempt to reunite utility with beauty, city with landscape. Biotechnics would promote new life thinking, leading to more developed human lives, more expanded psyches. As to geotechnics, it was the means for human beings to learn how to really and fully inhabit the earth.[125]

Geddes's 'geotechnics' is the prefiguration of White's own 'geopoetics', a parallel rejection of urban, industrial civilisation as the end and aim of human progress. For White the task is to get back to that ground and to define it outwith the assumptions of the national historical trajectory that still haunts MacDiarmid's and Gunn's rejection of modernity. In Geddes's work, it is the region and its cultural inheritance which is crucial, rather than the nation, and a region is defined by the geological structure of the land and the work that it makes possible for human beings, by the relation of country to city, and of city to river and sea. It is the regionalism of Geddes's 'Scottish Renascence' rather than the nationalism of MacDiarmid's 'Scottish Renaissance' to which White is inheritor, a renascence more concerned with Celtic traditions of identification with the land than with the construction of a proletarian society or the adoption of 'synthetic Scots'. 'If Geddes was and is mainly known as a town-planner, a city-surveyor,' White comments, 'he was also looking to a new exodus into "the outside world", that of the other animals, of plants and rocks':

> . . . perhaps one who knows
> even one rock thoroughly
> in all its idiosyncracy
> and relatedness
> to sea and sky
> is better fit to speak
> to another human being
> than one who lives and rots perpetually
> in a crowded society
> that teaches him
> nothing essential.[126]

What Geddes sought was what White was also determined to find, 'a great "single discipline", which is "complex indeed, but no more a mere maze than a mere chaos" and which leads to "a single presentment of the world", "a growing Cosmos, a literal Uni-verse".'[127]

Poetry has, for White, a broader and a deeper significance, for it is the response to a world in which 'the mind cries out for unity, for a unitive experience', it is the 'desire of a whole world',[128] and, as such, it is an act which is more than linguistic – a 'sheer experience of the nakedness and loveliness of everything, an ecstatic existence, expanding to the sense of cosmic unity'.[129] The achievement of this experience depends on being able to come close to the thingness of the world, its thisness – what Duns Scotus called its haecceitas. But that individuality is precisely what language, in its ordinary operation, refuses, because language brings the uniqueness of individual things into general categories – not this specific, unique tree but a tree, one of a type. To enter the 'white world' is, as in 'Letter to an Old Calligrapher', to circumvent this abstracting function of language itself:

> A hundred days
> along shore and mountain

with eye open
for heron and cormorant

now writing this
at the world's edge

in a silence become
a second nature

coming to know
in brain and in bone

the path of emptiness.[130]

As a linguistic structure the poem is a 'second nature', a duplication of the real, but behind the linguistic structure is another 'second nature', the second nature of 'silence', of the end of language and division and the beginning of unity.

From the 1970s to the 1990s, these 'white poetics' aligned Kenneth White with the reconceptualisation of the relationship of modern thought to the past of Western culture that characterised the work of Foucault, Deleuze and Derrida, and which can be traced to the influence of Edmund Husserl and Martin Heidegger, and through Heidegger to the Nietzsche by whom White was obsessed in his early years as a student in Glasgow. Nietzsche's demand for a transcendence of the Christian tradition and a recovery of the tragic world that was last experienced in ancient Greece, re-emerged in Husserl and Heidegger as the dismissal of the history of Western philosophy as a mistake, a mistake which could be corrected only by getting back to pre-Socratic insights in order to begin again:

hare pads
lightning flash
written rocks
begin again.[131]

Husserl, according to White, identified the rise of philosophy in ancient Greece as the beginning of a destructive dislocation of humanity from its engagement with a whole world:

What happened in the modern age was that rationality turned into rationalism, which means, among other things, a loss of the sense of

> world, a culture that rings more and more hollow (hardly helped by periodical attempts to give it more substance via naturalism, social realism or oneiric fantasy), and a proliferation of narrow specialities. How that move from 'full world' and knowledge of whole being to 'objective world', unilateral conceptions and endless series of sterile research came about is the history of Western philosophy, to which Husserl devoted a great deal of his thinking and teaching.[132]

White's poetry can be read as a dramatisation of that philosophical effort to undo the destructiveness of Western tradition, not only by an engagement with Eastern religious philosophies but by a return to European origins before the baleful effects of philosophy took hold: 'I'm idiomatic/I'm idiosyncratic/ /I'm pre-socratic'.[133] The means of that return to origins, White attributes to his discovery of shamanism, a discovery both biographical – his childhood creation of a hut which formed a kind of shrine full of magic objects – and intellectual, in his reading of Mircea Eliade's *Shamanism – the Archaic Techniques of Ecstasy*.

> As I read through that book, I came across more and more correspondences between what he was laying out and my own early experience. In other words, I had stumbled on to shamanism, had practised a kind of home-made shamanism, that is, an immemorial tradition going back to neolithic, paleolithic and prelithic times, elements of which can be found all over the world . . . This isn't really so surprising as it may sound. It's almost certain that, given enough scope, enough freedom, a child will go through all the past phases of humanity, from fishes to philosophers.[134]

Shamanism is, for White, one of the elements of Celtic tradition, so that both in his person and in his cultural inheritance he is able to re-enact the search for a new totality that Heidegger illustrates through a saying of Heraclitus: 'The (familiar) abode is for man the open region for the presencing of god (the unfamiliar one)'.[135] The Shaman is he who makes the gods, the unfamiliar ones, present themselves; he gives voice to that which lives beyond the boundaries of the community, thereby 'giving it breathing space'.[136] The shamanism through which White discovered the 'open world' connects directly, as his meditation on 'Heidegger at Home' reveals, to Husserl and Heidegger's effort to get back beyond Socratic philosophy:

On the steep slope
of a mountain valley
a little chalet
eighteen feet by twenty

all around
meadow and pinewood

when snow surrounded the house
that was the time for philosophy:
following all those
secret, silent paths
till cogitation turned into sight

like this high summer morning
and two hawks gliding
round and round
in the absolute light.[137]

The poem – ironically entitled 'Black Forest' – travels from the ordinary world – in which poetry is characterised by mere rhyme: 'valley', 'chalet' – towards that transcendence in which 'being' steps forth 'into the open region that lights the "between" within which a "relation" of subject to object can "be".'[138] Such moments of revelation, however, are precisely the ones that allow us to know ourselves to be 'at home' in the world, despite the alienation that modern civilisation imposes on us: the 'white world', he tells us, is 'where poetry and metaphysics meet'.[139] Without that meeting 'culture, as Nietzsche foresaw, would go to the dogs, that is, to what he called the "last men", hideously productive, but creatively nil'.[140] White's career, one might say, has been about finding a way back to Scotland, an other Scotland than the one he fled in 1968.

IV 'The time Scotland began to move'

In an interview with Colin Nicholson, Edwin Morgan noted that in the aftermath of the 1979 referendum, 'there was a sense of political numbness . . . I had been hoping there would be an Assembly, and the sense of let-down was very strong', but that he 'felt impelled to write a lot' in order to give voice to his 'determination to go on living in Scotland, and a hope that there might be some political change'.[141] From the publication of *A Second Life* in 1968, Morgan had become established as the 'international' Scottish poet – fellow-traveller with the Beats (in poems such as 'The Death of Marilyn Monroe'), experimenter with 'concrete' ('French Persian Cats Having a Ball') and 'sound' poetry ('Canedolia'), playful constructor of typographic witticisms ('Siesta of a Hungarian Snake'), almost more famous for his translations of European poets such as Montale or Mayakovsky than for his own writings. 'Seven Headlines' said it all in many variations:

absolu t e
m odern
men
If faut être absolument moderne[142]

Morgan was the 'absolute modern' and the modern was 'international' – as evidenced in his editorial role on the journal *Scottish International* from 1968. Though many of his poems were about local subjects – 'Glasgow Green', 'The Starlings in George Square' – or local encounters – 'Good Friday', 'In the Snack Bar' – they were framed by a style that declared its international affiliations, that saw Scotland anew through the medium of elsewhere ('A Chinese moment in the Mearns'), or celebrated modernity in Scotland ('The Opening of the Forth Road Bridge, 4.IX.64'). Implicitly, Morgan's poetry was the answer to the failure of Scotland to be fully part of the modern world: Scotland had to be made modern, because Scotland was a place resistant to modernity, resistant to renewal, left out of the technological transformations that were reshaping humanity's relationship with the cosmos:

Vostok shrieks and prophesies, Mariner's prongs flash –
to the wailing of Voskhod Earth sighs, she shakes men loose at last –
out, in our time, to be living seeds sent far beyond
even imagination [143]

The 'living seeds' of the future go forth from Russia and America, two of the cultures whose most important poets Morgan imitates or translates, as though, through him, Scotland might at least mimic the trajectory of a history it cannot itself perform, a history projected into a future that makes the past, the national past, the weight of past tradition, irrelevant to modern creativity. On this basis, for instance, Morgan would distinguish himself from the 'modernists' of the preceding generation: as compared with Pound or Eliot, he would prefer a poetry,

> relying less I think on earlier literature. I've the feeling of wanting to get away from that, I think; I'm a pretty strong anti-traditionalist in that sense. I really on the whole dislike history and tradition. I'm interested in what is happening, and I'm interested in what will happen, more than I'm interested in what has happened, I think, so that my long poem, if ever it comes out, will be rather different from the existing ones. It will perhaps be 'now' plus the future, rather than 'now' plus the past.[144]

'"Now" plus the future' suggests that Scotland, Scotland as a past, is irrelevant to Morgan's conception of poetry. As late as 1990, when the magazine *Cencratus* published a special issue on Morgan,[145] it linked him with Alexander Trocchi and William Burroughs, both of whom had been contributors to the 1962 Edinburgh Writers' Festival where Trocchi had famously challenged the relevance of Hugh MacDiarmid's work to contemporary Scotland. By framing Morgan with Burroughs and Trocchi it suggested that Morgan might be, like Trocchi, a poet of resistance to the traditions of Scottish literature – perhaps even a writer in 'exile', with Glasgow, where he had lived continuously since returning from service in the Second World War, as much a place of exile from the rest of Scotland as Paris or New York. It was as a native Glaswegian rather than a native Scot that he had described himself in a letter to Michael Schmidt in 1972 – 'I am really a very native Glasgow-loving root-clutching person'[146] – and his preference for Glasgow as distinct, and as distinctly different, was a view that Morgan retained even late in his life: he was reluctant, for instance, to attend the celebration of the establishment of his archive at the Scottish Poetry Library in Edinburgh because he thought it ought to be housed in Glasgow, and was only convinced to attend when he could defiantly wear a T-shirt with a picture of a Tunnock's Caramel Wafer on which was inscribed, 'Glasgow Takes the Biscuit'.[147]

Certainly many of those who interviewed Morgan in the 1970s regarded 'Scottishness' as something he would want to distance himself from: the assumption was that Morgan was part of 'a cosmopolitanism' that would be opposed to the rise of the Scottish nationalism that had taken psephologists aback by its successes in the 1960s. Morgan's response to such implications clearly came as a surprise to his interviewers:

> I think I am actually [a nationalist]. I think I would probably call myself that, though I don't feel very much attracted to the SNP. I'm not a member of any of the political parties, but I think in a sense that I feel Scottish and not English, and feel also that there is still a meaningful sense in which you could call yourself a Scottish writer, even though it's very hard to define this. In that sense I would still feel that there is enough that is distinct for it to be defined and developed, and, if possible, carried forward as a kind of tradition. I think there must obviously be a good deal of overlapping, both with English and with foreign international cultures – this is inevitable. But I would still feel quite strongly enough conscious of Scotland as an entity or the Scots person as being different from the Englishman, to want to keep this. In that sense I would call myself a Scottish nationalist . . . [148]

It was as a modernist from Scotland that Morgan established his reputation: that he was a Scottish nationalist was not evident to those who admired his adoption of innovative modernisms from around the world.

But for a poet who claimed to have no partiality for 'history and tradition', Morgan expended considerable energy from the 1950s to the 1970s in coming to terms with the poetic past of Scotland. In the early years of his time as a lecturer at the University of Glasgow he published, in 1952, 'Dunbar and the Language of Poetry', an essay which identified 'energy' as the key feature of Dunbar's work – 'What is immediately noticeable [. . .] is the *display* of *poetic energy* in forms that have considerable technical and craftsmanly interest'[149] – and between then and the late 1970s he had published essays on Gavin Douglas, William Drummond, Robert Fergusson, Robert Louis Stevenson, Hugh MacDiarmid, Edwin Muir, as well as general essays that reflected on 'Scottish Poetry in English' and 'The Resources of Scotland'. This continuous engagement with the Scottish poetic past had none of the obliterative intent behind MacDiarmid's 'Back to Dunbar' agenda in the 1920s: instead, Morgan patiently teases out what might still speak to contemporary readers, as, for instance, when he compares Stevenson with Gerard Manley Hopkins:

> of course it is impossible not to see the difference between a man who was a poet to his finger-tips and one who like Stevenson was an occasional poet whose main work lay elsewhere, in prose. But Hopkins is dazzling and it is important to give Stevenson his due. His verse is a genuine part of the tradition of Scottish poetry, which it extends in more than one direction, and in addition to that it holds out a range of poetic effects and pleasures which is, I believe, a good deal wider than we have been accustomed to assume.[150]

Stevenson is to be understood in terms of what he contributed to 'the tradition of Scottish poetry', and if, for many, it is difficult to relate 'to traditions that may seem more like locks than keys' ('The Resources of Scotland'),[151] Morgan nonetheless wants to open up those traditions and test what is usable: 'There comes a time when out of respect for itself a country must collect its resources, and look at its assets and shortcomings with an eye that is both sharp and warm: see what is there, what is not there, what could be there'.[152] It is also the time to evaluate what Scottish writers have contributed to 'world literature', a term invented by Goethe, the literary figure who dominated the early years of Thomas Carlyle's writing career, and it is Carlyle's truly international – and transdisciplinary – influence that Morgan seeks to emphasise:

> Engels admired Carlyle; so did James Joyce. To Engels, it was necessary to penetrate through the surface of Carlyle to find the serious and important social analysis. To Joyce, Carlyle was one of the great liberators of language and style, which is why he uses Carlyle so much in *Ulysses*, both in the Yes, the Everlasting Yea, of the conclusion, and in the remarkable parody of Carlyle which he brings in at the crucial moment of the birth of Mrs Purefoy's baby in the maternity hospital, again taking Carlyle as a celebrator, an anti-Malthusian, a yea-sayer to life.[153]

The 'international', in other words, not as an escape from Scottishness but as its fulfilment: for in Carlyle's style, with its mixture of the biblical and the Germanic, of Scottish with English, 'there are many parallels to be found in Scottish literature – Sir Thomas Urquhart, and the long satirical and flyting traditions, to say nothing of Scottish preachers or Scottish speech habits'.[154] Reintegrating into Scottish traditions the figure whose departure for London was often taken to be indicative of the death of those traditions, folds internationalism back into the national, as does reinterpreting MacDiarmid's late poetry in the context of the American long poem or Hans Magnus Enzensberger's *Mausoleum*, in which 'each poem is printed as a very clear collage of original poetry and documented writings or utterances of the great man in question'.[155] Far from asserting an internationalist nostophobia, Morgan's criticism of Scottish writers from the 1950s to the 1970s bespeaks a generous inclusiveness of those writers about whom something is known and a desire to discover more about what is unknown or known only partially: 'It is no use shying off from Macpherson's Ossian or Henry Mackenzie as if they were beneath serious concern. The history of drama in Scotland may be the blank it seems to be, and then again it may not; the fact is that until a complete history of it is written we are talking about it from insufficient knowledge'.[156] If the internationalism of Morgan's poetic experiments suggested the nostophobe's belief that creativity could be fulfilled only by escape from the constrictions of the national past, Morgan, the critic and teacher, was diligently attempting to recast that national past into one which could contribute to a creative future for the nation, and which could engage in terms of equality with other European cultures, as in his translation of Hölderlin's 'The Rhine':

> But the gods have their own
> undying life; and Heaven, if it needs anything,
> needs heroes, needs
> humanity, needs
> all things mortal. For
> spirits of Heaven can in themselves feel nothing,
> and therefore someone else (if I may say this)
> must surely feel, show sympathy
> for the sake of the gods
> who need him[157]

Hölderlin's poem insists that the gods wander among humanity, seeking what their godly status would deny them – emotion, sympathy, identification. Any stranger might be Zeus in disguise:

> Demigods besiege my thoughts now
> and I must seek them out, dear as they are,
> for their lives do often stir

my heart in its longing.
But what can I call him, the stranger
like you, Rousseau, who with a soul
unconquerable, strong to
endure, a firm understanding,
a sweet talent for listening
that he gave out the speech of the purest
like the wine-god, from a divine abundance.[158]

Hölderlin's encounter with 'the stranger' who comes like a god across his threshold is a celebration of theoxenia: '– Then gods and men celebrate their union/it is a celebration for all the living'. Morgan's translation of Hölderlin's poem may have been inspired by the fact that it is addressed to Hölderlin's friend Izaak von Sinclair, who was from a Scottish-German family that had been resident in Germany for two generations. Those who cross borders, like Rousseau and like Sinclair, those who come as strangers but are friends and inspirers, bring with them the possibility of encountering the gods:

Sinclair my friend! God may appear to you
on the sultry path under the fir-trees or
in a dark oak-wood sheathed with steel or
in clouds, you know him, since you know in your own youth
the strength of his goodness[159]

Such unexpected encounters with the stranger is a key theme in many of Morgan's poems, whether in the banal environment of 'In the snack bar' or the science fiction encounter in 'From the Domain of Arnheim' in which time travellers visit their primitive precursors: 'There are no gods in the domain of Arnheim', the speaker asserts but of course he is one who is godlike, or at least spirit-like, in his absent presence:

I know you felt
the same dismay, you gripped my arm, they were waiting
for what they knew of us to pass.[160]

A comic inversion of that encounter is dialogically presented in 'The First Men on Mercury'[161] and a celebratory version in 'Trio', when ordinary human beings on a Christmas shopping trip become visitors from the gods:

the guitar swells out under its silky plastic cover, tied at the neck
    with silver tinsel tape and a brisk sprig of mistletoe.
Orphean sprig! Melting baby! Warm chihuahua!
The vale of tears is powerless before you.
Whether Chist is born, or is not born, you
put paid to fate, it abdicates
                                        under the Christmas lights

Monsters of the year
go blank, are scattered back,
can't bear this march of three.[162]

A secular *theoxenia* can take place even in Buchanan Street.

For Morgan, the work of translation opened up poetic possibilities that had been closed down in the narrowing expectations of poets and poetry that had come to dominate poetry in English in Britain in the 1950s: as he put it in the 'Introduction' to *Sovpoems* in 1961, 'every "advance" in formalism is a further withdrawal from human relations and confidence – it snaps another link of trust between man and man'.[163] Soviet poetry, he asserts, offers a counterpoise to this diminished sense of how the poet relates to his social world: 'without the one big thing that the Soviet artist does have – interest, care, and positive confidence in and for man and society – there is too little to build on, and the arts become a sort of fascinating marginal fantasy, where talent and effort (and money) are devoted to convincing a sceptical world that the materials used are more interesting than the mind that shapes them or the end it shapes them to'.[164] Translation provides the opportunity to bring alternative conceptions of poetic purpose into one's own cultural sphere: by being hospitable to strangers one can find flights of poetic inspiration that go in alternative directions.

The very first issue of *Scottish International* in January 1968 offered an essay by Morgan on the theme of metamorphosis in the work of Andrei Voznesensky, prefaced by the assertion that a 'poetry which wants meaningfully to interlock with this age must be prepared to be vulnerable, fluid, various, adventurous and searching'.[165] The poem on which Morgan focuses and for which he provides his own translation is 'Wings':

The gods are dozing like slummocks –
Clouds for layabouts!
                                what hammocks!

The gods are for the birds.
The birds are for the birds.

What about wings,
all that paraphernalia?
It's too weird, I tell you,
What did the ancients see in these things?
Nearer
        and nearer
                to the fuselage
clouds press them in,
                to a vestige-
ality of winginess on our things,
our marvel-machines, strange
to them. Men have unslung
something new, men don't hang
out wings, men are with it, bang.
Man, men are winged![166]

The theme of the translation of men into (technological) gods is enacted in the translation into English of a Russian avant-gardism, inspired by the Soviet spaceflights, that gives new 'wings' to poetry in Scotland. Technological progress allows a Russian poet to consort with the gods – 'men become the gods they once adumbrated'[167] – but the hospitality of translation allows those gods to be guests in a previously flightless Scotland: a poetic theoxenia allows the god-like spirit of the Russian poet to offer creative nourishment to the Scottish domestic environment.

It was with precisely this aim that Morgan translated the Russian poet Mayakovsky into Scots: could Scots be 'hospitable' to a Russian modernist whose manifesto declared that poets should 'feel an insurmountable hatred for the language existing before them'?[168] Was Scots in the 1970s still capable of the kind of fusion with modernity that MacDiarmid had achieved in the 1920s? *Wi the Haill Voice: 15 Poems by Vladimir Mayakovsky* invited the moving spirits of modernism in Russia and in Scotland to be (god-like) guests at the (writing) table of Edwin Morgan:

> There is in Scottish poetry (e.g. in Dunbar, Burns, and even MacDiarmid) a vein of fantastic satire that seems to accommodate Mayakovsky more readily than anything in English verse, and

> there was also, I must admit, an element of challenge in finding out whether the Scots language could match the mixture of racy colloquialism and verbal inventiveness in Mayakovsky's Russian. I hoped Hugh MacDiarmid might be right when he claimed in 'Gairmscoile' that
>
> > . . . there's forgotten shibboleths o the Scots
> > Hae keys to senses lockit to us yet.[169]

Wi the Haill Voice exploits in its title the potential of Scots to create those effects which Mayakovsky's Russian contemporary, Alexei Kruchonykh, focused in the phrase 'the word is broader than its meaning':[170] '*Broad* Scots' creates a potentiality of meaning absent from English, so that 'Haill' is not only a translation of what is rendered in English as 'full', but 'haill' in the sense of 'whole', thereby challenging the prevalent assumptions that the very language of Scots is symptomatic of a fragmented culture, incapable of wholeness;[171] at the same time, it punningly invokes 'hail', to call from a distance, which is effectively what Morgan's translations allow Mayakovsky to do – to call from the distance of Russian and through the distance of Scots to a contemporary English-speaking audience. The theoxenic implications of this process are made manifest in the poem 'Vladimir's Ferlie' (rendered in English as 'An Extraordinary Adventure', the only poem, as Morgan notes in his introduction, of which there is an extant recording of Mayakovsky reading): it is a poem in which the poet rails at the sun for its summer heat, only to discover the sun descending to enter his cottage:

> It burst door, winnock, and winnock-frame:
> it brasht and breeshlt
> till it wan
> its pech, it spak fae the pit o its wame:
> 'Thon bleeze has never been retrackit
> Sae faur as this sin I was makkit!
> Ye caad me, poet?
> Whaur's yir trackie?
> I like my jeelie guid and tacky.'[172]

The modern god of an atheistic philosophy, the sun, comes to tea ('trackie') like the gods of old in their wanderings among mankind: a theoxenic celebration allows the poet to accept the sun's recommendation that he should 'gang furrit shinin gowd and shair!' ('go forward shining [like] gold and sure'), despite fatigue and criticism, and having been hospitable to the gods makes the poet himself godlike:

To shine ay and shine aawhere, shine
to the end o endmaist days –
that's aa!
This is the sun's
slogan – and mine![173]

Morgan's translation helps Mayakovesky achieve his ambition 'To shine ay and shine aawhere', an ambition that would be impossible without the hospitality that welcomes the stranger into the vernacular of another culture. Translation as theoxenia is the necessary prelude to, or accompaniment of, the enrichment of one's cultural resources. An essay from 1977 on 'Gavin Douglas and William Drummond as Translators', focuses on translation as the necessary route to a new national identity: 'we can see Douglas as indeed an exemplar of Renaissance vernacular revival, when country after country in Europe seized on translation of established classics as an act of linguistic independence and maturity, implying at the same time a culturo-national independence and maturity'.[174] For Morgan, translation was not the verbal equivalent of exile or of joining a 'colourless or promiscuous internationalism',[175] it was a way of infusing the national territory, the national psyche, with virtues, with literary opportunities that it might not have had within its own cultural evolution. That a Russian futurist could be comfortably entertained within Scots was proof that Scots was an integral part of European modernism, that MacDiarmid's achievement was not an isolated event of no significance to the 'wholeness' – indeed to the 'haleness', in the sense of 'health, fitness' – of Scottish culture. If the gods of modernism can come and take tea in Scots, then Scotland is indeed a fitting home for modern poetry.

And if politics in Scotland had failed then art must take its place, and *Sonnets from Scotland*, published in 1984, is Morgan's first statement of his refusal to submit to the political realities of the 1980s, an insistence that there are alternatives, that there have been and will be alternative Scotlands than the one produced in 1979 when 'A coin clattered at the end of its spin'.[176] *Sonnets from Scotland* also brings to a culmination Morgan's presentation of poetry as theoxenia, as the meeting place of gods and men, the intersection of the timeless with time, and of Scotland as a place hospitable to such minglings. The theoxenic frame of the sequence is a series of encounters with Scotland by unnamed visitors, space- or time-travellers, who encounter fragments of real or possible Scotlands from its earliest formation –

We saw Lewis
laid down, when there was not much but thunder
and volcanic fires [177]

– through its emergence from the ice age and the arrival of the first human beings to the coming of the Romans and of Christianity, and the first map makings of the late Middle Ages and reach forward to a variety of possible modern Scotlands – 'It was so fine we lingered there for hours'[178] – to the time when, by the building of 'The Solway Canal', Scotland is geologically separated from England and becomes its own 'northern island'.[179]

Playing with historical and geological timescales, the poems at once dwarf the relevance of the nation as the frame in which human beings live their lives but then project it out on to a universal scale – 'Scotland was found on Jupiter. That's true. / We lost all track of time, but there it was'.[180] The inhuman of the geological is also the context for human intimacy, so that 'Theory of the Earth' connects Robert Burns, the nation's bard, with James Hutton, the great eighteenth-century geologist who suggested not only the volcanic origins of rocks but that geology 'showed no vestige of a beginning, no prospect of an end',[181] facts which seem to be incorporated into Burns's 'A Red, Red Rose':

And I will luve thee still, my Dear
Till a' the seas gang dry. –

Till a' the seas gang dry, my Dear,
And the rocks melt wi' the sun.[182]

Morgan's poem sets poet and geologist in a vastness in which the Scotland that one celebrated and the other explored will have dissolved into nothingness:

They died almost
together, poet and geologist,
and lie in wait for hilltop buoys to ring,
or aw the seas gang dry and Scotland's coast
dissolve in crinkled sand and pungent mist.[183]

To be able to accept a timeframe in which the country that the sequence celebrates will 'dissolve' into near-nothingness and yet to assert the value of the lives that it frames is the tension which underlies *Sonnet from Scotland*; even if humanity's aspiration to consort with the gods is no more than an evolutionary accident – the product of

the force that could inter
such life and joy, in fossil clays, for apes
and men to haul into their teeming heads.[184]

– it is nonetheless to be celebrated. Thus 'At Stirling Castle, 1507' recounts an incident to which Morgan had already alluded in his essay on 'Dunbar and the Language of Poetry', noting how Dunbar, in the 'Fenyeit Freir of Tungland' 'can hardly wait to describe the charlatan aeronaut's "flight" from Stirling Castle, pursued and mobbed by all the birds of the air, attacking and crying alliteratively and cumulatively according to their characters';[185] in Morgan's sonnet the focus, however, is on the aeronaut's effort to fly when there is as yet no technology that can make flight possible:

He frowned, moved back, and then with quick crow struts
ran forward, flapping strongly, whistling cuts
from the grey heavy space with his black gear
and on a huge spring and a cry was out
beating into vacancy, three, four, five,
till the crawling scaly Forth and the rocks
and the upturned heads replaced that steel shout
of sky he had replied to – left, alive,
and not the last key snapped from high hard locks.[186]

Here, human ambition outstrips itself but prefigures in its very failure the 'wings' of Voznesensky's celebration, 'Man, men are winged!'. It also, however, prefigures the failure of Scottish politics in 1979, which is imaged in 'Post-Referendum' as a damaged, fallen angel, incapable of flight:

We watched the strong sick dirkless Angel groan,
shiver, half-rise, batter with a shrunk wing
the space the Tempter was no longer in.
He tried to hear feet, calls, car-doors, shouts, drone
of engines, hooters, hear a meeting sing.[187]

For both the flying man and the fallen angel, the time has not yet come when human control, whether in technology or in politics, can match the possibilities of the imagination, but if the technology and circumstances conspire, imagination can remake the world:

The universe is like a trampoline.
We chose a springy clump near Arrochar
and with the first jump shot past Barnard's Star.[188]

The improbable is the gateway to the world of the possible.

Morgan's personal commitment to theoxenia was to have significant ramifications in Scottish culture in the period between the first and second devolution referendums. In 'Five Berlin Poems', Liz Lochhead recalls a trip to Berlin in 1990, shortly after the fall of the Berlin Wall:

Today I got back from Berlin and the broken Wall.
With bits of it.
Smithereens of history, the brittle confetti
of chiselled-off graffiti,
trickle on to the brave blue dogeared cover
of my signed copy of *Sonnets from Scotland*
that I had with me and have just unpacked.[189]

'Unpacking' *Sonnets from Scotland* is set in balance with the historical transformation dramatized by the Berlin Wall, as though they were experiences of similar liberation, and Lochhead can celebrate Morgan because she too is a poet and dramatist of theoxenia, inviting the mythic from elsewhere – *Dreaming Frankenstein*, *The Grimm Sisters* – and the classics of European theatre – *Tratuffe*, *Medea* – to make themselves at home in Scotland. Scottish theatre had a long tradition of engagement with translation – Robert Kemp's Scots version of Molière's *L'École des Femmes*, *Let Wives Tak Tent*, was produced at the Edinburgh Festival in 1948, and versions of Ibsen's works were a staple of Scottish repertory[190] – but when the Royal Lyceum Theatre commissioned Lochhead to do a Scots version of Molière's *Tartuffe* in 1986, she developed or discovered a language that would locate the classic in a vernacular that was both historically rich and thoroughly modern: 'a totally invented . . . theatrical Scots, full of anachronisms, demotic speech from various eras and areas; it's proverbial, slangy, couthy, clichéd, catch-phrasey, and vulgar; it's based on Byron, Burns, Stanley Holloway, Ogden Nash and George Formby, as well as the sharp tongue of my granny.[191] It formed a medium in which she could not only 'hail' the classics into Scotland – further translations of Molière, of Chekov as well as from the Greek were to follow – but which also allowed her to dramatize the past anachronistically in what was, at least in part, the language of the Scottish present. When applied to Scottish history, as in *Mary Queen of Scots Got her Head Chopped Off* (1987), this collision of past and present – Riccio, Mary's secretary, uses a typewriter and productions of the play often set it in fashions and styles recognisable as particular decades of the twentieth century – underlines necromantically that 'history' is always the voice of the present. It also, however, takes a story which has travelled into the realms of high art in other cultures – Schiller's *Maria Stuart* (1800) and Donizetti's opera (1835) – and, theoxenically, brings it back to Scotland and transfers the tragedy of the interactions of regnal elites into a Scottish playground fight. The energy of the play's transformations of character – the actresses who play the queens also swap places to play each other's maids, as well as street children in Edinburgh – is in direct contrast to the fact that there can be no surprise about its plotline or its conclusion – the title states that fact baldly. Lochhead insisted that '*Mary Queen of Scots* is emphatically not a history play' but a 'metaphor for the Scots today',[192] and although this has been queried by Ian Brown,[193] it can be read, like *Sonnets from Scotland*, as the allegory of a nation that has lost its agency but which resists that loss by the very inventiveness with which it is articulated. Indeed, the title of *Mary Queen of Scots Got her Head Chopped Off* is balanced on the issue of agency – 'got' might imply that Mary was responsible for 'getting' her head chopped off, or that it was just the thing that happened to her – and the fact that the events that lead to Mary's death must repeat themselves is challenged by the experimentalism by which that repetition is framed: style becomes resistance to the facts of history.

Morgan's support for Lochhead's career – he wrote a 'Foreword' to *Dreaming Frankenstein and Collected Poems* in 1984, declaring that the volume showed that 'poetry in Scotland is evidently not lacking in health and flair'[194] – was matched by his support for Ian Hamilton Finlay in the early part of his career: it was Morgan who had directed Finlay to a letter about 'concrete poetry' by E. M. de Melo E Castro in the *Times Literary Supplement*, where Finlay discovered that 'it was just what in my little naïve, home-made, Scottish way, I had been thinking about'.[195] Finlay published his first concrete poetry in *Rapel* in 1963 and contributed to the first international concrete poetry festival in Brighton in 1967. His role as a pioneer in the movement was acknowledged when he and Morgan were nominated as the Scottish representatives on the committee of the international concrete poetry movement. This was not the only international network in which Morgan and Finlay were involved, as both had published in Gael Turnbull's *Migrant* magazine,[196] established in 1958 in Ventura, California, and which then led to Finlay's appearance in Migrant's new book list with his first collection, *The Dancers Inherit the Party* (1960). *Migrant* shows how the activities of Scottish migrants continued to impact on the homeland long after the end of Scotland's xeniteian Empire, but Finlay's progress from the folk simplicities of *The Dancers Inherit the Party*, through the phonetically transcribed Glasgow dialect of *Glasgow Beasts, an a Burd, haw, an Inseks, an aw, a Fush* of 1961, to the concrete poetry of the early 1960s, saw him also follow the example of *Migrant* by establishing in 1964, with his collaborator Jessie McGuffie, the Wild Hawthorn Press which launched, in the following year, the magazine *Poor. Old. Tired. Horse.* (a title taken from the poem 'Please' by Robert Creeley), of which 25 numbers had been produced by 1968. Edwin Morgan summarises it as a magazine in which 'well-crafted thing-y poetry was preferred to expressionist or confessional "depth"', and that while it did 'publish concrete poetry, semiotic poetry, and sound-poetry' it also included poets who 'dealt with the larger socio-political issues: Mayakovsky, József, Neruda, Günter Grass': the result, Morgan suggests was 'an eclecticism that two decades later seems to belong so much to the spirit of the sixties as to have gained more unity and harmony than it appeared to possess at the time'.[197] In 1966, in the midst of these creative shifts, Hamilton Finlay and his wife, Sue MacDonald-Lockhart, took over a small croft, called Stonypath, on the edge of the Pentland Hills, and they began to transform what was rough grazing into the garden that later became known, as a result of its opposition to the arts authorities in the Athens of the North, as Little Sparta. By name and by design, Little Sparta was a theoxenic project – its aim to create out of a domestic Scottish environment a place which would be ready to accommodate the arrival of the gods. Thus an old farm building was turned into a temple dedicated

TO APOLLO
HIS MUSIC   HIS MISSILES   HIS MUSES

and shrines which celebrated the patron god of the household were established. The Finlays' garden quite literally reshaped Scottish 'nature' to be a combination of local and classical architecture – Scottish buildings decorated with classical columns – and reshaped the landscape to embody versions of garden design from 'The Roman Garden' to the 'English Parkland'. The garden is a place where art and nature meet, whether in the lettering carved on stones and plinths and set amongst the foliage, or in the ways in which particular views are designed to replicate how previous art has envisaged nature, as in the 1979 exhibition *Nature Over Again After Poussin*. But the garden is also a place of war between humanity and nature: the garden imposes a pattern on nature which nature is always trying to disrupt – and all gardens do, in the end, succumb to nature's belligerence at being controlled. And the imagery of war is everywhere in Finlay's garden: a bird table is in the shape of an aircraft carrier, instead of a flute, classical figures in the statuary carry machine guns, the 'temple' of Apollo houses a guillotine and baskets for collecting heads. To be able to welcome the stranger who is a god-in-disguise you have to be able to defend yourself against the stranger who aims to destroy your creation. The garden both symbolises harmony – harmony between art and nature – and, at the same time, demonstrates the necessity of the violence by which that harmony is achieved – some plants are weeds, which cannot be allowed to flourish; as a card of 1973 states, 'Mower is less'.[198]

In its defiance of nature – the land is unpromising, the climate challenging – and of history – can such ambitious structures be built without the support of the state or some major sponsor?

– the Finlays' garden testifies to how will-power and creativity can transform the environment in which we live. But it also testifies to how every creation of the modern era is also a recollection of our distance from whatever it might mean to be 'at home' in the world: above and below a line drawing of a battleship are inscribed the lines

FOR THE TEMPLES
OF THE GREEKS

OUR HOMESICKNESS
LASTS FOR EVER[199]

In a Scotland whose eighteenth- and nineteenth-century achievements were expressed in imitations of Greek temples, this becomes doubly nostalgic, or doubly tragic. Art is always in search of the homeland from which it is always in exile – an exile by which each act of the recovery of the past confirms only that the past itself always gestures to an even deeper past which recedes from us the faster we pursue it.

Stonypath's transformation into Little Sparta, and the empty countryside's transformation not only into a flourishing garden full of statuary and poetry but by the rich allusiveness of its classical and modern imagery, might stand as an emblem of Scotland's theoxenic transformation in the last decades of the twentieth century. It was also, as it happens, a recuperation and reanimation of Scotland's tradition of the landscape garden as developed by Thomas Blaikie in France, where he was gardener to the royal family and responsible for the introduction of the '*jardin anglais*', and, equally, of the tradition of the domestic garden as developed by John Claudius Loudon, who made the style of the botanic garden – the 'gardenesque', as he called it – central to the gardens of the Victorian era. Finlay's garden invited the return of the gods to a Scotland that, in 1966 when he and Sue moved to Stonypath, had seemed far from promising territory.

V Vernaculars

During the Irish Revival of the 1890s, W. B. Yeats regularly invoked a quote he attributed to Victor Hugo: 'It is in the

Theatre that the mob becomes a people'.[200] Yeats's engagement with theatre in Dublin in the years before 1914 was aimed at creating 'a people' capable of the commitment required to produce a movement for political independence. In the 1960s and 70s, the rise of nationalism in Scotland seemed to have a similar dynamic, creating a theatrical energy that found a flourishing audience for the dramatic possibilities of the Scots language, whether in historical dramas such as Donald Campbell's *The Jesuit* (1976), or in the vernacular Scots of 'workplace' dramas such as Bill Bryden's *Willie Rough* (1972) or Roddy McMillan's *The Bevellers* (1976), or in the West of Scotland demotic of John Byrne's *The Slab Boys* (1978). The intersection of theatre and politics was made explicit in the work of John McGrath's 7:84 company, which combined the techniques of Brecht with the traditions of Scottish pantomime to produce what were intended to be socialist representations of Scottish working-class experience – *The Game's a Bogey* (1975) has as its focus the life the First World War Scottish communist leader John Maclean – but which, as in *The Cheviot, the Stag and the Black Black Oil* (1974), roused nationalist sentiments as much as socialist analysis. Touring the country to perform in ceilidh style in local venues, it looked like 7:84 had indeed found a 'people' with whom they could share their political vision. In the aftermath of the 1979 referendum, however, and the establishment of the Thatcher government, the political energy of 7:84 seemed to have as little chance of fulfilment as the demands for a Scottish parliament, and like many others in Scottish culture, 7:84 looked to the Scottish past for models of how it might challenge the Scottish present. Between 1982 and 1984 it recovered and re-presented a tradition of Scottish working-class drama which had entirely disappeared from Scotland's cultural consciousness, including, in 1982, Ena Lamont Stewart's *Men Should Weep*, first performed by the Unity Theatre Company in 1947; in 1984, Joe Corrie's *In Time of Strife*, first performed in 1926; and, in 1987, *The Gorbals Story*, first performed in 1946 and sufficiently successful in the London theatre to have been made into a film in 1950. The recovery of this tradition of working-class drama underlined not only that Scotland had its own distinct and powerful theatrical tradition – one that had disappeared from view in the country's cultural amnesia[201] – but that vernacular Scots was a medium through which the issues of a modern industrial society could be addressed.

The successes of Scottish theatre in the 1970s and 80s led to a regular questioning of why there was no national theatre company, dedicated to Scottish theatrical traditions.[202] As far back as 1970 a group of Scottish actors, including Andrew Cruickshank, Fulton Mackay, Roddy McMillan and Una McLean, had established the Scottish Actors Company in order that 'a space should be found for a Scottish, distinctive voice',[203] but the Scottish Arts Council had little enthusiasm for adding another national company to those it was often struggling adequately to fund. A proposal to build a new cultural venue in Edinburgh that would house the Lyceum, the Traverse and provide a home for Scottish opera stalled, and this unresolved possibility – known locally as the 'hole in the ground' – prevented any other route forward to the establishment of a National Theatre, with theatre funding dropping from 33 to 17 per cent of the Arts Council's budget. Nonetheless, theatre continued to thrive and to create space for 'a Scottish distinctive voice' but it was in the novel that that voice was to assert itself most vigorously after Polygon published, in 1984, James Kelman's first novel *The Bus Conductor Hines*. Francis Russell Hart had identified as one of the major difficulties of the Scottish novel an 'uncertain narrative voice' which cannot decide how distant or how close it ought to be to the speech of its characters: 'If local realities and affiliations matter, then authentic local speech matters. If local speech is seen as a test of cultural fidelity, then the faithful narrator may seem insular and the distanced narrator is hard pressed to seem anything but an accomplice of the betrayers'.[204] But just as Gray's *Lanark* subverts Hart's account of the 'problems' of the Scottish novel by redeploying them in a creative fashion, so Kelman overturns Hart's analysis by incorporating the terms of the problem into his own narrative technique. According to Kelman, what working-class writers are told by the literary establishment is that they should,

> Go and write any story at all, providing of course you stay within the bounds, not the bounds of decency or propriety or anything tangible; because that it not the way it works. Nobody issues such instructions. It is all carried out by a series of nudges and winks and tacit agreements. What it amounts to is: go and write a story about a bunch of guys who stand talking in a pub all day but if you have them talking then do not have them talking the language they talk.
>
> Pardon?

> Write a story wherein people are talking, but not talking the language they talk.[205]

As it cannot have its characters 'talking the language they talk', conventional literary realism defeats its own end: what it purveys is a 'reality-illusion' in which reality is actually rendered both inaudible and invisible. What Kelman developed was a style in which there is no disjunction between the language of the narrator and the language of the character – indeed, the character becomes his own narrator, describing his actions in the third person but doing so in the linguistic structures of first-person speech:

> But it couldnay get worse than this. He was really fuckt now. This was the dregs: he was at it. He had fucking reached it now man the fucking dregs man the pits, the fucking black fucking limboland, purgatory; that's what it was like, purgatory, where all ye can do is think. Think. That's all ye can do. Ye just fucking think about what ye've done and what ye've no fucking done; ye cannay look at nothing ye cannay see nothing it's just a total fucking disaster area, yer mind, yer fucking memories, a disaster area.[206]

The shift from third person 'he' to the self-addressing 'ye' reveals how fluidly the language of the novel adapts itself to Sammy's speech patterns. Instead of 'a story wherein people are talking, but not talking the language they talk', we are given a narration that works precisely by adopting as its own 'the language they talk'. In Kelman's novels the particularity of the vernacular in which a character would talk becomes the medium of the novel itself, thus reversing and inverting the usual hierarchy between the standard English of narration and the dialect in which characters speak. The result are narratives that are as fabulatory as Muriel Spark's or Alasdair Gray's, because the 'reality' they present consists equally of 'what ye've done and what ye've no fucking done', of what is believed to exist and what is believed not to exist: as Patrick Doyle in *A Disaffection* discovers, there is no end to language – 'you canni stop me talking. I just talk all the time'[207] – and in language the real and the unreal exist side by side: 'That poor old nonentity Vulcan, being once thought to exist, and then being discovered not to. Imagine being discovered not to exist! That's even worse than being declared fucking redundant, irrelevant, which was the fate of ether upon the advent of Einstein'.[208] In Kelman's novels the existent and non-existent continue to live side by side: in a disenchanted world, the discarded gods can find hospitality in speech.

By 1996 Scotland had neither a Parliament nor a National Theatre, but it had a voice; in fact, it had a wealth of voices.

Notes

1. Davie, G., *The Democratic Intellect: Scotland and Her Universities in the Nineteenth Century* (Edinburgh: Edinburgh University Press, 1961).
2. Davie, G., *The Scotch Metaphysics: A Century of Enlightenment in Scotland* (London: Routledge, 2001), p. 8.
3. Stewart, D., 'Dissertation Exhibiting the Progress of Metaphysical, Ethical and Political Philosophy, since the Revival of Letters in Europe', in Hamilton, W. Sir (ed.), *Collected Works*, Vol. 1 (Edinburgh: Thomas Constable and Co., 1854).
4. Davie, *Democratic Intellect*, p. 337.
5. Broadie, A., *The Tradition of Scottish Philosophy: A New Perspective on the Enlightenment* (Edinburgh: Polygon, 1990), p. 92.
6. Broadie, A., *A History of Scottish Philosophy* (Edinburgh: Edinburgh University Press, 2009), see particularly Chapter 5.
7. Davie, G., *The Crisis of the Democratic Intellect* (Edinburgh: Polygon, 1986), p. 162.
8. Ibid. p. 164.
9. Ibid. p. 260.
10. Ibid. p. 240.
11. Wilson, D. B., *Seeking Nature's Logic: Natural Philosophy in the Scottish Enlightenment* (Pennsylvania: Pennsylvania State University Press, 2009), p. 33–68.
12. Davie, *The Democratic Intellect*, p. 180.
13. Higgit, R., *Recreating Newton: Newtonian Biography and the Making of Nineteenth-Century History of Science* (London: Pickering and Chatto, 2007), p. 12ff.
14. Brewster, D., *The Life of Isaac Newton* (London: John Murray, 1831), p. 222.
15. Ibid. 264.
16. Ibid. 268.
17. Brewster, D., *Memoirs of the Life, Writings and Discoveries of Sir Isaac Newton* (Edinburgh: Thomas Constable and Co., 1855), II, pp. 374–5.
18. Ibid. 375.
19. Golinski, J., 'The Secret Life of an Alechemist', in Fauvel, J.,

R. Flood, M. Shortland and R. Wilson (eds), *Let Newton Be! A New Perspective on his Life and Works* (Oxford: Oxford University Press, 1988), p. 147.

20. Keynes, J. M., 'Newton the Man', in *The Royal Society Newton Tercentenary Celebrations 15–19 July 1946* (Cambridge: Cambridge University Press, 1947), p. 27.
21. Quoted Derek Gjersten, 'Newton's Success', in Fauvel, Flood, Shortland and Wilson (eds), *Let Newton Be!*, p. 26.
22. Rattansi, P., 'Newton and the Wisdom of the Ancients', in Fauvel, Flood, Shortland and Wilson (eds), *Let Newton Be!*, p. 187.
23. Gregory, D., *Elements of Astronomy, Physical and Geometrical* (London, 1715), pp. ix–x.
24. Westfall, R. S., 'Newton and Alchemy', in Vickers B. (ed.), *Occult and Scientific Mentalities in the Renaissance* (Cambridge: Cambridge University Press, 1984), pp. 315–35.
25. Lomas, R., *The Invisible College: The Royal Society, Freemasonry and the Birth of Modern Science* (London: Headline, 2002).
26. Brewster, D., *Memoirs of the Life, Writings and Discoveries of Sir Isaac Newton*, p. 374
27. Ibid. p. 313.
28. Normand, T., 'Natural Magic: Calum Colvin and the Legacy of Sir David Brewster', in Colvin, C. *Natural Magic|Natural Magic* (Edinburgh: Scottish Royal Academy, 2009), p. 7.
29. Images available at <http://www.calumcolvin.com/Ossian.html> (last accessed 09 September 2017).
30. Available at <http://www.calumcolvin.com/Burnsiana.html> (last accessed 18 May 2017).
31. Davie, *Democratic Intellect*, p. 185.
32. Hart, F. R., *The Scottish Novel: A Critical Survey* (London: John Murray, 1978), p. 407.
33. Massie, A., *One Night in Winter* (London, [1984] 1985).
34. Ibid. p. 43.
35. Ibid. p. 124.
36. Ibid. p. 124.
37. Ibid. p. 125.
38. Ibid. pp. 126–7.
39. Ibid. p. 142.
40. Ibid. p. 199.
41. Ibid. p. 65.
42. Ibid. p. 32.
43. Ibid. p. 199.
44. Ibid. p. 158.
45. Ibid. p. 112.
46. Ibid. p. 116.

47. Ibid. p 50.
48. Ibid. p. 236.
49. Robertson, J., *And the Land Lay Still* (London: Penguin, [2010] 2011), p. 244.
50. Gray, A., *Lanark: A Life in Four Books* (Edinburgh: Canongate, 1981), p. 243.
51. Ibid. p. 244.
52. Galloway, J., *The Trick is to Keep Breathing* (Edinburgh: Polygon, 1989), p. 79.
53. Kennedy, A. L., *So I am Glad* (London: Jonathan Cape, 1995), p. 5.
54. Welsh, I., *Marabou Stork Nightmares* (London: Jonathan Cape, 1995), p. 17.
55. Hart, *The Scottish Novel*, p. 295.
56. Massie, A., *Muriel Spark* (Edinburgh: Ramsay Head, 1982), p. 94.
57. Spark, M., *Territorial Rights* (London: Penguin, [1979] 1991), p. 172.
58. Ibid., p. 237.
59. Spark, M., *Symposium* (London: Penguin, [1990] 1991), p. 81.
60. Watt, I., *The Rise of the Novel* (Harmondsworth: Penguin, [1957] 1963).
61. Ibid. p. 32
62. Ibid. p. 31.
63. Ibid. p. 20.
64. Ibid. p. 62.
65. Ibid. p. 77.
66. Ibid. p. 78.
67. Ibid. p. 83.
68. Ibid. p. 86.
69. Ibid. p. 89.
70. Ibid. p. 87.
71. Ibid. p. 71.
72. Spark, *Robinson*, (London: Macmillan, 1958) p. 160.
73. Spark, M. and D. Stanford., *Emily Brontë: Her Life and Work* (London: Peter Owen Limited), p. 88. This was published in 1960, two years after *Robinson*, but Spark had been working on Brontë since editing her letters in 1953 and her book with Stanford had been commissioned in that year; see Stannard, M. *Muriel Spark: The Biography* (London: Weidenfeld & Nicolson, 2009), p. 136.
74. Spark, and Stanford, *Emily Brontë*, p. 95.
75. Spark, M., *Robinson*, p. 185.
76. Norquay, G. (ed.), *R. L. Stevenon on Fiction* (Edinburgh: Edinburgh University Press, 1999), p. 84

77. Spark, *Symposium*, p. 64.
78. Kennedy, A. L., *So I am Glad* (London: Jonathan Cape, 1995).
79. Banks, I., *The Wasp Factory* (London: Macmillan, 1984).
80. Whyte, C., *Euphemia MacFarrigle and the Laughing Virgin* (London: Gollancz, 1995), p. 109.
81. Meek, J., *Drivetime* (Edinburgh: Polygon, 1995).
82. Warner, A., *Morvern Callar* (London: Cape, 1996), p. 50.
83. Greig, A., *Electric Brae* (Edinburgh: Canongate, 1992),
84. Kelman, J. *The Busconductor Hines* (Edinburgh: Polygon, 1984), p. 168.
85. Banks, I., *Walking on Glass* (London: Macmillan, [1985] 1990).
86. Ibid.
87. This, we might say, is Banks's dystopic version of 'theoxenia'.
88. Welsh, I., *Trainspotting* (London: Secker & Warburg, 1993).
89. Kay, J., *Trumpet* (London: Picador, 1998).
90. Banks, I. M., *Player of Games* (London: Macmillan, 1988).
91. Kuppner, F., *A Concussed History of Scotland* (Edinburgh: Polygon, 1990), p. 192.
92. O'Rourke, D., *Dream State: The New Scottish Poets* (Edinburgh: Polygon, 1994), p. 65.
93. Hart, *Scottish Novel*, p. 406.
94. Gray, *Lanark*, pp. 500–1.
95. Ibid. p. 551.
96. Ibid. pp. 486, 493, 495.
97. Ibid. p. 489.
98. Ibid. p. 493.
99. See Manlove, C., *Scotland's Forgotten Treasure: The Visionary Romances of George MacDonald* (Aberdeen: Aberdeen University Press, 2017).
100. Macmillan, D., *Scottish Art 1460–1990* (Edinburgh: Mainstream, 1990), p. 318.
101. Fergusson, J. D., *Modern Scottish Painting* (Glasgow: William MacLellan, 1943), p. 69.
102. Fergusson, J. D., 'Art and Atavism: The Dryad', *Scottish Art and Letters*, Number 1, 1944, p. 48.
103. Bain, G., 'The Truth about Pictish Cultures', *Scottish Art and Letters*, Number 4, 1949, pp. 27–40. Bain's theories of Celtic art were collected as Bain, G. *Celtic Art, the Methods of Construction* (Glasgow: William MacLellan, 1944).
104. Fergusson, 'Art and Atavism', *Scottish Art and Letters*, p. 47.
105. See Antliff, M., *Inventing Bergson: Cultural Politics and the Parisian Avant-Garde* (Princeton, NJ: Princeton University Press, 1993), p. 106–134, who notes that the *Rhythm* group

in Paris was closely associated with those promoting a Celtic nationalist vision both of France and of Cubism.

106. White, K,. 'The Scot Abroad', *On Scottish Ground* (Edinburgh: Polygon, 1998), p. 105.
107. Ibid. p. 106.
108. Ibid. p. 107.
109. Ibid. p. 107
110. White, K., 'Pelagius', *Open World: The Collected Poems 1960–2000* (Edinburgh: Polygon, 2003), p. 9: 'but was there ever, I ask you/a brighter mind/a more diamond being/in all the murky history of knowledge?'
111. Note to 'Report to Erigena', *Open World*, p. 606.
112. 'Walking the Coast', XLIV, Ibid. p. 170.
113. White, 'Kentigern on Atlantic Quay', *On Scottish Ground*, p. 195.
114. Ibid. p. 195
115. White, 'Scotland, History and the Writer', *On Scottish Ground*, p. 153.
116. White, 'The Archaic Context', *On Scottish Ground*, p. 31.
117. White, 'The Alban Project', *On Scottish Ground*, p. 3.
118. White, 'A Shaman Dancing on the Glacier', *On Scottish Ground*, p. 41.
119. White, 'The Archaic Context', *On Scottish Ground*, p. 33.
120. White, 'Scotland, Intelligence, Culture', *On Scottish Ground*, p. 91.
121. White, 'On Rannoch Moor', *Open World*, pp. 100–1.
122. White, 'Into the White World', *On Scottish Ground*, p. 58.
123. White, 'The Island without a Name', *Open World*, p. 337.
124. Geddes P. and J. Arthur Thomson, *Biology* (London: Home University Library, 1925).
125. White, 'Looking Out: From Neotechnics to Geopoetics', *On Scottish Ground*, p. 147.
126. White, 'Walking the Coast, LII', *Open World*, p. 178.
127. White, 'Looking Out: From Neotechnics to Geopoetics', *On Scottish Ground*, p. 142.
128. White, 'Into the White World', *On Scottish Ground*, p. 60, p. 61.
129. Ibid. p. 64.
130. White, *Open World*, p. 106.
131. White, 'Chant', *Open World*, p. 57.
132. White, 'Talking Transformation', *On Scottish Ground*, p. 184.
133. White, 'Interpretations of a Twisted Pine', *Open World*, p. 213.
134. White, 'A Shaman Dancing on a Glacier', *On Scottish Ground*, p. 37.
135. Heidegger, M., 'Letter on Humanism', in Cahoone L. (ed.), *From Modern to Postmodern* (Oxford: Blackwell, 1996), p. 303;

originally published in Krell D. F. (ed.), *Martin Heidegger: Basic Writings* I (New York: Harper and Row, 1777), pp. 193–242.
136. White, 'A Shaman Dancing on a Glacier', *On Scottish Ground*, p. 38.
137. White, 'Black Forest', *Open World*, p. 92.
138. Heidegger, 'Letter on Humanism', in Cahoone L. (ed.), *From Modern to Postmodern*, p. 299.
139. White, 'The High Field', *On Scottish Ground*, p. 179.
140. Ibid. p. 179.
141. Nicholson, C., *Poem, Purpose, Place* (Edinburgh: Polygon, 1992), p. 76.
142. Morgan, E., *Collected Poems* (Manchester: Carcanet, 1990), p. 176.
143. Ibid. p. 199.
144. Whyte, H. (ed.), *Edwin Morgan: Nothing Not Giving Messages* (Edinburgh: Polygon, 1990), p. 34.
145. Ross, R., 'Editorial', *Cencrastus*, No. 38, Winter 1990/91.
146. Quoted in McGonigal, J., *Beyond the Last Dragon: A Life of Edwin Morgan* (Dingwall: Sandstone Press, 2010), p. 456.
147. Ibid. pp. 431–2.
148. White (ed.), *Nothing Not Giving Messages*, p. 40.
149. Morgan, E., *Crossing the Border: Essays on Scottish Literature* (Manchester: Carcanet, 1990).
150. Morgan, *Crossing the Border,* p. 156.
151. Ibid. p. 19.
152. Ibid. p. 23–4.
153. Ibid. p. 140.
154. Ibid. p. 131.
155. Ibid. 'MacDiarmid's Later Poetry', p. 193
156. Ibid. 'Towards a Literary History of Scotland', p. 12.
157. Morgan, E., *Collected Translations* (Manchester: Carcanet, 1996), p. 258.
158. Ibid. p. 259.
159. Ibid. p. 261.
160. Morgan, *Collected Poems*, p. 198.
161. Ibid. p. 267.
162. Ibid. p. 172.
163. Morgan, *Collected Translations*, p. 31.
164. Ibid. p. 31.
165. Morgan, E., 'Heraclitus in Gorky Street: The Theme of Metamorphosis in the Poetry of Voznesensky', *Scottish International*, No. 1, January 1968, pp. 21–6, at pp. 24–5.
166. Ibid. p. 25.
167. Ibid. p. 25.

168. Morgan, *Collected Translations*, p. 108.
169. Ibid. p. 113.
170. Ibid. p. 110.
171. This is the burden, for instance, of David Craig's *Scottish Literature and the Scottish People, 1680–1830*, of which Morgan writes in 1971: 'a mixture of Leavis and Marx that might seem to be unholy has worked in fact surprisingly well to produce a serious study of an important period in Scottish life and writing'; despite being 'refreshingly non-parochial, well-documented' it is 'yet at times rather wilfully unsympathetic' (*CB*, 11). 'Unholy' may not have been intended as a pun but Morgan is effectively turning back on Craig the accusation that Scotland was 'un-whole'.
172. Morgan, *Collected Translations*, p. 123.
173. Ibid. p. 125.
174. Morgan, *Crossing the Border*, p. 68.
175. 'Editorial', *Scottish International*, No. 1, January 1968, p. 3.
176. Morgan, *Collected Poems*, 'Post-Referendum', p. 449.
177. Ibid. 'Slate', p. 437.
178. Ibid. 'Clydegrad', p. 456.
179. Ibid. 'Solway Canal', p. 455.
180. Ibid. 'On Jupiter', p. 456.
181. James Hutton, 'Theory of the Earth; or an Investigation of the Laws Observable in the Composition, Dissolution, and Restoration of Land upon the Globe', *Transactions of the Royal Society of Edinburgh*, Vol. I (Edinburgh: J. Dickson, 1788), pp. 209–304, at p. 304.
182. Noble, A. and P. Scott Hogg (eds). *The Canongate Burns* (Edinburgh: Canongate, 2001) p. 412.
183. Morgan, *Collected Poems,* 'Theory of the Earth', p. 443.
184. Ibid. 'Carboniferous', p. 437
185. Morgan, *Crossing the Border,* p. 47.
186. Morgan, *Collected Poems*, 'At Stirling Castle, 1507', p. 442.
187. Ibid. 'Post-Referendum', p. 449.
188. Ibid. 'Travellers (1)', p. 447.
189. Lochhead, L., 'Five Berlin Poems', *Bagpipe Muzak* (London: Penguin, 1991), p. 77.
190. The *Fife Free Press*, for instance, advertised on 20 February 1954 a week of performances of Ibsen's *The Lady from the Sea* by the Perth Theatre Company.
191. Lochhead, L., *Tartuffe* (Edinburgh: Polygon, 1985), 'Introduction'.
192. Varty, A., 'Scripts and Performance', in Crawford R. and A. Varty (eds.), *Liz Lochhead's Voices* (Edinburgh: Edinburgh University Press, 1993), p. 162.

193. See, Brown, I., *History as Theatrical Metaphor: History, Myth and National Identities in Modern Scottish Drama* (London: Palgrave Macmillan, 2016), p. 160.
194. Lochhead, L., *Dreaming Frankenstein and Collected Poems* (Edinburgh: Polygon, 1984), p. v.
195. Quoted, Finlay, A., 'Afterword', Ian Hamilton Finlay, *The Dancers Inherit the Party & Glasgow Beasts, an a Burd* (Edinburgh: Polygon, 1996), p. 98.
196. See Richard Price's account of Turnbull and of *Migrant* in an essay: Price, R., 'Migrant the Magnificent', available at <http://www.poetrymagazines.org.uk/magazine/record.asp?id=19293> (last accessed at 14 June 2017); also available at <http://www.hydrohotel.net/EssaysMigrant1.htm> (last accessed 14 June 2017).
197. Morgan, E., 'Early Finlay', in Finlay A. (ed.), *Wood Notes Wild: Essays on the poetry and art of Ian Hamilton Finlay* (Edinburgh: Polygon, 1995), pp. 20–1.
198. Abrioux, Y., *Ian Hamilton Finlay: A Visual Primer* (London: Reaktion, 1985), p. 282
199. Ibid. p. 193.
200. Frayne, J. P. and Johnson C. (eds), *Uncollected Prose by W. B. Yeats: Later Reviews, Articles and Other Miscellaneous Prose 1897–1939* (London: Macmillan, 1975), p. 286.
201. The continuity of Scotland's theatrical tradition was the revealed by the contributors to: Findlay B., *A History of Scottish Theatre* (Edinburgh: Polygon, 1998).
202. Smith, D., '1950–1995', in Findlay B. (ed.), *A History of Scottish Theatre*, pp. 253–308 at p. 284; and Smith, D. 'Playing National: The Scottish Experiment', *Journal of Irish and Scottish Studies*, Vol. 1, No. 1, 2007, pp. 221–231.
203. Cruickshank, A., *Andrew Cruickshank* (London: Weidenfeld & Nicolson, 1988), pp. 105–6.
204. Hart, *The Scottish Novel*, p. 407.
205. Kelman, J. *And the Judges Said …* (London: Secker & Warburg, 2002), pp. 64–5.
206. Kelman, J., *How late it was, how late* (London: Secker & Warburg, 1994), p. 172.
207. Kelman, J., *A Disaffection* (London: Secker & Warburg, 1989), p. 313.
208. Ibid. p. 252.

5 Unsettled Will: Culture and Scottish Independence

I The Mystery

When David Cameron responded on the morning of 19 September 2014 to the outcome of the Referendum on Scottish Independence, he declared that remaining in the Union was the 'settled will' of the Scottish people: 'there can be no disputes, no re-runs – we have heard the settled will of the Scottish people'.[1] The almost unequalled turnout – 84.59% of the electorate voted – showed the extent of the commitment on both sides of the argument and reflected the intensity with which the debate had been conducted in the previous two years. Though the 'Yes' side lost 55:45, the surge in support for independence took it well beyond the 30% that had been the settled view in the polls since the 1990s, and in the week before the Referendum the will of the Scottish people had looked far from 'settled' when, after a single poll showed the 'Yes' campaign edging slightly ahead, the Prime Minister, the Deputy Prime Minister and the leader of the Labour party all abandoned Westminster and rushed north to make a joint 'vow' about increased powers for the Scottish Parliament if the Scottish people would only vote to stay in the Union.

The phrase 'the settled will of the Scottish people' was originally invoked by John Smith, leader of the Labour party from 1992 until his death in 1994, but it was used to counterbalance the 'settled will' of many Labour politicians in Scotland that devolution was a distraction from the main business of British politics, and likely to encourage rather than to nullify the appeal of the Scottish National Party. After all, when Scotland's commitment to devolution had last been tested in the Referendum of 1979, it had proved far from conclusive, with those in favour only marginally outnumbering those against and with almost the same percentage failing to register a vote. But what Cameron saw as a 'settled will' in Scotland in 2014 was to be radically challenged in the general election of May 2015, when the Scottish National Party (SNP) won all but three seats in Scotland and Labour lost 40 of its 41 seats. Had the electorate decided to punish Labour for working with the Conservatives in the 'Better Together' campaign? Or was an overwhelming majority for the SNP a signal that Scots had changed their minds, and now did want independence? Or was it the psephological consequence of the 45% who had voted 'Yes' committing to the SNP, while the 55% who had voted 'No' were split across a variety of parties? Was the overwhelming SNP majority a call for a second referendum, or was the 'settled will' of the majority still for the Union? Whatever the interpretation, the 'Brexit' vote in 2016 seemed to show a decisive split between opinion in Scotland (where 62% voted to stay in the European Union) and in England and Wales, where the vote was sufficiently decisive that the final outcome for the UK as a whole was 52% to leave and 48% to remain. That outcome was in turn to be put under considerable pressure, if not actual doubt, by the failure of Theresa May to gain the substantial majority she had hoped for in the 'snap' election of June 2017: were these outcomes which opened the way to a second independence referendum, as Nicola Sturgeon had claimed after the 'Brexit' vote, or did the stronger showing of the Unionist parties, who each gained seats at the expense of the SNP, show that such a referendum was unwanted by the 55%, who still formed the majority on the issue of independence?

In truth, the years between the first referendum in 1979, the second after the Labour Party's victory in 1997 and the third in 2014 have been years in which there has been no 'settled will' in Scotland: the establishment of the Scottish Parliament in 1999 was supposed to close the issue of Scotland's relationship with the Union but hardly was the new parliament building open than the Calman Commission was considering whether it ought to have broader powers, and before those recommendations could be enacted the 'vow' of greater powers offered by the three 'Better Together' party leaders led to the Smith commission, and to another set of proposals for increased powers. The constitutional settlement represented by the Scottish Parliament has been constantly unsettled by peoples' increasing willingness to commit their votes to the SNP – first in the Scottish parliament elections of 2007, when the SNP became a minority government, and then in 2011, when it won the outright majority that the proportional representation voting system in Scotland had been designed to prevent. The rise of the SNP from a fringe movement in the 1960s, to a small player in Scottish politics in the 1990s, to the dominant political force of the 2010s – it is now, in terms of membership, the third largest party in the UK[2] – has not only been remarkable but also, to many, remarkably mysterious: the *Herald*'s political columnist, Iain Macwhirter begins his book *Road to Referendum* with a question: 'Here's the mystery. How did Scotland go from being a willing and enthusiastic partner in the Union with England to the referendum on independence within the space of little more than a generation?'[3] That 'mystery', however, has not been answered at the end of Macwhirter's narrative: 'The theme of this book has been the rise, as if from nowhere, of Scottish Nationalism'.[4] Scottish nationalism arises from nowhere, propelled by a dynamic which seems to defy the logic of modern politics – sociological studies find that there is very little difference between social attitudes in Scotland and in England[5] – and also to defy the logic of Scotland's own history, in which it was a committed participant in the British Empire and a dynamic creator and defender of British institutions such as the British Broadcasting Corporation and the National Health Service. It is this that shocks opponents of the SNP such as former Prime Minster Gordon Brown who, in *My Scotland, Our Britain*, expresses dismay at 'the speed with which Scottish political nationalism has moved from the fringes to the mainstream, then to an electoral majority in the Scottish Parliament and now to threaten the very existence of Britain is extraordinary'.[6] Indeed, according to Brown, it is mystery even to those most acutely involved because neither the 'political nationalists who have driven the change, nor the Unionists who have resisted it, offer a clear sense of what really lies behind the rise of a hitherto unsuccessful party'.[7]

II The Accidental Parliament

It is easy to forget how unlikely a Scottish parliament, let alone an SNP government, seemed in the early 1990s, but one only has to look into Andrew Marr's account of the debate in his *The Battle for Scotland*, first published in 1993, or his 1993 contribution on Scottish politics to Paul Scott's *Scotland: A Concise Cultural History*, to see how far a possible Scottish parliament had been detached from any political reality. In the aftermath of the victory of Margaret Thatcher's successor, John Major, over Labour's Neil Kinnock in 1992, it looked to many commentators as though the Conservatives had established a permanent hold on power at Westminster and therefore erected an immoveable barrier to any form of devolution in Scotland. As Marr put it in what was then the final chapter of his book,

> Everything was changed, changed utterly. After the 1992 election Scottish politics, like British politics generally, functioned in a new world where assumptions about 'our turn' and 'it's only a question of time' had been rudely upended. Plausible new assumptions were that single-party rule at Westminster had become *the* rule and that the rule book of Britain was in the hands of an organization totally opposed to constitutional change for Britain.[8]

Major's victory was subsequently compounded by the death of the then Labour leader, John Smith, in 1994, which took from the party its most influential supporter of devolution, and though Labour had committed itself in its manifesto of 1992 to a Scottish parliament, many in the party remained uncertain whether such a parliament would protect Scotland from ever again having to suffer the consequences of Westminster policies for which Scots had not voted, or whether it would become a 'beacon for nationalism', as Donald Dewar later described proposals to build the new parliament overlooking Edinburgh on the top of Calton Hill.

The cause that had been known as 'home rule' and that had been the declared aim of the Liberal Party since the nineteenth century, and the policy of the Labour Party until the 1950s, and even, briefly, the policy of the Conservatives after Ted Heath's 'Declaration of Perth' in 1968 had, apparently, run into the sand: as Marr notes melancholically, 'the country that might have ruled itself but didn't, must remain a matter for conjecture'.[9] Despite the general support for Home Rule, however, no political party in Scotland was in favour of the Parliament that actually came into existence in 1999: Labour was resistant to proportional representation, which would constrain the power it had exercised in major areas of Scotland since the 1960s; the Liberal-Democrats favoured some form of federalism throughout the UK, not a devolution of power that left Westminster intact as the UK's centre of political authority; while the Conservative Party was, of course, against all forms of devolution and the SNP were as split as Labour, split between the 'gradualists' who saw devolution as a step to their ultimate aim and the 'separatists' who believed that they should campaign for nothing but complete independence. In 1992 the political parties in Scotland were no more capable of bringing about constitutional reform than they had been in 1979. Despite that oft-quoted appeal to the 'settled will of the Scottish people', there had been, in fact, no Scottish political consensus on the form that devolution should take, if, indeed, there was to be devolution at all. The Parliament happened, if not quite by chance, then through a series of apparently accidental and certainly unpredictable intersections of trains of events running in often contradictory directions.

In the first place, Tony Blair was not committed to devolution in the way that John Smith had been, and instead of devolution being a direct outcome of a Labour victory, a pre-legislative referendum was inserted into the process at a late stage in order to discover whether it was, indeed, the 'settled will' of the Scottish people. It was argued that this was necessary to prevent a devolution bill being subject to endless amendment and delay in Westminster, but many saw it as equivalent to the 40% rule that had scuppered devolution in 1979.[10] Secondly, there was the entirely unpredicted size of Tony Blair's majority in the 1997 election: Labour's commitment to devolution was based largely on the judgment that only by maintaining the number of its Scottish seats could it ever again take power at Westminster. The promise of devolution was, ironically, made unnecessary by the scale of Blair's majority: Labour's Scottish seats had not been fundamental to winning power, and the poor showing of the SNP in 1997 – as in 1992 – suggested that the offer of a separate Parliament to stop the progress of nationalism had been premature. Despite the existence of a manifesto promise,

Blair might simply have set aside the issue of Scottish 'Home Rule' as insignificant in relation to other issues he had to deal with, if not, indeed, at odds with the 'Cool Britannia' revolution over which he hoped to preside.

What, however, made the referendum of 1997 so different from that of 1979 was an organisation that Andrew Marr had pronounced already 'virtually dead' in 1993[11] – the Scottish Constitutional Convention. It was the work of the Convention, in producing a blueprint for the parliament, that turned the figments of political imaginings into a practical – and believable – proposal. And yet, in its origins, there could be no more haphazard organisation than the Constitutional Convention, which was dreamed up by two long-term campaigners for a Scottish Assembly, Alan Lawson, editor of the magazine *Radical Scotland*, and Jim Ross, a sometime contributor to the journal and someone who had formerly been a civil servant at the Scottish Office. Through the later years of the 1980s, *Radical Scotland* had warned – sometimes apocalyptically – of a 'doomsday scenario' in which Scotland voted persistently for left-wing parties but was ruled by right-wing governments in London: this 'democratic deficit' made Scotland powerless to defend itself against what were seen as 'alien' policies, threatening the extinction of Scotland as a distinct cultural, economic and political entity. Meeting for a coffee in Edinburgh's Grassmarket in 1987, Lawson and Ross decided that the campaign for a Scottish Assembly was never going to attract the support of the mainstream political parties, and that there needed to be a body which could represent the broad desire for a Scottish Parliament beyond mainstream politics. What they dreamed up they named the Scottish Constitutional Convention, and managed to get those committed to Scotland's cause among church leaders, trade unionists, festival organisers, together with a cross-section of politicians, to come together to sign a *Claim of Right* that made a Scottish parliament an issue not for the Westminster parties but for the Scottish people themselves:

> We, gathered as the Scottish Constitutional Convention, do hereby acknowledge the sovereign right of the Scottish people to determine the form of government best suited to their needs, and do hereby declare and pledge that in all our actions and deliberations their interests shall be paramount.[12]

Of course, the declaration had no legal status, but by its title it claimed the authority of generations of Scots from the *Claim of Right* issued by a Convention of the Scottish Estates to depose James VII from the throne of Scotland in favour of William of Orange, through the *Claim of Right* of 1842, in which the Church of Scotland sought to assert its independence from the British state, to the Covenant movement of 1949, organised by former SNP leader John MacCormick, which had tried to influence Westminster by gathering two million signatories to the declaration that, 'We, the people of Scotland who subscribe to this Engagement, declare our belief that reform in the constitution of our country is necessary to secure good government in accordance with our Scottish traditions and to promote the spiritual and economic welfare of our nation.'[13] Given how easily MacCormick's Covenant had been brushed aside, Lawson and Ross decided on an indirect appeal to the people through the leaders of 'civic Scotland'. At the Convention's opening meeting, Canon Kenyon Wright dramatised the competing forces involved in its deliberations: 'What if that other single voice we all know so well responds by saying, "We say no, and we are the state"? Well, we say yes – and we are the people'.[14] To claim to represent the people was a rhetorical flourish belied not only by the absence of both the Conservatives (who were against devolution) and the SNP (who wanted only independence), but by the absence of all those other parts of 'civic Scotland' which opposed devolution. Nonetheless, the Convention allowed the proposals put to the Scottish people in the 1997 referendum to be seen not simply as the proposals of the Labour government at Westminster but as already stamped with a 'national' authority. As a result, the outcome was an overwhelming vote for 'yes', with 1,775,045 in favour and only 614,400 against. That a parliament should come into existence in 1999 might have been the 'settled will' of the Scottish people, but that it was this particular parliament, from its supposedly non-confrontational horseshoe debating chamber to its D'Hondt mode of proportional representation, was the outcome of a series of accidental circumstances, that made it anything but a settled institution.

III Cultural Revolution

If politics and votes were the means of bringing the parliament into existence, they were not its direct cause: something more profound had brought about the shift in Scottish sentiment in the period between 1979 and 1997, for which the Scottish Poetry Library, now sited in a building close to the Parliament, might be taken as emblematic. A library devoted to the nation's poetry was an eccentric proposition in the aftermath of the 1979 referendum – wasn't there already poetry enough in the Edinburgh Public Libraries, in local libraries all over Scotland, in University libraries throughout the country? A group of activists led by the poet Tessa Ransford (1938–2015) took the alternative view that a poetry library could act both as a spiritual focus for the nation, and as a means of asserting its particular value to the world's culture. If a culture is defined by its languages, and if poetry is the highest expression of those languages, then an institution devoted to the nation's poetry is at the very core of a nation's conception of its identity. A plan was drawn up for a national institution devoted to the collection and dissemination of the nation's poetry, one sufficiently compelling to attract support from the then Director of the Scottish Arts Council, Walter Cairns, and, in 1984, turned into a material reality when it opened to the public just off Edinburgh's Canongate. Like many other cultural organisations in the period, the Scottish Poetry Library was a deliberate gesture of defiance in the face of the refusal of the Westminster political parties to deliver devolution, and a deliberate attempt to inspire the Scottish people with a sense of the traditions, achievements and the values of their own culture. When it moved to a new purpose-built location towards the bottom end of the Canongate in 1999 it was as if poetry pointed the way for Scottish politics and to the choice of the location for the new Parliament.

Cultural action, in effect, had become an alternative to the stalled nature of Scotland's political life in the long hiatus between 1979 and 1997 and led to a series of efforts to recuperate and articulate the value of Scotland's culture. Trevor Royle, who had worked for the Scottish Arts Council, produced the *Macmillan Companion to Scottish Literature* in 1983, the same year in which Alan Bold published *Modern Scottish Literature*, and in the following year Roderick Watson's *The*

Literature of Scotland offered an overview of the nation's literary history, one that was to be elaborated by the Aberdeen University Press four-volume, multi-author *History of Scottish Literature* (1987–8), which had emerged out of the magazine *Cencrastus*, also the source of Duncan MacMillan's *Scottish Art 1460–1990* (1990). These recuperations of the Scottish past were to be extended by Alexander Broadie's *The Tradition of Scottish Philosophy* (1990), Murray Pittock's *The Invention of Scotland* (1991), John Purser's *Scotland's Music: A History of the Traditional and Classical Music of Scotland from Earliest Times to the Present Day* (1992), Robert Crawford's *Devolving English Literature* (1992), Marshall Walker's *The Literature of Scotland since 1707* (1996), Charles Jones's *Edinburgh History of the Scots Language* (1997), Douglas Gifford's and Dorothy McMillan's *History of Scottish Women's Writing* (1997), and Bill Findlay's *A History of Scottish Theatre* (1998). These revaluations of Scotland's cultural history were augmented by the large number of texts recovered from near oblivion by the Canongate Classics series in the 1980s and 90s under the editorial direction of Roderick Watson – most notably, perhaps, the novels of Nan Shepherd and Willa Muir, but also the writings of John Muir and Mary Somerville – as well as by major anthologies of Scottish poetry, including Catherine Kerrigan's *An Anthology of Scottish Women Poets* (1991), Tom Hubbard's *The New Makars: The Mercat Anthology of Contemporary Poetry in Scots* (1991), Douglas Dunn's *Faber Book of Twentieth-Century Scottish Poetry* (1992), Daniel O'Rourke's *Dream State: The New Scottish Poetry* (1994), Roderick Watson's *The Poetry of Scotland* (1995) and David McCordrick's two-volume anthology of *Scottish Literature* in 1996, covering in Vol. 1 *Early Middle Ages to c1775* and, in Vol. 2, *1775 to Robert Louis Stevenson*.

These studies and collections revitalised the understanding of Scotland's past from the middle ages to the end of the twentieth century, but by far the most intense scrutiny was concentrated on Scotland in the eighteenth century. Early accounts, setting the ground for subsequent research included, Arthur Donovan, *Philosophical Chemistry in the Scottish Enlightenment: the Doctrines and Discoveries of William Cullen and Joseph Black* (1975), Anand C. Chitnis, *The Scottish Enlightenment: A Social History* (1976), Jane Rendall, *The Origins of the Scottish Enlightenment, 1707–1776* (1978), Bruce Lenman,

Integration and Enlightenment: Scotland 1746–1832 (1981), R. H. Campbell and Andrew S. Skinner, *The Origins and Nature of the Scottish Enlightenment* (1982), Richard B. Sher, *Scotland and America in the Age of the Enlightenment* (1990) and George Elder Davie, *The Scottish Enlightenment and Other Essays* (1991). Exploration of the sources and consequences of the Scottish Enlightenment were traced in John MacQueen, *The Enlightenment and Scottish Literature* (2 vols, 1982, 1989), Istvan Hont and Michael Ignatieff, *Wealth and Virtue: The Shaping of Political Economy in the Scottish Enlightenment* (1983), Vincent Hope, *Philosophers of the Scottish Enlightenment* (1984), Richard B. Sher, *Church and University in the Scottish Enlightenment: The Moderate Literati of Edinburgh* (1985), and John Robertson, *The Scottish Enlightenment and the Militia Issue* (1985). But the annus mirabilis of the rediscovery of the significance of eighteenth-century Scotland's Enlightenment was 1986 when the Institute for Advanced Studies in the Humanities (IASH) at the University of Edinburgh, together with the Edinburgh International Festival, launched a celebration of the Enlightenment in a partnership dubbed 'IPSE' – 'Institute Project Scottish Enlightenment' – over a six month period: Peter Jones, the Director of IASH summarised its activities in his prologue to a collection of essays entitled *Philosophy and Science in the Scottish Enlightenment* (1988):

> 225 IPSE lectures and seminars were attended by over 8000 people . . . Six IPSE International Conferences brought over 400 overseas delegates to Edinburgh, to participate in debate and investigation; forty IPSE International Fellows were elected to the Institute for periods of up to six months, to pursue research into all aspects of Scottish Enlightenment. 20,000 visitors went to the IPSE exhibition. 'A Hotbed of Genius', held in the Queen Street galleries of the Royal Museum of Scotland . . . IPSE commissioned three concerts for the festival, devised by Dr. David Johnson, and held in the Queen's Hall and in St Cecilia's Hall and . . . also commissioned a new adaptation for the stage, by Dr Roger Savage, of Hume's *Dialogues Concerning Natural Religion* . . .[15]

In addition, there were exhibitions of eighteenth-century Scottish art and of the Tassie medallions at the Univeristy of Edinburgh and, at the Royal Botanic Gardens, a celebration of the work of Dr John Hope, one of the most prominent figures in the development of the Edinburgh Botanic Gardens in the eighteenth century. Among the outcomes of the events of 1986 were David Daiches, Peter Jones and Jean Jones's (eds), *The Scottish Enlightenment, 1730–1790: A Hotbed of Genius* (1986) and David Daiches's *The Scottish Enlightenment: An Introduction* (1986). A host of other publications appeared in the following years, including Jennifer Carter and Joan Pittock's *Aberdeen and the Enlightenment* (1987), Peter Jones's own *Philosophy and Science in the Scottish Enlightenment* (1988) and *The 'Science of Man' in the Scottish Enlightenment: Hume, Reid and their Contemporaries* (1989), and, in the following decade, M. A. Stewart's *Studies in the Philosophy of the Scottish Enlightenment* (1990), David Allan's *Virtue, Learning and the Scottish Enlightenment* (1993), Paul Wood's, *The Aberdeen Enlightenment* (1993), Andrew Hook and Richard B. Sher's *The Glasgow Enlightenment* (1995), Alexander Broadie's *The Scottish Enlightenment: An Anthology* (1997) and Paul Wood's *Scottish Enlightenment: Essays in Reinterpretation* (2000).[16] In 1995, Edinburgh University Press began the publication of a new edition of the works of Thomas Reid, led by Paul Wood and Knud Haakonssen, while the Liberty Fund in the United States of America (USA) made available editions of the works of many eighteenth-century Scottish authors, such as Eugene F. Miller's *David Hume: Essays Moral, Political and Literary* in 1985 and the Glasgow edition of the works of Adam Smith.

This vast recuperation of the significance of eighteenth-century Scotland was to be given public and physical form with the siting, in 1996, of Sandy Stoddart's statue of David Hume on Edinburgh's Royal Mile: its position, close to but on the opposite side of the street from St Giles' Cathedral, and its form – Hume is dressed in a classical toga – a visual declaration of Hume's opposition to Christian belief.

By the time of the Devolution Referendum in 1997, a country whose past had been presented as threadbare, insignificant or crippled had acquired a culture overflowing with riches, not only making its 'Enlightenment' the focus of international concern but recuperating the prominent figures of its nineteenth-century xeniteian culture, so that Scott and Burns were again the objects of serious international literary scholarship. This historical transformation was matched by its wealth of contemporary popular culture as a result of the success its rock bands and its pop singers, from Runrig and the Proclaimers to Annie Lennox and Sharleen Spiteri, its comedians, from Billy Connolly to Gregor Fisher and Elaine C. Smith, and its internationally acclaimed actors from Sean Connery to Brian Cox, and to those, including Robbie Coltrane and Maurice Roëves, who had appeared in John Byrne's *Tutti Frutti* (1987) and Ewan McGregor and Robert Carlyle, who starred in *Trainspotting* in 1996. International awareness of the country was enhanced by the appearance in the same year – 1995 – of two Hollywood blockbusters, *Rob Roy*, starring Liam Neeson – who had previously appeared in the film version of William McIlvanney's *The Big Man* (1990) – and *Braveheart* (1995), starring Mel Gibson. Scotland was a country whose culture had gone from being reviled by its own intellectuals to being the object of intense international interest.

By no means were all of the people involved in this cultural transformation nationalists, nor did they intend their activities to contribute to some kind of national regeneration – indeed, some of those researching the Enlightenment saw eighteenth-century Scotland as an exemplar of a cosmopolitan internationalism – but nonetheless the effect was to make Scottish culture again distinctive and distinguished. The projective nationalism of its xeniteian empire was being recuperated as a resource which could underpin a resistant nationalism. The cultural transformation, stretching back to the impact of the Edinburgh Festival in the decade after its founding in 1947 and to that of the Scottish Arts Council in the decade after its establishment in 1967, preceded and gave value to the rise of political nationalism. The dynamics of this transformation are attributable to three causes. First, the end of the British Empire meant that the long-term purpose of the Union – which, from Scotland's perspective, had been the creation and maintenance of a Scottish empire – had disappeared. The mission to which Scotland had been committed throughout the period of its xeniteian expansion had to be recognised as over, with the result that the country had to rediscover its sense of historical purpose: when the SNP decided in the 1980s that its aim was not 'independence' but 'independence-in-Europe', it began to align its future with other small nations and regions in Europe, many of which had, of course, in the nineteenth century, taken their cultural inspiration from Scotland. Second, the secularization of the 1960s, and the rapid decline of membership of the Church of Scotland, resulted in the removal of one of the key ways in which Scotland's separate identity within the United Kingdom had been expressed: once Church membership no longer defined a semi-autonomous sphere of Scottish values, then those values needed an alternative mode of expression. Secularism, for both Scottish Protestants and Scottish Catholics, removed the institutional foundations by which a sense of Scottish difference was supported within the United Kingdom and thus made it possible for their continuing sense of difference to find an alternative political expression. And, third, the attempt to create a 'British' culture, which had been part of the aim and purpose of the British Broadcasting Corporation after the First World War, and of the British Arts Council after the Second World War, foundered in the 1950s in the face of American cultural dominance – the success of British popular music lay in its ability to exploit the dominant position of the English language, while adopting American musical styles – and as a consequence of the rise of multiculturalism after the 1960s. 'Britishness' in England retreated to the securer foundations of Englishness.

The former Prime Minster, Gordon Brown, has tried to make the case for 'Britishness' both on the necessary interconnectedness of the modern world and on the basis that modern identities – in an argument derived from the historian T. C. Smout – consist of 'concentric circles' of interdependent relations: Smout lists six markers of identity which encircle one another, beginning with family, then kin, locality then nation, which is in turn bounded by the state. There may be other encircling concepts – Empire, for instance, or Europe – but each circle sits comfortably in its appropriate space and each forms a circumference situated at an appropriate distance from the *cogito* at its core.[17] Brown refers us to his fellow Fifer Ian Rankin's account of how as a child he would write himself into his new diary, in an expanding series of locations that went from 17 Craignead Terrace in Bowhill, Cardenden by way of Scotland, Great Britain and the United Kingdom to 'The Universe'. As Brown notes, this repeats a structure which appears in James Joyce's fiction when Stephen Dedalus, in *Portrait of an Artist as a Young Man*, gives himself the following address:

Stephen Dedalus
Class of Elements
Clongowes Wood College
Salline
County Kildare
Ireland
Europe
The World
The Universe[18]

What Brown fails to take note of, however, is that in Joyce's formulation the United Kingdom has disappeared: although written years before Ireland's independence, Joyce had already written the United Kingdom out of the circles in which he saw himself as living. Not all circles are concentric with one another, and for migrant peoples like the Scots and the Irish, the trajectories of identity are more likely to resemble the extended ellipses of comets than the circles of planetary orbits. For many Scots, Canada and the USA are, in terms of the circuits of family connections, much closer than England: as for Joyce, for many Scots in the second half of the twentieth century, the United Kingdom simply ceased to exist as one of the circles of their identity, especially their cultural identity. When the Arts Council of Great Britain became, in the reorganisation of 1994, the Arts Council of England, it both formalised what its real purpose had been since the 1940s and acknowledged the irrelevance of Great Britain as a cultural boundary for those in Scotland, Wales and Northern Ireland. The infrastructure of the arts, as so often, was the predictor of the infrastructure of politics, for the United Kingdom's Westminster parliament, after devolution, might still pretend, in terms of economic policy and defence, to be a British parliament, but for domestic business it had, in fact, become, after 1997, the Parliament of England. Living between the surge of American cultural assertion and the decline of British culture, Scotland discovered the space in which to recover and reassert the national identity in which it had invested so heavily in the era of its xeniteian expansion. That cultural recovery was prologue to the SNP, which had managed at best only six seats in the House of Commons in the 1990s, capturing 28% of the vote in the first Scottish parliamentary election, thereby becoming immediately the second largest party in the parliament.[19] The subsequent rise of the SNP has been shaped not just by resistance to the failings of Westminster governments but by a cultural recuperation that restored to Scotland the value of its past and the continuing relevance of that past both to its own present and to a wider world which has come to see Scotland not only as a nation, but as a nation that has played a significant role in the development of the modern world.

There was, however, an underlying irony in this transformation of our understanding of the value of Scottish culture, for the SNP has been, since the 1960s, a party which resolutely avoided deploying culture as part of its political agenda: it was a party committed to the democratic right of Scots not to have a government for which they had not voted, and for Scotland to have a government which could bring about economic change in Scotland: its agenda has been, fundamentally, economic control rather than the preservation and promotion of a distinctive cultural inheritance. Ironically, it was the failure to convince the Scottish electorate on economic issues that proved decisive in the 2014 referendum as the 'Better Together' campaign pressed home its 'project fear' – fear for the future of pensions built up within the British tax system, fear about the Westminster government's refusal to allow Scotland to use the pound sterling, and, in a further irony in the light of the Brexit referendum of 2016, fear of possible exclusion from the European Union. The barque of a political nationalism which eschews culture as either a foundation or an aim of its political purpose has in fact risen on a tide of cultural engagement by which Scottish people have taken back ownership of their cultural past as the ground on which some of them, at any rate, can declare, with their medieval predecessors, that 'Fredome is a noble thing', and that we 'suld think fredome mar to prys/Than all the gold in warld that is' [we 'should think freedom more to prize/Than all the gold in world that is'].[20] The wealth of the nation is its accumulated culture, a culture which has impelled its political nationalism but which, more importantly, has guaranteed its continued distinction within the potentially obliterating context of English hegemony within the United Kingdom, or the equally obliterating power of American cultural globalism in the twenty-first century.

IV National Wealth

In John Ramsay McCulloch's edition of Adam Smith's *The Wealth of Nations*, first published in 1828, McCulloch offers the following justification of the science of political economy, and of the principle of the accumulation of wealth which it studies:

> The possession of a decent competence, or the ability to indulge in other pursuits than those that directly tend to satisfy our animal wants and desires, is necessary to soften the selfish passions, to improve the moral and intellectual character, and to insure any considerable proficiency in liberal studies and pursuits. Without the tranquillity and leisure afforded by the enjoyment of accumulated riches, these speculative and elegant studies which enlarge our views, purify our taste, and lift us higher in the scale of being, could not be successfully prosecuted. The barbarism and refinement of nations depend more on their wealth than on any other circumstance. No people have ever made any distinguished figure in philosophy or the fine arts, without having been, at the same time, celebrated for their riches and industry.[21]

Culture and refinement, for McCulloch, follow wealth: wealth, therefore, is the necessary foundation which has to be built before a culture can achieve 'refinement', and before distinction 'in philosophy or the fine arts' can be produced. McCulloch believed that he was here expressing the truth taught to us by Adam Smith's *Inquiry into the Nature and Causes of the Wealth of Nations*, and it is this version of Smith that has been promoted by the neo-liberalism that came to dominate Western politics in the last quarter of the twentieth century. In 1975, in Chicago, Margaret Thatcher declared that 'Adam Smith, in fact, heralded the end of the strait-jacket of feudalism and released all the innate energy of private initiative and enterprise which enables wealth to be created on a scale never before contemplated'.[22] 'Wealth creation' became the primary aim of political parties right and left, and nations were to be judged by their ability to generate wealth. To Mrs Thatcher, Scotland's refusal to adopt her free-market principles was deeply ironic, for 'Scotland in the eighteenth century was the home of the very same Scottish Enlightenment which produced Adam Smith, the greatest exponent of free enterprise economics until Hayek and Friedman'.[23]

If, after the economic disasters of 2008–9, few could still subscribe wholeheartedly to the view that free markets and free enterprise would, as McCulloch predicted and Thatcher insisted, create the wealth to allow human beings the 'enjoyment of accumulated riches', nonetheless, the bailout of the banks proved that no government had yet produced an alternative version of how the international economic system might be organised. But that such 'free-market' economies released people for those 'speculative and elegant studies which enlarge our views, purify our taste, and lift us higher in the scale of being' is hardly credible: the increasing gap between rich and poor, lengthening real working hours, the trivialisation of a public sphere infused by advertising, the retreat of the State from publicly-funded higher education and the retreat of higher education itself from any but pragmatic values, does not suggest that we have been, as societies, lifted 'higher in the scale of being'. If artworks are still being traded at inflated prices it is symptomatic not of a widely spread increase in 'speculative and elegant studies' but rather of the commercialisation of the art world as a 'hedge fund' for those with wealth that needs a secure location in a world of increasingly untrustworthy investment vehicles – not only the insecurity of the banks and the untrustworthiness of the bankers and the brokers, but increasingly of the governments which back them. Rather than 'soften the selfish passions' and 'improve the moral and intellectual character' of the nation, the neo-liberalism that has dominated government thinking since the 1970s produced, as a whole series of commercial and political scandals revealed in the years following 2009, a world distinguished by an amoral selfishness.

The irony of the assumption that the arts depend on 'opulence' is nowhere better symbolised than by the poet who was growing up while Smith was writing and revising his *Inquiry into the Nature and Cause of the Wealth of Nations* – Robert Burns. The social and economic context into which Burns was born was one in which it was almost impossible for small tenant farmers like his father or himself to accumulate wealth, and yet he was able to accumulate and pass on a body of work which was testimony not only to the creativity of the folk culture into which he had been born but to his own abilities to meld the various cultures in which he had educated himself. Equally, the 1980s, when much of the Scottish economy lay in ruins, was the period of the greatest efflorescence of Scottish art since at least the 1920s and perhaps as far back as the 1810s. What McCulloch's view of cultural refinement ignores is what Hanif Kureishi believes made Thatcher uneasy about 'culture': Thatcher, he suggested, was not simply a person 'of little cultural sophistication or understanding', but 'actively hated culture, as she recognised that it was a form of dissent'.[24] Those societies which made a 'distinguished figure in philosophy or the fine arts' were, for McCulloch, also 'celebrated for their riches and industry', and it was, presumably, those riches and industry which their fine arts 'celebrated'. Dissent is not part of the wealth of the nation – but in Scotland dissent has been crucial to the nation's wealth, as Scott's studies of the Jacobites in *Waverley* and the Covenanters in *Old Mortality* underline. Dissent, however, has come to be regarded as a disruption of the smooth working of free markets, even while those free markets have come to regard 'disruption' as a crucial aid to economic renewal.

The acceptance of the importance of the arts in modern economies – supported by evidence that 'creative' communities generate economic impact – has led to a stand-off between governments and the arts: on the one hand, governments want to encourage them as generators of innovation which could lead to wealth creation, but they do not want dissent to disrupt business planning. It is a contradiction which has come to dominate State provision of the arts in the era of neo-liberalism. It seemed, when the new devolved government in Scotland made 'Cultural Strategy' one of its earliest matters for consultation, that the politicians were going to repay their 'unacknowledged legislators' in the arts who had provided the foundations on which the parliament was established, with a new role for artists and the arts in Scottish life. What emerged, however, was less a strategy for culture than a strategy for how culture could deliver for other political imperatives. 'Cultural development', it declared, 'contributes to the image of Scotland as a modern, dynamic, and forward-looking society',[25] thereby, of course, immediately excluding from Scotland's new culture both the backward-looking, revivalist elements which have always been a part of it and the culture represented by Irvine Welsh's *Trainspotting*, which refuses to be hooked on forward-looking dynamism. More importantly, culture's role was to make a contribution 'to wider Scottish Executive priorities such as social justice, economic development, regeneration and equality'.[26] 'Culture', in other words, had become the medium through which the social and economic aims of the Scottish Executive could be managed and directed, so that creativity could be harnessed to economic performance. Thus, the cultural strategy argued, 'because Scotland's culture is dynamic' and because it has already shown the 'capacity to respond to new influences and to integrate them with existing traditions', it follows that 'the ability to adopt and adapt, allied to a capacity for innovation, mean that Scotland is well-placed to respond to the accelerating trend towards globalisation while maintaining a culture which remains modern, distinctive and relevant to the experience of Scots'.[27] The circularities of this last sentence reveal the profound quandary of the Executive's strategy: it needs to manage culture to make Scotland acceptable to globalised capital by developing its 'modern dynamism' while at the same time presenting culture as the already-existing 'experience and history of all Scotland's citizens'.[28] Individual Scots are thus both the origin of the culture for which the Strategy is developed and are mere spectators of it until both they and it have been massaged into an appropriately modern and dynamic form. The effect of this can be seen in the Scottish Arts Council (SAC) plan of 2001–2. Punningly entitled 'Work in Progress',[29] the real work in progress seems to be that of harmonising the SAC's work with the progress of the Executive's strategy, as each SAC action is keyed to a National Cultural Strategy priority, which in turn are then related to the Executive's social objectives, as though the SAC was simply the arm of government charged with carrying out the Executive's policies by proxy. Of course, 'he who pays the piper . . .', but ironically, and probably for the first time, a very large proportion of the SAC's funds did not, at that time, come from the government directly but from lottery funding, so that at the very moment when it might have been possible for the SAC to have the financial resources to set its own aims as cultural ones, it submitted itself to the Executive's conception of culture as the means of delivering other social objectives. This is clear in the various strategy documents produced on behalf of the departments of the SAC, such as the Literature Strategy:

> In the globalised world of the 21st century, where the knowledge and skills of a country's people will be crucial to success, literature

> will help to equip every Scot to live and work, and to reflect, communicate and engage, in this new and complex environment.
>
> Literature assists people to develop the essential skills of literacy, articulacy, independence of thought and enterprise.[30]

Literature is not the aim of the document nor the aim of the strategy: literature is a means to the fulfilment of the general government policy of making Scotland fit for enterprise. An anti-Thatcher movement of cultural and national dissent had turned, in the hands of New Labour, into an attempt to recast Scottish culture as an appropriate partner for global capital. Under the SNP administration, the Scottish Arts Council became 'Creative Scotland', an organisation that was responsible for the development of the 'creative industries' rather than the arts, and which came rapidly into conflict with the arts community.[31] Underlying the conflict was the fact that culture had come to be regarded as the consequence of wealth: culture must necessarily be in harmony with wealth and with wealth-creation, for it is by its economic wealth that a country will be valued.

These are not consequences that flow necessarily, however, from the theories of Adam Smith, as opposed to his nineteenth-century and twentieth-century interpreters, because, for Smith, what we would describe as the 'aesthetic' is the very foundation rather than the outcome of wealth, since the gold and silver, which became the medium of exchange in commercial societies, derive their value primarily from their 'beauty'. Indeed, 'the demand for the precious stones arises altogether from their beauty. They are of no use but as ornaments; and the merit of their beauty is greatly enhanced by the scarcity, or by the difficulty and expense of getting them from the mine'.[32] Beauty is not the consequence of wealth but its very foundation: things are valuable because they are deemed to be beautiful, and this is true, too, of how wealth gets its power in the world:

> We are then charmed with the beauty of that accommodation which reigns in the palaces and eoconomy of the great; and admire how every thing is adapted to promote their ease, to prevent their wants, to gratify their wishes, and to amuse and entertain their most frivolous desires. If we consider the real satisfaction which all these things are capable of affording, by itself and separated from the beauty of that arrangement which is fitted to promote it, it will always appear in the highest degree contemptible and trifling. But we rarely view

> it in this abstract and philosophical light. We naturally confound it in our imagination with the order, the regular and harmonious movement of the system, the machine or oeconomy of which it is produced.[33]

Our admiration – and envy – of the life of the wealthy is the product of the imagination, which sees in it 'something grand and beautiful and noble', worthy of 'all the toil and anxiety which we are so apt to bestow upon it' – but it is, nonetheless, simply an illusion. 'Power and riches' are, in fact, 'enormous and operose machines contrived to produce a few trifling conveniences to the body, consisting of springs the most nice and delicate, which must be kept in order with the most anxious attention, and which in spite of all our care are ready every moment to burst into pieces'.[34] Just as, in his essay on 'Astronomy', Smith sees scientific progress as a series of systems 'fitted to sooth the imagination',[35] each deceptively appearing to have produced order out of chaos, so the accumulation of wealth is a series of deceptions appearing to produce order in the world:

> It is this deception which rouses and keeps in continual motion the industry of mankind. It is this which first prompted them to cultivate the ground, to build houses, to found cities and commonwealths, and to invent and improve all the sciences and arts, which ennoble and embellish human life; which have entirely changed the whole face of the globe, have turned the rude forests of nature into agreeable and fertile plains, and made the trackless and barren ocean a new fund of subsistence, and the great high road of communication to the different nations of the earth.[36]

Economic activity, for Smith, is driven by the imagination – and, if we apply the lesson of the essay on astronomy to *The Wealth of Nations* itself, the science of economics is nothing more than imaginary systems 'fitted to sooth the imagination', each doomed – like the economies they describe – to crash when alternative imaginings collide or when their vision of order proves incompatible with experience.

This sceptical dimension of Smith's philosophy is one which is least acknowledged by those who, in the modern world, regard themselves as disciples of Smith's free market ideology. Thus George Sigler of the 'Chicago School' declares that Smith's great achievement was that

> he put into the center of economics the systematic analysis of behavior of individuals pursuing their self-interest under conditions of competition. This theory is the crown jewel of *The Wealth of Nations*, and it became and remains to this day, the foundation of the theory of the allocation of resources . . . Smith's construct of the self-interested individual in a competitive environment is Newtonian in its universality.[37]

Sigler's claim of a 'Newtonian universality' is precisely what Smith's 'History of Astronomy' denies: so believable is Newton's system to Smith as the consummation of the development of astronomy, that

> even we, while we have been endeavouring to represent all philosophical systems as mere inventions of the imagination, to connect together the otherwise disjointed and discordant phenomena of nature, have insensibly been drawn in, to make use of language expressing the connecting principles of this one, as if they were the real chains which Nature makes use of to bind together her several operations.[38]

Newton's theories present themselves as if they were real, but that reality, like those of all the preceding systems, is founded only on their appeal to the imagination. Smith's 'Newtonian universality' is, according to Smith himself, just as much an illusion as every previous claim to have produced a 'universal' truth – it is simply a 'deception which rouses and keeps in continual motion the industry of mankind' and of which he has not yet been disabused. The attempt to make economics a mathematical science based on the notion that homo sapiens is really homo economicus, and that the actions of such creatures can be charted with the same precision as Newton's charting of the forces that govern the planets, ignores the 'ground' upon which Smith built his system – the inevitably deceptive ground of the imagination.

If the imagination is the real motor of economic development then 'culture', rather than being the outcome of wealth, is its foundation. In a pragmatic rather than a philosophical context, this was the argument of David Landes's *The Wealth and Poverty of Nations*:

> If we learn anything from the history of economic development, it is that culture makes all the difference. (Here Max Weber was right

> on). Witness the enterprise of expatriate minorities – the Chinese in East and Southeast Asia, Indians in East Africa, Lebanese in West Africa, Jews and Calvinists throughout Europe, and on and on. Yet culture, in the sense of inner values and attitudes that guide a population, frightens scholars. It has a sulfuric odor of race and inheritance, an air of immutability.[39]

The idea may have frightened 'scholars' but it did not frighten politicians – what else was the Thatcherite campaign but an effort to change the 'culture of decline' in Britain? What else was 'Cool Britannia' in the Blair years but an effort to re-align the British economy with its most successful cultural export – popular music? What was telling in both cases, however, was that they were attempts to bring the national culture into line with the demands of wealth creation, with the 'universal' demands of economics, rather than an effort to make economics acknowledge the value of culture. Even Landes assumes that all his expatriate groups share the same economic motivations, but if 'culture makes all the difference' because of the 'inner values and attitudes that guide a population', then the difference in different cultures' attitudes to 'wealth creation' and to the satisfactions that it brings must be as important as their similarities. Here there is a telling difference in the two places where Smith uses the image of the 'invisible hand' as an explanation of how individual self-interest turns into social benefit. In *The Wealth of Nations* Smith writes:

> . . . every individual necessarily labours to render the annual revenue of the society as great as he can. He generally, indeed, neither intends to promote the publick interest, nor knows how much he is promoting it . . . he intends only his own gain, and he is in this, as in many other cases, led by an invisible hand to promote an end which was no part of his intention.[40]

'Gain', however, was not Smith's concern in the *Theory of Moral Sentiments* but 'happiness':

> They are led by an invisible hand to make nearly the same distribution of the necessaries of life, which would have been made, had the earth been divided into equal portions among all its inhabitants . . . These last too enjoy their share of all that it produces. In what constitutes the real happiness of human life, they are in no respect

> inferior to those who would seem so much above them. In ease of body and peace of mind, all the different ranks of life are nearly upon a level, and the beggar, who suns himself by the side of the highway, possesses that security which kings are fighting for.[41]

The 'invisible hand' that distributes 'happiness' does so on a very different basis from the one that distributes 'gain', though for Smith the value of a progressive economy, one still 'advancing to the further acquisition, rather than when it has acquired its full complement of riches', is precisely that it provides conditions in which 'the condition of the labouring poor, of the great body of the people, seems to be happiest and most comfortable'.[42] In such an economy 'happiness' and 'gain' seem to coincide but only as long as people are not obsessed with 'gain', because those who are will inevitably discover 'that wealth and greatness are mere trinkets of frivolous utility, no more adapted for procuring ease of body or tranquillity of mind than the tweezer-cases of the lover of toys; and like them too, more troublesome to the person who carries them about with him than all the advantages they can afford him . . .'[43]

The separation of 'happiness' from 'gain' is crucial to Smith's conception of human beings who are more than simply economic actors – who act not merely on the basis of their personal gain but on the basis of sympathy, altruism or justice. Much modern economic theory, on the other hand, has to insist on the fusion of 'happiness' and 'gain' in order to be able to treat each individual as a rational calculator of his or her own personal benefit: George Stigler's model of the rational consumer requires that, '(1) His tastes are consistent; (2) His cost calculations are correct; (3) He makes those decisions that maximise utility',[44] all of which leaves no room for past choice to change present tastes or for changing tastes to change cost calculations, effectively making economic values the only values relevant to human choice: 'happiness' equals 'gain'. As Amartya Sen has argued, 'the economic theory of utility, which relates to the theory of rational behaviour' assumes that an individual can be summarised by '*one* preference ordering . . .[which] is supposed to reflect his interests, represent his welfare, summarize his idea of what should be done', as well as 'describe his actual choices and behaviour' – 'a person thus described may be "rational" in the limited sense of revealing no inconsistencies in his choice behaviour, but if he has no use for these distinctions between quite different concepts, he must be a bit of a fool'.[45]

For Smith, on the other hand, choices are made not on the basis of rational economic calculation but on the basis of their aesthetic appropriateness: his 'impartial spectator' judges actions in terms of 'the sentiment or affection of the heart from which any action proceeds', and it is on 'the suitableness or unsuitableness, upon the proportion or disproportion, which the affection seems to bear to the cause or object which excites it, depends the propriety or impropriety, the decency or ungracefulness of the consequent action'.[46] The appropriateness of an action is not in its rational calculation but in its aesthetic 'proportion', its 'gracefulness': morality depends, like economics and politics, on the values of the imagination, and appropriate judgment depends on training the emotions through experience of the arts, which is why 'the idea of utility of all qualities of this kind, is plainly an after-thought, and not what first recommends them to our approbation'.[47] The wealth of the nation resides in its aesthetic value, and if poverty is ugly, opulence is not to be confused with beauty: the accumulation of capital is not as important to the nation as the accumulation of cultural capital. Financial capital, as was shown in the case of the Royal Bank of Scotland, is no guarantee of sustained independence; cultural capital guarantees a country's ability to resist dependence, even if, in Scotland's case, it has not proved – as yet – able to deliver political independence. But without cultural independence a country ceases to exist: the achievement of Scotland since 1707 or, more recently, after 1979, is that it has established the value of the culture on which its independence, whatever its political environment, can be maintained.

Notes

1. Available at <http://www.telegraph.co.uk/news/uknews/scottish-independence/11108256/Scottish-independence-David-Camerons-speech-in-full.html> (last accessed 23 September 2015).
2. At the time of writing it is 114,000, more than four times what it was at the beginning of the Referendum campaign.
3. Macwhirter, I., *Road to Referendum* (Glasgow: Cargo, 2014), p. 13.

4. Ibid. p. 375.
5. In their analysis of *The Scottish Electorate* of 1997, Brown, McCrone, Paterson and Surridge found few indicators of significant sociological difference between Scotland and England: 'in considering the influences on voting behaviour, we found relatively weak influences of social structure, and few differences in this respect between Scotland and the rest of Britain': Brown, A., D. McCrone, L. Paterson and P. Surridge (eds), *The Scottish Electorate: the 1997 General Election and Beyond* (Basingstoke: Palgrave, 1999), p. 70.
6. Brown, G., *My Scotland, Our Britain* (London: Simon & Schuster, 2014), p. 15.
7. Ibid. p. 19.
8. Marr, A., *The Battle for Scotland* (Harmondsworth: Penguin, 1993), p. 210.
9. Scott, P., *Scotland: A Concise Cultural History* (Edinburgh: Mainstream, 1993), p. 384.
10. Macwhirter, I., *Road to Referendum*, pp. 234–5.
11. Scott, *Scotland: A Concise Cultural History*, p. 384.
12. Marr, *Battle for Britain*, p. 205.
13. Ibid. p. 96.
14. Ibid. p. 206.
15. Jones, P. (ed.), *Philosophy and Science in the Scottish Enlightenment* (Edinburgh: John Donald, 1988), p. 1.
16. The new millennium saw no decrease in interest in the Scottish past with the continuing flow of publications including Murdo Macdonald's *Scottish Art* (2000), Aileen Christianson's and Carol Anderson's *Scottish Women's Fiction, 1920s to 1960s* (2000), Douglas Gifford, Sarah Dunnigan and Alan MacGillivray's, *Scottish literature in English and Scots* (2002), Ian Brown, Susan Manning and Murray Pittock's *Edinburgh History of Scottish Literature* (2007), Bill Bell's *Edinburgh History of the Book in Scotland* (2007) and Alexander Broadie's *A History of Scottish Philosophy* (2009), as well as the flood of books on Scottish history that followed on the success of T. M. Devine's *The Scottish Nation* (2000).
17. Smout, T. C., 'Perspectives on the Scottish Identity', *Scottish Affairs*, 6, Winter 1994, pp. 101–13.
18. Joyce, J., *Portrait of the Artist as a Young Man* (Harmondsworth: Penguin, [1916] 1976), pp. 15–16.
19. It had 35 seats to Labour's 56.
20. Barbour, J., *The Brus*, Bk 1, l. 225, 239–40, ed. A. A. M. Duncan, available at <http://www.arts.gla.ac.uk/STELLA/STARN/poetry/BRUS/text01.htm> (last accessed 16 October 2015); the standard nineteenth-century edition is Innes, C. (ed.), The Brus: *From a Collation of the Cambridge and Edinburgh Manuscripts*

(Aberdeen: Spalding Club, 1856), lines quoted p. 11, I. 47 and II. 61–2.

21. McCulloch, J. R., 'Introductory Discourse', Adam Smith, *An Inquiry into the Nature and Causes of the Wealth of Nations* (Edinburgh, [1828] 1863), pp. xv–xvi.
22. Quoted Stephen Copley, 'Introduction: reading the *Wealth of Nations*', in Stephen Copley and Kathryn Sutherland (eds), *Adam Smith's Wealth of Nations* (Manchester: Manchester University Press, 1994), p. 2.
23. Ibid. p. 2.
24. Available at <http://www.guardian.co.uk/books/2009/apr/11/thatcher-and-the-arts> (last accessed 15 December 2009.
25. *Creating our Future: Minding our Past: the National Cultural Strategy*: 'Summary' (Edinburgh: Scottish Executive, 2000), p. 2.
26. Ibid. p. 2.
27. Ibid. p. 5.
28. Ibid.
29. Scottish Arts Council, 12 Manor Place, Edinburgh EH3 7DD; 'This plan covers the period 1 April 2001 – 31 March 2002'.
30. Scottish Arts Council. *Literature Strategy 2002–2007* (Edinburgh: SAC, August 2002), p. 3.
31. The first director of Creative Scotland stood down in Dec 2012 only two years after his appointment, following a critical letter signed by a hundred leading figures in the arts in Scotland: see Higgins, C (2012), 'Andrew Dixon resigns as head of Creative Scotland', *The Guardian*, 3 December, https://www.theguardian.com/culture/charlottehigginsblog/2012/dec/03/andrew-dixon-resigns-creative-scotland (last accessed 23 March 2017).
32. Campbell, R. H., A. H. Skinner and W. B. Todd (eds), Adam Smith, *An Inquiry into the Nature and Causes of the Wealth of Nations*, Vol. 1 (Oxford: The Clarendon Press, 1976), p. 191.
33. Raphael D. D. and A. L. Macfie (eds), Adam Smith, *Theory of Moral Sentiments* (Indianapolis: Liberty Press, 1984), p. 183.
34. Ibid. pp. 182–3.
35. Smith, A., 'History of Astronomy', *Essays on Philosophical Subjects* (Indianapolis: Liberty Press, 1982), p. 46.
36. Raphael and Macfie (eds), Smith, *Theory of Moral Sentiments*, pp. 183–4.
37. Quoted Jerry Evensky, *Adam Smith's Moral Philosophy: A Historical and Contemporary Perspective on Markets, Law, Ethics and Culture* (Cambridge: Cambridge University Press, 2005), pp. 245–6.
38. Smith, A., 'History of Astronomy', *Essays on Philosophical Subjects*, p. 105.

39. Landes, D., *The Wealth and Poverty of Nations: Why Some Are So Rich and Some So Poor* (London: Abacus 1998), p. 516.
40. Campbell, Skinner and Todd (eds), Smith, *Inquiry into the Nature and Causes of the Wealth of Nations*, Vol. 1, IV, ii, p. 456.
41. Raphael and Macfie (eds), Smith, *Theory of Moral Sentiments*, pp. 184–5.
42. Campbell, Skinner and Todd (eds), Smith, *Inquiry into the Nature and Causes of the Wealth of Nations*, Vol. I, I, viii, p. 99.
43. Raphael and Macfie (eds), Smith, *Theory of Moral Sentiments*, p. 181.
44. Stigler, G., *The Theory of Price* (London: Macmillan, [1967] 1987), p. 52.
45. Sen, A. K., 'A Critique of the Behavioral Foundations of Economic Theory', *Philosophy and Public Affairs*, Vol. 6, No. 4, Summer 1977, pp. 317–44 at 338.
46. Raphael and Macfie (eds), Smith, *Theory of Moral Sentiments*, p. 67.
47. Ibid. p. 20.

Index